AGRICULTURAL TRANSFORMATION AND LAND USE IN CENTRAL AND EASTERN EUROPE

Agricultural Transformation and Land Use in Central and Eastern Europe

Edited by
STEPHAN J. GOETZ
TANJA JAKSCH
ROSEMARIE SIEBERT

Routledge
Taylor & Francis Group

LONDON AND NEW YORK

First published 2001 by Ashgate Publishing

Reissued 2018 by Routledge
2 Park Square, Milton Park, Abingdon, Oxon OX14 4RN
711 Third Avenue, New York, NY 10017, USA

Routledge is an imprint of the Taylor & Francis Group, an informa business

Publisher's Note
The publisher has gone to great lengths to ensure the quality of this reprint but points out that some imperfections in the original copies may be apparent.

Disclaimer
The publisher has made every effort to trace copyright holders and welcomes correspondence from those they have been unable to contact.

A Library of Congress record exists under LC control number: 2001091685

ISBN 13: 978-1-138-72778-6 (hbk)
ISBN 13: 978-1-138-72773-1 (pbk)
ISBN 13: 978-1-315-19073-0 (ebk)

Contents

List of Figures

List of Tables

List of Contributors

Albrecht Bemmann, Ph.D.
University of Technology, Dresden
Faculty of Forest, Geo and Hydro Science,
Institute of International Forestry and
Forest Products

Dieter Dräger, Ph.D.
Institute for Foreign Agriculture (IALA), Berlin

Stephan J. Goetz, Ph.D.
The Pennsylvania State University
Department of Agricultural Economics and Rural Sociology

Tanja Jaksch, Ph.D.
Institute for Foreign Agriculture (IALA), Berlin

Elke Knappe, Ph.D.
Institute of Regional Geography, Leipzig

Gudrun Loose, Ph.D.
Humboldt University of Berlin
Institute of Geography

Hermann Mertens, Ph.D.
Institute for Foreign Agriculture (IALA), Berlin

Rosemarie Siebert, Ph.D.
Center for Agricultural Landscape and Land Use Research (ZALF) e.V., Müncheberg
Institute for Socioeconomics

Translator:	David Fischbach, University of Leipzig
	Ursula Wappler, Berlin
Figures:	Renate Bräuer, Institute of Regional Geography, Leipzig;
	Rosemarie Janson, Institute for Foreign Agriculture (IALA), Berlin
Word processing:	Petra Jargow, Institute for Foreign Agriculture (IALA), Berlin

Acknowledgements

The editors gratefully acknowledge the co-operation, interest and advice of all the authors who contributed to this volume. We are also indebted to many organizations connected with the region, particularly the national statistical offices and the ministries of agriculture, whose help is greatly appreciated.

We are most grateful for permission to make extensive use of material from the following source: Zentrale Markt- und Preisberichtsstelle (ZMP), Berlin.

Rosemarie Siebert gratefully acknowledges support from the Federal Ministry of Consumer Protection, Food and Agriculture (BML) and the Ministry of Agriculture, Environmental Protection and Regional Planning of the State of Brandenburg (MULR).

Units

1 mm   Millimeter
$= \frac{1}{1000}$ meters
$= 0.001093$ yards
$= 0.003280$ feet
$= 0.039370$ inches

1 cm   Centimeter
$= \frac{1}{1000}$ meters

1 m   Meter
$= 1.0936$ yards
$= 3.2809$ feet
$= 39.37079$ inches

1 km   Kilometer
$= 1,000$ meters
$= 1,093.637$ yards
$= 3,280.8693$ feet
$= 39,370.79$ inches
$= 0.62138$ British or Statute Mile
$= 0.62138$ U.S. miles

1 ha   Hectare
$= 100$ acres
$= 10,000$ square meters
$= 11.96011$ square yards
$= 107\ 641.03$ square feet
$= 2.4711$ acres

1 km²	Square kilometer
	= 100 hectares
	= 1,000,000 square metres
	= 247.11 acres
	= 0.3861 square mile

1 l	Liter
	= 10 deciliters
	= 1.7607 pints
	= 7.0431 gills
	= 0.8804 quart
	= 0.2201 gallon

1 hl	Hektoliter
	= 100 liters
	= 22.009 gallons
	= 2.751 bushels

1 dt	(deci) Tonne
	= 100 kilograms
	= 1.9684 British hundred-weight
	= 2.2046 U.S. hundred-weights

1 t	Ton
	= 100 kilograms
	= 0.984 British ton
	= 1.1023 U.S. ton

Foreword

Lectori salutem–salute to the reader–is how the classical authors began their works. Those of us who worked on this volume cannot, of course, count ourselves among the classical authors, but we hope nevertheless to have provided a practical and useful service.

The growing world population continues to focus public attention on agriculture and nutrition in general and, more specifically, on the role of Central and Eastern European farmers in meeting the food needs of their fellow citizens. Opinions on the best path to follow, of course, differ. Some scientists insist that each unit of land needs to produce higher and higher yields. Others consider the correct way to be less intensive methods of production that ensure a sustainable use of land. They emphasize the need to protect the natural environment, especially within Europe where land is a relatively scarce factor of production.

Based on our own experience over the last decades, singular reliance on large-scale, industrial agriculture is not feasible. I believe that factors of production in agriculture cannot be dealt with in the same way as those in industry. The farmer must run his endeavors parallel to the vector of nature, encouraging favorable processes and avoiding damaging ones. A factory can be operated almost anywhere, regardless of the underlying technology and the surroundings. This is not true for agriculture, where technology has to be adapted to local circumstances and natural conditions.

Unfortunately, even today walls separate countries in Europe, although these walls are not made of concrete and brick. On one side of the wall, rich countries can afford a more benign form of agriculture, while on the other side those in positions of authority want to extract from the land everything it has to offer. The CEE countries described in this book have important choices to make. Farm-level productivity can be increased through mechanization and by using chemicals, but this has implications for farm workers who will lose their source of livelihood once these technologies are adopted. If the goal of policymakers is to keep village inhabitants where they are - because they have few if any alternatives in the cities - other choices of technique need to be considered, which do not displace labor to the same degree. Thus, while it is clear that farm work in these countries needs to be made less burdensome, one also needs to remember that those "freed" from agriculture must find other ways of making a living. It is particularly difficult, or even impossible, to create new jobs without the infusion of new capital. A peculiar trend is underway in Europe: an exodus from the land, coupled with a continually rising jobless rate.

This book does not aim to give general prescriptions. Instead, the authors attempt to give a clear and current picture of the upheavals and difficulties in the reform countries. In these countries, where former markets and mechanisms of exchange have fallen apart, where new states have come into being and where political and economic borders are changing, new insights and ideas need to be brought to bear on the relationships among land, people and the environment. The tasks required vary across countries, regions and in some cases even the plots of individual farms. All of this is occurring, depending on your point of view, in the shadow or with the illumination of globalization.

Once people were warned, "do in Rome as the Romans do." For the reform countries, Brussels or Washington has taken the place of Rome, but the old saying still holds true. People everywhere are trying to emulate the West, knowing full well that it is not a land of milk and honey. The task ahead is very difficult. We are only now realizing the full extent of the damage done to the natural environment during the last decades, when individuals had no incentive to protect the soil because it was considered to be communal property.

However, neither the exploitation nor the erosion of large plots of land has caused as much damage as the constant brainwashing of humans under socialism. One and a half generations of citizens have grown up under the constant pressure and influence of misguided ideas, and they acted accordingly. The process of catching up with the developed part of the world must include profound changes in attitudes among the peoples of these countries.

Prof. Dr. Péter von Sárközy (†)
Former Head,
Department of Economics,
University of Horticulture Budapest
and Chief Advisor to the Ministry
of Agriculture, Hungary, 1967-1973

Introduction

TANJA JAKSCH, ROSEMARIE SIEBERT AND STEPHAN J. GOETZ

The countries of Central and Eastern Europe (CEE) cover a territory that is more than six times larger than that of the European Union. The arable area within these countries is about twice the size of that in the EU. The sheer amount of land involved underscores the importance of ensuring that the land resource base in these countries is used in a sustainable manner. While the CEE countries are believed to have a large agricultural production and export potential, they for numerous reasons fail to utilize that advantage fully.

Recent political and economic upheavals in these countries have aggravated longstanding problems associated with land use, in some cases leading to dramatic reductions in soil fertility, drastic declines in crops produced for livestock feed, and detrimental longer-term consequences for the natural resource base. Considering these developments and the fact that general knowledge of the land use situation in the countries behind the former Iron Curtain tends to be fragmented at best, a major goal of this book is to describe changing land use patterns in this part of the world along with current agricultural transformation issues. This background information is important for those concerned with addressing questions about appropriate techniques and scales of agricultural production in these countries. The text is accompanied by numerous tables, figures and maps.

One of the most profound failures of socialism in the Soviet Union was the decision in the 1920s and 1930s to accelerate industrialization at the expense of agriculture. This entailed state redistribution of surpluses within the collective economy, from agriculture to industry. No attention was paid to the unique conditions under which agricultural production takes place, and an attempt was made to turn agriculture into a large-scale industry based on principles of mass production. Enforced by a state bureaucracy, this model of development was later implemented in other countries in Central and Eastern Europe and parts of the Third World. In the end, adherence to this model contributed to the demise of socialism.

This book updates and significantly expands upon a German language text, *Landnutzung in Mittel- und Ost-Europa*, originally published in 1996. Certain terms and concepts, such as *mechanization station* or *federation subject* lack an equivalent concept in the non-socialist world, and in these cases we retained the original term using a literal translation. Concepts of rurality are quite different in Europe than in the US: usually, the term *village* refers to a small rural place, while *town* (and city) is reserved for more urbanized places.

A number of chapters is this book are new, including *Chapter* 1, which examines agricultural transformation in CEE nations within a global perspective, taking into account lessons from past international agricultural development efforts. *Chapter* 2 introduces geographic features, major climates and soils, hydrographic conditions, and other factors defining and limiting land use options. *Chapter* 3 presents social and economic trends in rural areas and consequences of transformation for rural residents, presenting a general picture of natural population movements as well as changes in demographic and socioeconomic structures of the rural population.

While there are different ways of referring to the CEE region, including the European reference to *Middle Europe*, we have retained the label *Central* Europe, which is more common in the English-speaking world. We also distinguish among Baltic States, selected Former States of the Soviet Union and Eastern European Countries for purposes of organizing the book. These labels serve to group countries with common historical traditions and stages of development and, therefore, similar current transformation challenges and constraints. The Baltic States were of course also part of the Soviet Union, and at least the Eastern part of Russia also belongs to Eastern Europe. The choice of countries included was based on the expertise of the authors.

Our original objective for the individual country *Chapters* 4 to 15 was to present descriptive data in a unified and consistent manner. This goal was only partially achieved, however, because the sources and quality of information vary significantly across the CEE countries, and uniform data are not available. A consistent framework for statistical measuring and reporting based on EU-norms remains to be completed in most countries. As a result, the chapters do not all follow the same structure.

One of the main topics in the country descriptions is the comparison of land use before, on the eve of and after the beginning of the transformation process, depending on data availability. In some case its was possible to trace these processes down to the sub-national level. Building on an introduction to the natural preconditions of land use, sociological aspects, questions of settlement and employment in rural areas and ecological problems of each country are subsequently addressed, along with economic processes related to land use. Where data are available, separate sections are devoted to discussions of private farms, farming as a secondary source of income, and household farms in terms of their importance for food supplies and as sources of income for the rural population. Finally, a discussion of the livestock sector was added to the country chapters, which represents an addition relative to the 1996 text.

Chapter 16, which is also new, completes the book. It describes the importance of forestry and places the forest resources of the transformation countries into a global picture. This penultimate chapter also reviews important differences in historical conditions and traditions surrounding the concept of private property ownership in these countries.

The book presents detailed information about the types and development of land use in CEE countries over time, primarily from the perspective of economic geography. Most of the authors of this volume have worked in the CEE nations for many years, are fluent in the local language and have firsthand knowledge of conditions prevailing before 1990. Some of the data presented was obtained from original works that were not only untranslated but also unpublished (for example, in Poland and Belarus). Our goal is not only to present more information about this part of the world, but also to provide a better understanding of the extent and complexity of the task ahead, if a sustainable agricultural economy is to develop in this region.

1. Central and Eastern European Agricultural Transformation in a Global Perspective

STEPHAN J. GOETZ

[B]y 1989, thousands of books had been written on how to turn capitalism into communism but none on how to go back to capitalism. There was no model, no single precedent of a successful or unsuccessful attempt at traveling the road to freedom...

Samonis and Hunyadi, 1993, p. 3

1.0 Introduction

The decline in output in Central and Eastern European (CEE) transformation countries following economic and political liberalization around 1990 surprised many observers (e.g., Redmond and Hutton, 2000; Koester, 1998).[1] Changes in incentives facing individuals, pent-up demand and productive capacity, and integration into the global economic system had been expected to launch these economies rapidly onto paths of sustained economic growth. Instead, reduction of output was both deep and far-reaching across economic sectors of most transformation countries. Real GNP shrank between 1990 and 1999 in eight of the 12 countries studied here. Food production indices in 1999 were below 1989-91 levels in all 12 countries. In this context, Blanchard (1996, p. 117) asks, "Why does going from an inefficient system of production to a more efficient one involve a decline in output?"

The changes unleashed within the agricultural economies of CEE countries were in many ways unprecedented in scope.[2] They were *radical* in the sense of changing the roots of the economic system then in place, along with all of the rules, institutions and incentives facing decision-makers and mediating exchange. The changes involved wholesale restructuring of agricultural production and marketing systems and relationships,[3] making it difficult to predict how agriculturalists would in fact respond to liberalization. Yet scholars interested in the role and impact

1

of institutions and institutional design might have pointed to one of at least three historical antecedents in international agricultural development to caution that expectations of immediate production increases were unrealistic. Clues as to what was about to occur in the transformation countries could be found in lessons learned from land reforms in South America; forced land resettlement schemes in Indonesia; and structural adjustment responses in sub-Saharan Africa in the 1980s. In all three cases, a critical question was whether a market system and market agents were in place or would quickly emerge to articulate supply and demand by responding to any opportunities to earn profits.

In South America, markets were in place prior to land reforms and, in fact, they were well developed. However, these markets and market participants were set up to handle input delivery for and outputs from large farm operations (the *latifundistas*). The need to suddenly handle the output of numerous small operators *(minifundistas)* proved to be a significant challenge for the marketing system, at least in the short-run. In La Paz, Bolivia, agricultural products delivered from rural areas declined in the first three to five years following land reforms (Clark, 1968, p. 166). Blanchard (1996) argues that economic reforms at first lead to disorganization, and this is one explanation for the drop in output immediately after a major economic or land reform. Another consideration is that the greater the shock brought about by reform, the larger the resistance to change.

Experience around the world has shown there are three reasons why output may drop after land reform:[4] the marketing system cannot adapt immediately to new opportunities; scale economies previously in place no longer exist; and those formerly in positions of power may block the development of new marketing channels. Parallels with large-scale Soviet-style farms (*solkhovs*) are apparent here. Also, marketed surpluses may fall after land reform, even if output rises, if low-income producers retain more of their output for home consumption as their incomes rise. In CEE countries, these supply-side shocks to the food system occurred even as food demand collapsed because of economy-wide depressions and the evaporation of export markets in the FSU.

In contrast to the South American case, input and output market infrastructures simply did not exist in newly cleared regions of Indonesia, making it difficult for farmers forcibly relocated there to generate and market surpluses of food (see also Dorner, 1972, p. 42). High transactions costs, including lack of information, in many remote and thin African markets meant that the private sector lacked the necessary scale of operation and had difficulty responding to incentives ostensibly offered by market liberalization and withdrawal of parastatal agencies from agricultural input and output marketing. Farmers failed to produce surpluses for lack of markets, and markets failed to develop for lack of surpluses (Goetz, 1993).

The lessons drawn from past experience are that markets, prices and incentives matter, but so do institutions or "rules of the game" and the infrastructure needed to develop and support efficient marketing systems, including roads, market information systems for prices, grades and standards and effective credit systems. These prerequisites do not emerge automatically, but usually require carefully sequenced public investments. In this sense, Koester (1998, p. 284) writes "that it is not land reform *per se* that matters, but rather the type of land reform and the accompanying institutional changes."

A key lesson has also been that blanket recommendations do not work across different societies and economies. Instead, it is critical that local research and analytical capacity be created to deal with changing challenges and constraints that inevitably emerge over time in dynamic food production and marketing systems (Eicher and Staatz, 1998).

An important further question relates to the role of agriculture in the post-reform economic development of the CEE countries. Should surpluses be extracted from agriculture to support other sectors of these economies, should resource flows at least initially be reversed - flowing into agriculture - or should different sectors of these economies be allowed to develop independently of one another? Marx and Lenin clearly viewed agriculture as a sector to be exploited, with proceeds used to support accelerated industrialization (see also Hobbs, Kerr and Gaisford, 1997, p. 123). Western economists spent considerable time debating this important question, starting with the seminal work of Johnston and Mellor (1961).

It is perhaps too early to evaluate the proper role of agriculture in the context of the CEE countries but, again, historical precedents in other nations that have experimented with socialized agriculture (e.g., Tanzania) are plentiful, although these countries were not necessarily at the same level of industrial development. Will the CEE countries eventually shift resources released from extractive industries such as agriculture into secondary sectors of industry and manufacturing, as happened in virtually all industrialized countries, or will resources shift directly into the tertiary sector (services), altogether bypassing the manufacturing stage of development? In other words, is a transitory relative expansion of the manufacturing sector a necessary step on the path towards developing an advanced economy? In one of the first post-1990 studies of Poland and Hungary that is based on social accounting matrices, Cohen (1999, p. 218) finds "that there are growth biases in [these economies] towards primary sectors."

Agricultural transformation in the CEE countries is of interest to Western observers for at least three reasons. First, from a geo-strategic perspective, this part of the globe has the potential to be both an important buyer of agricultural products *and* a competitor. Second, much of the territory in these countries is forested, as is true of large parts of North America and Europe, and many common problems arise in terms of the optimal management of privately owned forest land. Third, from an economic development point of view, it is interesting to bring lessons learned in other countries around the world to bear on the transformation problems facing these countries. Finally, decision-making authority in the CEE countries is being radically decentralized just as nations such as the US accelerate the devolution of public decision-making authority to state and local units of government.

This chapter compares current macroeconomic and general economic foundations for growth in these countries in a global context, as well as selected trends and conditions in agriculture and rural areas. In addition, the transformation countries are examined in the context of trade in section 1.3. This chapter provides a general overview; subsequent chapters fill in descriptive details of agricultural transformation and land use patterns in each country.

1.1 Description of the national economies

An important fact not universally recognized by Western observers in 1990 was that the CEE countries were at markedly different stages of development. This was an important outcome of each country's historical development as well as Soviet-style planning, which categorized countries as agricultural, industrial-agricultural, or industrial (van Brabant 1998, p. 26), even though industrialization was the ultimate goal for each country. Only former East Germany and Czechoslovakia were considered to be industrial. Mixed agricultural-industrial countries included the Soviet Union, Poland and Hungary (and Cuba), while the agricultural group included Bulgaria and Romania (as well as Albania and Yugoslavia). Today, Bulgaria and Romania, along with Ukraine, rank at the bottom in GNP per capita (table 1.1) and they have the highest shares of GNP accounted for by agriculture.

As recently as 1995, per capita income ranged from $1,350 to $4,420 in these countries. Four years later, the range was $750 to $5,060, with a sharp decline occurring in Ukraine, and Lithuania experiencing the proportionately largest increase. Per capita GNP across these transformation countries is, therefore, diverging over time. In comparison, per capita GNP worldwide in 1999 was US $410 in low-income countries, $2,000 in middle-income countries and $25,730 in high-income countries (World Bank 2000, p. 275).

Table 1.1 Differences in the level of development of the countries

Country and [transforma- tion speed]*	Gross national product				Internet
	Level/capita current US $		Avg. ann. % change†	PPP US $/capita	Hosts per 10,000
	1995	1999	1990-99	1999	Jan. 2000
Belarus [s]	2,000	2,630	-4.3	6,518	0.9
Bulgaria [s]	1,370	1,380	-2.7	4,914	14.5
Czech R. [r]	4,420	5,060	0.9	12,289	109.8
Estonia [r]	3,010	3,480	-1.3	7,826	206.8
Hungary [r]	4,140	4,650	1.0	10,479	113.4
Latvia [r]	2,160	2,470	-4.8	5,938	57.3
Lithuania [r]	1,730	2,620	-3.9	6,093	34.4
Poland [r]	3,910	3,960	4.7	7,894	47.3
Romania [s]	1,400	1,520	-1.2	5,647	11.0
Russian F. [s]	2,250	2,270	-6.1	6,339	14.7
Slovakia [r]	2,940	3,590	1.9	9,811	48.0
Ukraine [s]	1,350	750	-10.8	3,142	5.4

Note: *r*=rapid adjustment, *s*=slow; †=gross domestic product.

Source: The World Bank, 2000 and Gomulka, 2000.

Economic collapse in the 1990s was most severe in Ukraine and the Russian Federation (table 1.1). Only Poland, Slovakia, Hungary and the Czech Republic achieved positive real GNP growth rates over this period according to World Bank (2000) estimates. These numbers must be viewed with caution, because they obviously do not include unreported economic activity, and a tendency existed under socialist planning to overstate output. Although economic problems of these countries during the Soviet era have been thoroughly documented (and continue in countries such as Cuba and North Korea), it is noteworthy that all 12 countries experienced positive growth, at least based on official data, ranging from 0.5 percent annually in

Romania to 3.5 percent in Latvia, in the decade just before the collapse of the Iron Curtain (1980-1990). Ukraine is now classified as a low-income country by the World Bank (*ibid.*). The Czech Republic, Estonia, Hungary and Poland are classified as upper middle-income countries, while Belarus, Bulgaria, Latvia, Lithuania, Romania and the Russian Federation are in the lower middle-income group, which also includes NATO member Turkey.

Another important consideration is that transformation countries liberalized their economies at different speeds and to different degrees (Gomulka, 2000). Only East Germany received full "shock-therapy," because the Federal Republic of Germany wanted to accelerate reunification and was willing and able to bear high costs of rapid transformation. Table 1.1 shows whether countries examined here pursued liberalization policies rapidly (*r*) or more slowly (*s*).

While there is no obvious relationship between speed of transformation chosen and annualized percent GNP growth between 1990 and 1999, it is noteworthy that all five countries choosing slow transformation had negative growth. Four of seven countries pursuing rapid adjustment experienced positive growth - as high as 4.7 percent in the case of Poland, which has benefited from booming exports to the EU: Polish exports of goods and services increased by nearly 11 percent annually between 1990 and 1999. Using an "index of reform progress" consisting of EBRD data on the extent of large- and small-scale privatization, enterprise restructuring, trade and foreign exchange, competitive policy, banking reform, securities markets and investment regulations, Sachs (1996, p. 129) finds that reform countries exhibiting more progress on this index had more rapid GNP growth between 1989 and 1995 than those showing less progress.

Also shown in table 1.1 are GNP per capita estimates for 1999 based on purchasing power parity; as the label implies, this measure holds constant the purchasing power of a unit of currency, converted into dollars, across countries. Using these numbers, the situation in the transformation countries does not appear quite as bleak (since the US $ is the basis of comparison, GNP and PPP GNP in the US are identical at $30,600 per person).

Significant differences exist across these countries in the spread of the Internet (table 1.1), as well as telephones and mobile phones, which are potentially important tools for rural entrepreneurs and farmers to communicate with input suppliers and buyers. In comparison, low-income countries world-wide averaged 0.37 Internet hosts per 10,000 people in January, 2000, while middle income countries had 9.96 and high income countries 777.22 hosts. A strong correlation exists between per capita GNP levels and use of information and communications technologies in these transformation countries. Also notable is that the five countries with the lowest number of Internet hosts per capita all chose a slower adjustment strategy.

Figure 1.1 shows a plot of output per capita versus population density. The lower trend line in the figure includes all 12 countries, while the three nations with the lowest GNP per capita have been dropped from the upper line - these nations are Ukraine, Romania and Bulgaria. Clearly, the relationship between density and income is much stronger when these latter countries are excluded. These three countries were the most agriculturally-oriented in 1999, as measured by the percent of GNP contributed by agriculture.

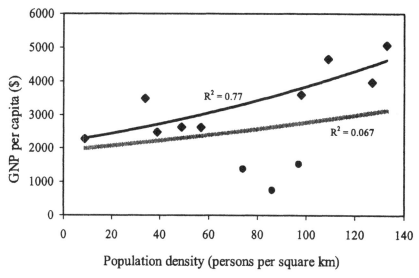

Figure 1.1   Effect of population density on GNP per capita, 1999

The positive correlation between population density and per capita GNP in figure 1.1 is noteworthy. The same phenomenon is observed within the US, and it is attributed to factors such as greater R&D spillovers among firms, less costly access to markets and other costs savings even under constant returns to scale technology, and more opportunities for specialization. Ciccone and Hall (1996) estimate that a doubling of employment density raises labor productivity by 6 percent in the US. The fact that a similar relationship holds in the transformation countries suggests that the same underlying forces exist regardless of a country's past and present political and economic systems. We may refer to this as the economic handicap of low population density.

Within these countries, the Gini index of income inequality varied from 19.5 in Slovakia and 21.7 in Belarus to 48.7 in the Russian Federation. This compares with Gini values of 41.5 for Turkey, 40.8 for the US, 30.0 for Germany and 24.7 for Denmark. The World Bank calculates this index such that a value of zero implies a perfectly even distribution of income, and 100 implies complete inequality. Of the 106 countries world-wide for which a Gini is reported, none has a lower value than Slovakia; the highest Gini value is 62.9 (Sierra Leone). Income inequality has a statistically weak negative effect on income growth in this sample of counties. In other words, lower income inequality tends to increase income growth, and vice versa.

CEE countries differ in terms of other economic indicators as well. The Baltic countries and Slovakia each contain five million or fewer people, which represent a relatively small domestic market. Belarus, Bulgaria, the Czech Republic and Hungary have 8-10 million people each, while Romania (22), Poland (39), Ukraine (50) and the Russian Federation (147 million) are considerably more populous. Detailed population estimates and densities are provided in individual country chapters.

The dominant labor market adjustment paradigm in these countries has been that public sector jobs diminished sharply after the reform, and continued to disappear as private sector employment expands (Johnson et al., 2000). However, private jobs do not grow as rapidly as public sector jobs disappear, and unemployment rises. Officially recorded unemployment rates (using most recent data available from the period 1994-1997) ranged from 2.7 percent in Belarus to 14.4 percent in Latvia. In Bulgaria, Estonia, Latvia, Poland, Slovakia and the Russian Federation, rates were above 10 percent; this compares with a 4.9 percent unemployment rate in the US, 7.1 percent in the UK, 9.8 percent in Germany, 12.4 percent in France and 14.4 percent in Finland.

The flipside of higher unemployment rates is that rates of "sick leave" (Samonis and Hunyadi, 1993, p.7) and of hidden unemployment in former public sector firms have fallen dramatically. Belarus and Romania, both pursuing more gradual transformation, had the lowest (2.7 percent) and second highest (13.7 percent) unemployment rates. The average unemployment rate of countries pursuing slow transformation (8.52 percent) was not materially different from that of the group pursuing rapid change (8.97 percent). Svejnar (1996) reviews econometric evidence related to flows of workers from unemployment to employment in selected reform countries, and in particular seeks to explain low unemployment rates in the Czech Republic.

Shares of females in the total labor force varied in 1998 from 44.5 percent in Romania to 50.3 percent in Latvia. In seven of the 12 countries, these rates were lower in 1998 than in 1980, but changes over time in most cases were small. In the US, the share of females in the workforce increased from 41.0 percent in 1980 to 45.7 percent in 1998. With few exceptions (such as Romania where 43 percent of females are employed in agriculture), females are more likely to be employed in services than in industry or agriculture, and their share in that sector is usually larger than is the case for the share of males. Even so, a trend towards the feminization of agricultural labor currently exists in some of these countries (e.g., Górz and Kurek, 1998; Turnock, 1998).

Adult illiteracy rates are extremely low in these countries, ranging in 1998 for females from zero percent in Latvia and Poland to three percent in Romania (data are not reported for the Czech Republic, Slovakia and Estonia). This compares with rates of 20 percent for females and 10 percent for males in other middle-income countries around the world. The Russian Federation has more scientists and engineers in R&D per million people (3,587) than any of the other transformation countries (the period is 1987-97, and data are for the most recent year available). This level is virtually identical to that of the US (3,676). The next highest countries are Belarus (2,248) and Ukraine (2,171). At the bottom are Latvia (1,049) and Hungary (1,099). Even so, Hungary leads these countries with the share of manufacturing exports in 1998 that were high-technology goods (21 percent).[5] Expenditures for R&D as a percent of GNP range from 1.20 percent in the Czech Republic to 0.43 percent in Latvia. In comparison, the US devotes 2.63 percent of GNP to R&D, and Sweden 3.76 percent.

Another powerful indicator of the depth of adjustments occurring in some of these countries during the 1990s is evident from changes in the amount of goods transported by road, measured in ton-kms hauled. In Bulgaria, for example, this number dropped from 13,823 ton-kms in 1990 to only 307 in 1998. In Hungary, the numbers were 1,836 and 14 ton-kms in 1990 and 1998 respectively. While these numbers must be viewed with caution, and the bulk of shipments in the former Soviet Union were by rail rather than by road (van Selm, p. 38), they do suggest that the volume of goods traded and transported within these countries has dried up remarkably. More importantly, this likely also reflects a greater subsistence orientation of agricultural production. The only other countries for which data are available at two different points in time are Poland, Slovakia and Romania. In all three of these, the volume has increased. Ton-kms hauled in the US rose from 1,073,100 to 1,534,430 over the period 1990 to 1998.

The share of roads that is paved is one indicator of the quality of a country's transportation infrastructure. Generally, unpaved roads can be serious impediments to transportation in these countries and they accounted for some of the large post-harvest losses occurring in Soviet agriculture.

This indicator has to be interpreted cautiously, however, and within the context of a country's level of development and population density. For example, in the US about 40 percent of roads are unpaved and yet the country has an excellent transportation system overall. In the transformation countries, the share of roads that are paved ranges from 22.1 percent in Estonia to 100.0 percent in the Czech Republic. Dirt roads can become impassable during periods of heavy rainfall, making it difficult for farmers in remote areas to access input and output markets.

These countries are also becoming more urbanized over time, with most increasing their urban population shares by six to eight percentage points between 1980 and 1999. Belarus experienced an increase of 14 percentage points (from 57 to 71 percent), while only Estonia saw a slight decrease in the urban population share; in the Czech Republic, the share stayed the same over this period, at three-quarters, while in Latvia the increase was one percentage point. Not counting Slovakia, where the urban population share is 57 percent, most countries have between 64 and 77 percent of their population living in urban areas; the latter ratio is identical to that in the US, while about 88 percent of the population in the UK and Germany is urbanized. This brings us to a more detailed discussion of conditions in rural areas in general and agriculture in particular.

1.2 Differences in agricultural economies and rural areas

As noted in the introduction, agriculture's relative contribution to output varies significantly across CEE countries. In 1999 this contribution ranged from only four percent in three countries to a maximum of 18 percent in Bulgaria (table 1.2). Agriculture's contribution to GDP has plummeted in most countries since transformation began (see, however, endnote 4). The largest decline occurred in Latvia, with 17 percentage points. It is difficult to think of two other pairs of numbers that more dramatically illustrate the depth of the transformation some of these countries have gone through in the last decade. Further, these smaller percentages are in most cases calculated from a smaller total GDP. In Latvia, for example, total GDP in 1990 was $12.49 billion, compared with only $6.66 billion in 1999.

The declining relative importance of agriculture over time evident in figure 1.2, is a hallmark of economic development (see also Siamwalla, 1995, p. 152). This is a natural evolution of shifting value-added functions from farms to off-farm sectors during the process of development and increasing specialization. More resources are allocated to producing other goods and services, in sectors that offer higher returns to labor, once basic food and fiber needs of an economy have been met, and more farm inputs are produced off rather than on the farm. Bulgaria is the only country in which agriculture's share in national output remained unchanged over the last decade.

Developed countries have gone through similar structural shifts in the relative contribution of agriculture to national output, but this transformation has been more gradual. For example, US agriculture contributed around 12 percent of total output in 1950. Fifty years later, this share has dropped to 2.6 percent (Debertin and Goetz, 2000), or by about 9.5 percentage points. In both industrialized and transformation countries, movement of labor out of agriculture is prompted by declining returns to labor. However, this is where similarities end. In the US, rising labor productivity based on the scientific industrialization of agriculture led to surpluses of workers who were readily absorbed by the manufacturing sector. In fact, release of labor from agriculture made possible the US manufacturing revolution; at the same time, food production and demand continued to expand.

The situation is very different in CEE countries, where collapsing effective demand for food coupled with price reductions to world market levels contributed to declining returns to farm labor. Here food output has not only stagnated but declined, and the release of workers from agriculture is posing a significant social burden. In the Soviet era, exports were the only major stimulus for agriculture. The collapse of COMECON, which had created a pronounced regional division of agricultural labor and strong reliance on trade, was an important factor contributing to the decline in agriculture. The collapse of markets also meant that funds for investments disappeared, and this negatively affected the transportation and processing sectors, which were already plagued by inadequate and deterio-rating stocks of trucks and equipment.

Even though the role of agriculture diminishes in a relative sense in the course of economic development, growth of the agricultural sector may play a critical role in stimulating growth in other sectors of the economy.

An immediate question is whether agricultural growth in these countries affects growth in other sectors in the same way as it has in Asia, sub-Saharan Africa and Latin America - that is, in a positive manner (Mellor, 1995, figures 1.1-1.3, pp. 2-4). When we plot data for the 12 countries studied here, the same relationship exists as that also found in other countries. More specifically, figure 1.3 shows that countries experiencing less contraction in agriculture also tended to have less shrinking (or faster growth) of services and industry GDP between 1990 and 1998. While it is too soon to draw definitive conclusions from the data, the shapes of the two trend curves in the figure are noteworthy; they imply a diminishing effect of agricultural growth on industry growth, and an increasing effect on services growth over time.

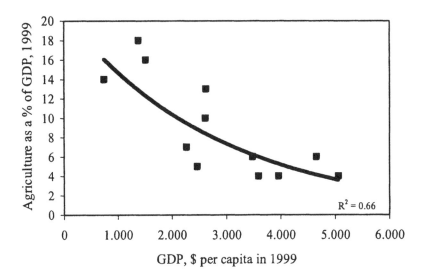

Figure 1.2   Value added in agriculture as a percent of GDP versus GDP per capita, 1999

The contribution to GDP of industry (including manufacturing) in the transformation countries also shrank between 1990 and 1999, which means that services have become much more important, proportionally, in total output. In Latvia, Estonia and Slovakia, value added by services as a percent of GNP increased by more than 30 percentage points. In 1990, services accounted for less than one-half of GDP in all of the countries; today services account for more than one-half of GDP in ten of the 12 countries. It is premature, however, to conclude that these countries have altogether by-passed the manufacturing growth stage and will become increasingly services-dominated. In comparison, in middle-income countries world-wide, the share of services in GDP increased from 47 to 55 percent, while in the US it rose from 70 to 72 percent over this period. Only Hong Kong (85 percent) and Panama (74 percent) have higher shares of GNP accounted for by services than the US.

Output of food in 1996-98 has declined, in some countries sharply, from 1989-91 levels. Estonia, Latvia and Ukraine rank at the bottom on this measure, while only Romania is close to maintaining food production levels of a decade earlier (table 1.2). A positive relationship exists between rural population density and the index of food production in 1996-98 relative to 1989-91. Rural population density - people per square kilometer of arable land - varies from 27 in the Russian Federation to 156 in Slovakia, and countries with higher rural population densities (or fewer hectares of arable land per capita) were more likely to produce as much food in 1996-98 as they had almost a decade earlier. Conversely, arable land per capita ranges from 0.28 in Slovakia to 0.86 in the Russian Federation (table 1.2); comparable numbers are 0.67 ha/capita for the US, 0.10 for the UK, 0.14 in Germany and 0.31 in France. Considerable variation also exists in the amount of arable land as a percent of all land; this ranges from 7.5 percent in the Russian Federation to 57.1 percent in Ukraine, which has a rural population density of 50 persons per km^2.

Tractors used in agriculture are most plentiful in Poland and Baltic countries; these numbers are considerably lower than those in Germany (991 per thousand farmers), the UK (883) or the US (1,484). Bulgaria (63 per 1,000 workers), Romania (84) - the two agrarian societies - and Ukraine (89) - the region's breadbasket - ranked at the bottom on this indicator. Using the most recent year for which data are available, annual agricultural wages between 1995 and 1999 ranged from US $410 in Belarus to $1,864 in Romania; data are available only for seven of the countries examined here. In Belarus, wages had plummeted from $1,641 in 1980-84, and they fell from $2,417 to $659 in the Russian Federation. Agricultural wages fell in four of six countries for which such data are available.

Measured as value-added per worker, agricultural productivity in 1999 was highest in Bulgaria, at $5,135, followed by $4,771 in Hungary. This compares with $39,001 in the US, $36,889 in France and $22,759 in Germany. Ukraine ($1,454) and Poland ($1,751) were at the bottom on this measure. Clearly, considerable agricultural productivity differences exist across these countries. In the four countries for which data are available, value-added in manufacturing exceeds that in agriculture: the largest discrepancy occurs in Poland, with $1,751 in agriculture and $7,637 of value added per worker in manufacturing. The smallest gap is found in Romania, with $3,101 and $3,482, respectively. This implies that shifting workers out of agriculture and into manufacturing will raise total output.

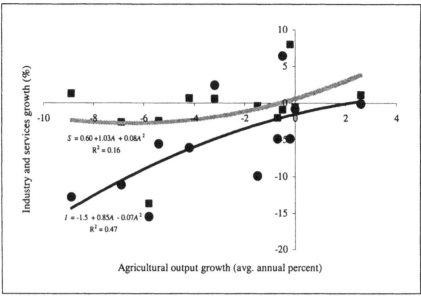

Figure 1.3 Effect of agricultural output growth on growth in other sectors, 1990-1998

Note: A=agriculture, I=industry, S=services.

When value added in agriculture per worker is plotted against arable land per capita, as a crude proxy for farm size and the relative scarcity of land, a negative relationship emerges - as expected (figure 1.4). As land becomes relatively more scarce per worker and farms smaller, agricultural productivity - measured here with respect to labor - increases, although the relationship is admittedly weak. This pattern is borne out repeatedly in other countries and time periods (e.g., Tomich, Kilby and Johnston 1995, pp, 124-7; Goetz 1998 for data from Egypt; see also the discussion in Lerman, 2000 and Feder, 2000). While it would be interesting to test whether the same relationship existed 10 or 20 years ago, lack of accessible and reliable data make such a comparison impossible. In some of the subsequent chapters authors argue that land holdings have become too small and fragmented in the transformation countries to permit efficient agricultural production and mechanization. In that case, we would no longer expect to observe the relationship in figure 1.4.

Table 1.2 Agricultural statistics for the transformation countries

Country	Agric. in GDP (% of VA) 1990	1999	Index of food Production ('89-91=100)	Arable Land (ha/cap.)	Tractors per 1,000 Farmers
Belarus	24	13	65.9	0.60	124
Bulgaria	18	18	67.8	0.51	63
Czech Rep.	8	4	79.7	0.30	164
Estonia	17	6	47.0	0.77	495
Hungary	15	6	76.3	0.47	156
Latvia	22	5	48.1	0.70	312
Lithuania	27	10	69.2	0.79	263
Poland	8	4	88.2	0.37	281
Romania	20	16	95.9	0.41	84
Russia	17	7	64.4	0.86	106
Slovakia	7	4	74.7	0.28	92
Ukraine	26	14	52.3	0.65	89

Note: Data for food production are from the most recent year available in the period 1996-98; for arable land and tractors the period is 1995-97.

Source: The World Bank, 2000.

Another important difference across these nations is the mix of public and private control over land prior to 1990. For example, in Poland the share of farmland that was privately held has always been large, making the transition to private enterprise and free markets relatively easier than in other countries (Takács-György, 1999, p. 4). Following reforms, new landowners in the other transformation countries usually had three primary options (other than selling or leasing the land): putting their land into a cooperative or leaving it there; forming joint stock companies or partnerships; or creating sole proprietorships. Using data from Romania on a sample of 1,394 households, Rizov et al. (2000) find that farm operators' human capital level and endowments of capital are important determinants of the type of organization chosen. In particular, farmers with higher levels of human capital (and entrepreneurial ability) are significantly more likely to farm on their own than in cooperation with other farmers.

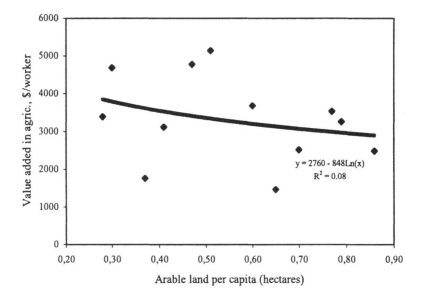

Figure 1.4   Value added in agriculture per worker versus arable land per capita, 1999

The food price index is our last indicator of the depth of adjustments occurring in agricultural sectors of these countries. Average annual percent growth in the food index between 1990 and 1998 ranged from 14.9 percent in Slovakia to an unimaginable 485.9 percent in Belarus. In four countries the index averaged above 100 percent annually. Relationships among monetization, hyperinflation and food industry employment are examined for the case of Yugoslavia in Miljkovic and Garcia (1996).

1.3   Central and Eastern Europe in the global economy

Trading of goods within Soviet republics was extensive prior to 1990. These trading patterns were centrally dictated, and not based on comparative advantage, however. As mentioned above, some countries emphasized agricultural production (or other primary sectors), while industrial production was the focus of others. For example, TV sets and refrigerators were produced mainly in Russia, Ukraine and Belarus (van Selm, p. 37), while East Germany (Trabants, Wartburgs), Russia (Volga and Lada), Romania (Dacia), Poland (Polski Fiat) and Czechia (Škoda) specialized in the production of cars, and Hungary produced Ikarus buses.

These countries are of strategic interest to the US and the EU because they have the potential over time to be significant competitors for agricultural commodities on world markets - if they can solve the organizational and institutional problems now plaguing their agricultural sectors and rural areas. Conversely, these countries are also important markets for US farm commodities and processed foods, and US farmers have a stake in economic conditions prevailing in these countries. With their large land holdings, many of the former state and collective farms would appear to benefit more from the types of agricultural equipment used on farms in the US Midwest or Great Plains, than the equipment developed for typically smaller West European holdings.

Recent data show just how sensitive Russian food imports are to domestic economic conditions. Russia in 1999 dropped out of the top 15 destinations for US agricultural exports for the first time in at least the last decade, after being 10th in 1996; the Former Soviet Union ranked 4th as recently as 1991. US agricultural exports to Russia dropped from about $90 million in each of the first seven months of 1998 to zero in September of that year, following the crisis in August.[6]

Ukraine and Belarus, both slow-adjusting countries, saw exports of goods and services on average shrink by 3.6 and 11.1 percent annually between 1990 and 1999. In contrast, the five countries with the highest average growth in exports were all rapid transformers - the Czech Republic, Estonia, Hungary, Slovakia and Poland each had export growth rates of 8 percent or more. In fact, figure 1.5 shows that countries able to aggressively expand exports of goods and services since 1990 also experienced significantly faster GDP growth (or slower shrinking of output). These countries have the potential to become key actors on global food markets - both as exporters and as importers, by virtue of their geographic locations. In the Soviet era, countries such as Bulgaria had guaranteed markets for their agricultural products, and there were no incentives to innovate or to produce higher-quality products because the Russian market did not reward such efforts. In contrast, Hungary exported to Europe and was forced to operate at higher levels of efficiency and quality, and was thus better prepared to take advantage of new export opportunities after 1990.

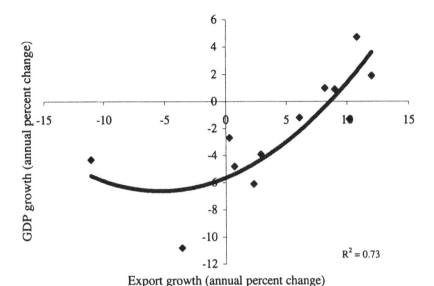

Figure 1.5 Effect of export growth on GDP growth, 1990-1999

1.4 Conclusion

> There are never enough bureaucrats and reform experts to go around; the experts become experts in the process of applying the reform. If a reform is to be carried out successfully, it must win the active participation of the people directly affected by the reform, the farmers who best know the conditions of their rural community; the principle of local involvement applies to land reform just as it does to the other aspects of agricultural development. ...So long as the would-be beneficiaries are treated as mere on-lookers ... the reform has little hope of success.
>
> Dorner, 1972, p. 50, quoting Millikan and Hapgood, 1967.

Building market economies - including the institutional, social and human dimensions - in CEE countries from the ground up has proven far more difficult than originally anticipated. It has also proven more difficult than rebuilding Europe's industries and physical infrastructure after World War II through massive capital transfers under the Marshall Plan. In Western Europe, the *soft infrastructure* needed to motivate economic activity and mediate exchange, including rules, regulations and property rights that could be enforced, were in place and well-defined before the war. In the transformation countries, decades without private property rights and the ability or obligation to make economic decisions - beyond those occurring within the boundaries of the household - have created generations of citizens who have no experience with, and thus have some degree of difficulty functioning in, a free market environment where economic outcomes are not always predictable. This unpredictability is currently compounded by regulatory uncertainty as well as political and economic instability in many of these countries.

To answer the question, what needs to be done to get agriculture moving (again) in these countries, the temptation arises to compare conditions and prospects for agricultural development in the transformation countries with those of under-developed countries around the world. After being liberated from colonial rule, leaders of many developing countries thought that agriculture would best be developed by relying on publicly-owned firms that operated on a large and capital-intensive scale. The move to private, small-scale farming and reliance on free markets came about only gradually (Mellor, 1995, pp. 9-10). Even so, a concern has always existed that completely unregulated markets and privatization could be counterproductive if they allowed the eventual creation of monopolies.

African agriculture, for example, has experienced many failures, but success stories also abound. Both levels of human capital (primarily formal education) and natural resource endowments in the form of soils (organic matter content) and moisture levels, would appear to favor CEE countries. Yet African farmers have largely been in charge of their own destinies - *poor but efficient* in the words of Schultz - for many generations. This element has been missing in the centrally planned economies, and its impact cannot be discounted. This is not to say that economic agents in CEE are not self-motivated and cannot flourish in a free enterprise system. But the amount of time, retraining and rethinking needed to accomplish this has probably not been sufficiently recognized.

In making comparisons with underdeveloped countries, it is important to remember that these transformation countries are middle-income countries, and at generally higher levels of economic development. The opportunity to grow one's own food on a private piece of land is not necessarily viewed as progress by those engaging in such activities after 1990, especially in light of the fact that input and output markets are in rudimentary stages of development. The fact that many people are moving back into rural areas to grow and in some cases process their own food is more properly viewed as a step down the economic development ladder.

Although systems and procedures of exchange were in place in CEE countries, and food system participants may have been the same before and after 1990, the food system was not set up to efficiently articulate supply and demand. Hobbs et al. (1997, p. 124) describe the problem this way: "The vertical segmentation of this hierarchical [food system] tended to foster conflict as middle level management had little or no incentive to cooperate" with food system participants higher up or further down the food system. Over time, "collective farm workers lost the more holistic perspective over the farm business associated with farmers in modern market economies."

Locally-targeted research will be needed along with incentives for entrepreneurs to bring the latest research discoveries into practice. This crucial step was usually missing in the Soviet system. Furthermore, farmers need basic education in business management and entrepreneurship concepts to be able to identify and invest in the types of technology that are appropriate for their conditions. Local consumption linkages and expenditure patterns need to be better understood, and an emphasis placed on private small-to-medium enterprises and entrepreneurship to help accommodate the large numbers of farmers who have become redundant in agriculture. For social scientists, finally, an intriguing question is whether social capital exists in rural areas of the CEE countries and, if so, what role it might play - as a complement to existing human capital stocks and new investments in physical infrastructure in promoting the growth and development of these rural economies.

Notes

[1]   van Seln (1997, Table 3.1., p. 29) lists the precise dates at which Soviet Republics gained sovereignty and independence.

[2]   Sachs (1996, p. 128) describes the following four steps needed to accomplish economy-wide reforms in the transformation countries: 1. systematic transformation (including changes in or creation of laws, institutions and administrations); 2. financial stabilization; 3. structural adjustment (including changes in resource allocation); and 4. a framework that stimulates rapid growth.

[3]   In this context, the term "transition countries" used, for example by the World Bank, is overly benign, as it implies a gradual shift from one system or steady state to another. Instead, we use the term "transformation," as it more accurately describes the changes from the ground up that are occurring in these countries. See also Stark (1992).

[4]   This requires careful measurement. In some countries food consumed on the farm is not counted in national accounts, which can suggest a drop in food output following land reform when in fact none occurred.

[5]   This includes exports such as hard drives for laptop computers manufactured for IBM.

[6]   See: www.ers.usda.gov/briefing/russia/issuethree.htm. Accessed 10/09/2000.

References

Blanchard, Olivier (1996), 'Theoretical Aspects of Transition', *American Economic Review* (Proceedings), vol. 86, pp. 117-22.

Ciccone, Antonio and Robert E. Hall (1996), 'Productivity and the Density of Economic Activity', *American Economic Review*, vol. 86, pp. 54-70.

Clark, Ronald J. (1968), 'Land Reform and Peasant Market Participation on the Northern Highlands of Bolivia', *Land Economics*, vol. 44, pp. 153-172.

Cohen, S.I. (1999), 'European Structural Patterns Applied to Transition Economies: Assessment for Poland and Hungary', *Socioeconomic Planning Sciences*, vol. 33, pp. 205-219.

Debertin, David L. and Stephan J. Goetz (2000), 'Technology Gains and Farmer Well-Being: Some Evidence from the Data,' selected poster pres. at AAEA ann. meeting, Tampa, FL.

Dorner, Peter (1972), *Land Reform and Economic Development*, Penguin Books, Baltimore, MD.

Eicher, Carl and John M. Staatz (1998), editors, *International Agricultural Development*, John Hopkins University Press, Baltimore, MD.

Feder, Gershon (2000), "From Transition to Development: The Economics and Policies of Rural Transition in East Asia, the Former Soviet Union, and Central and Eastern Europe: Discussion," *American Journal of Agricultural Economics*, vol. 82, no. 5, pp. 1156-8.

Goetz, Stephan J. (1993), 'Interlinked Markets and the Cash Crop-Food Crop Debate in Land-Abundant Tropical Agriculture,' *Economic Development and Cultural Change*, vol. 41, pp. 343-61.

Goetz, Stephan J. (1998), 'Assessment of FSR's EIHS Producer Data for Use by MVE in Constructing Pre-Reform Benchmarks,' prep. for Abt Assoc. and USAID/Cairo, *mineo*, 5pp.

Górz, Bronislav and Wlodzimierz Kurek (1998), 'Poland,' in D. Turnock (editor), *Privatization in Rural Eastern Europe: The Process of Restitution and Restructuring*, Edward Elgar, Northampton, MA, USA, pp. 169-99.

Gomulka, Stanislav (2000), 'Ten Years of Retrospect: Secrets of Successful Macroeconomic Policies,' *Transition*, Aug.-Oct., pp. 16-9.

Hobbs, Jill E., William A. Kerr and James D. Gaisford (1997), *The Transformation of the Agrifood System in Central and Eastern Europe and the New Independent States*, CAB International, Oxon, UK.

Hutton, Sandra and Gerry Redmond (2000), 'Poverty in Transition Economies: An Introduction to the Issues,' in S. Hutton and G. Redmond (eds), *Poverty in Transition Economies*, Routledge Studies of Societies in Transition, London, pp. 1-13.

Johnson, Simon, Daniel Kaufmann and Oleg Ustenko, (2000) 'Formal Employment and Survival Strategies after Communism,' *Transition Newsletter*, Aug.-Oct. www.worldbank.org/html/prddr/trans/WEB/abstracts/forempab.htm

Johnston, Bruce F. and John W. Mellor (1961), 'The Role of Agriculture in Economic Development,' *American Economic Review*, vol. 51, pp. 566-93.

Koestner, Ulrich (1998), 'Introduction,' *European Review of Agricultural Economics*, vol. 25, pp. 281-8.

Lerman, Zvi (2000), "From Common Heritage to Divergence: Why the Transition Countries are Drifting Apart by Measures of Agricultural Performance," *American Journal of Agricultural Economics*, vol. 82, no. 5, pp. 1140-8.

Mellor, John W. (1995), 'Introduction,' in J.W. Mellor (ed), *Agriculture on the Road to Industrialization*, John Hopkins University Press, Baltimore, pp. 1-22.

Miljkovic, Dragan and Roberto J. Garcia (1996), 'Employment in Agribusiness and Purchases of Agricultural Products: The Effects of Monetization in Yugoslavia,' *Journal of Agricultural and Applied Economics*. vol. 28, pp. 357-68.

Millikan, M.F. and D. Hapgood (1967), *No Easy Harvest*, MIT Press, Boston, MA.

Rizov, Marian, Erik Mathijs and Johan F.M. Swinnen (2000), 'Post-Communist Agricultural Transformation and the Role of Human Capital: Evidence from Romania,' selected paper presented at the AAEA annual meeting, Tampa, FL.

Sachs, Jeffrey D. (1996), 'The Transition at Mid Decade,' *American Economic Review* (Proceedings), vol. 86, pp. 128-33.

Samonis, Valdas and Csilla Hunyadi (1993), *Big Bang and Acceleration: Models for the Postcommunist Economic Transformation*, Nova Science Publ., Inc., Commack, NY.

Siamwalla, Ammar (1995), 'Land-Abundant Agricultural Growth and Some of Its Consequences: The Case of Thailand,' in J.W. Mellor (ed), *Agriculture on the Road to Industrialization*, John Hopkins University Press, Baltimore, pp. 150-74.

Stark, David (1992), 'Path-Dependence and Privatization Strategies in East Central Europe," *East European Politics and Societies*, 6, Winter, pp. 17-54.

Svejnar, Jan. (1996), 'Enterprises and Workers in the Transition: Econometric Evidence,' *American Economic Review* (Proceedings), vol. 86, pp. 123-7.

Takács-György, Katalin. (1999), 'Difficulties of the Transition in Agriculture in Central Europe in the 1990's,' selected paper presented at the AAEA annual meeting, Nashville, TN.

Tomich, Thomas P., Peter Kilby and Bruce F. Johnston (1995), *Transforming Agrarian Economies: Opportunities Seized, Opportunities Missed*, Cornell University Press, Ithaca, NY.

Turnock, D. (1998), 'Introduction,' in D. Turnock (editor), *Privatization in Rural Eastern Europe: The Process of Restitution and Restructuring*, Edward Elgar, Northampton, MA, USA, pp. 1-48.

van Brabant, Jozef M. (1998), *The Political Economy of Transition: Coming to grips with history and methodology*, Routledge Studies of Societies in Transition, London.

van Selm (1997), *The Economics of Soviet Break-Up*, Routledge Studies of Societies in Transition, London.

World Bank, *2000 World Development Indicators*. Avail. at www.world-bank.org

2. Climate, Soils and Agricultural Potential

GUDRUN LOOSE

2.0 Introduction

Natural conditions, which are predetermined by climate, water, soil and vegetation, strongly influence a region's basic agricultural potential. Judicious use of that potential - i.e., utilizing but not exhausting it - and efforts to increase the potential through scientific and technological innovation should be key principles underlying land use. It is especially important to consider these principles in places where land use patterns are undergoing rapid and fundamental change. Far-reaching social transformation processes in CEE countries are leading to profound land use changes. To make these transformations ecologically and economically sustainable, natural land use potentials need to be considered carefully.

2.1 Climate

Macroclimate

Central and Eastern Europe can be divided into two areas in terms of climate: a large part with temperate climate, and a much smaller part with Mediterranean climate. The Rhodope mountain range in the southeast forms a natural boundary between these regions. Additionally, the extreme north of Eastern Europe (Kola Peninsula and areas north of 63° latitude) have a subpolar climate (Kupfer, 1954). This differentiation of CEE climate is the result of atmospheric circulation patterns. The temperate zone[1] has year-round circulation of extra-tropical cyclonal westerlies, while the Mediterranean zone[2] is differentiated by seasonal alternations of extra-tropical westerlies and tropical trade winds.

A general westerlies drift dominates in the extra-tropical westerlies circulation, but this drift can change frequently and abruptly. The unsettled drift results from permanent cyclonal activities; the primarily eastward depressions (cyclones) incorporate airstreams of different origins (from arctic to tropical) through suction effects, each with specific properties. According to Hendl (1967), northerly airstreams are on average much colder throughout the year than those coming from the south, and airstreams coming from the ocean are much warmer in winter and cooler in summer than those of continental origin. Maritime airstreams contain more water vapor and, as a rule, also more clouds than comparable streams of continental origin. The latter are also highly permeable to radiation and therefore allow a rather strong variation of air temperatures during the course of a day.

Since precipitation in the westerlies circulation is also strongly linked to cyclonal activity - most precipitation comes from clouds rising along the front of a cyclone - cyclone-borne disturbances lead to precipitation that is erratic in terms of when it occurs, variable in quantity, and interspersed with irregular dry periods (Hendl, 1967). Hence, circulation that is influenced by extra-tropical cyclonal westerlies circulation gives rise to highly unsettled weather patterns with strong variations in both temperature and precipitation, and with year-round precipitation.

Unsettled weather is also typical of winters in Mediterranean Europe, when extra-tropical cyclonal circulation spreads to that region. However, winters are milder because of more intensive radiation (at lower latitudes) and vast stretches of warm Mediterranean water. In contrast, southern Europe comes under the influence of the Etesians during the summer, i.e., of northeasterly trade winds of tropical trade wind circulations. This settled airstream with its stable stratification results in intensive radiation, few clouds and little rainfall, which produces warm and dry summers. Therefore, the Mediterranean climate has an unfavorable seasonal distribution of precipitation, with a winter peak and a minimum in summer.

In addition to general circulation, a number of other factors influence climatic conditions in CEE, and contribute to their further differentiation. The area stretches from about the 40th to 70th north parallels, and latitude-dependent variation of radiation strongly influences temperatures. In general, annual average air temperatures increase with declining latitude, as is apparent from rising annual mean temperatures (table 2.1). Due to seasonal variations in radiation duration and intensity in more northern regions, however, certain differences appear over the course of a year. In the winter, radiation intensity and duration both decline rapidly at higher latitudes. Temperatures therefore fall more sharply towards the north than in the summer, when declining radiation intensity is compensated for to some extent by longer radiation and greater daily input of energy.

In addition to latitude-dependent temperature variations, strong zonal influences with highly complex effects are present. These are described as "maritimity" and "continentality", and they depend on relative distributions of seas, oceans and continental land mass. Because of Europe's strong segmentation by peripheral seas (Baltic Sea, Mediterranean Sea, Black Sea, Caspian Sea), cyclones can bring maritime influences of the Atlantic Ocean far to the East. However, high pressure domes over Central Asia during the winter block the advance of Atlantic depressions, diverting them to the north, where they are trapped and push up on top of each other over the Baltic states (Blüthgen and Weischet, 1980). In general, continentality over the European mainland increases from west to east and southeast. According to Ivanov (1959), climate conditions in Poland, the Czech Republic, northern parts of Slovakia, the Baltic states, north, west and central Belarus, northwest Ukraine, and Russia's northern regions adjacent to the Baltic Sea are classified as lightly continental (continentality 101-121) (figure 2.1).

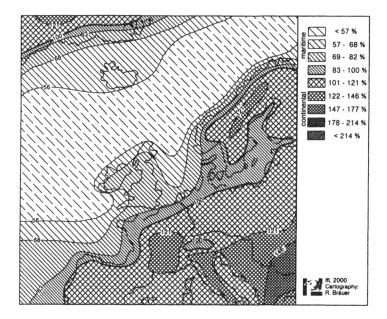

Figure 2.1 Continentality according to Ivanov

Source: Adapted from Blüthgen and Weischet, 1980.

Increasing continentality is characterized by rising temperature amplitude in the course of both the day and the year,[3] declining annual total precipitation, and a shift of maximum precipitation from the winter into summer. Declining Atlantic influences towards the east and southeast are primarily due not to declining frequency of maritime airstreams, but rather to increasing modification of these streams by the underlying continent (Hendl, 1967). Air in the lower atmosphere is heated up strongly in the summer and cooled down even more in the winter. Thunderstorms with heavy convective rainfall often develop over hot continental areas in the summer, which means that the amount of precipitation is higher in the summer than in the winter with its cyclonal peak. Even though precipitation peaks in the summer, humidity falls and aridity rises with increasing continentality since high temperatures cause potential evaporation to sometimes exceed actual amounts of precipitation (table 2.1).

According to Mohrmann and Kessler (1959), all of CEE, except for the Tatra Mountains, has a precipitation deficit from July to September, which increases from mountains to lowlands, from coastal regions inland, and especially from the cooler north towards the hot (during the summer) south, where the deficit may be more than 400 mm (figure 2.2). As long as plants find sufficient moisture in rhizospheres to overcome short-term or moderate rainfall deficiencies, they will not wilt, although their growth comes to a standstill. The critical physiological threshold lies between a 100 to 200 mm deficit, depending on the plant species. Above this threshold, irrigation is essential for plant survival; below the threshold irrigation is still recommended for optimal plant growth (Blüthgen and Weischet, 1980).

In addition to latitude-dependent radiation and different degrees of continentality, CEE's topography further contributes to climatic differentiation. Different elevations above sea level, from lowland to mountain ranges, result in different thermal conditions; the temperature on average drops by 0.6°C per 100 m increase in altitude. This creates both cool plateaus and summit locations and warmer basins and lowlands, but the continental influence is always preserved. Therefore, winters are colder and summers hotter in the Walachian Basin than in the Bohemian Basin. Mountains have a particularly strong influence on precipitation, as they intensify the frontal up-slide of cyclones. But here again, western mountain ranges receive more precipitation, due to their lower degree of continentality, than high mountains in southeastern Europe. Unlike the windward sides of mountains, where precipitation is abundant, adjacent leeward basins are at a disadvantage. In these basins, summer thunderstorms are necessary to keep annual precipitation above 500 mm. Within the mountain ranges, highly diversified climate patterns develop depending on the topography, with major contributions from favorable radiation on south-facing slopes, temperature inversions (lakes of cold air in valleys and clearings, warmer slopes), stronger wind as well as barrier and *foehn* effects. These climatic conditions and climate-affecting factors together create a highly diversified climate in CEE countries. The climate differences, in turn, result in different conditions for farming and agricultural land use potentials.

Agroclimate and agricultural land use potential

Relationships between weather or climate and agriculture are extremely complex. This is due to spatial and temporal variability of meteorological elements on the one hand, and to wide-ranging demands of plants and farm animals, on the other. Weather and climate requirements vary not only between cereals and root crops or among the cereals, but also among different varieties of cereals.

Agriculture's primary demands on weather and climate relate to warmth and moisture; a deficit or surplus of these factors sets back agricultural activities. Consequently, temperature and moisture regimes provide fundamental information about agricultural land use potentials. Attention needs to be paid not only to average conditions (annual means and totals), but also to temporal dynamics during the course of a year and variations between years. Following Bourke and Rosini (1984) and particularly Seljaninov (1972),[4] agroclimatic conditions in CEE can be described as follows.

In northernmost Eastern Europe - coastal regions of the Barents Sea north of the 65th parallel - prospects for agriculture are severely limited. Here temperature sums for the period with continuous daily temperature means above 10°C are less than 1,000 degrees. Growing seasons are usually less than 90 days, and the range of crops that can be grown is small. Even in the summer the risk of ground-level frost exists. Tubers and green vegetables can be grown only in locations with favorable topoclimate, and places with the most favorable thermal conditions are also suitable for growing early potatoes, cabbage and spring-sown cereals. These crops are grown close to their thermal tolerance limit, however, and even slight negative temperature deviations have immediate and far-reaching consequences. Severe winter killing of pasture grasses and cereals may occur, especially in winters with only a thin snow cover.

Table 2.1 Climatological normals for select climate stations 1931-1960 (Roman numerals denote the month)

Station	Annual mean temperature (°C)	Mean temperature of coldest month (°C)	Mean temperature of warmest month (°C)	Temperature amplitude (deg.)	Annual Precipitation (mm)	Maximum precipitation (mm/month)	Minimum precipitation (mm/month)	Relative humidity (%)		
								Annual mean	Maximum in month	Minimum in month
Poland										
Szczecin	8.4	-1.1	17.7	18.8	527.0	61 / VII	27 / II	81.0	89 / XII	72 / V
Krakow	7.7	-3.3	17.5	20.8	686.0	97 / VI	32 / II	80.0	87 / XII	73 / V
Warszawa	7.8	-3.3	18.0	21.3	515.0	71 / VI	21 / II	78.0	88 / XII	68 / V
Czechia										
Brno	8.7	-2.5	18.5	21.0	493.0	72 / VI	24 / I a II	75.0	85 / XII	65 / IV
Ostrava	8.2	-2.4	17.8	20.2	701.0	104 / VI	27 / I	77.0	84 / XII	71 / IV
Praha	7.9	-2.0	17.1	19.1	527.0	77 / V	23 / II	77.0	85 / XI to I	70 / IV a V
Slovakia										
Poprad	5.8	-5.0	15.5	20.5	579.0	90 / VI	23 / I	76.0	82 / XII	70 / IV
Hurbanovo	10.0	-1.5	20.2	21.7	523.0	57 / VIII	27 / III	74.0	85 / XII	65 / IV
Hungary										
Budapest	10.4	-1.6	20.8	22.4	516.0	63 / VI	29 / III	73.0	86 / XII	63/IV a VII
Debrecen	9.9	-2.6	20.3	22.9	566.0	80 / VI	30 / II	77.0	88 / XII	69/V a VII
Pécs	10.4	-1.4	20.5	21.9	619.0	84 / VI	32 / II	73.0	85 / XII	65 / VII

Table 2.1 continued

Station	Annual mean temperature (°C)	Mean temperature of coldest month (°C)	Mean temperature of warmest month (°C)	Temperature amplitude (deg.)	Precipitation per annum (mm)	Maximum precipitation (mm/month)	Minimum precipitation (mm/month)	Relative humidity (%)		
								Annual mean	Maximum in month	Minimum in month
Romania										
Bucuresti	10.6	-2.4	22.0	24.4	595.0	77 / VI	32 / X	70.0	87 / XII	57 / VIII
Sibiu	8.5	-4.0	18.7	22.7	627.0	99 / VI	26 / II	74.0	86 / XII	66 /IVa.VII
Timisoara	10.6	-1.6	21.1	22.7	593.0	76 / VI	36 / II	73.0	86 / XII	62 / VII
Bulgaria										
Sofia	10.0	-1.5	20.7	22.2	579.0	78 / V	31 / I	69.0	79 / XII	62 / VIII
Sandanski	14.0	2.4	24.6	27.0	481.0	63 / XI	23 / IX	65.0	78 / XII	54 / VII
Varna	12.1	1.9	22.0	23.9	471.0	50 / XI	31 / IX	77.0	82 / I	70 / VIII
Estonia										
Tallinn	5.1	-5.5	16.3	21.8	667.0	84 / VIII	29 / II a III	81.0	87 / XII	74 / V
Tartu	4.8	-7.1	16.5	23.6	589.0	86 / VIII	23 / II	-	-	-
Latvia										
Riga	6.2	-4.7	16.9	21.6	636.0	79/VII a VIII	25 / II	-	-	-
Dau-gavpils	5.5	-6.7	16.9	23.6	634.0	83 / VII	27 / II	-	-	-

Table 2.1 continued

Station	Annual mean temperature (°C)	Mean temperature of coldest month (°C)	Mean temperature of warmest month (°C)	Temperature amplitude (deg.)	Precipitation per annum (mm)	Maximum precipitation (mm/month)	Minimum precipitation (mm/month)	Relative humidity (%)		
								Annual mean	Maximum in month	Minimum in month
Lithuania										
Vilnius	6.0	-6.1	16.9	23.0	683.0	78 / VII	38 / II	-	-	-
Silute	6.8	-3.8	16.7	20.5	797.0	95 / VII	34 / II	-	-	-
Belarus										
Minsk	5.8	-6.9	17.3	24.2	677.0	88 / VII	34 / II	80.0	90 / XI	67 / V
Brest	7.4	-4.5	18.0	22.5	611.0	80 / VII	31 / II	-	-	-
Vitebsk	5.1	-8.2	17.1	25.3	663.0	92 / VII	30 / II	-	-	-
Ukraine										
Kharkiv	7.5	-6.9	20.3	27.2	519.0	75 / VII	32 / III	74.0	89 / XII	58 / V
Kyiv	7.7	-5.6	19.3	24.9	649.0	88 / VII	35 / X	76.0	88 / XII	63 / V
Odesa	10.1	-1.7	21.5	23.2	464.0	49 / VII	26 / X	76.0	86 / XIIa I	63 / VII

Table 2.1 continued

Station	Annual mean temperature (°C)	Mean temperature of coldest month (°C)	Mean temperature of warmest month (°C)	Temperature amplitude (deg.)	Precipitation per annum (mm)	Maximum precipitation (mm/month)	Minimum precipitation (mm/month)	Relative humidity (%) Annual mean	Maximum in month	Minimum in month
Russia										
Kazan	3.8	-13.0	19.6	32.6	548.0		27 / II a III	75.0	85 / XII	62 / Va VI
St. Petersburg	5.0	-7.8	17.7	25.5	635.0	81 / VIII	30 / II	79.0	88 / XII	66 / V
Moskva	5.0	-9.3	18.2	27.5	691.0	94 / VII	34 / III	77.0	86 / XII	64 / V
Murmansk	0.0	-11.3	12.6	23.9	492.0	79 / VIII	19 / III	78.0	84 / XIa.XII	68 / VI
Soci	14.0	5.9	22.7	28.6	1,573.0	203 / XII	90 / V	-	-	-
Rostov	9.7	-4.6	23.0	27.6	596.0	77 / XII	33 / X	72.0	87 / XIIa I	58 / VII a. VIII

* *Note*: These are the most recent data available on a consistent basis across these countries. In general data represent the period 1961 – 1990 with exception of data of relative humidity for Poland, Romania, Estonia, Lithuania, Ukraine and Russia, which are related to the period 1931 – 1960.

Source: Adapted from WMO (1996), *Climatological Normals (CLINO) for the Period 1961 - 1990*, Geneva; WMO (1962), *Climatological Normals for Climate and Climate Ship Stations for the Period 1931 - 1960*, Geneva.

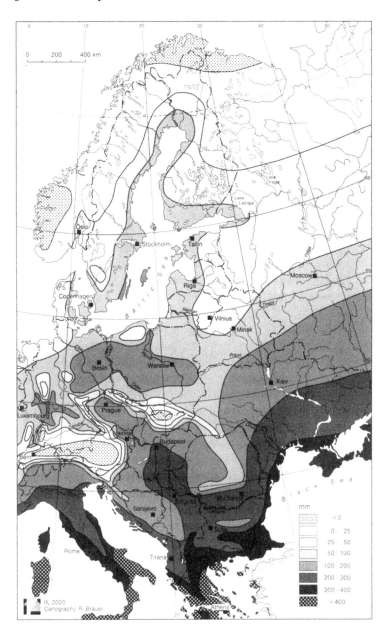

Figure 2.2 Precipitation deficit during July-August-September in Europe

Source: Adapted from Mohrmann and Kessler, 1959.

Europe between 60° and 45° north - i.e., the bulk of CEE, except for the immediate northern and southern fringes - has the most favorable climate for agricultural production. On average, temperatures and precipitation are sufficient. General thermal problems occur only for thermophilic crops, such as corn or grapevines, when their cultivation is extended further to the north. Greater variability of weather conditions, however, causes substantial seasonal and annual variations that affect agriculture. Yields are already influenced by more frequent occurrences of widespread weather events in some years or seasons (Klaus, 1986). Almost all over Europe, for example, the increasing prevalence of northwesterly winds is causing grain yields to decline. More pronounced or prolonged temperature and rainfall variations are a problem, as they may lead to shorter growing seasons - mostly as a result of long and cold springs - and also to periods of excessive moisture or drought.

Field operations (seedbed preparation, sowing, cultivation and harvesting) cannot be carried out when soils are too wet. Under these conditions, crops also suffer from less vigorous growth, lower yields and greater risk of disease. Cereals may lodge and - like hay - fail completely. From an agronomic point of view, drought occurs when the amount of plaint-available soil moisture becomes inadequate beyond a critical period. This is caused primarily by periodically and/or seasonally inadequate precipitation and high rates of evaporation. Most crops are particularly susceptible to drought during germination, as young plants, and during periods of intensive growth, when they - like farm animals - are also more susceptible to diseases.

Within the large temperate European zone, temporal variation in weather conditions goes hand in hand with significant spatial differences in climate, as discussed earlier. A significant increase occurs in the annual sums of continuous daily mean temperatures above 10°C: from 1,000 degrees in the north to as much as 4,000 degrees in the southernmost part. The growing season extends over more than 150 days in southern parts of Belarus, in Ukraine and southern parts of Russia, and over more than 210 days on the Balkan Peninsula. In addition, the frost-free period increases up to 190 and 240 days, respectively (particularly along the western coast of the Black Sea). A wide range of crops can be grown under these conditions: tubers, potatoes, spring- and autumn-sown cereals, corn for silage, canola and flax. Fruits and berries can be grown in regions with temperature sums up to 2,500 degrees, that is, up to about the Warsaw-Kiev-Kuibyshev line. Corn for grain, sugar beet, sunflowers, soybean and hard-shelled fruits (nuts and almonds) are important crops in regions where temperature sums are even higher and, in places with mild winters, grapes are an important crop.

Despite generally favorable thermal conditions during the growing season, a certain risk of damage to crops exists, especially in central parts of the East European Lowlands, east of the Riga-Lvov-Krivoy-Rog line to the Danube River delta. Here winters are bitterly cold with mean temperatures between -5 and -15°C during the coldest month, and as low as -15 to -20°C at the foot of the Ural Mountains. Long frost periods endanger fruit trees and, particularly in years with little snow cover, fall-seeded cereals and oil seeds.

As do thermal conditions, moisture conditions also vary significantly from the north to the south/southeast. Northern regions, generally above the Riga-Minsk-Moscow-Kirov line are excessively wet, and drainage is required in many places. In the region immediately to the south, to about the line from the northern edge of Kisalföld and Alföld-Bucharest-Kishinev-Kuibyshev-Orsk, water supply is sufficient and reliable throughout the growing season, with less than a 25 percent probability of drought. South of that line, moisture conditions are poor, with up to 50 percent probability of drought, and the annual drought period increases rapidly to an average of 100 days further south. In many places options for offsetting moisture deficits are limited, as sufficient surface water is not available.

Mediterranean conditions occur in Eastern Europe only south of the Rhodope Mountains - i.e., further south than in western or Central Europe - which is related to the orographic structure of the Balkan Peninsula. Therefore, cultivation of typical subtropical crops, such as citrus fruit, olives or cotton, is not important in Bulgaria. However, the more intensive solar radiation favors cultivation of highly thermophilic crops, such as apricots, peaches, grapes and tobacco. Other typical features of Mediterranean climate, such as water shortages that occur not only during average dry summers but also throughout the year, or occurrences of weather extremes - heavy rain, hail, heat waves, etc. - also exist in certain regions.

A more detailed description of agroclimatic conditions in Europe can be found in the *Agro-Ecological Atlas of Cereal-Growing in Europe*, although the coverage of Eastern Europe does not extend all the way to the Ural Mountains. Altogether 45 agroclimatic sub-regions are identified for relevant countries in CEE (figure 2.3). The mountain regions (Sudetes, Beskids, Eastern and Southern Carpathians, Balkan Mountains and Rhodope complex) are excluded, as the climate conditions in these regions are extremely diverse and do not fit well into a general classification scheme (Thran and Broekhuizen, 1965).

Figure 2.3 Agro-climatic sub-regions

Source: Adapted from Thran and Broekhuizen, 1965 and Broekhuizen, 1969 (Agro-Ecological Atlas of Cereal Growing in Europe, vol. I and. II).

Legend for figure 2.3: Agro-climatic sub-regions in CEE

Sub-regional climate conditions and type of farming

1	Invariably wet, cool, fairly mild in summer, icy in winter
	Transition from livestock farming to arable farming; intensive arable farming in the south; cattle and sheep farming; no fruit growing (except strawberries)
2	Invariably wet, cool, cool in summer, icy in winter
	Transition from livestock farming to arable farming; intensive arable farming in the south; cattle and sheep farming; no fruit growing
3	Moderately wet, moderately cool, fairly mild in summer, frost in winter
	Very intensive arable farming; fruit growing (apples) feasible
4	Invariably wet, moderately cool, fairly mild in summer, icy in winter
	Arable farming; some grassland farming; fruit growing (apples, plums) quite feasible
5	Invariably wet, moderately cool, fairly mild in summer, frost in winter
	Arable farming and grassland farming; fruit growing (apples, pears, cherries, plums) to some extent feasible
5a	Wet, moderately cool, fairly mild in summer, frost in winter
	Arable farming and grassland farming; fruit growing (apples, pears, cherries, plums) to some extent feasible
6	Moderately wet, moderately cool, fairly mild in summer, cold in winter
	Arable farming; limited amount of grassland farming
7	Wet, temperate, fairly mild in summer, cold in winter
	Arable farming; some grassland farming
8	Wet, moderately cool, fairly mild in summer, cold in winter
	Arable farming; grassland farming
9	Invariably wet, moderately cool, fairly mild in summer, frost in winter
	Arable farming; grassland farming
10	Very wet, moderately cool, cool in summer, cold in winter
	Arable farming; grassland farming
11	Very wet, temperate, cool in summer, cool in winter
	Arable farming; some grassland farming
12	Very wet, moderately cool, cool in summer, cold in winter
	Fodder farming; arable farming; some cattle farming on mountain pastures
13	Moderately wet, moderately cool, mild in summer, icy in winter
	Arable farming; little grassland farming
14	Moderately wet, temperate, fairly mild in summer, frost in winter
	Arable farming and some grassland farming
14a	Moderately wet, temperate, mild in summer, frost in winter; annual temperature: 7.5° to 8°C
	Arable farming and grassland farming
14b	Periodically wet, temperate, fairly mild in summer, cold in winter
	Arable farming and some grassland farming
15	Moderately wet, temperate, mild in summer, frost in winter; annual temperature: 8° to 9°C
	Arable farming and some grassland farming
16	Same as 15, except that spring is somewhat warmer and rain is more plentiful in the summer
17	Invariably wet, temperate, fairly mild in summer, cold in winter
	Arable farming; in some districts also grassland farming

17a   Periodically wet, mild, mild in summer, cold in winter
Arable farming and some grassland farming

18   Moderately wet, temperate, mild in summer, frost in winter
Arable farming, some grassland farming; some hops, fruit and vegetable growing

19   Moderately wet, temperate, fairly mild in summer, cold in winter
Arable farming; grassland farming; clover pasture

20   Invariably wet, temperate, cold in winter, mild in summer
Arable farming; grassland farming; clover pasture

20a   Wet, temperate, fairly mild in summer, cold in winter
Arable farming; grassland farming; clover pasture

20b   Invariably wet, mild, fairly mild in summer, cold in winter
Arable farming; grassland farming; clover pasture; sheep pasture

21   Invariably wet, mild, mild in summer, cold in winter, mild in spring
Grassland farming; arable farming; clover pastures

22   Invariably wet, temperate, fairly mild in summer, cold in winter
Arable farming; hardly any grassland farming

22a   Wet, mild, fairly mild in summer, cold in winter, mild in spring
Arable farming; grassland farming; vegetable growing

23   Wet, mild, mild in summer, cold in winter
Arable farming; hardly any grassland farming;
Viticulture and fruit growing on 15% to 30% of the agricultural area

24   Wet, mild, fairly mild in summer, cold in winter
Arable farming; viticulture and fruit growing 15% to 40%;
Grassland farming; much clover pasture

25   Very wet, temperate, fairly mild in summer, frost in winter
Arable farming; grassland farming

26   Wet snow forest mountain climate: short cool summer, longer frost winter
Mostly arable farming where technically possible;
Otherwise cattle farming and grassland farming on meadows, mountain pastures and rough grazing land

27   Very wet, temperate, mild in summer, frost in winter
Arable farming where technically possible;
Otherwise grass land farming

28   Invariably wet, mild, fairly mild in summer, cool in winter, mild in spring
Arable farming; hardly any grassland farming

28a   Invariably wet, mild, fairly mild in summer, mild in winter, mild in spring
Arable farming; grassland farming (milk and meat)

29   Invariably wet, mild, mild in summer, cool in winter
Arable farming; grassland farming (milk and meat);
In the north-west 60% of the agricultural area is pasture, in the north-east 30% to 50%, in the south and south-east less than 20%

35   Dry at times, moderately warm, dry in summer, warm in summer, tepid in winter
Arable farming; viticulture and fruit growing;
Frequent irrigation

36   Wet, moderately warm, warm in summer, cool in winter
Arable farming; viticulture; olive-oil production in the south; milk and meat in the north; silkworm farming in all districts owing to the cultivation of white mulberry

37   Wet, mild, mild in summer, cool in winter (annual temperature: 12°C)
Arable farming, field crops, hardly any viticulture; 20% to 30% pasture

38   Invariably very wet, temperate, fairly mild in summer, cool in winter (average altitude)
Arable farming; much grassland farming

39   Wet, mild, mild in summer, cool in winter (annual temperature: 10°C)
      Arable farming; 30% to 40% grassland farming, especially for meat production;
      viticulture, tobacco in the south-east

39a   Invariably wet, mild, mild in summer, cool in winter
      Arable farming; much grassland farming, especially fattening on pasture

40   Very wet, mild, mild in summer, cold in winter
      Arable farming; viticulture; grassland farming; milk and meat production

45   Moderately wet, mild, fairly mild in summer, mild in winter
      Intensive arable farming

46   Wet, temperate, cool in summer, mild in winter
      Intensive arable farming; grassland farming

54   Dry, warm, warm in summer, warm in winter, wet in autumn, dry in summer
      Intensive arable farming with a large number of irrigated sites; sheep and goat
      breeding on a great deal of wasteland; mountain and forest pasture; fruit growing
      and viticulture predominant

60   Moderately wet, mild, mild in summer, frost in winter, moderately dry in late
      summer
      Arable farming; grassland farming in the west; some viticulture and fruit growing
      in the east

60a   Moderately wet, mild, warm in summer, cold in winter, dry in midsummer
      Arable farming; viticulture and fruit growing on 15% to 45% of the agricultural
      area, lentils

61   Wet, mild, mild in summer, frost in winter
      Fruit growing and viticulture on 15% to 45% of the agricultural area; grassland
      farming

61a   Very wet, mild, mild in summer, frost in winter, dry in winter
      Fruit growing and viticulture on 15% to 45% of the useful area;
      Grassland farming

62   Occasionally wet, mild, mild in summer, frost in winter,
      moderately dry in late summer
      Arable farming; grassland farming

63   Moderately wet, mild, warm in summer, cold in winter, moderately dry in late
      summer
      Arable farming

64   Moderately wet, mild, mild in summer, cold in winter, moderately dry in late
      summer
      Arable farming and grassland farming

65   Wet, moderately warm, warm in summer, cool in winter
      Arable farming; grassland farming on mountain slopes with cattle, sheep and goats

66   Wet, moderately warm, warm in summer, cold in winter, dry in late summer
      Arable farming; much grassland farming; both very intensive

67   Wet, moderately warm, warm in summer, tepid in winter, dry in summer
      Arable farming; fruit growing and viticulture

68   Wet, mild, warm in summer, mild in winter, dry in late summer
      Arable farming with irrigation

69   Occasionally dry, moderately warm, hot in summer, tepid in winter, dry in
      summer
      Arable farming with irrigation; fruit growing and viticulture (almonds)

70   Frequently dry, warm, warm in summer, warm in winter, dry in summer
      Arable farming; cultivation of industrial crops

71   Wet, warm, warm in summer, warm in winter, dry in summer, sunny in winter
      Arable farming with irrigation

73	Frequently dry, warm, warm in summer, warm in winter, dry in summer
74	Occasionally wet, moderately warm, warm in summer, tepid in winter, dry in summer
75	Occasionally wet, moderately warm, warm in summer, tepid in winter, dry in summer
77	Occasionally wet, cold, cool in summer, icy-cold in winter, wet in late summer, cold in autumn; gradual rise in temperature in spring
78	Occasionally wet, cool, cool in summer, icy in winter; wet in late summer and autumn, cold in autumn; rapid rise in temperature in spring
79	Wet, cool, fairly mild in summer, icy in winter; wet in late summer, mild in spring (rapid rise in temperature), cold in autumn
80	Wet, cold, cool in summer, icy in winter, wet in late summer, mild in spring (rapid rise in temperature)
81	Occasionally wet, cold, cool in summer, icy-cold in winter (coldest month – 13.0°C); wet in late summer, cold in autumn
82	Occasionally wet, cold, cool in summer, icy-cold in winter (coldest month – 13.7°C); wet in late summer, cold in autumn
85	Wet, cool, fairly mild in summer, icy-cold in winter, wet in late summer, mild in spring (rapid rise in temperature)
86	Occasionally wet, cold, fairly mild in summer, icy-cold in winter, wet in early and mid-summer, cold in autumn
86a	Occasionally wet, cold, cool in summer, icy-cold in winter, wet in early and mid-summer, mild in spring (rapid rise in temperature)
87	Occasionally wet, cool, fairly mild in summer, icy in winter, wet in early and mid-summer, mild in spring (rapid rise in temperature); number of frost-free days: 120
87a	Occasionally wet, cool, fairly mild in summer, icy in winter, wet in early and mid-summer, mild in spring (rapid rise in temperature); number of frost-free days: 125
87b	Occasionally wet, cold, fairly mild in summer, icy-cold in winter, wet in late summer, mild in spring (rapid rise in temperature)
88	Occasionally wet, cold, fairly mild in summer, icy-cold in winter, wet in early and mid-summer, mild in spring (rapid rise in spring)
92	Wet, cool, fairly mild in summer, icy in winter; wet in early and mid-summer; mild in spring with rapid rise in temperature; number of frost-free days: 140
92a	Wet, cool, fairly mild in summer, icy in winter; wet in early and mid-summer, mild in spring with rapid rise in temperature; number of frost-free days: 130
93	Occasionally wet, cool, fairly mild in summer, icy in winter, wet in late summer, mild in spring with rapid rise in temperature
93a	Wet, cool, fairly mild in summer, icy in winter; wet in late summer, mild in spring with rapid rise in temperature
94	Occasionally wet, moderately cool, mild in summer, icy in winter, wet in early and mid-summer, mild in spring with rapid rise in temperature; number of frost-free days: 140
95	Wet, moderately cool, mild in summer, icy in winter, wet in early and mid-summer, mild in spring with rapid rise in temperature
95a	Occasionally wet, moderately cool, mild in summer, icy in winter, wet in early and mid-summer, mild in spring with rapid rise in temperature; number of frost-free days: 165
96	Wet, temperate, mild in summer, icy in winter, wet in early and mid-summer, mild in spring with rapid rise in temperature
97	Occasionally wet, temperate, mild in summer, icy in winter, wet in early and mid-summer, mild in spring with rapid rise in temperature

98	Occasionally wet, temperate, mild in summer, icy in winter, dry in late summer, mild in spring with rapid rise in temperature
100	Wet, temperate, mild in summer, frost in winter; wet in early and mid-summer, mild in spring with rapid rise in temperature
101	Occasionally wet, temperate, mild in summer, frost in winter, wet in early and mid-summer, cool in spring with gradual rise in temperature
102	Occasionally dry, temperate, mild in summer, icy in winter, wet in early and mid-summer, mild in spring with rapid rise in temperature
102a	Frequently dry, mild, warm in summer, frost in winter; wet in early and mid-summer, mild in spring with rapid rise in temperature
103	Occasionally wet, mild, mild in summer, frost in winter; wet in early and mid-summer, cool in spring with gradual rise in temperature
104	Occasionally dry, mild, warm in summer, frost in winter; wet in early and mid-summer, cool in spring with gradual rise in temperature (warm in autumn)
105	Occasionally wet, mild, warm in summer, frost in winter; wet in early and mid-summer, mild in spring with rapid rise in temperature
106	Occasionally wet, mild, warm in summer, frost in winter; wet in early and mid-summer, spring with short days
107a	(North) Very wet, moderately warm, warm in summer, tepid in winter; rainy season in autumn and winter, warm in autumn; number of frost-free days: 190
107b	(South) Very wet, moderately warm, warm in summer, tepid in winter; rainy season in autumn and winter, warm in autumn; number of frost-free days: 195
108	Occasionally dry, mild, warm in summer, frost in winter; rainy season in spring and winter, cool in spring with gradual rise in temperature
109	Occasionally dry, moderately warm, warm in summer, cold in winter; rainy season in autumn and winter, mild in spring with rapid rise in temperature
110	Occasionally dry, moderately warm, warm in summer, mild in winter; rainy season in autumn and winter, warm in autumn
111	Frequently dry, moderately warm, hot in summer, mild in winter; dry in summer, warm in autumn
112a	(North) Dry, moderately warm, hot in summer, mild in winter; dry in summer, warm in autumn
112b	(South) Frequently dry, moderately warm, warm in summer, cold in winter; rainy season in spring and winter, cool in spring with gradual rise in temperature
113	Dry, warm, hot in summer, tepid in winter; rainy season in spring and winter, coolin spring with gradual rise in temperature
114	Wet, sultry, hot in summer, warm in winter; arid in summer, rainy season in autumn and winter, warm in autumn
115	Arid, hot, hot in summer, warm in winter; arid in summer, warm in autumn
117	Wet, cool, fairly mild in summer, icy in winter; wet in late summer, in spring rapid rise in temperature

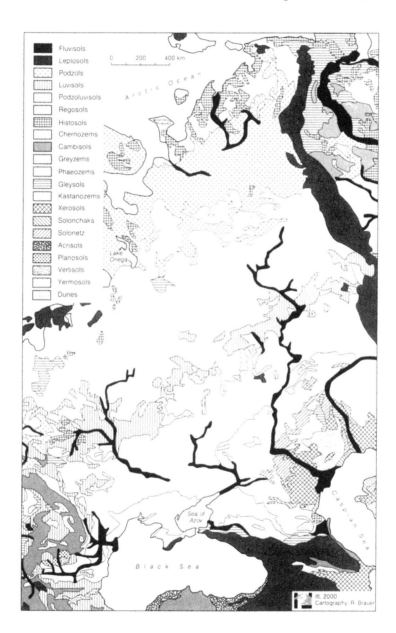

Figure 2.4 Main soils associations (generalized)

Source: FAO/UNESCO (1978): Soils of the World 1:5,000,000

2.2 Soils

Soil is an important agricultural input. It provides a place for crops to root and it supplies them with water and nutrients. Through melioration, irrigation, fertilization and different forms of cultivation, crops can be raised in areas where they would not naturally grow. Prior experience with intensive agricultural production shows that soil protection is critical if soil is to retain its fundamental role in the future.

Climate and soil interact closely with one another. Climatic conditions have affected soil development over thousands of years, giving rise to the soil types that exist today. Soil quality can alter agricultural potential set by agro-climatic conditions - especially by changing the supply of water and nutrients. Excellent soil conditions can to some extent compensate for unfavorable agro-climatic conditions.

Primary soils and their agricultural potential

Soil is the product of many processes that occur on or near the Earth's surface. Soil-forming factors, including parent material, climate, water, flora and fauna, and human activity, over time determine soil-related processes such as weathering, mineralization and humification, and horizontal and vertical mineral shifting. The number and diversity of soil-forming processes and their interactions with one another have left behind an enormous diversity of soil types. These can be grouped according to different criteria, and soil cover and distribution patterns can be fully characterized.

A guide for soil groups is needed for larger, more structured areas or, more specifically: "[s]oil groups that have formed under the influence of climate, relief, and substrata conditions typical for a region or under geological development of 'standard areas'" (Ewald, 1989, p. 337). In CEE, this generalized soil geography leads to a close correlation between pedologic conditions, on the one hand, and environmental and orographic conditions, on the other. In Eastern European lowlands, primary soil groups change with environmental conditions, which vary among zones. In central and southeastern Europe, the strong orographic surface continuum leads to less rigid zonal soil associations (figure 2.4). In general, soils influenced by water dominate in the north, while steppe-like conditions prevail in the south. Major soil groups in CEE can be described using the FAO's classification system,[5] based on FAO (1993), Ehwald (1989), Schmidt-Lorenz (1986), Heininger (1994), and FAO (1981) - as follows:

Histosols are hydromorphic, organic (marshy) soils. They are characterized by formation and accumulation of peat and formed in very wet and/or cold conditions. As a result, organic materials decompose very slowly. Even with little biomass production, a thick humus horizon can build up. These soils exist in areas with excessive precipitation under suitable soil surface conditions (in-filling zones of lakes, valleys floors, depressions, etc.)

Histosols are loosely packed and retain large amounts of water. In northern regions, they are characterized by permafrost. Usually they are acidic and nutrient-poor. Because of their weak supply of nutrients and the influence of water and permafrost, they have only limited agricultural potential (primarily for grazing). Drainage is feasible only in agro-climatically favorable areas. The process leads to subsidence, whereby the surface sinks, peat layers compress, and the topsoil humus disperses. Large areas of Histosols occur in northern and central parts of Russia, in Byelorussia, in northern and central Ukraine, and in Poland's lowlands. They often occur together with other poorly drained soils (Gleysols, Fluvisols) and Podzols. Numerous smaller areas with favorable topography can be found in parts of CEE.

Gleysols are mineral soils with distinct hydromorphic characteristics (gleys). Permanent or predominant influence of groundwater, backwater, or persistent moisture leads to the typical gley appearance. This includes pale grey spots, bands or horizons in water-saturated regions and yellow, orange, or red spots of iron along with black spots of manganese in non-saturated layers. Gleysols are nutrient-rich. However, their waterlogged state, inherently reduced oxygen supply, and de-nitrification (reduction of nitrates to nitric oxides not usable by plants or pure nitrogen) limits their agricultural potential. They are best suited for grazing.

Gleysols are widespread in northern Russia, where they are associated with other hydromorphic soils and are subjected to permafrost. During snow-melting periods, frozen sub-soils add an immense amount of soil moisture. In the rest of CEE, Gleysols occur in lowlands (such as in the foothills of the Baltic ridge or in the Colchis lowlands) and in depressions and valleys.

Fluvisols are alluvial soils with little or no profile differentiation (wetland soils). They developed under conditions of regular flooding. Early, post-Pleistocene sediments left by this flooding vary greatly, depending on sedimentation conditions. The multiple layers can have a wide range of texture, humus content, chemical makeup and nutrients, but usually these soils are nutrient-rich.

Fluvisols occur in connection with bodies of flowing water. The largest areas are river plains of the Volga, Danube, Oder, and Theiss. Agricultural potential depends strongly on hydrographic conditions. Fluvisols in floodplains of rivers and those with very wet subsoils can only be used as grasslands. Wetlands with little hydromorphic characteristics and soil regions protected by dikes are highly productive for dryland crops (grains, horticulture, fruits), although the high clay content requires strict water management.

Podzols develop on porous parent substrata with low fertility. They occur in CEE mostly on glacial or periglacial sands. Soil formation is determined by podzolization (shifting of organic material and sesquioxides from upper to lower soil layers). This causes the surface to bleach and acidify, while the subsoil cements to the point of impermeability (laterite).

Podzol soils are nutrient poor and suffer from lack of nitrogen, potassium, and phosphates. They dry out quickly due to their porous nature, but if an impermeable layer (laterite) has formed, seasonal waterlogging can occur. Due to their limited agricultural potential, Podzols are mainly used for grazing. Intensive measures (deep plowing, lime application and fertilization) can improve their potential under favorable agroclimatic conditions. Podzols mainly occur in northern and central Russia and in Poland, but they are also found in the Czech Republic, Hungary and Romania.

Luvisols are characterized by lessivation (migration of clay particles, including their humus and iron oxide shells, from surface soils to sub-soils, forming an upper horizon with low clay content and a lower horizon rich in clay). This migration often leads to soil packing, which in turn can cause waterlogging. The migration of soil particles is enhanced by frequent fluctuation of flooding and drying.

In CEE, Luvisols are formed as brownish soils, mostly on glacial and periglacial deposits (sands, clays, loesses). The older soils in southern Europe have a more distinctly reddish color caused by longer rubification (the expelling of hematitc iron oxides to the mineral surface). Luvisols are often associated with Cambisols, and owe their high agricultural potential to a number of factors. They contain a large amount of weatherable minerals and a relatively large amount of nutrients. They have good alkaline saturation and moisture storage, and are well aerated unless the subsoil has become too dense. In temperate zones, Luvisols are among the most important agricultural soils, with a wide range of uses. On slopes, however, they are prone to erosion and mud build-up. Melioration is sometimes necessary when the subsoil has become too dense. In CEE,

Luvisols are used for grains, sugar beet, and fodder crops. In southern Europe they are also used for vines and horticultural crops. Tree crops and grazing are preferred in mountainous regions.

Podzoluvisols are soils that show signs of podzolization as well as lessivation (bleached soils, Dernoposols). They have a bleached clay- and sesquioxide-depleted horizon that penetrates the underlying clay horizon along an irregular border. Most Podzoluvisols are more acid and have a lower nutrient saturation than Luvisols. Rooting and water uptake can be impeded by the dense clay layer and, in northernmost areas, by permafrost.

Podzoluvisols form a broad belt from Poland through the Baltic States and Byelorussia to the Ural Mountains. They are seldom used in less favorable, colder regions. In thermally more favorable conditions, they are used as green land or for crops (winter grains, potatoes, sugar beet). Here they require careful tillage and fertilization.

Planosols are soils with abrupt changes in texture between an upper layer with little clay and a deeper layer with high clay content. They develop mostly in flat or lowlands, where they are regularly subjected to temporary flooding from precipitation or at least hydromorphic episodes on the surface (gley formation). Their parent materials are Pleistocene sediment with high clay content or alluvial and colluvial deposits of varying mineralogy.

Planosols are in general low to moderately fertile. They are limited by a low structural stability on the surface, a tendency to waterlog in the subsoil, and seasonal alternation of wetness and drought. They are mainly used as green land but also for wheat and sugar beet, requiring careful fertilizer and water management. In CEE, these soils are only found on a larger scale in flatlands of Rumania's Danube valley.

Cambisols are moderately developed soils with predominantly middle or fine texture and stable structure. The characteristic brown coloring is the result of weathered silicates, release and oxidation of iron, and formation of clay-minerals. An appreciable accumulation of clay does not occur because the high content of iron and aluminum compounds lowers the clay mineral's mobility.

Because Cambisols develop on a wide variety of materials and surfaces (usually late Glacial or Holocene), their properties vary widely. They are usually pH-neutral to acid, have good water storage, and drain well. Their soil fauna is active, and they are moderately fertile. They have a high agricultural potential for crops (wheat, barley, oats, corn potatoes, sugar beet) and grazing (cattle, sheep). The topography, however, is important in determining how they are used. Cambisols are common in hills and mountains of central, central-eastern, and southeastern Europe; they are often associated with Luvisols.

Chernozems are very dark (dark brown to black), deep soils (black soils) rich in humus and nutrients. They have developed since the last glacial period on loose sediments (particularly loess), and under a highly productive cover of grass vegetation. The most important soil-forming processes include intensive mull formation, clay-humus formation, and good soil homogenization brought about by a well-populated and active fauna.

Chernozems have very high natural fertility as a result of their high humus and nutrient content, porosity, good water storage capacity, and neutral pH. The main crops grown are wheat, barley, corn and sugar beet along with horticultural crops. Drought stress and short growing periods limit this exceptional potential, however. Chernozems span a broad band from southeastern Europe, through the Ukraine and southern Russia, to the Ural Mountains. They also occur in the Bohemian basin.

Phaeozems developed out of alkaline sediments. They have a prominent, dark surface soil with high humus content and alkaline saturation. The subsoil is rich in clay. These soils resemble the moist degradation stage of Chernozems due to their intense saturation and erosion processes under moist conditions. Phaeozems are porous, well aerated soils with stable structure, high nutrient content, and large reserves of weathered minerals. They are mostly found in mountain-surrounded basins of the Czech Republic, Slovakia, Hungary, Romania, and Bulgaria. Their high agricultural potential is suitable for grains, corn, sugarbeet, tree crops, vines and tobacco.

Greyzems are dark brown to dark gray soils, rich in nutrients and humus (Gray Forest Soils/Grey Soils). They combine characteristic processes of Chernozems - intensive accumulation of calcium saturated humus-acids and mull formation - with processes characteristic for Luvisols and Cambisols - formation of iron-stabilized humus, clay formation, clay migration, and browning. They also form a geographic belt in southeastern and eastern Europe between Chernozems in the south and Luvisols or Podzoluvisols in the north.

Greyzems, along with Chernozems and Phaeozems, make up some of the most valuable farmland. In the cold, northernmost regions of the Ukrainian and Russian steppe zone, low temperatures limit their use. Here cold-resistant grains, potatoes, and some sugar beet are grown.

Kastanozems are chestnut colored soils containing carbonates. The surface horizon is rich in humus, although not as rich or as deep as that of Chernozems. They are characterized by de-carbonation in the topsoil and lime (sometimes gypsum) accumulation at even relatively shallow depths. The deeper layers are partially sodic. The chemical make-up is a definite sign that soils are dry for a good part of the year, limiting these otherwise nutrient-rich soils. They are suitable for wheat and cotton cultivation. Their high potential can only be reached through irrigation, although this can lead to erosion and high sodicity. The results of dry farming are erratic, usually requiring some form of improvement in water-soil conditions such as black fallow ground. Due to low biomass production, Kastanozems used for grazing only last when used extensively.

Kastanozems occur in southern Europe on the northern coast of the Black Sea and in foothills of the Caucasus, stretching out south of the Ural mountains into Asia. They are associated with Solonetz-Soils with increasing dryness.

Solonetz-soils are highly alkaline and rich in sodium (alkali or sodium soils). They have a dense, dark or light gray A-horizon with low clay content, which quickly turns plastic when moist and hardens rapidly when dry, forming polygon-shaped cracks. The very dense subsoil is rich in clay and has a characteristic columnar structure. The sodium accumulation can be caused either by natural processes (intensive weathering of sodic parent substrates, influence of sodic groundwater, erosion of former Solonchak-soils as a result of increased humidity), or through human intervention (such as irrigation or lowering of groundwater levels).

In Europe, Solonetz-soils occur especially in southern Russia (Caspian lowlands) and on a smaller scale in Hungary and Rumania. They have low agricultural potential. They have few nutrients, and their high sodium content is toxic to most crops. The high density and unfavorable soil structure (fluctuating from soaked to dried out) limit water circulation and rooting and make working the soil very difficult. Solonetz-soils are mainly used for extensive grazing. In cooler, more favorable agroclimatic conditions they can be reclaimed for crops through intensive melioration (deep tilling, application of gypsum and pyrite and leaching with calcium-rich water).

Leptosols are poorly developed, shallow soils on a crumbling layer of hard rock (sometimes called Lithosols, Ranker or Rendzina). The soil formation is limited to a small humus accumulation. There are notable differences in texture, mineralogy, acid and base content, and humus content, depending on the parent material and formation conditions. Their shallow depth makes

Leptosols susceptible to drought, waterlogging, and erosion. When used agriculturally, they are easily destroyed.

In Europe, Leptosols are limited to mountain regions (especially the Ural Mountains and Caucasus). Due to the topography of the land, Leptosols are usually forested and mostly have only a grazing potential.

Regosols are inorganic, undeveloped soils on a rocky subsurface. Parent materials are usually colluvial and recent alluvial deposits. Except for a small accumulation of humus, distinct soil horizons have not been able to form. Regosols are low in organic matter and have little mineral or organic exchange. Often soil materials cohere poorly due to coarseness. Regosols are, therefore, subject to erosion.

Regosols are limited to the western permafrost zone of Russia, where they are often associated with Gleysols and Histosols. They usually remain under their natural vegetation and are periodically used for reindeer grazing.

Major soil groups need to be subdivided for large scale surveys based on topography-dependent changes (the principle of soil-catenae). These more refined soil units produce a much more differentiated mosaic. A detailed explanation cannot be given here but can be found in the Europe volume of the FAO/UNESCO Soil Map of the World and in national soil maps (FAO/UNESCO, 1981). It is important to note that CEE has a high, though regionally extremely varied, pedological potential. Exact, local knowledge of soil conditions is imperative for successful agricultural management - that is, to insure lasting yields and to reduce soil deterioration over time.

Soil damage from human use

Soil quality and potential change over time. Changes can be induced by nature (climatic shifts and changes, volcanic eruptions, changes in drainage areas, lakes drying up, among others) or by humans as they use land. Changes can improve or worsen and degrade soil quality.

Natural soil degradation occurs in combination with various pedogenetic processes such as podsolization, lixiviation and salt accumulation, or it is induced by certain ecological conditions as in the case of erosion, solifluction or water logging. Human influence can either raise soil resistance to natural degradation processes, or it can be primarily responsible for soil degradation (FAO, 1979). Soil exploitation can accelerate or intensify degradation processes, even extending them to ecosystems where they did not otherwise exist. Anthropogenic soil damage can include soil sealing, soil packing or accumulation of toxic materials.

Soil degradation occurs through chemical, physical and biological processes that depend on and affect each other (figure 2.5). Agricultural exploitation can endanger the soil in different ways. Crops extract soil nutrients. A negative humus balance diminishes organic matter content. Large machinery and livestock can compact topsoil. Tillage and lack of soil cover can cause erosion of soil and humus particles by wind and water. Soluble salts can accumulate as a result of improper irrigation. Organic and inorganic materials from fertilizers and pesticides can contaminate the soil.

Soil degradation leads to a long-term reduction in agricultural potential by directly affecting plant growth (Heiniger and Herweg, 1994). Restricted aeration and limited oxygen supply make it more difficult for plants to sprout and root. Rooting area shrinks, leading to reduced nutrient availability, less water and too little anchoring in the soil. Supply of nutrients and ability to store them is reduced (due to toxicity from isolated elements such as sodium and aluminum). Microbiological balance is destroyed (nutrient mineralization is impaired), making plants susceptible to diseases. Accumulation of soluble salts reduces soil water supply and changes plant metabolism. Soil flora and fauna dwindle, further worsening total nutrient circulation as well as plants' water, air and energy supply.

Although stages and effects of soil degradation are more or less known, quantitative or geographical surveys have only provided a fragmented picture (Craswell, 1993). Quantitative assertions are mostly based on estimates, while those making geographic assessments have drawn their conclusions from land use intensity. This suggests a general west-to-east slope of degradation in CEE. Starting in flatland areas of Bohemia and Moravia and lowlands of northwest and southwest Hungary, degradation is reduced in stepwise fashion in easterly and northeasterly directions. It reaches a minimum in the Volga region and in non-black-earth regions of Russia (Nefedova et al., 1992). Extreme deviations from this general trend can occur within a locality, however (see descriptions for specific countries), and in less intensively exploited areas extensive degradation processes also occur.

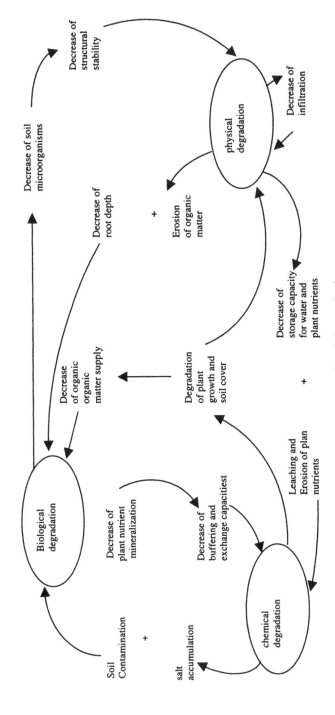

Figure 2.5 Major interactions between different types of soil degradation

Source: Adapted from Heiniger and Herweg, 1994.

For Europe as a whole, an estimated 22 percent of the area (218.8 million ha) has been degraded as a result of human activity (Oldeman et al., 1991). Sixty million ha have a low degree, 144.3 million ha a medium degree, 10.8 a high degree, and 3.1 million ha an extreme degree of degradation. Damage is primarily caused by water erosion (114.6 million ha), wind erosion (42.1), chemical processes such as salinization, acidification, and accumulation of toxic substances (25.7), and physical processes such as crusting, packing, sealing and humus reduction (36.4 million ha). Annual rates of soil loss due to erosion are between 10 and 20 t/ha (Pimental, 1993). This is comparable to farmland loss due to erosion in the US (16 t/ha annually). Several million more acres are believed to have even higher rates of loss (Ploey et al., 1991).

One of the most severely degraded regions in Europe is the black-earth zone (Chernozems zone) of Ukraine and Russia. At the end of the 19th century over 70 percent of farmland in eastern and southeastern Russian lowlands showed signs of soil degradation, and substantially diminished yields (Karavayeva et al., 1991). Degradation has continued since then. The humus content of the steppe zone in central parts of the Russian lowlands, for example, decreased from 7-10 percent in 1881 to 4-7 percent in 1981. In the southeast, it decreased from 9-11 percent to 6-8 percent. Humus reserves have declined by over 30 percent (*ibid.*).

Destruction of natural vegetation and permanent plowing, under influence of continental climatic conditions, has increased erosion enormously. Gully erosion (ovrag formation) has made even slightly sloped areas unusable. In addition to water erosion, wind erosion has damaged the black earth zone, despite the fact that surfaces vulnerable to this kind of soil removal are uncommon in the natural steppe. As a result, a substantial part of the land is degraded. In Ukraine approximately 25 percent of Chernozems are affected, although 18 percent are eroded to a lesser degree, 5 percent to a medium extent, and 2 percent heavily (Karavayeva et.al., 1991).

Irrigated Chernozems have become more and more susceptible to compacting, salinization and alkalinizaion. Some have even been degraded to Gleysol- or Solonetz-type soils. It is estimated for the European part of the former Soviet Union that 20 percent of irrigated fields have turned to wasteland and up to 50 percent to bog. Forty to fifty percent of agriculturally exploited soils in Hungary suffer from acidity, waterlogging or salinity (Nefedova et al., 1992). A special soil degradation problem exists in radioactively contaminated regions of Russia, Byelorussia and Ukraine, following the Chernobyl catastrophe. Even 10 years after the disaster, the extent of ecological and economical damage can hardly be measured (see the country analyses).

Conclusion

Soil degradation - especially in terms of its consequences for agricultural production - is a dramatic problem. The immediacy is clear when looking at the time required for soil to regenerate and form: according to Pimental, it takes 500 years to develop 2.5 cm of topsoil. The most favorable estimates for regeneration are about 1 t/ha per year; this compares with ten to twenty times higher annual rates of soil loss at present. Past and current damage done - measured on a human time scale - is irreversible. Regeneration - if possible at all - would take thousands of years. It is therefore of utmost importance to at least halt soil degradation by instituting effective soil management systems. Ecologically-oriented production methods, adapted to local agroclimatic, pedological and hydrological conditions, based on closed circulation of biomass and nutrients, a range of locally suitable crops and techniques, and additional protective and conservation measures, are foundations of such a management system.

2.3 Summary and prospects

The large region of CEE has an impressive agricultural potential. Natural conditions vary substantially within this area from north to south, and east to west. Individual sub-regions have different agricultural potentials and profiles, creating opportunities for interregional and interstate exchange of agricultural products.

Continuing soil degradation–due to improper farming techniques and overexploitation in the past and the present - has greatly impaired the natural agricultural potential, however. Soil degradation, accelerated by anthropogenic influence and coupled with other environmental problems (especially water pollution), threatens the future agricultural potential of large areas. Ecologically adapted farming systems are indispensable for the future. This can only be achieved if and when the current transformation processes in CEE create the necessary political, economic and social pre-conditions. Without supporting measures such as agricultural education and advice and financial assistance; suitable technologies; and ecologically-oriented price policies, the majority of farms will not be able to introduce sustainable farming systems or to use them over the long term.

Along with existing problems of adapting farming systems to natural conditions, new demands will arise in the future. Further changes in the climatic conditions can be expected, and they will have consequence for the natural requirements of agricultural production. In the last hundred years, the average yearly temperature has risen globally between 0.3 and 0.7°C

(Parry and Carter, 1988). Current estimates are that global temperatures will increase by between 1.5 and 4.5°C, assuming the carbon dioxide content in the atmosphere doubles between the years 2050 and 2100 (Brouwer and Chadwick, 1991) or even by as much as 5.5°C (Parry and Carter, 1988).

According to Brouwer and Chadwick (1991), Europe can expect (until the year 2030) a general rise in the average annual temperature of at least 1°C in northern Europe and 0.5°C in southern Europe. In CEE this will be accompanied by a slight increase in annual precipitation (Brouwer and Chadwick, 1991). The summers will become warmer and dryer, while the winters become cooler and wetter. Long-term forecasts (from 2030 to 2075) see an increase in the average annual temperature of between 3 to 4°C. In this case, all seasons will be affected by the warming. The winter will experience the greatest increase–by up to 7°C in the north and by about 2°C in Mediterranean Europe. Average annual precipitation north of the 50th parallel will increase up to 150 mm, while decreasing considerably to the south–with a decline of up to 300 mm in the Mediterranean region. A rise in the sea level by 40 to 160 cm is expected to accompany these environmental changes. Changes in the coastal lowlands, affecting nearby rivers and streams, will follow.

Basically, climate change will most likely lead to a change in the length of the growing season. In northern Europe, the rise in temperature will increase these periods, while the longer drought periods will shorten them in the south. The northern borders for raising certain crops (sugar beet, winter wheat, summer barley, potatoes) will shift 5 to 7 degrees latitude to the north. Large areas of forest in the non-black-earth zone would become attractive for farming, while the zone itself would most likely produce surpluses (Hekstra, 1991).

Ecological consequences of global warming, however, should not be ignored. A study of the region around St. Petersburg illustrates this issue. The study assumes a rise in temperature of 2.2°C, and a rise in precipitation of 127 mm by the year 2035. With a linear application of fertilizer until 2010, yields of winter rye will increase about 5 percent. Subsequently, yields will decrease by 23 percent because rising groundwater levels (+38 percent) will reduce soil fertility by 42 percent. The accompanying intense leaching of soil nutrients will greatly burden surface waters (+225 percent) (Pitovranov et al., 1988).

No detailed forecasts can currently be made of how climate conditions will in fact change within the various regions of CEE, or the consequences these changes will have for farming, and what effects farming will in turn have on the ecosystem. However, it is clear that agriculture and agricultural production practices will have to adapt to these changing climate conditions.

Notes

[1] "Temperate climate" (Alisov, 1954) is similar to the terms *feuchtgemäßigtes Klima* (Flohn, 1950), *Klima der planetarischen Frontalzone* (Kupfer, 1954), and *temperiertes Zyklonaklima* (Hendl, 1963).

[2] "Mediterrranean climate" is similar to the terms *subtropisches Klima* (Alisov, 1954; Kupfer, 1954), *subtropisches Winterregenklima* (Flohn, 1950), and *Kernpassat-Wechselklima mit winterlicher Zyklonalwitterung* (Hendl, 1963).

[3] For extra-Mediterranean Europe, Hendl reports an increase of the annual temperature variation of about 0.5°C per degree of longitude (Hendl, 1967).

[4] Seljaninov presented a world map of agroclimates in 1972. In the underlying agroclimatic classification he first identifies temperature-dependent agroclimatic zones that are defined by the average annual sum of continuous daily mean temperatures above 10°C (so-called growth-active temperatures for the majority of crops). The limiting thresholds of temperature sums result from the thermal requirements of the range of crops concerned. Further subdivision of the thermal zones is based on the degree of moisture as determined by the optional use of a hydrothermal coefficient or of a drought index (Seljaninov, 1972; see also Hupfer, 1991).

[5] The FAO-classification was developed for the FAO/UNESCO Soil Map of the World 1:5,000,000, published from 1971 to 1981. The classification criteria follow those of the US-classification, the most important being the diagnostic soil horizons. The FAO-classification deviates, however, from the US-taxonomy in criteria definition and nomenclature.

In 1985 many changes were made to the classification that were not transferred to the Soil Map of the World 1:5,000,000. The classification now lists 29 major soil groups: Fluvisols, Gleysols, Regosols, Leptosols, Arenosols, Andosols, Vertisols, Cambisols, Calcisols, Gypsisols, Solonetz, Solonchaks, Kastanozems, Chernozems, Phaeozems, Greyzems, Luvisols, Planosols, Podzoluvisols, Podzols, Lixisols, Acrisols, Alisols, Nitisols, Ferrasols, Plinthosols, Histosols, and Anthrosols (FAO, 1993).

References

Alisov, B.P. (1954), *Die Klimate der Erde*, Berlin, 277 pp.

Blüthgen, J. and Weischet. W. (1980), *Allgemeine Klimageographie*, Berlin, New York, 887pp.

Bourke, A. and Rosini E. (1984), 'The Impact of Climatic Fluctuations on European Agriculture', in H. Flohn and R. Fantechi (eds), *The Climate of Europe: Past, Present and Future*, vol. II, Dordrecht, Boston, Lancester, pp. 269-314.

Broekhuizen, S. (ed.) (1969), *Atlas of the Cereal-Growing Areas in Europe*, vol. II, Amsterdam, London, New York, pp.156, 60 maps.

Brouwer, F.M. and Chadwick, M.J. (1991), 'Future Land Use Patterns in Europe', in F.M. Brouwer, A.J. Thomas and M.J. Chadwick (eds), *Land Use Changes in Europe*, Dordrecht, pp. 49-78.

Craswell, E.T. (1993), 'The Management of World Soil Resources for Sustainable Agricultural Production', in D. Pimentel (ed.), *World Soil Erosion and Conservation*, University Press, Cambridge, pp. 258-276.

Ehwald, E. (1989), 'Bodengenetik, Bodensystematik, Bodengeographie', in G. Müller (ed.), *Bodenkunde*, Berlin. pp. 262-339.

FAO (1979), *A Provisional Methodology for Soil Degradation Assessment*, Rome (FAO).

FAO (1993), World Soil Resources: An Explanatory Note on the FAO World Soil Resources Map at 1:25,000,000 Scale, Rome (FAO), 64 pp., 4 maps.

FAO/UNESCO (1978), *Soil Map of the World 1:5,000,000*, Sheets V-1, V-2, Edition 1/ 1978, Paris (UNESCO).

FAO/UNESCO (1981), *Soil Map of the World 1:5,000,000*, vol. V: Europe, Paris, UNESCO, 90 pp., 1 map.

Flohn, H. (1950), 'Neue Anschauungen über die allgemeine Zirkulation der Atmosphäre und ihre klimatische Bedeutung', *Erdkunde*, 4, Bonn, pp. 141-162.

Frei, E. and Peyer, K. (1991), *Boden – Agrarpedologie*, Bern, Stuttgart, 190 pp.

Heiniger, O. and Herweg K. (1994), *Die Ressource Boden*, Bern, 56 pp.

Hekstra, G.P. (1991), 'Climatic Change and Land Use Impact in Europe', in F.M. Brouwer, A.J.Thomas and M.J. Chadwick (eds), *Land Use Changes in Europe*, Kluwer Academic Publishers, Dordrecht, pp. 117-207.

Hendl, M. (1963), *Einführung in die physikalische Klimatologie*, II, Systematische Klimatologie, Berlin.

Hendl. M. (1967), 'Einführung in die Klimaverhältnisse Europas', *Zeitschrift für den Erdkundeunterricht*, No. 11, Berlin, pp. 409-423.

Hupfer, P. (1991), Das Klimasystem der Erde: Diagnose und Modellierung, Schwankungen und Wirkungen, Berlin, 464 pp.

Karavayeva, N.A., Nefedova, T.G. and Targulian, V.O. (1991), 'Historical Land Use Changes and Soil Degradation on Russian Plain', in F.M. Brouwer, A.J. Thomas and J.J.Chadwick (eds), *Land Use Changes in Europe*, Kluwer Academic Publishers, Dordrecht, pp. 351-377.

Klaus, D. (1986), *Statistische Zusammenhänge zwischen Ernteertrag und Großwettergeschehen in Europa*, Stuttgart, 48 pp.

Kupfer, E. (1954). 'Entwurf einer Klimakarte auf genetischer Grundlage', *Zeitschrift für den Erdkundeunterricht*, 1, Berlin, pp. 5-13.

Michael, Th. (1996), 'Bodendegradation. Dimension, Ursachen und Folgen eines globalen Umweltproblems', *Zeitschrift für den Erdkundeunterricht*, 5, Berlin, pp. 200-209.

Mohrmann, J.C.J. and Kessler, J. (1959), Water deficiencies in European Agriculture. A Climatological Survey, Wageningen, 60 pp., 10 maps.

Müller, G. (ed.) (1989), *Bodenkunde*, Berlin, 380 pp.

Nefedova, T.G. et al. (1992*), Nutzung und Probleme der Umwelt im mittleren und östlichen Europa*, Begleittext zu den Kartenblättern im Atlas Ost- und Südosteuropa. Deutsche Fassung, Wien, 30 pp.

Oldeman, L.R., Engelen, V.W.P. and Pulles J.H.M. (1991), 'The Extent of Human - Induced Soil Degradation', in L.R. Oldeman, R.T.A. Hakkeling and W.G. Sombrock (eds), *World Maß of the Status of Soil Degradation*, An Explanatory Note, Wageningen, Nairobi, pp. 27- 33.

Parry, M. and Carter, T.R. (1988), 'The Assessment of Effects of Climatic Variations on Agriculture: Aims, Methods and Summary Results', in M.L. Parry, T.R. Carter and N.T. Konijn (eds), *The Impact of Climatic Variations on Agriculture*, vol. I, Assessments in Cool Temperate and Cold Regions, Kluwer Academic Publishers, Dordrecht, pp. 11-95.

Parry, M.L. and Carter T.R. (1991), 'Climatic Changes and Land Use Potential in Europe', in F.M. Brouwer, A.J. Thomas and M.J. Chadwick (eds), *Land Use Changes in Europe*, Kluwer Academic Publisher, Dordrecht, pp. 209-231.

Pimentel, D. (1993), 'Overview', in D. Pimentel (ed.), *World Soil Erosion and Conservation*, University Press, Cambridge, pp. 1-5.

Pitovranov, S. E., Kiselev, V.I., Iakiments, I.N. and Sirotenko, O.D. (1988), 'The Effects of Climatic Variations on Agriculture in the Subarctic Zone in the USSR', in M.L. Parry, T.R. Carter and N.T. Konijn (eds), *The Impact of Climatic Variations on Agriculture*, vol. I, Assessments in Cool Temperate and Cold Regions, Kluwer Academic Publishers, Dordrecht, pp. 623-707.

Ploey, J. D., Imeson, A. and Oldeman, L.R. (1991), 'Soil Erosion, Soil Degradation and Climatic Change', in F.M. Brouwer, A.J. Thomas and M.J. Chadwick (eds), *Land Use Changes in Europe*, Kluwer Academic Publishers, Dordrecht, pp. 275-292.

Schmidt-Lorenz, R. (1986), 'Die Böden der Tropen und Subtropen', in S. Rehmö (ed.), *Grundlagen des Pflanzenbaus in den Tropen und Subtropen*, Stuttgart, pp. 47-92.

Seljaninov, G.T. (1972), 'Agrokimaticeskaja karta mira', in I.A. Goldberg (ed.), *Agroklimaticeskij atlas mira*, Moskva, Leningrad, pp. 2-3, 24-25 and Map 1-2.

Semmel, A. (1993), *Grundzüge der Bodengeographie*, Stuttgart, 123 pp.

WMO (1962), *Climatological Normals for Climate and Climate Ship Stations for the Period 1931 to 1960*, Geneva.

WMO (1996), *Climatological Normals (CLINO) for the Period 1961 - 1990*, Geneva.

Thran, P. and Broekhuizen, S. (eds) (1965), *Agro-ecological Atlas of Cereal-Growing in Europe*, vol. I, Agro-Climatic Atlas of Europe, Amsterdam, London, New York, pp. 36, 125 maps.

3. Social Change and Trends in Rural Areas

ROSEMARIE SIEBERT

3.0 Introduction

The years 1988-1989 marked a fundamental turning point for the former socialist CEE countries. The transition to free markets in these countries is a complex and longer-term process that follows diverse patterns, and one that is influenced heavily by historical tradition and national interests, by differences in the level of economic development, and by the political sophistication and cultural modernity of the societies concerned (Geier, 1994; Weidenfeld, 1995).

Significant differences existed among the former socialist countries even before 1988 in the underlying preconditions for social change and economic transformation. For example, the agricultural sector in Poland has always played an important role because of the dominance of family farms, which in 1989 cultivated about 80 percent of the country's agricultural land (Agra-Europe, 32/97). This dominance of family farms in Poland was not diminished, as it was in other countries, in the days of the Soviet Empire. In the other CEE countries, large cooperative and state farms almost completely dominated the agricultural sector. Hungary had a few highly efficient, large cooperative farms, while the large-scale agricultural enterprises in Russia and the Ukraine were generally less successful.

The economic transformation strategy chosen by a country has important consequences for rural areas and the people who live there. Rural villages and towns in CEE were disadvantaged relative to cities well before 1988; in fact, rural areas tended to be marginalized. Farming was usually the only income source in rural areas, non-agricultural jobs were virtually non-existent, and the physical infrastructure was deficient and sometimes altogether missing. This, in turn, led to out-migration of parts of the rural population.

Current transformation policy in most CEE countries fails to account for specific problems and conditions of rural areas. As a rule, these countries lack mature regional development policies, and investments needed to improve the infrastructure are not made because public financial resources are lacking. In most cases, decisions about the use of available funds do not favor rural areas. For example, rural construction programs in Russia for roads and railroads, gas and water supply lines, and housing have been discontinued because of a lack of funds (Gerloff, 1994). It has become clear that structural change in the transformation countries has caused even greater social differences, and a deterioration of material living conditions for large parts of the rural population.

3.1 Population density and distribution

Population densities vary significantly across the CEE countries. Romania (with 98 inhabitants/km^2), Hungary (110), Slovakia (108), Poland (123) and Czech Republic (131) are more densely populated. In contrast, the successor states of the former Soviet Union are sparsely populated: most average fewer than 50 inhabitants per square kilometer. Lithuania (56 inhabitants/km^2) and the Ukraine (85) are exceptions (Statistisches Bundesamt, various years). Considerable variation also exists in the population densities within individual CEE countries: in industrial centers, these densities are very high, while they are low in rural areas.

In the last 30 to 40 years, the distribution of population between rural and urban areas has reversed itself, following a trend similar to that occurring in the U.S. and other developed countries. Around 1950, the rural population still accounted for 60 to 80 percent of the total CEE population. By the late 1980s the share of people living in rural areas had declined to between 30 and 40 percent.

Figure 3.1 Population density

3.2 Demography and migration

Since the early 1990s, the demographic structure of the CEE countries has changed dramatically. Deteriorating living conditions and uncertainty about the future have contributed to declining numbers of live births, a trend that is evident in all countries, and pronounced in a few. In Bulgaria, Russia, Romania and the Ukraine, but also in Estonia and Hungary, birth rates are on the decline. Russia, for example, had a small excess of births over deaths until 1991, but since then natural population growth has been negative. Some regions still have an excess of births, but the number of regions with an excess of deaths over births is increasing.

In Bulgaria, natural population growth turned negative in 1989. This was due mainly to the social and economic uncertainty prevailing in the country (Meyerfeld, 1996). More than 20 percent of the rural areas in Bulgaria are experiencing significant population declines because of negative growth (Geschev, 1995). In the Ukraine, the population was shrinking in 7 out of 10 rural districts as early as 1989 (Redenko, 1995).

Decades of rural exodus have created a profound imbalance in the age structure of the rural population in the transformation countries. In particular, population pyramids of many rural communities have become inverted. As young and skilled people left their rural villages and towns in the wake of industrialization even before 1990, the share of elderly residents increased noticeably.

In many countries this trend has continued well into the present. In the Hungarian lowlands (Alföld), for example, primarily young males continue to leave their rural homes because of dramatic decline in agricultural employment and the lack of non-farm jobs. A critical need exists in these areas to create jobs, or to stimulate local entrepreneurship outside of agriculture. Years of rural exodus have led to a dwindling in many small rural villages and towns in the number of young and skilled workers that industrial firms typically seek when making location decisions. Today, experts believe that up to 2,000 villages in the Alföld region will become ghost towns as the population continues to age (Agrarinformationsdienst Osteuropa, 1994).

In the Czech Republic, an estimated 650,000 - mostly young - people left rural areas between 1980 and 1990, seriously distorting the population's age structure (Agrarinformationsdienst Osteuropa, 1994). Remote rural communities in Romania lost 20 to 30 percent of their population between 1956 and 1992 (Knappe and Benedek, 1995). Among the regions most severely affected between 1977 and 1992 were the low mountain ranges in the central western part of the Oltenia region, the Gedic Piedmont, parts of the Danube basin, the Banat highlands and the central and western parts of the Transylvanian plain (Janos, 1995).

In Bulgaria, 2.5 million, mostly young people left rural areas for industrial centers between 1946 and 1979. As a result of this exodus, the share of the elderly population in rural areas rose sharply, and Bulgaria was the first country in Europe in which the death rate in rural areas exceeded the rate of births (Meyerfeld, 1996).

In countries such as Russia, Bulgaria and Romania, in contrast, a reverse migration from urban to rural areas is now underway. In Bulgaria, the nascent return migration from cities to rural areas is largely explained by the granting of land ownership rights (Geschev, 1995). Similarly, in Romania increasing numbers of urban residents are moving back to rural towns and villages (Nemenyi, 2000). Here, too, the prospect of acquiring land for agricultural or horticultural uses is a major incentive to resettle in rural areas. Other motivating factors include high urban unemployment and comparatively low costs of living in rural areas (Agra-Europe, 21/97).

In Russia, the number of rural residents had declined for decades, but a reversal has occurred with economic reforms. Between 1991 and 1994, the rural population increased by 3.1 percent, from a total of 38.8 million to 39.9 million (Agra-Europe, 44/94). This increase was due not to natural population growth (i.e., an excess of births over deaths), but to increasing migration of Russians, particularly of refugees from former Soviet republics, into rural regions. Since 1990, about one million Russians (5 percent of the resident population) have left the Russian north, the Far East and Siberia to settle in central Russia, and more than 600,000 settled in rural areas of Russia (Ugarov, 1997).

Rural population growth in Russia is also driven by urbanites seeking to farm to meet their food needs. Moreover, out-migration from rural areas into cities has slowed recently. This appears to be associated with free market incentives and the creation of private enterprise, and new legal arrangements in Russia. Specifically, migrants receive land for their own use, and they also own the output produced on the land (Patsiorkovski et al., 2000). As is true in Romania, rising levels of unemployment, high crime rates and drastic increases in the cost of living are making cities less attractive.

Another reason for the declining rural exodus in Russia is the fact that many young people - the demographic group with the highest propensity to migrate - have already left. While the recent country-wide share of people of retirement age was 23 percent and that of working age was 51 percent, retirees already account for between 30 and 35 percent of the population in many parts of rural Russia (Agrarinformationsdienst Osteuropa, 1994).

Changes in administrative boundaries have also contributed to growth of the rural population, at least according to official definitions. In particular, some former towns have been downgraded to rural settlements, in the process adding about 700,000 residents to the rural population.

The population pyramid of many rural communities was disturbed not only by the longstanding migration to cities. Ecological disasters, such as the Chernobyl nuclear reactor accident, have also changed demographic conditions, producing single-parent families, declining birth rates, and high mortality rates in the most severely affected regions (Rudenko, 1993).

3.3 The advent of unemployment

With a collapsed political system, and the transition from a state-controlled to a free market economy, the transformation countries are now also facing unemployment. This phenomenon is new, at least in its present open form. Restructuring and privatization in the agricultural sector have displaced labor and, owing to the still high proportions of people engaged in farming (up to 30 percent of the overall labor force), this has caused far-reaching social problems in rural areas. The problems are aggravated by the fact that agriculture was typically the only industry providing jobs in rural areas, and the inherited industrial and social infrastructure was such that no new jobs were created once the farm economy shrank. Lacking entrepreneurial skills, most former farm workers saw no alternative but to join the ranks of the unemployed.

While specific labor market conditions vary from country to country, unemployment rates generally did not peak in the years immediately following reforms. The primary reason is that public subsidies were used to keep the rate of unemployment artificially low, which led to high rates of concealed unemployment in many reform countries; this became known as "unemployment on the job". This type of unemployment is becoming more transparent as transformation proceeds.

The former Soviet republics reported very low official unemployment rates in the early reform years. Belarus, the Ukraine, Russia, and to some extent the Baltic states, were reluctant to take the political risks associated with spectacular growth in open unemployment. They initially shifted the labor adjustment problems to agricultural operations through shortened workdays, unpaid forced leave, etc. (Heinrich et al., 1996). Since then, reported unemployment rates have also increased in these countries (ZMP, 2000).

In Poland and Hungary, in contrast, unemployment reached dramatic levels early in the transformation process. In Hungary, the 1.1 million workers on average unemployed between 1989 and 1994 included as many as 600,000 jobless in agriculture. Following the collapse of output markets, privatization of state farms, transformation of cooperative farms, and transfer of former agricultural input-supplying activities to independent enterprises, large numbers of workers were displaced in the agrarian sector. The drop in employment was about 32 percent across all agricultural enterprises, and as high as 72 percent among cooperative farms (Agrarinformationsdienst Osteuropa, 1995).

Unemployment is generally a significant problem in rural Hungary. In industrially backward regions that are less suitable for agricultural production, up to one-half of all workers are estimated to be unemployed (*ibid.*). Hardest-hit are places with populations of fewer than 1,000 in the northeastern and southwestern parts of the country. These regions also have the highest rate (70 percent) of long-term unemployed persons, i.e., of those seeking work for more than 180 days. The rural unemployment rate continued to exceed the national average rate of 9.6 percent in 1998 (ZMP, 2000).

In Poland, the rural unemployment rate was 17 percent in February 1994 (Agrarinformationsdienst Osteuropa, 1994). However, the rate varied considerably by farm type. Unemployment was lowest (6.2 percent) in the private farm sector, but well above the average in areas with a large share of state farms, particularly in northern Poland (e.g., 30.5 percent in Slupsk) (DIW et al., 1995). Excess supply of rural workers in Poland was estimated at between 750,000 and one million in 1994 (*ibid.*). Three years later (1997), 1.5 million people were without work in Poland's rural communities (Agra-Europe, 16/97).

The emergence of a highly diversified informal sector in Poland has tended to offset the adverse social and economic consequences of high unemployment. Further, as a result of overall economic growth, unemployment has declined somewhat since 1997 even though significant regional differences persist. In particular, unemployment rates remain high in sparsely populated areas, particularly in northern Poland where the economy is less diversified (Kühne, 2000).

In Romania, Slovakia, and Bulgaria unemployment rates in 1994 were between 12 and 15 percent. In Bulgaria, employment of rural workers declined by 28 percent; in many of the mountain regions, the decline was as high as 40 to 50 percent within only two years (1990 to 1992) (Geschev, 1995; Kostova, 1997). In view of conditions in agriculture, the number of people released from farming is likely to increase even further. The number of long-term unemployed alone rose to more than 400,000 by mid-1994. The unemployment rate in Bulgaria reached 18 percent in 1999 (ZMP, 2000). An important reason for this increase, in addition to the deteriorating conditions in agriculture, is the deindustrialization that has occurred in the last few years.

In Slovakia, the number of individuals employed in primary agriculture declined by 52 percent between 1990 and 1994; this rate was well above the average rate of decline in employment in other sectors of the economy. Also, while the unemployment rate nationally was 15 percent in 1995, jobless rates were much higher in the southern and eastern regions of the country (Blaas, 1993; Agrarinformationsdienst Osteuropa, 1995; Blaas and Wolz, 1998). By 1999, the national average unemployment rate was 19 percent (ZMP, 2000).

In Romania, the official number of unemployed workers has so far remained stable, largely because more employees were placed on shortened work schedules and involuntary leave, and many workers went to work on small family farms. In the Czech Republic, official unemployment rates to date have been comparatively low. While the agricultural labor force also declined dramatically - from 531,000 in 1989 to 225,000 by 1994 - this decline largely consisted of elderly workers (Agrarinformationsdienst Osteuropa, 1994). Workers employed in activities that supported agriculture, such as building and repair teams, were another group that suffered from employment cutbacks. In addition, many highly skilled workers, with uncertain job prospects in rural areas, left to pursue employment opportunities elsewhere. Recently, unemployment rates have also increased here, however, reaching 9 percent in 1999 (ZMP, 2000).

Knowledgeable observers believe that unrecorded or concealed unemployment rates in many CEE countries are high (Werner, 1994; Heller, 2000). In some countries, many of those affected have been unemployed long-term and no longer appear in official statistics. Further, not all workers who have become redundant report that they are unemployed and, hence, they are not officially counted; rates of underreporting are especially high among females. In Poland, for example, the estimated jobless rate, including concealed unemployment, was 35 percent in 1997 (Agra-Europe, 16/97), but official statistics show a much lower rate of only 14.1 percent. In addition, official statistics do not capture the large number of workers who were forced into early retirement on meager pensions that are not fully inflation-adjusted, for example, in Hungary, Poland and the Czech Republic.

Female workers and young adults are especially affected by redundancy. In some countries they are estimated to account for up to 80 percent and 40 percent of the unemployed, respectively (Heinrich and Koop, 1996). Unless new jobs are created in rural areas in the foreseeable future, young and highly skilled workers will continue to move away.

Growing unemployment has been described as a "complex social deculturalization process," with a wide range of effects (Geier, 1995). Unemployment not only leads to massive wasting and destruction of social, community, and individual experience and achievements (i.e., human capital), but also to a dramatic deterioration of the material well-being of the individuals concerned. This deterioration afflicts not only the unemployed, but it increasingly affects growing shares of the general rural population–particularly in Russia, Belarus, the Ukraine, Romania, and Bulgaria.

3.4 Changing standards of living

Although inflation has declined significantly after reaching exorbitant levels in 1991 and 1992 following price liberalization, it remains relatively high in the transformation countries. Even though nominal incomes have increased in all of the countries studied here, real incomes of large population segments are declining which, in turn, is reducing standards of living. In many CEE countries, the adjustment process has led to widespread impoverishment of farmers and large shares of the rural population (Kühne, 2000; Benedek, 2000). Income from employment, the primary source of revenue for private households, is trending downward (Hämmerling, 1993). This is primarily due to the increasing relative importance of transfer payments, which reflects rising unemployment and increasing numbers of retirees.

Food is becoming an increasingly important item in private household expenditures. In many countries, more that 50 percent of household income is now devoted to buying food. Bread is scarce in Romania; milk, butter, yoghurt, cheese and sugar are almost non-existent. When these products are available, they are imported by private traders and sold at prices that are high relative to prevailing wages and pensions. The quality of the population's nutrition has already been poor for a number of years, and may now be deteriorating even further. Many Romanian farmers live below the poverty line (Agrarinformationsdienst Osteuropa, 1994; Benedek, 2000).

A few years into the transformation process, consumers' purchasing power in Bulgaria declined to only one-half of 1990 levels. About 55 percent of the rural population and almost 90 percent of retirees are estimated to live below subsistence levels. Bulgaria had the lowest standard of living of all CEE countries in 1997 (Atanassova, 1999). In Poland, almost 60 percent of the farm population lived at or near the poverty line in 1992, while 20 percent of the rural population received social security (Agra-Europe, 16/97). In Hungary, according to official statistics, about 30 percent of the population lives below official subsistence levels (DIW et al., 1995), while in Lithuania this applies to 75 percent of the families (Künstling and Kuodys, 1994).

Unemployment, loss of income, and inflation erode both consumer purchasing power and consumer demand, and domestic demand for agricultural products has declined accordingly in a number of transformation countries. In Russia, consumption of meat, milk, butter, sugar and fruit declined to as little as 50 percent of the 1986-1990 average (Gerloff, 1995). Domestic grain consumption in Hungary declined by 15 percent (Bauernzeitung, 1995), and milk and dairy consumption by 40 percent (Hrabovszky, 1995).

High rates of unemployment, and declining real wages and purchasing power, are forcing many individuals to seek new income sources to survive. A return to barter trade is occurring in many countries. Large sections of the rural population, particularly in the Czech Republic, Bulgaria, Russia, Lithuania and Belarus, are forced to increasingly rely on own-farm production to survive.

For many rural residents, farming as a supplemental activity has become a major source of self-sufficiency. More specifically, because of rapid increases in grocery prices, large segments of the population can survive only by growing their own food or by receiving food from relatives who farm. Lithuania, for example, has about 500,000 part-time farms with an average size of between 0.15 and 3 hectares each. In Slovakia, several rural groups in 1993 were completely self-sufficient, producing a variety of goods for their own consumption (Agrarinformationsdienst Osteuropa, 1994). In response, to economic uncertainty, high unemployment and lack of job prospects, many Slovakian farmers have reluctantly taken their land and agricultural equipment out of the reformed cooperatives to farm on their own, primarily on a subsistence basis (Wolz and Blaas, 1998). It is important to understand that, despite the appeal and promise of private farming, this represents a setback in the standard of living for most of these families. This situation is unlikely to change unless markets develop and production credits are made available to farmers so that they can purchase inputs.

In the Czech Republic, nearly three-quarters (73 percent) of the rural population was farming part-time in 1993 (Agrarinformationsdienst Osteuropa, 1994). Russia at the same time had about 16.6 million individual part-time farms. Surveys of private family farms in rural Russia reveal that they are presently meeting two-thirds of their subsistence needs from own-production (Agrar-Europe, 41/98; Heller, 2000). In Belarus, this part-time farming accounted for only 15 percent of both farm- and arable land, but for 66 percent of perennial crops, 32 percent of all cows, 34 percent of hogs and 64 percent of sheep, goats and poultry production. In Estonia, own-production now accounts for 15 percent of the food consumed in urban households, and for 36 percent in rural households (Brandt, 1998).

Continually declining standards of living of large parts of the rural population is not the only trend that has emerged in these countries. The transformation strategy chosen by CEE states is also changing social relations. Familiar groups and prior social systems are disintegrating, individuals are separated from their social bonds, and new social forms are emerging (Geissler, 1993). Privatization, which has developed considerable momentum in some rural areas, is at the core of these changes in the social fabric.

The re-establishment of a social stratum of independent farmers is proceeding at different rates across these countries. There are now numerous private landowners, while other rural workers have virtually no possessions. As polarization within the societies increases, perhaps most strongly in Russia, groups of newly poor have emerged. With a growing proportion of impoverished people on the one hand, and a small group of individuals with growing property and influence, on the other, the potential for social conflict is real.

3.5 Summary

Structural economic change in the CEE countries has increased social and economic differences between these countries and Western Europe even more. The next few years will likely see an increase in social problems in rural areas. In some countries more labor is likely to become superfluous in the short-term, as the free market economy gains a stronger foothold, leading to high rates of unemployment. The ability to cushion these processes is severely curtailed by a lack of public funds in the CEE countries. This, in turn, will lead to greater social differentiation and, possibly, growing social conflicts. The already wide gap in standards of living between the East and the West is likely to become even wider.

References

Agra-Europe 44/94, 31. Oktober 1994.
Agra-Europe 16/96, 15. April 1996.
Agra-Europe 16/97, 21. April 1997.
Agra-Europe 21/97, 26. März 1997.
Agra-Europe 32/97, 11. August 1997.
Agra-Europe 41/98, 12. Oktober 1998.
Agrarinformationsdienst Osteuropa (1992-1996), Berlin.
Atanassova, T. (1999), 'Die Auswirkungen der Finanz- und Wirtschaftspolitik des durch den IWF etablierten Wirtschaftsrates auf die bulgarische Landwirtschaft', *Berichte über Landwirtschaft*, 77, Münster-Hiltrup, pp. 282-290.
Agrarinformationsdienst Osteuropa, 2. - 6. Jahrgang, 1992-1996; Berlin.
Bauernzeitung, December 1, 1995.
Benedek, J. (2000), 'Sozialer Wandel im ländlichen Raum Rumäniens', *Europa Regional*, 2, Leipzig, pp. 42-54.

Blaas, G. (1993), Agriculture in Slovakia - A Forced Re-Structuring? 15th Congress of European Society for Rural Sociology, Wageningen.

Blaas, G. and Wolz, A. (1998), 'Economic Situation and Structural Changes in Slovakian Agriculture', *Eastern European Countryside*, 4, Torun, pp. 99-116.

Brandt, H. (1998), 'Die estnische Landwirtschaft in der Transformation. Situation und Ausblick im Frühjahr 1998', *Berichte über Landwirtschaft*, 76, Münster-Hiltrup, pp. 649-659.

DIW et al. (Deutsches Institut für Wirtschaftsforschung Berlin, Institut für Wirtschaftsforschung Hamburg, Institut für Wirtschaftsforschung München, Institut für Weltwirtschaft Kiel, Institut für Wirtschaftsforschung Halle und Osteuropa-Institut München) (1995), *Wirtschaftslage und Reformprozesse in Mittel- und Osteuropa*, Sammelband, Berlin.

Geier, W. (1994), 'Soziologische Ansätze zur vergleichenden Sozial- und Kulturgeschichte Ost- Ostmittel- und Südosteuropas. Disziplinäre und methodologische Aspekte', *Kultursoziologie*. Ambitionen, Aspekte, Analysen, Leipzig, pp. 1, 5-19.

Geier, W. (1995), 'Indikatoren zur Analyse der Umbrüche im Osten Europas', *Kultursoziologie*. Aspekte, Analysen, Argumente, Leipzig, 1, pp. 5-28.

Geissler, R. (1993), *Sozialer Umbruch in Ostdeutschland*, Opladen.

Gerloff, J.-U. (1995), 'Die Wirtschaft Rußlands 1994', *Erdkundeunterricht*, 9, pp. 344-348.

Geschev, G. (1995), Der Wandel der demographischen Entwicklung und der ländlichen Siedlungsstruktur in der Republik Bulgarien, in F.-D. Grimm, (ed.), *Der Wandel des ländlichen Raums in Südosteuropa*, München, pp. 173-184.

Hämmerling, A. (1993), 'Bulgarien. Wirtschaftliche Rezession setzt sich fort', Institut für Wirtschaftsforschung Halle (IHW), *Mittel- und Osteuropa: Beiträge zu den Wirtschaftsreformen*, 2, pp. 69-77.

Heinrich, R.P., M.J. Koop et al. (1996), 'Sozialpolitik im Transformationsprozeß Mittel- und Osteuropas', in H. Siebert, (ed.), *Kieler Studien*, 273, Tübingen (Institut für Weltwirtschaft an der Universität Kiel).

Heller, W. (2000), 'Zur sozioökonomischen Transformation im ländlichen Raum Rumäniens', *Europa Regional*, 2, Leipzig, pp. 32-40.

Hrabovszky, J.P. (1995), 'Die Transformation der Produktions- und Infrastruktur in der ungarischen Landwirtschaft', in F.-D. Grimm, (ed.), *Der Wandel des ländlichen Raums in Südost-europa*, München, pp. 46-57.

Ianos, I. (1995), 'Gegenwärtige Trends in der Entwicklung des ländlichen Raumes in Rumänien', in F.-D. Grimm, (ed.), *Der Wandel des ländlichen Raumes in Südosteuropa*, München, pp. 125-142.

Knappe, E. and Benedek, J. (1995), 'Der Wandel des ländlichen Raumes im Gebiet um Cluj – Napoca', *Europa Regional*, 4, Leipzig, pp. 1-14.

Kostova, D. (1997), 'The Employment Crisis in the Rural Regions of Bulgaria', *Eastern European Countryside*, 3, Torun, pp. 91-102.

Kühne, O. (2000), 'Die regionale Entwicklung des Arbeitsmarktes im Transformationsprozess Polens', *Europa Regional*, 1, Leipzig, pp. 33-42.

Künstling, D. and Kuodys, A. (1994), 'Stand und Probleme der Privatisierung der litauischen Landwirtschaft', *Europa Regional*, 1, Leipzig, pp. 21-26.

Meyerfeldt, M. (1996), 'Demographische Transformationsprozesse in Bulgarien', *Europa Regional*, 1, Leipzig, pp. 24-31.

Nemenyi, A. (2000), 'Rural Households in Romania – Struktur, Income, Consumti', *Eastern European Countryside*, 6, Torun, pp. 121-128.

Patsiorkovski, V.; O' Brien, D.J. and Dershem, L. (2000), 'Changes in Households and Institutions in Rural Russia from 1991 – 1999', *Eastern European Countryside*, 6, Torun, pp. 55-66.

Rudenko, L. (1993), 'Das Kernkraftwerksunglück von Tschernobyl. Geographische Aspekte der Folgen in der Ukraine', *Europa Regional,* 1, Leipzig, pp. 31-37.

Rudenko, L. (1995), 'Die Veränderungen im ländlichen Raum der Ukraine seit drei Jahrzehnten und die gegenwärtigen Lebensbedingungen der Bevölkerung', in F.-D. Grimm, (ed.), *Der Wandel des ländlichen Raums in Südosteuropa,* München, pp. 207-214.

Statistisches Bundesamt, *Länderberichte* 1992-1996, Wiesbaden.

Statistisches Bundesamt (1992), *Länderbericht Tschechien 1992,* Wiesbaden.

Statistisches Bundesamt (1993), *Länderbericht Russische Förderation 1993,* Wiesbaden.

Statistisches Bundesamt (1994a), *Länderbericht GUS-Staaten 1994,* Wiesbaden.

Statistisches Bundesamt (1994b), *Länderbericht Ungarn 1994,* Wiesbaden.

Statistisches Bundesamt (1995a), *Länderbericht Bulgarien 1994,* Wiesbaden.

Statistisches Bundesamt (1995b), *Länderbericht Staaten Mittel- und Osteuropa 1994,* Wiesbaden.

Statistisches Bundesamt (1995c), *Länderbericht Rumänien,* Wiesbaden.

Statistisches Bundesamt (1996), *Länderbericht Polen,* Wiesbaden.

Ugarov, A. (1997), 'Transformation der Landwirtschaft in Rußland in eine marktorientierte Struktur', *Berichte über Landwirtschaft,* 212. Sonderheft, Münster Hiltrup, pp. 51-67.

Weidenfeld, W. (1995), 'Demokratie und Marktwirtschaft in Osteuropa. Strategien für Europa', *Schriftenreihe der Bundeszentrale für politische Bildung,* 329, Bonn.

Werner, K. (1994), 'Die Transformationsökonomien Mittel- und Osteuropas im Jahre 1994', Institut für Wirtschaftsforschung Halle (IWH), *Mittel- und Osteuropa: Beiträge zu den Wirtschaftsreformen,* 4, Halle, pp. 7-27.

Wolz, A. and Blaas; G. (1998), 'Die Transformation der landwirtschaftlichen Produktionsstrukturen in der Slowakei und ihre zukünftige Entwicklung', *Berichte über Landwirtschaft,* 76, Münster-Hiltrup, pp. 309-323.

Zentrale Markt- und Preisberichtsstelle GmbH ZMP (2000), *Agrarmärkte in Zahlen: Mittel- und Osteuropa 2000,* Bonn.

BALTIC STATES

4. Estonia

ELKE KNAPPE

4.0 General setting

Geography and topography

Estonia is the northernmost of the three Baltic States. The land is fairly flat, with numerous lakes and bogs; the latter cover more than one-fifth of the territory. Lake Peipus, Estonia's largest lake, covers an area of 3,555 km² and extends over 150 km, with a maximum depth of only 15 m. The total Estonian territory of 45,200 km² includes 45 percent forestland and 32 percent farmland.

Climate

Estonia's climate is primarily maritime with some continental influence, particularly in southern parts of the country. Average annual precipitation is about 500 mm in coastal regions and about 700 mm in central parts of the country. Average temperatures are 13-16°C during the summer and between -3 and -6°C in the winter, for a relatively short growing season of only about 170 days/year.

Population

In late 1998, Estonia had a resident population of 1,453,844, 30 percent of which lived in villages (i.e., in rural areas). The ethnic structure of the population changed dramatically while Estonia was part of the Soviet Union (table 4.1). Before this period, most Russians living in Estonia were descendants of orthodox believers who for religious reasons had emigrated from the Novgorod region into eastern Estonia in the late 18th and early 19th Centuries.

Under Soviet rule, large numbers of Russian workers poured into Estonia, settling primarily in the northeastern parts of the country and in

Tallinn (Reval), the capital. This marked the beginning of a sharp increase in the Russian-speaking population. At the same time, opponents of the Soviet system and those merely accused of opposition were deported to Siberia. In fear of reprisal, tens of thousands of Estonians left their country, with most emigrating to Canada and the United States. As a result of refugees leaving the country, and the effects of war and deportations, Estonia lost about 210,000 residents.

Table 4.1 Ethnic composition of Estonia's resident population

	1934	1989	1998
Estonians	88,2	61,5	65,1
Russians	8,2	30,3	28,1
Ukrainians	-	3,1	2,5
Belorussians	-	1,8	1,5
Finns	-	1,1	0,9
Latvians	0,5	0,2	0,2
Lithuanians	-	0,1	0,2
Poles	-	0,2	0,2
Others	3,1	1,7	1,3

Source: Adapted from Statistical Office of Estonia, 1999*c*.

Administrative structure

Tallinn (Reval), the Estonian capital, has a population of about 480,000. Administratively, the country is subdivided into 14 districts (*Maa*), each of which is governed by a district town (figure 4.1).

History

Estonia's history as an independent state is relatively short, as is true of neighboring Latvia. After the war of liberation from Russia (1918-20), Soviet Russia recognized the country's independence in the Peace Treaty of Tartu. Estonia suffered less during World War I than Latvia and Lithuania, as fighting reached the country late and with reduced force, resulting in a smaller loss of lives and industrial plants. The end of the war marked the beginning of a period of considerable economic growth. Living standards in Estonia improved consistently and were comparable to those in neighboring Finland.

These developments came to an abrupt end in 1940, when Estonia was annexed by the Soviet Union under the Hitler-Stalin Pact. Estonia was turned into the Estonian Soviet Socialist Republic, and the Soviet economic and political system was forced upon the country. This entailed a radical transformation of the country's entire economy: uranium and oil shale mining increased sharply, the Tallinn harbor was developed to a significant extent, and the city became a center of mechanical engineering. The Narva textile factory complex (*combine*), with a labor force of 12,000, was the largest in the Soviet Union.

Economic structure and transformation

Estonia is poor in mineral resources: uranium, oil shale as well as peat, gypsum and sand are the only resources worth mining. The Soviet Union spent large sums of money on the industrialization of Estonia and developed strong economic ties with the country. Industrial production was mainly concentrated in the capital, while Pärnu was important for its harbor and Tartu as a university center.

Economic integration evaporated with the collapse of the Soviet Union and with Estonia once again becoming a sovereign state. This also marked the beginning of rigorous economic restructuring. The process was initially painful for the economy, but some successes were soon evident. Estonia was the first Baltic State to abandon the Ruble and to introduce its own national currency, the Estonian Kroon.

Privatization of large industrial complexes proceeded at a steady pace, as the state progressively withdrew from the economy. As a result, Estonian markets were no longer protected from imports, which especially affected the agricultural sector. In many cases imported goods are cheaper than domestic products, which, in turn, reduces demand for local products and makes it difficult for domestic producers to sell their goods.

Investments from abroad are substantial. Estonia ranks third - after Hungary and the Czech Republic - among CEE countries in terms of total foreign investments, 38 percent of which come from Finland and 24 percent from Sweden (Organization for Economic Co-operation and Development, 2000).

In addition to manufacturing, transit trade from Russia into Western and Northern Europe, and tourism are major contributors to the economy. Most of the tourists (more than 90 percent) come from Finland, usually for one-day visits to Tallinn.

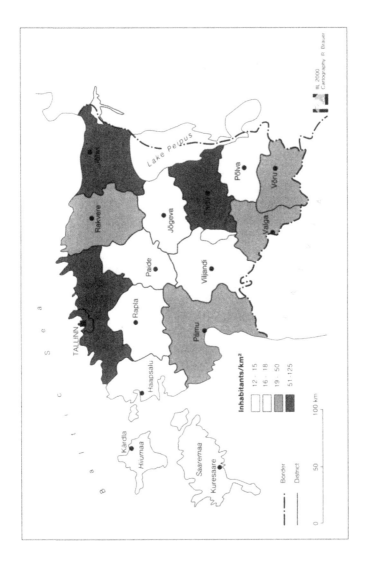

Figure 4.1   Administrative structure and population density

Estonia's foreign trade reflects the country's orientation towards Western Europe. In 1998, for example, 54 percent of Estonia's exports went to EU countries, and imports from the EU accounted for 66 percent of total imports. Imports from Russia comprised only 18 percent and exports only 25 percent. Estonia, like the other Baltic States, has a negative foreign trade balance.

4.1 Agricultural policy

Estonia's agricultural policy is as consistently liberal as the country's overall economic policy. Having become independent again in 1991, Estonia started to privatize land by way of restitution to former landowners. Vouchers were issued to those who had worked on state (*kolkhoz*) farms so that they could also acquire private property.

Some land has not been reclaimed by former owners, and is available for sale. This land is managed by a trust company, which is also in charge of its sale or restitution, a process that is often complicated by the difficulty of furnishing proof of title and a lack of documents. Even in 1999, large tracts of land still needed to be properly recorded and entered into the land register. Finally, much of the farmland, especially in peripheral (remote) regions, is of low quality and largely remains unused.

Estonia's Government has started to prepare the country's farming sector for entry into the EU by phasing out subsidies, and by liberalizing domestic prices as well as food imports from the EU. This has created tension in agriculture, most severely affecting newly established family farms and emerging input suppliers as well as food processing or marketing firms (Simo, 1998).

The share of agriculture in GDP declined from 12 percent in 1992 to as little as 5.9 percent in 1997, and the share of people engaged in farming dropped from 14 percent to 6.9 percent during this period. Thus, agriculture is becoming less important as a source of income for the rural population. Creation of new non-farm jobs is not keeping up with declining demand for agricultural labor, which is causing serious problems especially in peripheral regions of southern Estonia. Selective out-migration and a deteriorating infrastructure accentuate these problems. Even as subsidies are being phased out, the government is providing targeted low-cost loans to more-efficient farms, in the hope that they will emerge as models for the less efficient farms.

4.2 Land use

Structure of land use

Estonia covers a total land area of 45,200 km², which is currently used as follows:

Farmland	1.433 million ha
arable land	1.12 million ha
Forest land	2.016 million ha

Agricultural land use

Natural conditions Most soils in Estonia are podzols; in the northern and northwestern parts these are less fertile, sodded calcareous soils, while southern and central regions have somewhat better calcareous soils. The A-horizon is generally shallow, and irrigation and drainage together with regular fertilization and liming are essential for successful farming. Climate and soils are particularly suitable for animal husbandry, but Estonia also traditionally produces a wide range of crops.

Farm types and sizes While Estonia was part of the Soviet Union, all agricultural production was carried out on large collective (*kolkhoz*) farms. In 1989, each *kolkhoz* on average farmed 4,140 ha. Privatization has produced a structure of farms (table 4.2) that differs substantially from the structure that had existed previously.

Table 4.2 Farm types and sizes in Estonia, 1998

	Part-time family farms		Full-time family farms		Corporate farms	
	total ha	ha/farm	total ha	ha/farm	total ha	ha/farm
Farmland	190,700	1.1	526,000	12.7	377,700	429.4
Arable land	103,700	0.6	397,200	9.6	360,200	469.6
No. of farms	177,071		41,446		767	

Source: Adapted from Statistical Office of Estonia, 1998*a*.

Estonia now has many part-time farms, which to some extent have come to dominate the country's farm structure (table 4.2). Families primarily grow crops to meet subsistence needs (i.e., to survive), especially in economically depressed areas, but from time to time they also sell surpluses through emerging private markets. At present, this kind of subsistence farming has a stabilizing function, and for many families it is the only way in which they can remain in their familiar environments.

Even full-time family farms have comparatively small plots of land, which provide them with only limited income. These families can survive through farming alone only by reducing consumption levels. The average family farm has only 9.6 ha of arable land, which is not enough to farm efficiently (Elmet and Kivistik, 1999).

Only 0.7 percent of full-time family farms have more than 100 ha of arable land, the size considered to be the minimum needed for efficient grain production in Estonia (Statistical Office of Estonia, 1998*b*). Table 4.3 shows that most farms have between 10.1 and 20 ha each.

Table 4.3 Number of full-time family farms by size

Year	< 5ha	5.1-10ha	10.1-20ha	20.1-30ha	30.1-50ha	50.1-100ha	>100ha
1995	1,634	1,827	3,750	2,721	2,488	1,027	66
1996	3,490	2,898	5,272	3,574	3,175	1,273	85
1997	2,901	3,644	6,364	4,299	3,800	1,574	140
1998	4,941	5,865	9,545	6,216	5,519	2,347	238
1999	6,269	7,147	11,446	7,247	6,380	2,677	280

Source: Adapted from Kivistik, 1999.

In terms of area farmed, corporate farms better satisfy the pre-conditions for efficient scales of operation. However, these farms also face serious capital constraints, as well as low producer prices and high costs of production, making it difficult for them to benefit fully from their size.

Crop production

Since Estonian agriculture traditionally emphasized livestock production, most crops are grown for feed (grain and green forage), but they also include potatoes, vegetables, flax and sugar beet. Because of adverse climatic conditions, crop yields are not very high. During 1994-98, average crop yields were as follows (Ministry of Agriculture, 1998):

Grain:	1.7 tonnes/ha
Potatoes:	14.0 tonnes/ha
Sugar beet:	24.0 tonnes/ha
Spring-sown rape:	1.1 tonnes/ha

Part-time farmers account for most of the vegetables produced. With high labor requirements, their output of vegetables makes up 23 percent of agricultural output (value-added), but uses only 12 percent of the country's arable land. This implies that part-time farmers use their land more intensively, based mainly on the high input of manual labor for cultivating, tending and harvesting of vegetables.

Livestock production

Livestock production, and milk production in particular, is the most important component of Estonian agriculture. Livestock numbers by farm type are shown in table 4.4.

Table 4.4 Livestock numbers by farm type, 1998

	Part-time family farms		Full-time family farms		Corporate farms	
	Total	Per farm	Total	Per farm	Total	Per farm
Cattle	50,800	0.3	57,400	1.4	199,300	259.8
Cows	30,500	0.2	32,600	0.8	95,500	124.5
Pigs	20,800	0.1	27,200	0.7	278,400	362.2
Sheep & goats	20,500	0.1	10,300	0.2	-	-
Poultry	843,200	4.8	160,300	3.9	1,632,200	2,128

Source: Adapted from Statistical Office of Estonia, 1999a.

Only corporate farms have large livestock herds (table 4.4). Many full- and part-time family farms have only one cow or pig to meet their own-consumption needs. A total of 2,612 dairy herds were registered at the Estonian Dairy Control Center in 1997, and 83 percent of these herds contained fewer than 50 animals (Kivistik, 1999), placing them below the minimum amount needed for efficient milk production. This fragmentation of livestock holding, which is a direct consequence of privatization, is retarding the development of a competitive agricultural industry in Estonia.

The average number of dairy cows on different types of farms at the same time reflects different milk marketing practices. While milk from cows kept by part-time farmers in most cases is consumed or processed directly on the farm, a portion of the milk produced on full-time family farms is shipped to the dairy industry and then sold on markets. The third group - large farms - produces milk only for markets.

Until the early 1990s, milk production was the main source of income for many farmers, but declining numbers of dairy cows suggest that this is no longer the case today. In 1992, Estonia still had 708,300 head of cattle (of which 264,300 were dairy cows), but in early 1999 that number had declined to 307,500, including only 158,600 dairy cows (Statistical Office of Estonia, 1999*b*). Such drastic declines have obviously affected the dairy processing industry. Many processing operations have become unprofitable, some have closed, and the unmet market demand for certain dairy products (such as cheese) was immediately met by imports.

In 1997, milk and dairy products (such as milk powder) still made up 20 percent of Estonia's total exports of agricultural goods. Despite the decline in total quantities, these exports remain a major factor in the country's economy. Only fish and fish products had a larger share (30 percent) of exports (Statistical Office of Estonia, 1999*c*). Most of these products are exported to Russia.

4.3 Forestry

About 45 percent of Estonia's territory is covered with forests, and the wood products industry plays an important role in the national economy.

In 1997, forest property was distributed as follows:

Private property:	162,300 ha
State property:	1,158,800 ha
Others:	695,500 ha
Total:	2,016,600 ha

Logging intensity has increased noticeably in recent years (table 4.5). Spruce is the dominant tree species, particularly on sites that are intensively harvested.

Table 4.5 Logging rates as a percent of standing crop

Year	Logging rate (%)
1992	0.77
1993	0.85
1994	1.24
1995	1.30
1996	1.37
1997	1.87

Source: Adapted from Statistical Office of Estonia, 1999*c*.

Forest privatization is proceeding at a relatively slow rate. In the long run, however, the government will pull almost completely out of forestry, and only some 700-1,000 hectares will be state-managed in the future. Plans exist to establish a forest owners' organization; one of its goals will be to ensure compliance with forest sustainability provisions.

References

Elmet, H. and Kivistik, J. (1999), 'Integration of the Baltic Sea Countries to the Common Agricultural Policy of the EU', Proceedings of the 66th EAAE Seminar, Tallinn, pp. 221-227.

Kivistik, J. (1999), *Stand der internationalen Wettbewerbsfähigkeit der Estnischen Agrar- und Ernährungswirtschaf*, Tallinn.

Ministry of Agriculture (1998), *Agriculture in Estonia*, Tallinn.

Organization for Economic Co-operation and Development (2000), *Economic Surveys 2000*, Paris.

Simo, K. (1998), 'Estonian Agriculture on its Way to the European Union', *Transactions of the Estonian Agricultural University*, Tartu pp. 31-37.

Statistical Office of Estonia (1998a), *Agriculture in figures*, Tallinn.

Statistical Office of Estonia (1998b), *Agriculture 1998*, Tallinn.

Statistical Office of Estonia (1999a), *Agriculture in Figures 1996-1998*, Tallinn.

Statistical Office of Estonia (1999b), *Estonian Statistics 1999*, Tallinn.

Statistical Office of Estonia (1999c), *Statistical Yearbook 1998*, Tallinn.

5. Latvia

ELKE KNAPPE

5.0 General setting

Geography and topography

Latvia takes up the western fringe of the East European lowlands, and has
an average altitude of 87 m above sea level. Lowlands and elevated plains
120 m above sea level are the dominant topographical forms. North of the
river Daugava (Düna) is the Central Latvian hill country, which is
separated by the river Gauja from the West Livonian hill country. The
Courland hill country lies south of the river Daugava. The Latvian territory
of 64,600 km² includes 39.8 percent farmland, 41.0 percent forested land
and a large number of small lakes, which make up 1.7 percent of the area.

Climate

Latvia's climate is determined by its geographic location and topography. It
is a transition climate from the maritime to the continental type, and is
moderated by the nearby Baltic Sea. Summers are cool and moist, with a
relatively small amount of evaporation.

Population

In late 1998, Latvia's total population was 2,458,403; the population's
ethnic background is shown in table 5.1. The policy of "Russianization"
implemented when Latvia was part of the Soviet Union led to dramatic
increases in the Russian-speaking population, especially in urban areas.
Even today, ethnic Latvians are a minority in Riga and Daugavpils, the
largest cities in the country.

Administrative structure

The Latvian capital of Riga, with a 1998 population of 805,997, is by far the largest city. Daugavpils, the second largest city, has only 120,000 inhabitants. Administratively, the country is divided into 26 districts (*rayons*) (figure 5.1). The historical subdivision of the country into four primary regional units continues to this day: Kurzeme (West Latvia), Zemgale (South Latvia), Vidzeme (North Latvia) and Latgale (East Latvia).

Table 5.1 Ethnic composition of Latvia's resident population (%)

	1935	1995
Latvians	77.0	56.7
Russians	8.8	30.3
Belarussians	1.4	4.3
Poles	2.6	2.6
Ukrainians	0.0	2.7
Germans	3.3	0.0
Lithuanians	1.2	1.4
Jews	4.9	0.0
Others	0.8	2.0

Source: Adapted from Apstiprinajusi Latvijas Republikas Izglitibas un Zinatnes Ministerija, 1996.

History

On August 21, 1991, Latvia proclaimed its independence from the Soviet Union, and the Constitution of February 15, 1922 was re-instated. The intent was to symbolize the continuation of Latvia as a sovereign state, a sovereignty that had only been interrupted by the period of Soviet annexation. Latvia had gained independence as early as November 1918, but in 1919 had to defend itself against attempts to create a Soviet Latvia. The Russian Red Army was defeated with the support of Poland, and on August 2, 1920, a peace treaty was signed in Riga, in which Soviet Russia not only recognized Latvia's independence but also relinquished control of Latvian territory.

Against this background of political and economic autonomy, Latvia began to cope with the aftermath of World War I. After an economic depression, Latvia became a major exporter of agricultural goods, primarily butter and pork. When the Soviet Union annexed Latvia in 1940 during World War II, Latvian GDP per capita was almost twice that of the Soviet Union.

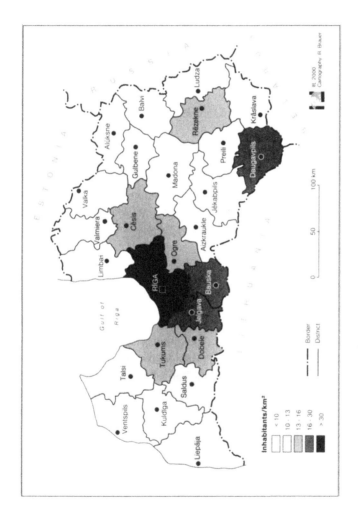

Figure 5.1 Administrative structure and population density

From 1940 to 1991, Latvia was a Soviet Republic and, as a result, firmly integrated into the Soviet system. The integration was associated with intensive industrial development and growing demand for labor. This labor was supplied primarily by Russia's central regions, which contributed to a substantial increase in the number of Russians in Latvia's resident population. A collective (*kolkhoz*) farming system based on the Russian model was proclaimed as a goal for rural areas. Many farmers who resisted collectivization were deported.

As a result of deportations, refugees leaving the country, and the ravages of war, Latvia lost about 320,000 inhabitants during the 1940s and 1950s. This was a severe loss for the country, because many of the refugees and deportees were agricultural and intellectual leaders.

Economic structure and transformation

As a Soviet Socialist Republic, Latvia continued to be a major agricultural producer, but was subject to central planning that emphasized the development of the country's industrial potential. Major cities, especially the capital of Riga, but also Daugavpils, Ventspils and Liepaja and others, benefited the most from this emphasis.

Latvian manufacturing workers, who tended to be highly skilled, produced TV sets, mopeds, milking equipment, telephones and railway wagons, and the country's economic integration into the Soviet economy was strong both in terms of export of products and imports of inputs. Not surprisingly, the collapse of the Soviet Union had profound effects on Latvia's economy. Engineering and chemical products, building materials and manufactured food products could suddenly no longer be readily sold on Russian markets. It soon became clear that the largely obsolete industrial complex, with its often over-sized plants and a lack of both suppliers and markets, would have to be privatized if it was to compete on world markets. Latvia's progress on the road to modernization is evident from recent growth of real GDP (table 5.2).

Today, nearly all industrial and agricultural enterprises in Latvia are in private hands (Central Statistical Bureau of Latvia, 1998*a*). The successful implementation of free markets led to further increases in investments from abroad (table 5.3). Most of the investments originate, by volume, in Denmark, Russia, the United States, Germany, Singapore, Great Britain, Sweden and Switzerland.

Table 5.2   Gross domestic product relative to previous year

Year	% of previous year
1995	99.2
1996	103.3
1997	106.5
1998*	103.8

Note: *Decline due to the ruble crisis in Russia

Sources: Central Statistical Bureau of Latvia, 1998c, Ministry of Economy, 1999.

Table 5.3   Direct investment from abroad

Year	Million USD
1996	504
1997	675
1998	927

Source: Ministry of Economy, 2000.

Major industrial centers in Latvia include the capital of Riga-which is a center both of industry, finance and services–and the cities of Daugavpils, Liepaja, Ventspils, Jelgava and Rezekne. The economic dominance of Riga is undisputed: with about 33 percent of the country's total population, the city produced 54 percent of GDP in 1996. In Daugavpils, Latvia's second largest city, Russian immigrants had worked mainly in the engineering and chemical industries, which were particularly vulnerable to the collapse of the Russian economy. Not surprisingly, the current unemployment rate is high in Daugavpils (Report on the Development of Eceonomy of Latvia, 2000).

Seaports, especially Liepaja and Ventspils, are of strategic importance to the country's economy. Ventspils was the largest oil terminal in the Soviet Union, and today oil trading is once again the city's main source of income. Another pipeline from Russia through Belarus into Ventspils is planned, which will further increase this seaport's importance.

5.1   Agricultural policy

Latvia's agricultural sector has traditionally played an important economic role. Between World Wars I and II, private farm ownership dominated in Latvia, as a result of land reform and the expropriation of mostly Balto-German land-owners, who had owned sizable tracts of land. After early start-up problems, Latvia soon became an exporter of bacon, beef and dairy products.

With the Soviet Union's occupation in June 1940, these developments ended abruptly. Latvian farmers were forced to form collective farms based on the Soviet model. Large-scale operations were created, with an average size of 5,000 to 6,000 ha each; these units specialized in meat, milk, egg and poultry production. However, Latvia could not feed the large livestock herds using only local resources, and feed concentrates had to be brought in from other parts of the Soviet Union. The Latvian Soviet Socialist Republic accounted for only 0.4 percent of the farmland, but for as much as 2 percent of the entire livestock production of the Soviet Union.

With Latvia gaining independence once again, institutional arrangements governing agricultural production were also reformed. From 1989 on, farmers could leave the *kolkhoz* farms to set up independent farms (according to the Private Farms Act of 1989). The Land Reform Act followed in 1991. According to this Act, former owners had to notify the land committees by June 22, 1992 if they were interested in land restitution. The Privatization Act of July 10, 1992, terminated state ownership of land. Key elements of this Act are as follows:

• Those who can prove that they owned land before July 21, 1940 received title to the land, if they register their claim; rights of current users are accommodated to the extent possible (for example, if users had erected a building on the land, they would be compensated).
• After privatization, land can be rented out.
• The former collective (*kolkhoz*) and state (*sovkhoz*) farms are dissolved or turned into privately-owned farms.
• Unclaimed land may be given to peasants who have little or no land.
• Foreigners may not buy land, but can lease land for up to 99 years.
• In cases where former land owners do not want to have their land back, or no longer want to farm, or where the land can not be returned (for example, if it had been developed for housing), compensation is made in the form of vouchers. Holders of vouchers have the first claim to buying the property.

Source: Latvijas Valsts agraras ekonomicas instituts, 1999.

The Latvian Government supports the development of private farms through protectionist measures, such as import taxes, and by granting loans for mechanizing and modernizing farming operations. Because many farmers own few assets, and even though loan terms are often highly favorable to borrowers, the heavy reliance on debt has led to financial difficulties and eventual foreclosures of numerous farm businesses (Gulbe, 1998).

Fertilizers, pesticides, seeds and plants, electricity and fuels are relatively expensive, and farmers are often unable to use these inputs on an adequate scale. Liberalization of producer prices led to sharp price declines, especially for meat and dairy products. This, in turn, has significantly reduced the profitability of farming.

Another problem for rural areas is the fact that a range of social services and activities that used to be provided by the collective and state farms are no longer available. This includes construction and maintenance of housing, kindergartens, schools, shops, municipal cultural centers, local road systems, and so forth. These activities, which are now divorced from agricultural production, have to be carried out by local governments or private firms. Lacking financial resources, local governments in most cases can provide only public services. And, in rural areas, private investors and contractors are scarce (Tisenkopf and Zobena, 1999).

Poor infrastructure and a lack of local jobs are primary reasons why especially younger workers seek to leave rural areas. However, out-migration is often tempered by a lack of opportunities in urban areas and low urban wages, and it has not reached a large scale. In rural areas, families can still be supported through subsistence farming, and many rural residents take advantage of this option. Thus, subsistence farming is currently a stabilizing force in rural areas.

5.2 Land use

Structure of land use

Latvia's land area is currently used as follows:

Farmland	2.4 million ha
arable land	1.7 million ha
Forest land	2.8 million ha
Meadows, pastures and fallow	0.9 million ha

Agricultural land use for crop production

Latvia's soils are comprised of the following:

Sodded podzols	52 percent	Wet land	23 percent
Sodded calcareous soils	4 percent	Boggy soils	19 percent
Alluvial soils	2 percent		

A large share of soils has a relatively low pH, and requires regular liming when used as farmland. More than 90 percent of soils used for agricultural production have excessive moisture, and their water content needs to be controlled through drainage systems. This is an additional financial burden on agricultural production.

Traditionally, agriculture has been an important factor in Latvia's economy, and today 16 percent of the country's workforce remains engaged in farming. However, the share of agriculture in GDP is declining (by 1998 it was only 7.8 percent). While privatization in agriculture has been completed officially, entering all landowners into the land register will require much more time. Lack of documentation and proof of ownership, as well as disputes over plots, are the main reasons why this process is being drawn out. The present-day structure of farms in Latvia is shown in table 5.4.

Table 5.4 Sizes of different farm types

Type of farm	*Farmland (ha) 1997*	Farmland (ha) 1998
State farms and corporate farms	140,688	270,574
Full-time family farms	1,297,856	1,347,030
Part-time family farms	119,789	83,494
Household (subsistence) farms	765,613	741,099

Source: Adapted from Central Statistical Bureau, 1999.

State farms are nowadays mainly concerned with training farmers in crop production methods and animal husbandry.

Corporate farms are successors of former *kolkhoz* farms. They are found mainly in eastern Latvia, where soils are poor, transportation is inadequate and non-agricultural jobs almost non-existent. Demand for land to set up family farms in these regions remains extremely limited.

Full-time family farms are farms that were given back in the process of privatization to former owners, or their heirs, and are now farmed full-time by farmers and their families.

Part-time family farms also operate on private land. Farming supplements income from non-agricultural jobs (mainly in the craft trades), which are their main sources of income. Reflecting the relatively large share of land farmed, these full- and part-time family farms also account for relatively large shares of total agricultural output (table 5.5). The average size of these farms is only between 15 and 20 hectares, so that they may not be able to achieve sufficient scales of operation to be competitive under EU conditions.

Household farms are operated on leased land or land held in usufruct. Household farmers mostly live in rental apartments and do not own land. They produce exclusively for subsistence needs and their output tends not to appear in official statistics.

Table 5.5 Crop production shares of different farm types (1998)

	State and corporate farms (%)	Full- and part-time family farms (%)
Grain	18.0	82.0
Potatoes	3.7	96.3

Source: Adapted from Agriculture in Latvia, 1998.

For Latvia as a whole, the decline in crop production that started following reforms has now slowed, and crop yields per hectare are stabilizing or even increasing (tables 5.6 and 5.7).

Table 5.6 Trends in crop production (1,000 t)

	1981-85	1995	1996	1997	1998
Grain	1,277.0	693.7	968.6	1,043.5	970.2
Potatoes	1,684.0	863.7	1,081.9	843.3	694.1
Vegetables	243.8	223.7	179.5	149.7	119.6
Sugar beet	364.4	250.0	257.8	387.5	597.0
Flax	4.7	0.8	0.79	0.96	1.34

Sources: Central Statistical Bureau of Latvia, 1998*b*,1999.

Table 5.7 Yield trends for selected crops (100 kg/ha)

	1981-85	1995	1996	1997	1998
Grain	17.7	16.9	21.5	21.4	20.5
Potatoes	145.0	115.0	138.0	121.0	118.0
Vegetables	160.0	122.0	108.0	107.0	99.0
Sugar beet	273.0	264.0	259.0	357.0	365.0
Flax	3.0	5.5	5.9	6.2	6.2

Sources:. Central Statistical Bureau of Latvia, 1998*b*,1999.

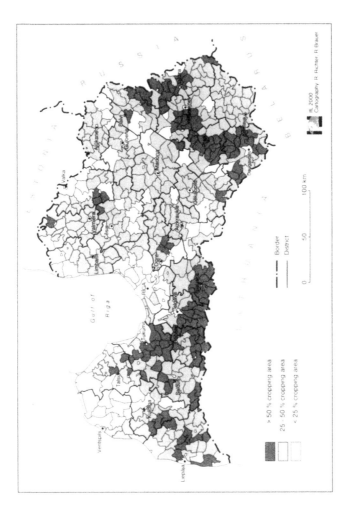

Figure 5.2 Agricultural land use

Average crop yields in Latvia are low compared to yields in Central and Western Europe. This is due to adverse climate and also to out-dated agronomic practices, including use of low-quality seed, limited use of fertilizers and pesticides, and lack of mechanization.

Average yields are highest in central Latvia and lowest in Latgale, in eastern regions of the country (figure 5.2).

Livestock production

Problems also exist in the livestock sector, which experienced a substantial expansion while Latvia was part of the Soviet Union. At that time, and as indicated earlier, large amounts of feed were imported from other regions of the Soviet Union. The early transition to private farming in Latvia was associated with declining livestock numbers, largely because feed supplies dried up. This decline accelerated once Russian markets collapsed; simultaneously, problems with domestic product quality became apparent.

As Latvian markets opened to products from Scandinavia and Western Europe, quality differences became obvious and consumers developed strong preferences for imported products, which in some cases were cheaper than local products. Today, both producers and the food industry have become much more quality-conscious. Investments were made to modernize the processing industry, and this contributed to stabilization of livestock numbers (table 5.8).

Table 5.8 Trends in livestock numbers (1,000 head)

	1990	1994	1995	1996	1997	1998
Cattle	1,439	551	537.1	509.4	476.9	434.4
Of which cows	535	312	292	277.4	262.8	242.1
Pigs	1,401	501	522.8	459.6	429.9	421.1
Sheep	165	86	72.1	55.5	40.7	29.4
Horses	31	27	27.2	25.8	23.3	22.0
Poultry	10,321	3,662	4,198	3,790.7	3,551	3,208.8

Source: Central Statistical Bureau of Latvia, 1998*b*.

As table 5.8 shows, livestock numbers declined most dramatically in the early 1990s. Since then the rate of decline has slowed, with only the number of sheep dropping noticeably in 1998.

The Latvian Government recognized early on that structural change and the transformation process would exceed the agricultural sector's capacity to keep pace. A modern, competitive agricultural sector is likely to develop only with public assistance (as was true in the US and the EU). New approaches, such as specialization and production of niche products, are being explored to make traditional agriculture more profitable. Examples include seed multiplication, the cultivation of medicinal plants and spices, and organic farming. Organic foods will have a ready market in and around large cities.

5.3 Forestry

Forests are an important part of Latvia's natural wealth. Some 2.8 million ha, or 6 ha per capita are forested, out of which 1.4 million ha are state-owned. 1.2 million ha are privately owned, while the remainder belongs to entities such as corporate bodies and public institutions.

Trees include pine, spruce, birch, white alder, aspen, European alder, ash and oak. Annual utilization is approximately 8 million m³ of wood. Exports of wood and wood products account for about one-third of all exports, thus contributing significantly to Latvia's overall trade balance.

References

Apstiprinajusi Latvijas Republikas Izglitibas un Zinatnes Ministerija (1996), *Pasaule Geografias Atlants*, Riga.

Central Statistical Bureau of Latvia (1998*a*), *Agriculture Farms in Latvia*, Riga.

Central Statistical Bureau of Latvia (1998*b*), *Agriculture in Latvia*, Riga

Central Statistical Bureau of Latvia (1998*c*), *Latvia - Statistics in Brief*, Riga.

Central Statistical Bureau of Latvia (1999), *Monthly Bulletin of Latvian Statistics*, Riga.

Gulbe, I. (ed.) (1998), *Agriculture of Latvia*, Riga.

Latviajas Valsts agraras ekonomikas instituts (1999), *Latvijas lauksaimnieciba 1998: politika un attistiba*, Riga.

Ministry of Economy (1999), *Economic Development of Latvia (1999)*, Riga.

Ministry of Economy (2000), *Economic Development of Latvia (2000)*, Riga.

Report on the Development of Economy of Latvia. Juli 11, 2000, http://www.lem.gov.lv.

Tisenkopf, T. and Zobena A. (eds) (1999), Social Aspects of Sustainable Agriculture: Experience in Nordic and Baltic Countries, *Jelgeva*.

6. Lithuania

ELKE KNAPPE

6.0 General setting

Geography and topography

Lithuania, the largest and southernmost of the three Baltic States, stretches over an area of 65,300 km². Situated in the East European Lowland Plain, the country's topography is typified by till plains and terminal moraines with many lakes, bogs and vast forests.

The Nemunas (Memel), Lithuania's longest river, flows into the Courland Lagoon. The large number of lakes is characteristic of eastern parts of the country, the largest being Lake Druksiai, which spreads over 4,479 ha with a maximum depth of 33m. About 54 percent of the land is farmland, and 28 percent is forested.

Climate

Lithuania's climate is of a transitional type, between continental and maritime. Climate conditions are relatively favorable for agriculture, with annual precipitation ranging between 500 and 600 mm and mean temperatures between -4.8°C in January and 17.2°C in July. At 170 to 200 days, the growing season is somewhat longer than that in Estonia and Latvia.

Population

In 1999, Lithuania's population was 3,704,830, with some 2,500,000 living in cities. The population's ethnic background is much more homogeneous than that of the other two Baltic States. The Russian-speaking population lives mainly in Vilnius, the capital, and in the industrial centers. The Polish minority population settled primarily in and around Vilnius, a region that was part of Poland until World War II.

After World War II, Lithuania - like Latvia and Estonia - became a full-fledged Soviet Republic, and many workers immigrated from Russia. At the same time, numerous native Lithuanians (about 80,000 in 1949 alone) fell victim to a rigorous deportation policy. Following its return to a sovereign state, citizenship and nationality requirements were less strict in Lithuania than in Latvia and Estonia. Any individual who on the day of the declaration of independence had a permanent residence in Lithuania could become a citizen. This liberal policy toward granting of citizenship is explained in part by the fact that ethnic Lithuanians were by far the largest group in the country (table 6.1).

Table 6.1   Ethnic composition of Lithuania's population (%)

	1979	1989	1998
Lithuanians	80.0	79,6	81.4
Russians	8.9	9.4	8.3
Poles	7.3	7.0	7.0
Belarussians	1.7	1.7	1.5
Ukrainians	1.0	1.2	1.0
Jews	0.4	0.3	0.1
Latvians	0.1	0.1	-
Tatars	0.1	0.2	-
Romany	0.1	0.1	-
Others	0.4	0.4	0.7

Source: Adapted from Methodical Publishing Center, 1999.

Administrative structure

With a population of 580,100, the capital of Vilnius is Lithuania's largest city. Kaunas is the second largest city, with 410,800 inhabitants, and Klaipeda ranks third with 202,346 inhabitants. The country has three administrative divisions: counties (*Apskritys*) are the largest unit, followed by districts (*Rajonai*) and municipalities (*Seniunijos*) as the smallest units (figure 6.1). Lithuania has a total of 110 cities and towns, 10 counties, 44 districts, and 446 municipalities.

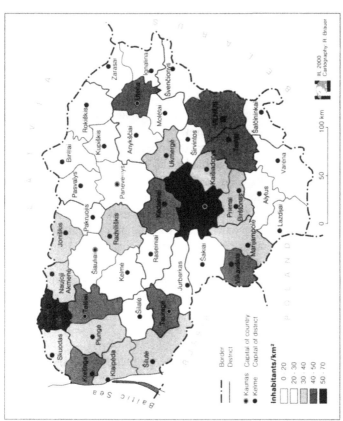

Figure 6.1 Administrative structure and population density

History

With a long history as an independent state, Lithuania's past is quite different from that of Latvia and Estonia. The Grand Duchy of Lithuania was founded in 1236, when King Mindaugas united Lithuanian tribes. In 1385, the Union Treaty of Krewo formalized the Lithuanian/Polish union. Many Lithuanians subsequently converted to Christianity. Following the third division of Poland, Lithuania became part of the Russian Empire in 1795. This marked the beginning of Russianization. Lithuanian books were banned and orthodox religion was favored.

After World War I, Lithuania declared itself an independent republic, but in January 1919 Soviet troops occupied a large part of the country. After Russian forces retreated, a peace treaty was signed in Moscow in 1920 and the Lithuanian constitution took effect in 1922. At that time, Germany and Great Britain became the principal importers of Lithuanian goods, which were mostly agricultural.

Since Poland refused to return the occupied region around Vilnius, Kaunas served as Lithuania's capital until 1938. When Soviet troops again invaded the country - this time at the government's behest - Vilnius once more became a Lithuanian city. Lithuania subsequently annexed the Memel region, which had come under French administration after World War I.

Lithuania's independence ended once again after World War II, when it became an integral member of the Soviet Union as the Lithuanian Soviet Socialist Republic. Collectivization of agriculture began in 1949, and large cities were turned into industrial production centers. The seaport of Klaipeda was declared a military base and, hence, a *closed city*.

Social transformation

The Soviet Union's collapse cleared Lithuania's path to renewed independence, and in 1991 it was again recognized as a sovereign state. Democratic structures had to be established, the state-controlled economic system had to be transformed into a free market system, and the economy, tailored entirely to the needs of the former Soviet Union, had to be fundamentally reorganized. Independence coincided with a decline in both industrial and agricultural output.

Lithuania can potentially benefit from its geographic location as a crossroad for East-West trade, and as a transit route between the Kaliningrad region and Russia. Other strategic factors include oil refining at Mazeikiai, which is the only oil refinery in the Baltic region, and the seaport of Klaipeda with its modern container terminal.

Lithuania is also poor in mineral resources, and only sand, gypsum, peat, rock salt and amber are mined. Oil deposits have been discovered, but extraction has not yet started. The Lithuanian economy is dominated by manufacturing industries, primarily food processing and textiles, as well as the energy sector. Wood processing is becoming more important over time, as discussed below.

Privatization of the economy has occurred in two stages: in the first stage, privatization of former public enterprises was mainly in the form of vouchers being issued to residents; these vouchers give their holders a stake in the enterprise. In the second stage, Lithuania's State Privatization Agency was charged with selling public companies to interested parties both at home and abroad. Today, major Lithuanian trading partners include Russia, Belarus, the Ukraine and, especially, Germany, Denmark, Latvia and Poland.

6.1 Agricultural policy

Before accelerated industrialization was imposed by the Soviet Union, Lithuania was a predominantly agrarian country. Forage production benefited from abundant rainfall, providing an excellent basis for animal production (milk and meat)(figure 6.2).

As part of the Soviet Union, Lithuania's agricultural system was collectivized, with large state (*sovkhoz*) and cooperative (*kolkhoz*) farms focusing primarily on cattle and hog production. These large farms were dissolved immediately after landed property was privatized, and former landowners or their heirs could either reclaim their land or seek compensation. According to a 1997 law, even former landowners who left Lithuania are entitled to restitution, which is expected to entail the relocation of more than 10,000 families living on presently unclaimed land.

Land ownership was first limited to 50 ha, then to 150 ha. Today, more than 80 percent of all land is again in private hands. However, the new family farms are very small, averaging 8.5 ha each in 1994, 7.6 ha in 1996, and 11.7 ha in 1997 (Government of the Republic of Lithuania, 1998). With rapid declines in subsidies, these new farms face enormous start-up problems.

At 10.1 percent (in 1998), the share of agriculture and forestry in GDP is higher in Lithuania than in Latvia or Estonia. The share of people engaged in farming is also relatively high, but trending downward: 24.2 percent in 1996 versus 21.8 percent in 1998 (Fyodorov and Korneevets, 1999).

6.2 Land use

Structure of land use

Land use depends heavily on soil water regimes, and large tracts of land cannot be farmed without being drained. The proportion of arable land in the country's overall farmland is high (86 percent) (Künstling and Kuody, 1994).

Agricultural land use

Most Lithuanian soils are sodded podzols, which dominate in coastal regions and on ridges, while boggy podzols dominate in lowlands. The sodded calcareous soils of the Central Lithuanian Plain and lowlands, and alluvial river meadows, are the most fertile in the country. Sodded podzol gleys are also fertile, but many are too waterlogged to be used agriculturally (Rudert, 1992).

Crop production

Crop production in Lithuania reached a peak during the Soviet period, and experienced steep declines after 1990. Declining crop yields, particularly of grains (table 6.2), have led to rising food imports.

Table 6.2 Crop yields in Lithuania (in 1,000 t)

Crop	1990	1997	1998	1999
Grains	3,265	3,052	2,717	2,100
Potatoes	1,573	1,830	1,849	-
Sugar beet	912	1,002	959	940

Sources: Adapted from Methodical Publishing Center, 1999; ZMP, 2000.

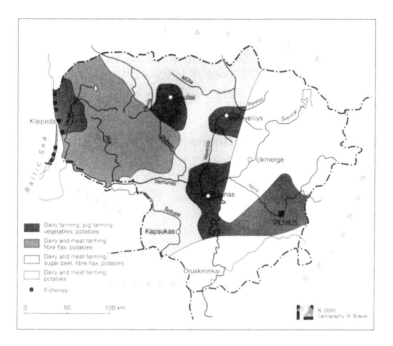

Figure 6.2 Agricultural production in Lithuania

Crop production is dominated by grains, which make up 48 percent of total crop output. Forage production ranks second, but demand for forages has declined as a result of shrinking livestock herds. Vegetables, industrial crops and tubers take up only a small share (5 percent) of area cropped. Unlike trends in the other two Baltic countries, area used to produce potatoes shows a moderate increase, because many part-time farmers grow potatoes to feed their families (table 6.3).

Table 6.3 Potato area in the Baltic states (1,000 ha)

	1993	1997	1998
Estonia	43	35	32
Latvia	88	63	53
Lithuania	122	125	136

Source: Adapted from ZMP, 2000.

The relatively low crop yields largely reflect low application rates of pesticides and fertilizers, and the relative scarcity of seeds. Inadequate machinery and equipment (one tractor per 100 ha of farmland in 1998) and high-cost fuel account for poor soil preparation, which in turn depresses yields.

With privatization, full- and part-time family farms now account for much of the crop output. They grow 97 percent of potatoes, 80 percent of vegetables and 60 percent of grains (Statistikos Departamentas pri Lietuves Respublikos Vyriausybes, 1998).

Crop yields of full-time family farms in 1997 were (in 100 kg/ha):

Grains:	25
Potatoes:	166
Vegetables:	145
Sugar beet:	309

Source: Statistikos Departamentas pri Lietuves Respublikos Vyriausybes, 1998.

Livestock production

Livestock is a long-established industry in Lithuania. Beef, pork and milk yields reached high levels, which were comparable to those attained in European countries, during independence between World Wars I and II.

Animal production was also the dominant agricultural sector under Soviet rule. Even at that time, many farm households engaged in intensive animal husbandry, which was a significant source of income. Pork producers suffered the most after 1990, mainly because of the decline in feed production (table 6.4). Because of the decline in pork production, Lithuania has lost its former position as an important pork exporter. Increasing grazing of cattle has to some extent compensated for a relative lack of feed concentrates.

Table 6.4   Trends in hog and cattle numbers (1,000 head)

	1996	1997	1997	1998
Hogs	1,270	1,128	1,200	1,168
Cattle	1,065	1,054	1,016	928
Cows	86	590	582	541

Source: Adapted from Methodical Publishing Center, 1999.

Part-time family farms continue to contribute significantly to overall livestock production; in 1996 their share of the total output was 35 percent. Full- and part-time family farms together account for 70 percent of Lithuania's livestock output (Schwierz, 1999). Remaining large farms and cooperative farms have lost much of their former dominance and the use of less efficient production methods by family farms has reinforced reductions in livestock numbers. In addition, animals are often kept under sub-optimal conditions that do not conform to modern sanitary standards. Milk yields are also low. In 1998, average milk yield per cow was only 3,120 kgs, compared with an average of 5,530 kgs in the 15 EU countries in 1997 (Klohn and Windhorst, 1999).

6.3 Forestry

Forest stands in Lithuania are unevenly spaced. The largest timber stands are found in eastern and southeastern parts of the country, with smaller and medium-sized forests of between 500 and 5,000 hectares each. Pine dominates in the largest stands, most of which are found on poorer sandy soils, while spruce trees grow on more fertile soils. Most of the forestland is owned by the state.

Annual logging volume is over 4 million m³ (table 6.5). To improve the viability of commercial logging, drainage systems have been installed on more than 300,000 ha of forestland. Both wood exports and wood processing by the furniture industry have recently expanded as a share of Lithuania's economy.

Table 6.5 State forest felling (in 1,000 m³)

	1985	1995	1998
Forest felled	3,008	5,281	4,122
Felling for afforestation purposes	1,767	2,121	2,137
Thinning and sanitary felling	1,189	2,915	1,911

Source: Methodical Publishing Center, 1999.

References

Fyodorov, G. M. and Korneevets, V.S. (1999), *Baltiskij Region Kaliningrad*, Kaliningrad.

Government of the Republic of Lithuania, Department of Statistics (1998), *Lithuania in figures*, Vilnius.

Klohn , W.and Windhorst, H.-W. (1999), *Die Landwirtschaft in Europa*, Vechta.

Künstling, D. and Kuody, A. (1994), 'Stand und Probleme der Privatisierung der litauischen Landwirtschaft', *Europa Regional*, 2, Republik Litauen 1995; Leipzig (Institut für Länderkunde), pp.21-26.

Methodical Publishing Center (1999), Statistical Yearbook of Lithuania, Vilnius.

Rudert, Ch. (1992), 'Republik Litauen – Ressourcen und wirtschaftliche Bedingungen', *Institut für Ausländische Landwirtschaft*, Berlin.

Schwierz, A. (1999), *Agrarmärkte in Zahlen*, Bonn.

Statistikos Departamentas prie Lietuves Respublikos Vyriausybes (1998), *Lietuvos zeme sukis*, Vilnius.

Zentrale Markt- und Preisberichtsstelle GmbH (ZMP) (2000), *Agrarmärkte in Zahlen: Mittel- und Osteuropa*, Bonn.

FORMER STATES OF THE SOVIET UNION

7. Belarus

DIETER DRÄGER

7.0 Background to the transformation

In the Belarus Republic, transition to democracy and free markets began late in 1991 following the break-up of the Soviet Union. Farms, firms and other enterprises, about 75 percent of which had been centrally controlled by Soviet authorities, had to be integrated into a new national regulatory framework. This process required, most importantly, the strengthening of workers' management skills. Another task that had to be tackled early on was the creation of a national tax and currency system.

An even more complex task was transforming the interdependent trading network with other regions of the Soviet Union, based on centrally-planned division of labor, into foreign trade relations grounded in market conditions. In the import-dependent power supply, chemicals and metals processing industries, as well as in the export-oriented branches of the agro-industrial complex, and the consumer goods, tool-making and mechanical engineering industries, the current outlook is rather bleak. About 80 percent of trade still occurs with successor states of the Soviet Union. Compared to 1991, imports and exports have declined by more than 50 percent. Terms of trade have also turned against Belarus, mainly as a result of rising fuel prices.

The Belarus reform program pins its hopes on a gradual evolution towards a socially-oriented market economy, combining a wide range of ownership and business organizations with competition and individual responsibility. In the long-run, economic activity is to respond both to internal and external markets conditions, while conforming with national resource constraints. Reforms are presently proceeding only at a modest pace (Gusakov, 2000).

According to Belorussian experts, fundamental reform of corporate and business structures has yet to begin. Slow transformation of companies into private enterprises with a well-defined and recognized legal basis, continued state regulation, limited progress in developing market infrastructure and an inappropriate subsidy system all hamper the process whereby companies adjust to new economic realities. Further, falling output and significant reductions in real income have resulted in decreasing consumption and poorer living conditions for much of the population. Table 7.1 contains indicators reflecting economic conditions in the 1990s.

Table 7.1 Year-to-year variation in selected economic variables (%), based on constant prices

	1990	1991	1992	1993	1994	1995	1996	1997	1998
GDP	-0.2	-1.2	-9.6	-11.0	-13.0	-10.0	2.8	10.4	8.3
Indust. output	2.1	-1.0	-9.4	-10.0	-17.1	-11.7	3.5	18.8	11.0
Agric. output	-8.7	-4.9	-8.5	3.7	-14.4	-4.7	2.4	-4.9	-4.0
Investment	9.0	4.0	-29.0	-15.0	-11.0	-31.0	-5.0	20.0	25.0
Retail turnover	14.7	-8.1	-22.0	-14.2	-10.0	-23.0	31.0	18.0	21.0
Imports plus exports*	-	-	-	-	23.7	84.2	22.6	27.9	-2.4

Note: * Calculated from imports plus exports in $ (US) at current prices

Sources: Compiled from data in Institut für Wirtschaftsforschung, 1999; Ministerstvo statistiki i analiza, 2000.

7.1 General setting

Territory, population and administration structure

The territory of the Belarus Republic covers an area of 207,600 km². Its national boundary has a length of 2,969 km; neighboring countries are Poland to the west, Ukraine to the south, Russia to the east, and Lithuania and Latvia to the north.

Belarus' population of 10.18 million in early 1999 gives it an average of only 49 inhabitants per 1 km². About 70 percent of the population lives in urban areas, and two-thirds of these live in larger cities with more than 100,000 inhabitants each. Population growth was relatively modest in past decades, with an annual growth rate of only 0.5 percent between 1980 and 1995. Since 1994, the population has decreased for the first time since the end of World War II: by 1999, the population had dropped by 187,999 relative to the 10,367,000 recorded in 1994. The regional differentiation of the population and other regional data are shown in table 7.2 and figure 7.1

The Belarus Republic's administrative structure is shown in table 7.3 and figure 7.1. The country is subdivided into the capital of Minsk as an independent territorial unit with nine urban *rayons* (districts), and six *oblasts* (regions). *Rayons* and autonomous towns are the next lower administrative level. On average, 58,000 inhabitants live in each *rayon*.

Table 7.2 Territory and population, 1994

	Territory (1,000 km²)	Population Total (1,000)	Urban (1,000)	Rural (1,000)	Inhabitants per km²
Republic Belarus	207.6	10,367.3	7,073.9	3,293.4	49
Brest oblast	32.8	1,519.7	918.3	601.4	46
Vitebsk oblast	40.1	1,451.1	961.1	490.0	36
Gomel oblast	40.4	1,606.0	1,085.1	520.9	40
Grodno oblast	25.0	1,216.7	741.7	475.0	49
Minsk capital	0.2	1,693.3	1,692.9	0.4	8,467
Minsk oblast	40.0	1,611.0	801.4	809.6	40
Mogilev oblast	29.1	1,269.5	873.4	396.1	44

Source: Ministerstvo statistiki i analiza, 1995.

Table 7.3 Administrative structure of the Belarus Republic (January 1994), number of units

Belarus/Oblast	Rayons	Towns	Urban rayons	Urban-type settlements	Rural communities	Villages per rural community
Belarus	118	102	25	109	1,452	17
Oblasts:						
Brest	16	20	2	9	225	10
Vitebsk	21	19	3	26	248	27
Gomel	21	17	4	17	280	10
Grodno	17	12	2	21	192	23
Minsk-capital	-	1	9	3	-	-
Minsk	22	20	-	22	307	17
Mogilev	21	13	5	11	200	16

Source: Ministerstvo statistiki i analiza, 1994.

Geography and climate

The land is flat to lightly rolling, averaging 160 m above sea level, and with Mount Dzerzhinsk (Minsk *oblast*) as the highest (345 m) and the valley of the Neman River (Grodno *oblast*) as the lowest (80-90 m) elevations. Many rivers traverse the country. Their waters discharge either into the Dnepr and its tributaries and eventually into the Black Sea, or into the Neman and Dvina Rivers and from there into the Baltic Sea.

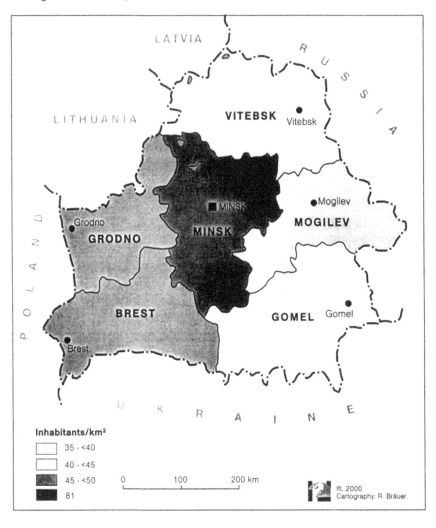

Figure 7.1 Administrative structure and population density (1993)

The northern and northwestern parts of the country in particular have many small lakes. Altogether, Belarus has 10,800 lakes, most of which expand over less than 50 km². Sodded podzols and bogs dominate. The climate is moderately continental. Winters are relatively mild and summers moderately warm, often with early and late frosts. Mean temperatures are -7°C in January and 19.9°C in July. Annual precipitation averages 641 mm (table 7.4), about two thirds of which falls during the growing season.

Table 7.4 Regional meteorological data, Belarus

Parameter	Meteorological stations*								
	1	2	3	4	5	6	7	8	9
Annual precipitation, mm 1990-1995 average	651	651	520	634	599	568	581	631	608
During that period:									
maximum	816	766	593	714	658	673	672	790	726
minimum	550	541	454	534	478	415	475	501	520
Annual mean temperatures, °C 1990-1995 average	6.2	6.8	6.8	6.4	5.7	8.4	7.9	7.3	7.4
During that period:									
maximum	7.0	7.7	7.6	7.3	6.5	9.2	8.7	8.2	8.2
minimum	5.3	5.8	5.9	5.6	4.8	7.7	7.1	6.4	6.4
Rain factor (acc. to Lang) 1990-1995 average	105	96	76	99	105	68	73	86	82

Notes: * Meteorological stations: 1 = Verchnedvinsk, Vitebsk *oblast*; 2 = Minsk;
3 = Marjina Gorka, Minsk *oblast*; 4 = Oshmyani, Grodno *oblast*; 5 = Gorki,
Mogilev *oblast*; 6 = Brest; 7 = Pinsk, Brest *oblast*; 8 = Vasilčvici, Gomel *oblast*;
9 = Gomel.

Source: Ministerstvo statistiki i analiza, 1996.

The growing season extends over 190 to 205 days. The sum of positive temperatures during the growing season is between 2,100 and 2,500° C.

7.2 Agricultural policy

Stated initially as fundamental premises[1] of the reform process in Belarus, the following goals are at the heart of agricultural policy in the 1990s:

- Improvement of the legal and regulatory basis for agrarian reform;
- Advancement of the competitive position of agricultural production through an efficient policy of prices, taxes, loans and subsidies, through investment within the framework of product-oriented public target programs, through development of market infrastructure and international cooperation, and through promotion of agricultural research, basic and advanced training, information and extension;
- Reform of ownership of farms, as well as of upstream and downstream firms and sectors (input suppliers and marketing/processing firms);

- Improvement of living standards of the rural population and demographic stabilization through employment policies, investments in rural infrastructure, and strategies for raising income levels.

In the short term, the most urgent task for agricultural policy is addressing the present agricultural and food industry crisis, i.e., declining production, reduced input use, rising farm debt, and erosion of real incomes of workers. In the medium term (5 to 7 years), the aim is to produce reliable food supplies and net agricultural exports by more efficiently utilizing the vast agricultural potential.

Belarus, like other transformation countries, considers reform of land ownership as central to restructuring the farm sector. So far, however, legislation to address problems surrounding land entitlements has been politically controversial and has not advanced as much as in some of the other transformation countries. According to the Act "On the right of land ownership" of September 1993, agricultural land - with few exceptions - continues to be state-owned; land is merely provided to users either for permanent use or on a rental basis, without a transfer of title.

Land use and rental fees are used to fund public programs that encourage soil protection and sustainable uses of land. More than 90 percent of farmland, including land operated by full-time family farms, continues to be state-owned. Foreign persons or corporations are not allowed to acquire private land, but may rent it for up to 99 years. Owners of private plots may establish small, part-time farms (*dachas*) or vegetable plots to meet subsistence needs, engage in weekend farming, or construct homes.

Further steps towards de-nationalizing land are urgently needed, particularly in connection with reforms of former state corporations and businesses. The following options are currently being discussed: privatization of land used by full-time family farms, and more freedom of choice for collective (*kolkhoz*) and state (*sovkhoz*) farms that have been assigned land for permanent use by the government. These farms would be permitted to transfer land through ownership shares to their employees, who would in turn be allowed to remove their shares to create full-time family farms, to extend their part-time family farms or to use land in other ways, such as in independent units within *kolkhoz* and *sovkhoz* farms, or in new joint ventures (partnerships). The underlying idea is to gradually approach characteristics of private land ownership and a free market economy. In this context, agricultural policy documents point out that it is important to take advantage of concentrated and specialized forms of agricultural production, and of the scale economies that can be achieved on large farms. This is a key reason why the government continues to insist on owning farmland.

Traditional *kolkhoz* and *sovkhoz* farms are being internally restructured through the establishment of relatively independent crop or livestock production units within these large-scale farms. Integral to this approach is the privatization of farming assets, mainly through transfers of state or collective assets into shared property.

To smoothen the transformation to a market economy, the government is allowing new types of farm businesses, such as family farms, cooperatives and corporations to develop alongside the existing, traditional types. The expectation is that the resulting competition will allow only the most profitable business forms to survive. However, specific legislation needed to define the legal status of these new businesses, and their rights, is lagging far behind, and this regulatory uncertainty is slowing down the overall transformation.

The pronounced increase in the number of new, small-scale farms is another sign of change. The share of small producers in agricultural land use doubled from 7.3 percent in 1990 to 15.1 percent in 1999. Part-time family farms operated both by agricultural workers who continue to be employed on large farms, and by retirees in rural areas, account for most of these small-scale farms. For increasing numbers of rural residents, farming "on the side" is essential to meet subsistence needs. In 1998, the amount of land available to part-time family farms averaged only 0.8 hectares, however.

Together, these smallholders cultivate 1.4 million ha of farmland. In comparison, 2,641 full-time family farmers cultivated 58,200 ha in 1999, for an average of 22 ha per farm. About 83 percent of farmland is in the hands of corporate farms, most of which are traditional *kolkhozes*, with an average size of 3,050 ha. By the end of 1998, almost 50 percent of *kolkhoz* or *sovkhoz* farms had begun to reform themselves. Altogether, however, only 81 have completed the transformation into new corporations or cooperatives. Current land use patterns for different farm types are shown in table 7.5.

Improving rural economic conditions is another major agricultural policy concern in Belarus. Progress in this area is expected to give a major impetus to agrarian reforms. The last decades have seen dramatic declines in the rural population, from almost 79 percent of the total population in 1960 to 30 percent in 1998 or, in absolute terms, from 5.6 to 3.1 million. This decline was particularly pronounced in the 1970s and 1980s. Between 1990 and 1998 the rural population again fell noticeably, by 368,000 persons or 11 percent.

Table 7.5   Agricultural land use by type of user, 1999

| | Farmland | | Arable land | | Forests* | |
Land users	1,000 ha	%	1,000 ha	%	1,000 ha	%
Total	9,307.2	100	6,186.6	100	8,225.0	100
Farms and small producers	9,193.6	98.78	6,141.6	99.27	1,239.0	15.06
Kolkhoz farms	5,644.5	60.65	3,667.8	59.29	902.0	10.97
Sovkhoz farms	1,975.1	21.22	1,324.3	21.41	329.0	4.00
Other joint ventures	103.4	1.11	73.3	1.18	2.0	0.02
Full-time family farms	58.2	0.62	47.8	0.77	6.0	0.07
Small producers	1,412.4	15.18	1,028.4	16.62	-	-
Forestry enterprises	45.0	0.48	12.4	0.02	6,251.0	76.00
Other land users	68.6	0.74	32.6	0.53	735.0	8.94

Note: * As of January 1, 1994

Sources: Compiled from data in Gusakov, 2000; Ministerstvo statistiki i analiza, 1994.

This evolution goes hand in hand with deteriorating demographic conditions, characterized in the mid-1990s by:

- Birth rates being below death rates, which accounts for one-fifth of the drop in the rural population;
- Disparity of the gender ratio: more men than women up to 45 years of age, but more women than men in older age groups;
- Average life expectancy of 64 years for men and 75 years for women; and
- The share of the population able to work has declined to 45 percent as more and more younger people have left rural areas.

Compared with other CIS member countries, Belarus has its own unique rural socioeconomic conditions. Creating economic conditions that raise rural incomes is seen as the most important task of national agricultural policy. This has to be directed first and foremost at farms, as livelihoods of more than two-thirds of rural families depend directly on income from agriculture. Furthermore, social and cultural facilities in villages, as well as important parts of the physical infrastructure, such as roads and lanes, were originally set up by *kolkhoz* and *sovkhoz* farms and are being maintained by them even today. This means that agricultural policies, including subsidies designed to improve conditions in agriculture are, indirectly, also social policy measures.

Rural areas will be developed based on the Act "On the socio-cultural and economic development of the village and of the agro-industrial complex". Local conditions are to be taken into consideration when the former property of large farms is to be redistributed to local residents. Other main functions of this Act include the support of housing development in rural areas and creation of new jobs, mainly in the manufacturing and services sectors. These are also intended to stem out-migration of people who are able to work and, therefore, to contribute to a better long-run rural demographic structure.

Almost 60 percent of the retired population lives in rural areas. Caring for older generations, as well as low-income families and unemployed workers, remains a special concern of agro-social policy. The current thinking is that large farms - including those converted into private corporations - will continue to provide social functions (such as soup kitchens) in addition to supporting family subsistence farms. Thus, certain vestiges of socialized agriculture are expected to remain in place.

7.3 Land use

Overall structure of land use

Land use in Belarus is officially recorded and reported both by type of use and by allocation to different sectors. Therefore, land reported under agricultural uses includes farmland as well as forestland and developed land, if that land can be attributed to farms and small producers. At the same time, farmland is also reported by other user categories, such as industries. Agriculture uses 56.6 percent of the national territory (table 7.6). In 1994, this area included 77.7 percent farmland, 10.4 percent forest land, and 11 percent other land (waters, bushes, bogs, developed land and roads). Table 7.7 shows land uses by oblast, with silvicultural use ranking first, followed by agricultural and grassland uses.

Table 7.6 Structure of land use, 1999

Land uses	1,000 ha	%
National territory (total)	20,760.0	100.0
Agriculture	11,571.9	56.6
Forestry	6,832.4	32.9
Industry, military, transport, communications	846.4	4.1
Protected areas, health resorts	678.3	3.3
Settlements	379.1	1.8
Land reserve	237.0	1.1
Other users	34.5	0.2

Source: Gusakov, 2000.

Belarus was greatly affected by the Chernobyl (Ukraine) nuclear reactor disaster in 1986. Radiation load from ^{137}Cs with its 30 years half-life is a long-term problem. According to measurements taken in 1991, about 46,000 km² (22 percent of the national territory) are contaminated with at least 1 Ci ^{137}Cs/km², affecting 3,370 towns and villages and a population of 1.9 million. About 16,600 km² of land are loaded with 5 Ci/km² or more. *Oblasts* Gomel and Mogilev suffer the most from heavy radioactivity. Sixty percent of the contaminated land lies in the Gomel oblast (figure 7.2*)*. Most of the population (126,000 persons) was evacuated from the most severely affected areas (with 15 Ci/km² or more). In the Gomel, Mogilev and Brest *oblasts*, 87 percent, 15 percent and 12 percent of the population, respectively, live in areas where contamination is as high as 15 Ci/km². Consequences for public health, particularly that of children, are serious. Thyroid tumors among children have increased seven-fold, and by as much as 22-fold in the Gomel region (Spaar and Schuhmann, 2000).

Another urgent concern is supplying residents of contaminated zones with relatively safe food. Specific rules and control mechanisms have been set up for agricultural production and for consuming local products. However, these rules and mechanisms are implemented only when funds are available. Some 1.8 million ha of forestland (24 percent of woods) are subject to special use regulations. The use of forests in heavily contaminated areas is forbidden.

Agricultural land use

Structure of agricultural land use The total amount of farmland in Belarus decreased from 9.8 million ha in 1970 to 9.3 million in 1999, with heavily contaminated soils set aside after the Chernobyl disaster accounting for more than one-half of this decrease. Aside from this, the size and structure of farmland are relatively stable (table 7.8). Special mention should be made, however, of shifts in permanent grassland. Between 1960 and 1997, the area of meadows decreased by almost 50 percent (from 2.4 million to 1.3 million ha) while pastures increased from 1.2 to 1.7 million ha. This entailed an overall decrease of permanent grassland from 3.5 to 2.9 million ha. In Soviet times, Belarus specialized in producing meat and milk, as well as potatoes. These sub-sectors, along with forages, benefited from large capital investments, which ceased after 1990.

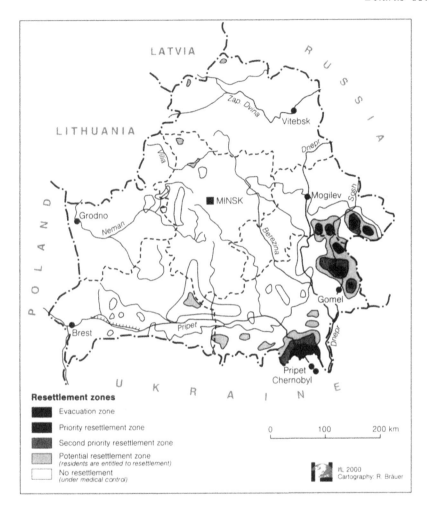

Figure 7.2 Areas resettled because of radioactive contamination

Table 7.7 **Land use patterns by** *oblast,* **1994, in percent of the total land**

	Belarus	Brest oblast	Vitebsk oblast	Gomel oblast	Grodno oblast	Minsk oblast	Mogilev oblast
Forests	39.6	35.3	36.4	42.3	36.4	40.0	38.7
Arable land and permanent crops	30.1	26.5	30.2	22.1	36.2	32.6	35.6
Grassland	15.0	18.2	12.9	13.6	15.3	14.4	16.1
Waters, bogs, waste land, miscellaneous	9.6	16.3	14.4	11.6	7.7	7.6	6.0
Nature conservation	2.1	0.7	1.8	7.0	1.4	0.4	-
Settlements	1.8	1.8	2.3	1.5	1.6	2.2	1.4
Industry/transport	1.8	1.2	2.0	1.0	1.4	2.8	2.2
Territory total	100.0	100.0	100.0	100.0	100.0	100.0	100.0

Source: Adapted from Ministerstvo statistiki i analiza, 1994.

In view of climate and soil conditions in Belarus, drainage projects have been particularly important. While about 700,000 ha of drained land were used agriculturally in the 1950s, this number had increased to 1.8 million ha by 1970, 2.3 million by 1980, and 2.9 million ha by 1997. The draining of permanent grassland accounts for a significant share of these increases, especially since 1980 (Skarapanov, 1995). Arable land now accounts for 43 percent and grassland for 57 percent of drained area. The Belorussian Polesie marshland is a regional center for drainage projects.

Table 7.8 Farmland structure in Belarus, 1960-1997

	1960		1980		1990		1997	
	1,000 ha	%	1,000 ha	%	1,000 ha	%	1,000 ha	%
Farmland total	9,738	100	9,646	100	9,415	100	9,306	100
Arable land	6,050	62.2	6,196	64.2	6,105	64.8	6,175	66.4
Meadows	2,350	24.1	1,475	15.3	1,323	14.1	1,291	13.9
Pastures	1,200	12.3	1,824	18.9	1,834	19.5	1,696	18.2
Permanent crops	138	1.4	151	1.6	153	1.6	144	1.5
Principal forage area	5,225	53.6	5,337	55.3	5,711	60.6	5,537	59.5

Source: Spaar and Schuhmann, 2000.

Regional differences in soil types, water and temperature regimes have resulted in different land use patterns across *oblasts* (tables 7.9, 7.10 and 7.11). These differences are most obvious in the arable land to grassland ratio, and in patterns of areas seeded.

Oblasts Brest and Gomel and the southern part of Minsk have the largest proportion of boggy peat and podzol soils and, therefore, an above-average amount of grassland, but in northern zones - Vitebsk and the northern parts of oblasts Grodno, Minsk and Mogilev - arable land accounts for 70 percent or more of the area.

Uses of arable land Cereals/grain legumes and forage crops dominate, each accounting for more than 40 percent of arable land, followed by potatoes, industrial crops and vegetables (table 7.12). This basic structure has not changed much over the last 40 years, except for certain variations of individual crop shares. Along with the priority given to milk and beef production, field forage crops have expanded at the expense of other crops. Cultivation of industrial crops dropped during the last decades, while cereals hectarage varied between 46 percent (1960), 41 percent (1970), 50 percent (1980) and around 44 percent (1990s) of the total.

According to the Institute for Agricultural Economics (Institut agrarnoj ekonomiki) in Minsk, if the stability of future national food supplies is to be ensured, cereals and grain legumes should account for 51 percent, field forage for 32 percent, potatoes and vegetables for 11 percent, and industrial crops for 6 percent of crop area. Since 1980, barley has pushed rye out of first place, while oats and wheat rank third and fourth. These structural changes were associated with the fact that, as indicated above, Belarus has specialized in milk and meat production, which has increased the demand for feed grains since the 1970s. The structure of cereals production in the 1990s shown in table 7.13 reflects changing demand patterns as well as declining yields.

Further structural changes in cereals production are considered essential to meet and even exceed growing domestic grain demand. The government's target is for grain legumes to once again equal 10 percent of all cereals output. To accomplish this, adequate seed supplies are needed along with appropriate technology for both cultivation and harvesting of these crops. Wheat is also to account for about 10 percent of all cereals. In addition to an increase in production of *triticale*, corn for grain is to be promoted and account for about 6 percent, mainly in the southern regions. Rye would then decline to about 30 percent, while barley would stabilize at 40 percent (but with a strongly reduced share of malting barley).

Table 7.9 **Major soil groups in the Belarus Republic, 1996, in percent**

Soil type	Belarus Republic	Oblast					
		Brest	Vitebsk	Gomel	Grodno	Minsk	Mogilev
Sodded calcareous soils	0.2	0.4	0.1	0.1	0.1	0.4	0.2
Sodded podzols	45.1	22.6	43.3	33.0	59.9	48.0	53.8
Boggy sodded podzols	22.6	26.3	29.0	29.6	15.6	21.8	25.0
Boggy sodded calcareous soils	9.0	14.3	10.1	7.6	10.2	7.6	6.3
Alluvial soils	8.7	5.9	2.2	10.9	4.7	2.9	5.8
Boggy peat soils	14.4	30.5	15.3	18.8	9.5	19.3	8.9

Source: Smeän and Bogdevic, 1996.

Table 7.10 Share of soil type in arable land, 1985, in percent

Oblast	Clay and loam	Sandy Loam	Sand	Peat
Brest	7.9	51.5	25.8	14.8
Vitebsk	66.2	27.1	4.9	1.8
Gomel	18.2	36.0	34.7	11.1
Grodno	26.7	62.3	9.9	1.1
Minsk	42.8	41.6	6.2	9.4
Mogilev	48.3	42.8	7.6	1.3
Belarus Republic	37.6	42.5	13.6	6.3

Source: Senko et.al, 1986.

Table 7.11 Farmland by *oblast*

	Farmland (1,000 ha)		Arable land (%)		Permanent grassland (%)	
Oblast	1990	1995	1990	1995	1990	1995
Brest	1,461	1,456	58	58	40	40
Vitebsk	1,739	1,702	69	71	30	28
Gomel	1,451	1,413	60	62	38	36
Grodno	1,292	1,284	69	70	29	29
Minsk	1,894	1,872	67	70	31	28
Mogilev	1,506	1,424	67	69	31	29

Source: Ministerstvo statistiki i analiza, 1995.

Potato area has declined continuously from 18 percent in 1960 to about 12 percent in the 1990s, and a further decline to 10 percent or 600,000 ha is expected. Solutions to pressing technological, phytosanitary and seed problems are urgently needed. The expectation is for industrial potatoes to be grown in closer proximity to processing plants. The estimates for potato production include export demand for food potatoes, potato products and seed potatoes (Gusakov et.al, 1995).

Traditionally, flax ranked first among industrial crops, but production and marketing problems have contributed to a marked decline in the area allocated to this crop. In 1960, flax was still grown on 270,000 ha (5 percent of arable land), but this declined to 149,000 ha (2.5 percent) by 1990 and as little as 72,000 ha (1.8 percent) by 1997. Finding new uses for flax products, modernization of the processing industry and improvements in production technology - supported by a program advancing research, development and investment - may allow the flax industry in Belarus to survive. Flax is expected to be cultivated on 130,000 ha in the next few years, with regional concentrations (75 percent) around Vitebsk, Minsk and Grodno.

Both sugar beet and rapeseed (colza) are important crops in several locations, especially in *oblasts* Brest, Grodno and Minsk. The scope for producing these crops is limited, however, by insufficient processing capacity. Chances for expanding colza production to 150,000 ha appear good. Vegetable growing increased during the 1990s, with cabbage, carrots and red beet accounting for more than 80 percent of output. As with potatoes, most of the output (83 percent of crop area) comes from small producers.

Table 7.12 Cropping patterns in Belarus

	Crop area							
	1,000 ha				in percent			
	1980	1990	1995	1997	1980	1990	1995	1997
Total crop area	6,308	6,126	6,150	6,207	100	100	100	100
Cereals and grain legumes	3,139	2,645	2,692	2,718	49.8	43.2	43.8	43.8
Winter rye	1,074	917	969	855	17.0	15.0	15.8	13.8
Winter wheat	119	125	141	200	1.9	2.1	2.3	3.2
Spring wheat	90	15	36	96	1.4	0.2	0.6	1.6
Barley	1,218	1,030	1,033	885	19.4	16.8	16.8	14.3
Oats	391	360	337	325	6.2	5.9	5.5	5.2
Other cereals	-	8	39	76	-	0.1	0.6	1.2
Buckwheat	44	18	18	19	0.7	0.3	0.3	0.3
Grain legumes	203	172	119	262	3.2	2.8	1.9	4.2
Industrial crops	290	248	205	156	4.6	4.0	3.3	2.5
Flax	234	149	98	72	3.7	2.4	1.6	1.2
Sugar beet	52	46	55	47	0.8	0.7	0.9	0.8
Rapeseed	-	49	48	28	-	0.8	0.8	0.4
Misc.	4	4	4	9	0.1	0.1	0.0	0.1
Potatoes	787	638	725	700	12.5	10.4	11.9	11.3
Vegetables	54	41	77	83	0.8	0.7	1.2	1.3
Forage crops	2,038	2,554	2,451	2,550	32.3	41.7	39.8	41.1

Source: Ministerstvo sel'skogo hozâjstva, 1998.

Forage production dominates agricultural land use in Belarus. In the 1990s, 75-80 percent of farmland was used for these crops. Together with feed potato production, most of which comes from small producers and accounts for 3 percent of farmland, the principal forage area is a relatively stable basis for forage production. However, crop yields in the principal forage area vary greatly, and the intensity of cultivation is declining. Feed grains are grown on about 1.4 million ha, or 15 percent of the farmland.

Table 7.13 Cereals production patterns, in percent

	1960	1970	1980	1990	1995	1997
	55	34	34.2	34.7	36.0	31.5
Oats	15	11	12.4	13.6	12.5	11.9
Barley	10	28	38.8	38.9	38.4	32.6
Wheat	6	18	6.7	5.3	6.6	10.9
Buckwheat	5	2	1.4	0.7	0.7	0.7
Grain legumes	8	7	6.5	6.5	4.4	9.6
Miscellaneous	-	-	-	0.3	1.4	2.8

Sources: Ministerstvo sel'skogo hozâjstva, 1998; Centralnoe statisticeskoe upravleie, 1971.

Table 7.14 shows the declining share of permanent grassland in the principal forage growing area of Belarus; this decline was accompanied by falling crop yields. From the point of view both of agricultural sustainability and profitability, substantially increasing the efficiency of permanent grassland farming has become a priority.

Table 7.14 Size and structure of forage areas

	1985		1990		1997	
	1,000 ha	%	1,000 ha	%	1,000 ha	%
Principal forage area[a]	5,760	100	5,711	100	5,537	100
Meadows	1,455	25.3	1,323	23.2	1,291	23.3
Pastures	1,901	33.0	1,834	32.1	1,696	30.6
Perennial field forage	1,444	25.1	1,497	26.2	1,542	27.9
Corn, green and for grain	387	6.7	69	8.2	200	3.6
Fodder beet	157	2.7	139	2.4	133	2.4
Other forage crops[b]	416	7.2	449	7.9	675	12.2

Notes: [a] Total of permanent grassland and field forage area
[b] Except feed potatoes and feed grain

Sources: Ministerstvo statistiki i analiza, 1998.

Economic aspects of land use

Over time, the value of livestock output has exceeded that of crops. From 1960 to 1990, livestock production increased by 134 percent and its share in total agricultural output rose from 50 percent to about 63 percent. In comparison, crop production increased by 37 percent, and total agricultural production by 84 percent. Because of relatively slow growth in yields, forage had to be grown on increasingly larger areas, and feed grain and protein feeds had to be imported, to meet requirements of the expanding livestock herds in Belarus.

This was the background for a pattern of trade-dependent agricultural production and intensive integration into the former Soviet economy. The underlying production and trade relationships fell apart in the 1990s when agricultural production, and livestock production in particular, suffered severe declines (table 7.15). These changes not only reflect movement towards market conditions, but also firm-level adjustment problems (such as a lack of credit) that have arisen with reforms.

Table 7.15 Patterns and average growth of agricultural production in the 1990s*

	Unit	1990-1992	1993-1995	1996-1998
Total production	Mill. Rubles	11,141	9,520	8,627
Production per ha of Farmland	Rubles	1,185	1,019	927
Crop production				
Total	Mill. Rubles	4,557	4,476	3,828
Per ha of farmland	Rubles	485	479	411
Livestock production				
Total	Mill. Rubles	6,584	5,044	4,799
Per ha of farmland	Rubles	700	540	516

Note: * Gross output based on 1983 prices.

Source: Calculated from data in Ministerstvo statistiki i Analiza, 2000.

Livestock production data are summarized in table 7.16. Livestock numbers and performance increased up to 1990, but major challenges have arisen in ensuring efficient organization of animal production. In the 1990s, dramatic cost increases were no longer compensated for by commensurate increases in output prices, and the livestock sector entered a state of crisis.

Recovery of the livestock sector will require a radical and nationwide reorganization of animal production, both at the farm-level and within the meat processing industry, in addition to capital investments leading to technological improvements (Gusakov et.al, 1999). Targets for future livestock output, calculated using national food security considerations, are contained in table 7.17.

Further intensification is required for crop production as well, especially in terms of raising yields if minimum needs of the population are to be met from domestic sources. Grain production is one priority to this end, but traditional export-oriented branches, such as potato and flax production, are also to be developed more strongly according to government plans. At the same time, imports of vegetable oils and oilseeds, fruit, vegetables, sugar, protein feeds and certain cereals will be expanded (Gusakov, et.al, 1999) as a net exporter. Benchmarks for future production of commercial crops are reported in table 7.18.

Table 7.16 Livestock production and productivity over time

	1960	1990	1997
Number of head (in 1,000; year end)			
Cattle	3,666	6,975	4,802
of which: cows	2,037	2,362	1,999
Pigs	3,164	5,051	3,686
Sheep, goats	1,213	445	186
Poultry	18,645	50,600	40,500
Horses	519	217	233
Large animal units/100 ha farmland	42.0	65.8	48.7
Milk yield per cow (kgs)	1,818	3,220	2,859
Per-capita output (kgs)			
Milk	393	727	501
Meat	49	115	62
Eggs (pieces)	106	356	338

Source: Spaar and Schuhmann, 2000.

Table 7.17 Medium-term targets for animal production

	1997	2002	2005
Meat (1,000 t)	631	750-770	800-840
Milk (1,000 t)	5,132	5,680-6,160	6,000-6,500
Fat cheese (1,000 t)	37	40-41	45-48
Butter (1,000 t)	72	84-87	95-100
Fresh milk products (1,000 t)	813	920-950	1,000-1,100
Eggs (mill. pieces)	3,459	3,780-3,880	3,900-4,000

Source: Gusakov et al., 1999.

To achieve these targets, it will be necessary to sustain the productivity of arable land, to continue to better utilize the land's potential, and to improve productivity of permanent grassland. Presently about 56 percent of the arable land is considered to be more productive, while the remainder is less productive (Smeân, 1995).

Table 7.18 Average crop output and yields

	Harvested output (1,000 t)			Yields (100 kg/ha)		Output (kg/capita)
	1989/91	1996/98	Target 2005	1989/91	1996/98	1996/98
Cereals	7,200	5,688	8,200-8,500	25.8	23.6	552
Potatoes	9,549	8,466	10,000-11,000	147	119	823
Vegetables	854	1,190	1,350-1,400	186	142	116
Fruit	463	380	600-620	47	.	37
Sugar beet	1,479	1,231	1,650-1,700	315	243	120
Flax	64	37	.	4.7	5.0	3.6
Rapeseed	50	35	120-125	12.5	8.0	3.4

Source: Gusakov et al., 1999.

The most pressing tasks in terms of improving land management include:

• Draining waterlogged soils; existing drainage systems cover 20 percent of arable land and 51 percent of permanent grassland, i.e., a total of 2.9 million ha or 31 percent of farmland. On 50 percent of the drained area, systems urgently need repair and maintenance to counteract growing risks of secondary encroachment of swamps (Skarapanov, 1995).
• Liming 30 percent of arable land and 40 percent of permanent grassland.
• Preservation of the present humus content (2.2 percent) of soils by applying larger quantities of organic manures, as application rates have fallen from 8 t in 1980 to only 4 t per ha of farmland Smeân and Bogdevic, 1996).
• To preserve the relatively favorable phosphorus and potassium status of soils and secure a good nutrient balance, higher inputs of fertilizer are required for about 50 percent of arable land, as mineral fertilizer input has decreased from 214 kgs of pure nutrients per ha (1990) to as little as 95 kgs (1997).
• Field-specific rehabilitation measures on 1.4 million ha (15 percent) of farmland suffering from radioactive contamination.

National development schemes and increasing international cooperation are needed to accomplish these tasks. Other prerequisites include expeditious reforms of former state farms and businesses, including the settlement of ownership relations, legal reforms, and new land use strategies to meet the demands of a market economy.

7.4 Forestry

Forestry enterprises and organizations use 32.9 percent of the national territory. Most of this is forestland (91.8 percent or 6.25 million ha), a fraction is farmland (1.2 percent) and the remainder is other land. Together with forestlands managed by agricultural and other users, a total of 8.23 million ha (39.6 percent) of the national territory is in silvicultural uses; this includes land targeted for future reforestation. Some 7.4 million ha are covered with woods, with about 70 percent coniferous and 30 percent deciduous trees.

The average annual timber harvest between 1990 and 1993 was 9 million m³, 40 percent of which went into industrial processing, with the remainder used for timber, fuel and as raw material for wood-based industries. With an average forest age of 40 years, future logging rates are expected to be much higher. Therefore, forestry and the wood industry are considered to have a good development potential in rural areas of Belarus.

Between 1990 and 1993, about 26,200 ha of new forests were planted annually, which is about the same area as that cleared of trees. Cutting for maintenance purposes on 275,000 ha annually contributed one-third of the overall timber harvest. All in all, the output of the forestry sector was below that of the 1980s, but the decline was less pronounced than that in agriculture and other areas of the national economy. The use and replacement of woods in wetlands and in areas contaminated with radioactivity poses special problems.

Note

[1]   See also the state program for reforming the agro-industrial complex, adopted by the Council of Ministers on August 6, 1996.

References

Centralnoe statisticeskoe upravlenie Sovete ministrov SSR (1971), *Selskoe hozâjstvo SSR*, Moscow.

Gusakov, V.G., Iljina, Z. M. et al. (1995), *Osnovnye napravleniâ strukturnych preobrazovanij seljskochozâjstvennogo proizvodstva Respubliki Belarus na period do 2005 goda (rekomendacii)*, Belorusskij naucno – issledoratel'skij institut ëkonomiki i informacii APK, 113 pp., Minsk,

Gusakov, V.G., Moroz, U. D., Iljina, Z.M et al. (1999), *Koncepcijâ i Prgramma prodovol'stvennoj bezopasnosti Respubliki Belarus,* Belorusskij naucno-issledovatel'skij institut ëkonomiki i informacii APK 140 pp., Minsk.

Gusakov, V.G. (2000), 'Naucnye principy razvitiâ i mehanizm ёffektivnogo funkcionirovaniâ APK', *Agroekonomika*, vol. 1, Minsk, pp.3-24.

Institut für Wirtschaftsforschung Halle (1999), 'Die wirtschaftliche Lage der Republik Belarus', 15. Report, Research Series, Booklet 8, Halle, pp.1-40.

Ministerstvo seljskogo chozâjstva i prodovol'stviâ Respubliki Belarus (1998), *Agrpromyšlennyj kompleks Respubliki Belarus*, 68 pp., Minsk.

Ministerstvo statistiki i analiza Respubliki Belarus (1994), 'Narodnoje chozâjstvo Respubliki Belarus', Statisticeskij ezegodnik, Minsk.

Ministerstvo statistiki i analiza Respubliki Belarus (1995), 'Narodnoje chozâjstvoRespubliki Belarus', Statisticeskij ezegodnik, Minsk.

Ministerstvo statistiki i analiza Respubliki Belarus (1996), *Statisticskij bulletenj*, No.5, Minsk.

Ministerstvo statistiki i analiza Respubliki Belarus (1998), 'Narodnoje chozâjstvo Respubliki Belarus', Statisticeskij ezegodnik, Minsk.

Ministerstvo statistiki i analiza Respubliki Belarus (2000), Narodnoe hosâjstvo Pokazateli 1990-1999, http://www.president.gov.by/minstat

Senko, F.P. et. al (1986), *Sistemy vedeniâ seljskogo hozâjstva Belerusskoj SSR*, Minsk.

Skarapanav, S.G. (1995): 'Prablemy racyânaljnaga vykarystannâ zâmelnago fondu Belrarusi', *Vesci Akadëmii agraruych navuk Belarusi*, vol. 3, Minsk, pp. 42-51.

Smeân, N.I. (ed.) (1995), 'Pocvy, ich evolûciâ, ochrane i povyšenie proizvoditeljnoj sposobnosti v sovremennyh socialjno - ekonomiceskich uslovijach', Materialy I. Sëzda Belorusskogo obschestva pocvovedov, Minsk, Gomel.

Smeân, N.I., Bogdevic, J.M. (1996), 'Pocvennobiologiceskij potencial Belorusi', unpubl., Minsk.

Spaar, D. and Schuhmann, P. (eds) (2000), Natürliche Grundlagen der Pflanzenproduktion in den Ländern der Gemeinschaft Unabhängiger Staaten und des Baltikums, pp. 345, Agri-Media, Bergen Dumme.

8. Russia

TANJA JAKSCH AND DIETER DRÄGER

8.0 Background to the transformation

The long process of political change that began under President Gorbachev led to radical reforms in the early 1990s, which were designed to thoroughly transform the national economy into a free market system. The most important steps toward eliminating central planning were the liberalization of prices; the privatization of firms, which allowed producers to make their own production and sales decisions; the creation of private banks; and stronger integration into the world economy.

Price formation was largely governed by supply and demand conditions, and supply initially caught up with demand - a situation that rarely existed in the past. Along with the rapidly expanding and deepening process of transformation, however, a number of negative developments soon occurred. In particular, GDP, investments and retail sales have declined.

As was true in other CEE countries, agricultural production fell drastically. Since 1989, Russia's international rank has slipped from 7th to 49th in the ratio of food production to consumption (Ministry of Housing, Spatial Planning and the Environment, 1995). With rising food prices, food consumption has declined and current consumption levels are well below normal requirements. This is closely related to the decline in average life expectancy since 1991 (Woprossy statistiki, 1994).

After perhaps overly rapid privatization in agriculture, a more evolutionary process is now being followed. Privatization is currently based on the co-existence of large-scale (*kolhkoz* and *sovkhoz*) farms and independent, small-scale family farms. These smaller farms are expected to expand production rapidly, because they require less capital and can lease additional land.

In parallel to the initial decline in agricultural production associated with rapid early restructuring, soil nutrients are being depleted, which largely explains declining grain production (Spaar and Schuhmann, 2000).

Fertilizers are estimated to replace only about one-third of the nutrients absorbed by crops and weeds (Spaar and Schuhmann, 2000). Lack of capital has brought the once large-scale national drainage program to a halt, with the area meliorated declining by 634,000 ha since 1993. Water-logging, which together with salinization and erosion affects 106 million ha of farmland, has become a serious problem. Lack of administrative and organizational capacity, as well as capital, impede the development and implementation of sustainable land use regulations that have been recommended by land use experts (Radugin, 1992).

Russia's economy began 1999 with a continuing recession, coupled with currency instability and a non-functioning banking system. Foreign debt, amounting to 120 percent of GDP, intensified the problems created by economic restructuring. Agricultural production declined due to poor grain harvests. Real wages fell by 12 to 15 percent, and total investments declined from the previous year's low level by a further 7 percent (bfai, 1999*b*, 1999*c*).

8.1 General setting

The Russian Federation has a territory of 17,075,400 km² and a population of 148.3 million (Eastern Europe and the commonwealth of Independent States,1997). It has the largest land area of any country. The Russian Plain takes up most of European Russia. It is covered with ice-age deposits in the north and *loess* in the south. The Smolensk-Moscow elevation forms the end-moraine of the Dnieper ice-age, while the Valdai hills form the end-moraine of the Valdai ice-age. To the north, the plains and hills of the Baltic Shield (Karelian and Kola Plateau) adjoin the Eastern European Plains (Eastern Europe and the Commonwealth of Independent States, 1997).

The Eastern European Plains end to the south at the Caucasus, which makes up a small part of Russia, and it terminates at the Ural Mountains to the east. The large expanses of Siberia and the Far East stretch beyond the Ural Mountains, with the Altay and Sayan Mountains to the south, along with the mountains around Lake Baikal and Transbaikalia.

Permafrost stretches across approximately 9 million km² in the north. The tundra zone is a 50 km (European part) to 300 km (Asian part) wide strip of land. The Taiga covers a 1,000 km wide strip of land from the Baltic Sea to the Pacific. To the south, the forest steppe follows as a narrow transition area. Here patches of deciduous trees alternate with open areas that are farmed today, but once formed a fertile meadow-steppe (IALA, 1991).

Along the lower Don, in Ciscaucasia, and in the foothills of the southern Ural Mountains, Russia has a share of the forest-free meadow steppe belt. Almost all of the rich black soil in this area is used for farming. A strip of semi-desert stretches along the Caspian Sea (Gerloff and Zimm, 1978).

About 108 million residents live in cities and 40 million in rural areas; the rural population has grown by one million since 1989. For years, the number of workers employed in agriculture has remained at 10 million, representing about 14 percent of the total workforce. About 120 million people are of Russian nationality. The largest non-Russian groups include the Tartars with 5.5 million and Ukrainians with 4.4 million.

After the break-up of the Soviet Union, migration led to a separation of the different nationalities. Russians were repatriated from other CIS countries, while Ukrainians, Belarussians and Jews, among others, left Russia. The net effect of this migration on the total population has been negligible, however. Basic data for Russia's regions are provided in table 8.1.(see also figure 8.1) Population density varies greatly across the large Russian territory.

Table 8.1 Russian land area and population, 1994

Federation, Region	Area 1,000 km²	Population 1,000	Inhabitants per km²	Rural pop. share (percent)
Russia-total	17,075.4	148,366	8.7	27
Northern	1,466.3	6,022	4.1	24
Northwestern	196.5	8,136	41.4	13
Central	485.1	30,118	62.1	17
Volga-Vyatka	263.3	8,464	32.2	31
Central Black Earth	167.7	7,840	46.8	39
Volga	536.4	16,808	31.3	27
Northern Caucasus	355.1	17,518	49.3	44
Ural	824.0	20,421	24.8	26
Western Siberia	2,427.2	15,138	6.2	29
Eastern Siberia	4,122.8	9,200	2.2	29
Far East	6,215.9	7,788	1.3	24
Kaliningrad	15.1	913	60.5	22

Source: Goskomstat, 1995.

Table 8.2 shows the different administrative divisions of Russia's regions, including the number of so-called *federation subjects*. These are administrative units covering particular groups of people, ethnic minorities or other "special areas." Federation subjects are represented in parliament by an independent federation council. Also shown is the number of urban settlements and rural communities in each district.

Table 8.2   Administrative divisions of Russia's regions

Region	Number of Federation Subjects	Districts	Cities	Urban Settle-ments	Rural Commu-nities
Northern	6	82	63	155	923
Northwestern	4	62	62	90	734
Central	13	302	248	396	4,243
Volga-Vyatka	5	143	63	172	2,048
Central Black Earth	5	122	50	85	1,893
Volga	8	214	90	167	3,127
Northern Caucasus	9	179	96	102	2,093
Ural	8	229	144	265	3,436
Western Siberia	9	205	84	152	2,461
Eastern Siberia	10	157	71	197	1,641
Far East	10	144	66	279	1,281
Kaliningrad	1	13	22	5	96

Source: Goskomstat, 1995.

8.2   Agricultural policy

As of 1992, all 24,300 existing *kolkhozes* and *sovkhozes* were legally re-structured. One-third of these had re-registered by 1994 and retained their former status. Three hundred were turned into stock companies, 11,600 became limited liability corporations, 1,900 agricultural cooperatives, 400 became farming operations of other firms (including retail or wholesale firms) or organizations as well as military installations, 900 became farmer associations, and 2,300 took on other business forms.

Reformers expected a large number of agricultural workers to leave the large-scale Soviet-style farms and to establish their own small farms after receiving their shares of land and equipment. Based on the experience with small private plots prior to 1990, these new farms were expected to produce large amounts of food. This, however, has not occurred. In early 1998, there

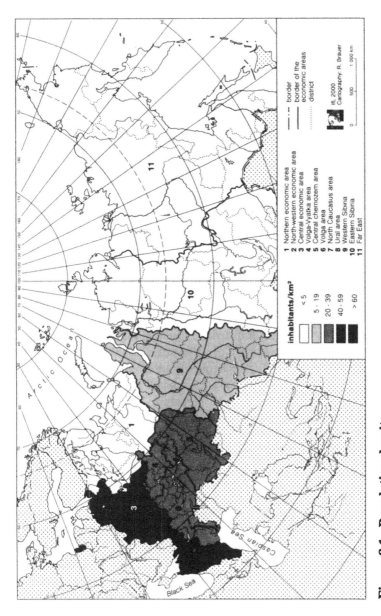

Figure 8.1 Population density

Source: **Statistisches Bundesamt, 1993.**

were only 274,300 small-scale family farms. The following factors explain why the number of farms is small:

- The 1998 economic crisis, coupled with political and financial insecurity.
- Capital scarcity.
- Attempts by managers to keep large-scale farms intact (using both carrots and sticks they seek to prevent farmers from leaving; for example, some managers simply refused to transfer land, or failed to pass on subsidized credit to those wishing to leave).
- The collective thinking and behavior of Russian farmers based on longstanding traditions included a strong sense of security offered by large-scale farms.

Source: Miloserdov, 1995.

It is difficult to determine the relative importance of each factor in explaining actual developments.

Historical legacy is also important for understanding the circumstances under which land is actually being privatized. Prior to communism, land was considered to be communal property, which was redistributed by village leaders every 12 to 18 years based on the size of farm families. Building on this tradition, the draft federal law "On Farming Businesses" of February 1997 charged managers of large-scale farms with *distributing* land to former workers, rather than explicitly transferring the land to them. In other words, it was often not clear to recipients of land that they were to become legal owners of the land in perpetuity. Further, the system of distribution led to corruption and cronyism. The fact that the draft law is not yet being enforced properly has also impeded the development of a market economy in agriculture. These underlying problems have been recognized, and Russian legislators continue to work on the draft federal legislation.

More than half the family farms have an area of up to 20 ha each, a fourth have 21 to 50 ha, and only 7 percent have over 100 ha. On small farms, sunflowers (representing 10 percent of all output), sugar beet (3.5 percent) and grain production (5 percent) dominate. The share of livestock production is low on these farms, because this activity requires relatively large amounts of capital. Small farms produce less than 2 percent of total output of milk and livestock for slaughter (Nowoe selskoja chostjaistwo, 1999).

The transfer of land to citizens for establishing small, part-time farms and gardens has expanded the number of small-scale producers. Their share of total output has risen from 28 percent in 1991 to 48 percent in 1998. In particular, their share of potato production rose from 67 percent to 92 percent and that of vegetables from 46 percent to 70 percent over this period. The share of cattle rose from 20 percent to 47 percent, cows from 28 percent to 36 percent, swine from 22 percent to 31 percent and sheep and goats from 31 percent to 43 percent (ZMP, 1999; Selskaja Shizn, 1998).

On the marketing side, farmers are shifting from selling produce to state purchasing organizations to alternative marketing channels. These include local farmers' markets, private trading networks and restaurants, and barter trade. State purchases of oil seed and sugar beet have fallen much more than purchases of other commodities. Here, direct sales are now occurring to private processors through contracts. Some of the processed products are then returned to growers who sell them on local markets or use them for barter trade, or to pay workers in-kind. Recently, the share of imported meat and milk products in total supply has grown significantly.

The rate of increase in prices of industrial products and services has slowed somewhat relative to increases in agricultural product prices. In 1992-93, agricultural output prices increased 8.8-fold, while input prices increased 13.5-fold (Woprossy statistiki, 1994). The economic slowdown and delays in payments for goods have hurt many farmers financially. More than half of all family farms are estimated to be losing money.

8.3 Land use

Forested areas stretch across 768.4 million ha (table 8.3), representing 45 percent of Russia's territory and almost one-third of the Earth's forests. Most of the forests are found in Siberia and the Far East. For logistical reasons, including market access, more than half of the logging occurs in the European and Ural regions.

Russia has an agricultural area of 222 million ha, that includes 130 million ha of arable land, an amount equal to the total arable land of the EU. Nature and landscape reserves were extended from 21.4 million ha in 1990 to 35.7 million in 1997.

Table 8.3 Land use in Russia

Type of area	1,000 ha	Percent
Forest Area	768,400	45
Agricultural Area	222,000	13
Reindeer Pastures	324,000	19
Water Area	68,300	4
Other Areas	324,400	19
Total	1,707,500	100

Source: Goskomstat, 1997.

The continental, northern location of Russia tends to create generally unfavorable conditions for agricultural production. The main agricultural area is located in the middle and southern parts of European Russia. Agriculture in Siberia is limited to a strip of land narrowing to the east along the southern border, especially in the region of Novosibirsk-Tomsk. Farther to the east, only scattered and fragmented patches of agricultural activity are found, in part because yields are highly variable. Crops are threatened by frost, drought and high summer precipitation in some areas.

In 1997, some 937,000 ha of orchards existed in Russia along with 103,000 ha of vineyards. Production of these crops has been decreasing over the last 10 years, and they currently cover only half the area covered in the early 1980s. Tea plantations cover 1,600 ha. About 5.2 million ha of the arable land are suitable for irrigation, while 5 million ha are drainable.

Nearly 80 percent of farmland is still farmed by *kolkhozes, sovkhozes* or organizations emerging from these farms. Small-scale farms use 4.4 percent of the area, while subsistence farms and gardens cover 3.3 percent. Other users of land, such as urban residents, farm 13 percent of the land as a secondary source of income and food (ZMP, 1998; bfai 1998; Miloserdov, 1995).

Crop production

Over half the arable land nationally was taken up by grains prior to 1990. Summer grains, especially wheat and barley, dominate all other types of grain. Table 8.4 shows national cropping patterns at two points in time. The large increase in the share of fallowed land is noteworthy.

Table 8.4 Cropping patterns, in percent

Crop	1988	1998
Grains	55.2	37.9
Sugar beet	1.2	0.6
Oil seed	3.1	3.1
Potatoes	2.8	2.3
Vegetables, melons	0.7	0.5
Feed vegetables	36.3	24.3
Fallow land	0.7	31.1

Sources: Institut für Ausländische Landwirtschaft, 1991; ZMP, 1999.

Russian attempts to increase crop yields prior to transformation were not always successful (table 8.5). Even in years of record grain production, 20 percent of the farms harvested less than 10 dt/ha. Higher wheat yields were achieved only in the northern Caucasus (28.3 dt/ha in 1988) and the central Black Earth region (21.8 dt/ha). In other major farming areas, such as the Volga and Ural regions and western Siberia, yields were 13.0, 10.3 and 13.7 dt/ha, respectively.

Table 8.5 Quantities harvested and yields of selected crops

Crop		Average 1981-1985	1988	1998
Grains	1,000 t	98,986	102,807	47,800
	dt/ha	14	15.6	9.4
Sugar beet	1,000 t	25,101	32,716	10,800
	dt/ha	166	222	134
Sunflowers	1,000 t	2,328	2,953	3,000
	dt/ha	10	12.1	
Potatoes	1,000 t	38,439	33,692	31,000
	dt/ha	104	102	96
Vegetables	1,000 t	12,129	11,481	10,000
Flax	1,000 t	152	126	33
	dt/ha	2.9	2.6	3.1
Silage corn	1,000 t	164.8	190.8	46.0
	dt/ha	163.0	202.0	112.0

Sources: Institut für Ausländische Landwirtschaft, 1991; ZMP, 1999.

Notorious problems in Russia's food system included high harvest, transportation, storage and processing losses, which reduced the amount of food available for consumption. These losses amounted to an estimated 20 percent of potatoes harvested and 12 percent of all vegetables, for example. The limited empirical evidence available suggests that post-harvest losses continue to be a concern. Further, since the beginning of transformation, yields of four of the five crops shown in table 8.5 for which data are available have deteriorated.

Regional aspects of agricultural land use

Northern and Northwestern Region The northern region includes the area of the Kola Peninsula, Karelia and the area south of the White Sea, covering 5.5 million ha. The northwestern region is made up of the areas around St. Petersburg, Novgorod and Pskov.

Agricultural output in this region almost exclusively serves to provide local populations with fresh vegetables and livestock products. In recent years, planting of feed crops has increased even as livestock inventories fell in response to the high cost of imported feed from other Russian regions. Vegetable production around St. Petersburg has expanded, providing fresh produce to city residents.

Table 8.6 Production of grains, meat and milk by region, in kgs/capita

Region	Grains	Meat	Milk
Russian Federation	661.3	56.4	326.7
Northern	73.8	37.4	225.3
Northwestern	46.5	32.8	194.9
Central	316.1	38.0	258.6
Volga-Vyatka	653.5	65.9	436.4
Central Black Earth Region	1,447.9	96.1	525.9
Volga	1,079.0	70.7	392.0
Northern Caucasus	1,266.8	71.7	310.1
Ural	657.8	58.6	351.6
Western Siberia	747.2	64.2	421.0
Eastern Siberia	549.7	54.7	290.7
Far East	137.2	34.4	163.6
Kaliningrad	412.9	67.0	520.1

Source: Goskomstat, 1995.

Central Region The central region includes 12 regions around Moscow. Here twenty million ha are used agriculturally, representing 10 percent of the total agricultural area of Russia. Grains and feed, along with industrial crops, dominate land use in this region. Planting of grains for human consumption has fallen in the last 10 years, from about 40 percent of total cultivation to 25 percent, as production of grains for livestock has expanded. Winter wheat and rye are cultivated in equal amounts in this region.

The share of potato and vegetable planting has increased around large cities of the region. In areas such as Yaroslavl, Vladimir, Kostroma, Smolensk, Ryasan and Tula, vegetable production rose substantially, in sharp contrast to other farming regions in Russia. Feed production, in particular, has increased as farmers attempt to expand livestock production. In Tula and Smolensk, vegetable production has expanded, displacing produce shipped in from the south.

Volga-Vjatka-Region. This region includes around 10 million ha of agricultural land and stretches north of the central region to the Ural Mountains. Unlike trends in other regions, vegetable and livestock production have recently fallen sharply.

Rye dominates grain production here, but its share is falling due to increased summer wheat planting. The share of winter wheat is low, at about 5 percent. The share of potato cultivation is above the national average, but it is declining as planting of vegetables expands.

Central Black Earth Region This region has over 13 million ha of Russia's best land, and the quality of the soils also influences cropping patterns. Winter wheat traditionally dominated grain cultivation, taking up a third of the land. However, winter wheat production has decreased to 20 percent of the land in the last 10 years as feed grain production expanded. Half of the sugar beet, over 500,000 ha, is cultivated in this region but the area is gradually falling, from 770,000 ha in 1985.

With three million ha, area devoted to major feeds is below the national average. The high natural fertility of soils leads to high yields of all crops. Due to limited water supplies, the irrigated area (comprising only 3 to 4 percent of the agricultural area) is minimal.

Volga Region. This region along the middle and lower Volga contains about 40 million ha of agricultural area. Planting patterns here have shifted dramatically in recent years. The share of winter wheat has almost doubled at the expense of winter rye and summer wheat.

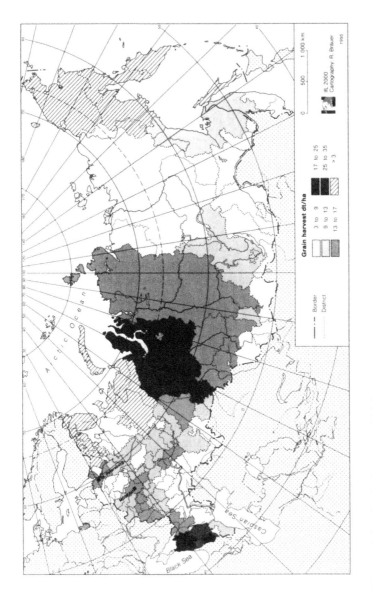

Figure 8.2 Grain harvest, 1994

Planting of sunflowers dominates industrial crops in this region, with one-third of total Russian arable land, especially in the areas of Srstov, Volgograd and Samara. The share of vegetable planting is also above the national average. Cropping patterns have remained relatively stable in the last few years.

Northern Caucasus Region. This region contains high quality land throughout. Since 1990, however, agricultural production has fallen by one-third. Every fifth ton of national grain output is harvested here. Grains take up almost half of the arable land, with half of this area covered by winter wheat. The nationally highest grain yields are obtained in the Krasnodarer area of the region.

Planting of sunflowers has risen dramatically in the last years, and now makes up more than 40 percent of area cultivated to this crop in all of Russia. Sugar beet area has remained relatively stable. Potatoes cover one fourth of the total area cultivated, and the area has recently risen slightly. This crop is increasingly consumed locally rather than being exported out of the region.

Cultivation of vegetables in this region contributes about one-third of total Russian vegetables production. In addition, the production of potatoes and vegetables has shifted from large-scale public farms to small-scale, subsistence family farms, in the process raising the share of subsistence consumption in total consumption.

Ural Region. This region contains over 34 million ha of farmland, making it the second largest agricultural region in European Russia, after the Volga region. Grains are the main crops, making up one-half of total cultivation. Of this, 40 percent is used for summer wheat planting. Industrial crops have a stable share in the region with 80,000 ha of sugar beet and 250,000 ha of sunflowers. The potato and vegetable harvest is mainly consumed locally.

Siberia. Siberia is divided into Western Siberia, Eastern Siberia, and the Far East. The agricultural area of all three regions together comprises over 60 million ha, or more than a fourth of Russia's arable land. Agricultural intensity decreases from west to east and from south to north.

Summer wheat dominates grain planting with more than 50 percent of the area planted in Siberia; in the Far East it amounts to only 25 percent. Industrial crops are almost exclusively planted in Western Siberia. Sugar beet area, however, has fallen by one half (30,000 ha) compared to previous years. Sunflower cultivation has almost doubled to 230,000 ha, most of which is consumed locally, and has displaced imports. Planting of potatoes and vegetables has increased, augmenting local supplies of these products (ZMP, 1999).

Livestock production

Nationally, livestock inventories have changed dramatically in the last few years. At 27.3 cattle and 29 hogs per 100 ha of arable land, livestock holdings have always been comparatively low, but they have declined further during the transformation. Sheep inventories were reduced to less than a third of 1989 levels, while swine inventories have been cut in half (table 8.7).

An important problem is poor quality of livestock feed, especially in terms of adequate protein levels. This leads to long fattening periods, of up to 26 to 30 months for cattle, and 14 to 16 months for hogs in some regions. Milk yields have declined over time (table 8.8), and are below 2,000 kg/cow in some areas.

Table 8.7   Livestock inventories (million head)

Livestock	1989	1998
Cattle	59.8	31.7
Cows	20.8	14.5
Hogs	39.8	17.3
Sheep	62.7	18.8
Poultry	646.2	360.0

Sources: Institut für Ausländische Landwirtschaft, 1991; ZMP, 1999.

Table 8.8   Production and yields in the livestock sector

Product		1988	1998
Meat (slaughter weight)	1,000 t	9,813	4,659
Cattle, Calves	1,000 t	4,150	2,000
Swine	1,000 t	3,399	1,560
Milk	1,000 t	54,534	33,197
Eggs	Mill.	49,144	32,549
Wool	1,000 t	227	48
Milk/Cow	kg	2,703	2,233
Eggs/Hen	pc	242	234
Wool/Sheep	kg	3.8	2.9

Sources: Institut für Ausländische Landwirtschaft, 1991; ZMP, 1999.

In 1990, efforts aimed at improving swine and poultry production, and the introduction of improved cattle breeds that yielded more meat, were supposed to rapidly increase meat production. As of 1999, results of these efforts are not encouraging.

In 1998, two thirds of the processed meat consumed in Russia was imported. The feed grains deficit for large-scale hog and poultry production facilities was estimated at 3.8 million t in 1999. Declines in imports since then have reduced the domestic availability of meats and meat products considerably. The production of meat, milk, and eggs, especially on large-scale farms, has declined significantly. By 1998, 55 of 236 large-scale poultry facilities, 23 of 64 hog, and 45 egg-laying facilities had folded. In 1990, three million tons of pork were processed by slaughterhouses; by 1998 this had dropped to only 554,000 tons.

As a result of rising prices for feed and other inputs, livestock production has shifted to small-scale family farms, where output is used mainly to meet subsistence needs. In part, this shift is encouraged by the fact that workers on large-scale farms are partially paid in-kind with feed grains, which they in turn use on their own farms. The feed situation has worsened as a result of poor harvests and import reductions.

The abrupt reduction of meat imports in the fourth quarter of 1998 left a significant supply gap on Russian markets. One indication of the magnitude of this adjustment is the fact that one-third of all EU pork exports went to Russia prior to the currency crisis. Commodity groups in Russia are trying to persuade the government to provide loans in the amount of 2.5 billion rubles for a poultry farm improvement program. The groups are pushing for reduced import tariffs on feed, breeding stock, veterinary medicine and equipment; in exchange, tariffs on manufactured goods imports are to be raised.

A substantial potential for raising livestock and crop output is believed to exist in the small-scale family farming sector, as well as in changing land lease arrangements that, for example, allow rural non-farm workers and urban residents to farm "on the side" (i.e., to moonlight). Some observers believe that this is the only way to move agriculture ahead in the short-run and to assure adequate national food supplies, given the uncertainty that presently surrounds private markets.

References

Bundesstelle für Außenhandelsinformation (bfai) (1998), *Märkte der Welt 1997/98*, Köln.
Bundesstelle für Außenhandelsinformation (bfai) (1999a), *bfai-Info Osteuropa*, 2, Köln.
Bundesstelle für Außenhandelsinformation (bfai) (1999b), *bfai-.Info Osteuropa*, 5, Köln.

Bundesstelle für Außenhandelsinformation (bfai) (1999c), *Russland zum Jahreswechsel 1998/1999: Wirtschaftstrends*, Köln/Moskau.

Eastern Europe and the Commonwealth of Independent States (1997), *Regional surveys of the world*, Rochester.

Gerloff, J. U. and Zimm, A. (1978), *Ökonomische Geographie der Sowjetunion*, Haack, Gotha.

Goskomstat (1995), *Selskokozjajjstvo Rossii*, Moscow.

Goskomstat (1997), *Selskokozjajjstvo Rossii*, Moscow.

Institut für Ausländische Landwirtschaft (IALA) (1991), *Die Landwirtschaft in der Sowjetunion*, Berlin.

Interfax, http://www.maximov.com/interfax/interfax_website.htm

Miloserdov, R. (1995), 'Problemy razvitija raznykh form predprijatijj v selskom khozjajjstve Rossii V', Kolloqium zu Fragn der Agrarreform in Russland (4.11.1993), Berlin.

Ministry of Housing, Spatial Planning and the Environment (1995), *Agriculture and Rural Areas in Central and Eastern Europe*, The Hague,

OECD (1995), *Agricultural Policies, Markets and Trade in the Central and Eastern European Countries: selected New Independent States, Mongolia and China*, Monitoring and Outlook, Paris.

Nowoe selskoja chostjaistwo 1/1999, Moscow.

Selskaja Shizn, Moskva, (various years), Moscow.

Spaar, D. and Schuhmann, P. (eds) (2000), *Natürliche Grundlagen der Pflanzenproduktion in den Ländern der Gemeinschaft Unabhängiger Staaten und des Baltikums*, Agri Media, Bergen Dumme.

Radugin, N. (1992), 'Agrarnaja reforma: dva goda spustja', *Zemlja i Ljudi 49*, Moscow.

Russia Food Market (1998), Sankt Petersburg.

Woprossy statistiki 1/1994, Moscow

Zentrale Markt- und Preisberichtsstelle GmbH (ZMP) (1996), *Agrarmärkte in Zahlen: Mittel- und Osteuropa 1995*, Bonn.

Zentrale Markt- und Preisberichtsstelle GmbH (ZMP) (1998), *Agrarmärkte in Zahlen: Mittel- und Osteuropa 1997*, Bonn.

Zentrale Markt- und Preisberichtsstelle GmbH (ZMP) (1999), *Agrarmärkte in Zahlen: Mittel- und Osteuropa 1998*, Bonn.

Zentrale Markt- und Preisberichtsstelle GmbH (ZMP) (2000), *Agrarmärkte in Zahlen Mittel-und Osteuropa 1999*, Bonn.

9. Ukraine

HERMANN MERTENS

9.0 Background to the transformation

Prior to World War I, Ukraine was known as *Europe's breadbasket*. Large areas of fertile land and a relatively favorable climate for crop growth accounted for high grain production levels. In 1930, the USSR forcibly collectivized the agricultural sector, binding it to an inefficient planned economy. This not only resulted in drastic declines in grain production, but also led to severe famines in 1931 and 1932. These events decimated the country's farms and paralyzed individual incentive for many years.

Following widespread destruction during WW II, the farm sector did not recover until the 1960s. Total agricultural output rose slowly between 1970 and 1990, but remained far below the country's potential, with average annual growth of only 1.2 percent. Between 1981 and 1985, poor harvests reduced output levels of grain, the most important crop, to below the 1971-75 annual average. From 1986 to 1990, total grain production increased, reaching more than 50 million t in 1997.

Political and economic events in the 1990s brought about Ukraine's independence but also once again led to dramatic reductions in agricultural output. Total output in 1995 was only 65 percent of 1990 levels. After two disastrous grain and sugar beet harvests in 2000, the government discussed the need to import grain for the first time in decades, and raw sugar imports more than doubled. Until then, sugar imports had been used solely to utilize all of the capacity of sugar processing plants. Output of livestock products has also fallen drastically and the index of gross agricultural product was expected to fall below 50 in 1999 (1989-1990=100).

Explanations for shrinking agricultural production can be found in an unsuccessful transformation strategy for Ukraine's overall economy. Consequences have included growing unemployment and inflation, increasing foreign debt, falling production and declining consumer purchasing power. One of the main obstacles, now as in the past, has been than $65 per capita, compared to $720 in Poland or $1,910 in Hungary (FAZ, 2000).

Agricultural policy since independence has failed to break away definitively from institutions and structures established during the Soviet period. This includes, among other factors, haphazard privatization of farms, *de facto* continuation of the state monopoly over land, and continuation of centralized product purchasing by state organizations at official prices. A serious barrier - and consequence - is the lack of private markets and price formation mechanisms, which also impedes the development of input markets and efficient production of inputs (Agra Food East Europe, No. 207).

9.1 General setting

Territory and population

Ukraine covers an area of 603,700 km². Along the east-west-axis it extends over more than 1,300 km, and 893 km along the north-south-axis. Neighbors to the west are Poland, Slovakia and Moldova, to the north Belarus and Russia, which form the eastern border toward the Black Sea. Ukraine encompasses the southwest part of the eastern European lowland, and it has little topographical variation. It is bordered to the southwest by the Carpathian Mountains (rising to 2,061 m above sea level), to the south by the Crimean Mountains (to 1,545 m a.s.l.) and the Black Sea, and to the north and east by the Belarus and Russian lowlands. The Dnieper, the most important river, divides the country into a western side with the Volyn-Podilsk Plateau, and an eastern side containing the Donets Hills. While the Volyn-Podilsk Plateau rises above 400 m at some points, the Donets hills remain just below this level.

A growing majority (71 percent) of the 48.8 million people in Ukraine was living in cities in 1999. The workforce consists of 22.4 million people; 3.9 million (17.4 percent) of these have jobs in agriculture. Average population density is 80.8 persons/km². Population centers are the Donets Basin, the metropolitan area of Kiev, and the western administrative regions (figure 9.1). The population's ethnic composition is 73 percent Ukrainian and 22 percent Russian. The remainder is made up of ethnic groups from neighboring countries.

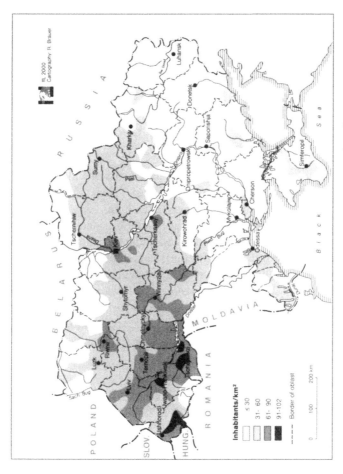

Figure 9.1 Administrative structure and population density

State and administration

In August 1991, Ukrainian leaders declared the country's independence. More than 90 percent of citizens confirmed the declaration in a subsequent plebiscite. In December, the presidents of Russia, Ukraine, and Belarus signed the so-called Minsk Declaration, forming the Commonwealth of Independent States (CIS).

The current form of government is a Republic. Legislative authority is held by parliament (Verchovna Rada), while the President and his cabinet provide executive leadership. Parliament is still dominated by anti-reform parties, while the President and Chief of the Cabinet remain at odds over transforming the economy to a free enterprise system, which has become an almost unavoidable political goal after detachment from the USSR. As noted above, the current constellation of political power has limited transformation to only fragmented progress, especially in terms of privatization.

According to most foreign observers, nine years of independence have led to little change in economic momentum. This is true despite the strengthened position of President Leonid Kutchma, who was first elected in 1993 and reelected in 1999. In January 1995, a decree was issued to accelerate privatization in agriculture and industry, and in the following July, parliament approved a constitutional agreement to strengthen reform powers. Neither action has led to any substantial changes.

The country has 24 administrative regions (*Oblasts*) with 485 districts and the autonomous Crimean Republic. There are 437 cities, six with over a million inhabitants–Kiev, the capital with a population of 2,622,000, Kharkiv, Dnipropetrovsk, Donetsk, Odessa and Zaporizhya.

Economic situation

Ukraine belonged to the more-developed economic areas within the former Soviet Union. Three regions can be distinguished within the national economy.

- The Donetsk-Dnipr Region in the southeast is considered the industrial center of Ukraine, with about 37 percent of the area and 42 percent of the population (98.9 inhabitants per km^2) along with mining and industrial complexes. Important branches of industry are: chemicals, machinery, ferrous and non-ferrous metallurgy, fuels and energy. Light manufacturing and food industries are also important. The center of this area is the Donetsk region, the most highly developed region of the former USSR. Forty-four percent of Ukraine's bituminous coal is found here along with sizeable deposits of rock salt, large amounts of iron, manganese and quicksilver ore, as well as limestone and chalk.

- The southeast region covers 46 percent of the territory and includes 43 percent of the population. It is considered to be the most important industrial-agricultural region. Major industrial sectors include: machinery, light manufacturing and food industries, chemicals and wood products. In this region, the wood products sector has access to 76 percent of national forests and 82 percent of wood supplies. The Kiev area is the largest contiguous industrial area in the region.
- The southern region is the smallest economic area, making up 19 percent of the area and 15 percent of the population. The autonomous Crimean Republic belongs to this region. Because of proximity to the Black Sea, shipbuilding and fish processing are concentrated here. Agricultural machinery and equipment, and tool machinery manufacturing as well as transportation technology are also important.

The country has a relatively well-constructed transportation infrastructure. About half of the streets are paved, and major roads connect industrial regions. The railway runs on electricity and connects the major industrial areas via transportation hubs. Ukraine's ports have year round access to the world's oceans through the warm waters of the Black Sea and to central Europe via the Danube. The country, especially the economic center of the "Donets Basin," is a transit and distribution area for energy supply lines.

Economic performance has declined dramatically in the last years. GNP per capita in 1998 fell to 38 percent of its 1990 level. In 1995, GNP as well as manufacturing and construction output were shrinking by 10 percent annually, compared with about 5 percent for agricultural output. Annual inflation was in the five-digit range but has been brought under control, falling to 12 percent in 2000. Real investment has declined dramatically and shows no signs of recovery so far. Table 9.1 documents the year-to-year decline of Ukraine's economy.

Foreign and domestic observers forecast that GNP in 2000 may rise for the first time in 9 years. However, favorable developments in the last months of 1999 do not signal, in their opinion, an improvement that can stand on its own. The need for reform is immense. Most important is strengthening property rights of individuals, consistently continuing privatization, making the legal and regulatory environment more transparent, and improving foreign investors' confidence. In agriculture, emphasis is being placed on promoting self-sufficiency of farms and easing land transfers. There are increasing indications that buying and selling of land will be made legal. One concern is the (often long-term) debt owed by farms, which undermines their ability to purchase modern inputs and also limits the development of a vibrant input supply industry (Schubert, 1995).

Table 9.1 Trends in selected economic indicators

Indicator	1991	1993	1995	1997	1998	1999[a]	2000[b]
GNP (1990=100)	88.4	65.5	44.5	38.7	38.1	37.7	38.4
Industrial production (1990=100)	95.2	79.5	45.3	42.2	41.6	42.6	42.8
Gross agric. production (1990=100)	87	81	65	58	52	50	51
Investments (1990=100)	92.9	52.6	29.4	22.6	21.0	20.6	21.8
Inflation rate (consumer prices in %)	91	2,000	10,156	401	20	18	12
Household deficit (% of GNP)	-	6.5	7.6	-	-	1.1	-
Foreign exchange balance ($ mill. US)	+307	-476	+231	-2,896	-2,039	-260	-

Notes: [a] Preliminary data; [b] Forecast

Source: Adapted from Kommission für die Erforschung der Agrar- und Wirtschaftsverhältnisse des europäischen Ostens, 1997; bfai, 2000a-c.

Climate

Temperate, continental weather dictates the county's climate, except in a small strip along the southern Crimean coast where Mediterranean climate and winter rain predominate. Damp and relatively warm winds from the Atlantic region prevail in western Ukraine. They bring sufficient precipitation and tend to moderate extreme deviations in temperature.

As Atlantic influences fade into a more continental climate, precipitation decreases and temperature contrasts strengthen. While an average of 750 mm of rain falls in Lviv in the west, only 550 mm fall in Kharkiv in the east. With only few exceptions, precipitation falls primarily during the favorable crop growth period. At least one-third of the precipitation falls from May to August, even in the more arid regions (table 9.2).

A dry zone runs along the southern coast from the Danube delta to the Straits of Taganrog, including the northern Crimea. Only about 350 mm of precipitation fall here annually. Regional distinctions similar to those for rainfall can be observed for temperature differences: as the average yearly temperature falls, the difference between summer and winter temperatures increases, and colder winters become more common (table 9.3).

Table 9.2 Precipitation in selected locations, 1971-1980 avg., in mm

Station	Mai	June	July	August	May-August (% of total)	Annual average
Kharkiv	50.2	58.6	82.5	51.7	45	545.8
Kiev	41.3	65.3	101.7	52.9	42	624.0
Lviv	76.7	99.8	110.1	80.8	44	773.4
Odessa	42.0	40.9	51.9	33.5	36	467.7
Simferopol	50.4	60.9	45.2	45.9	40	606.2

Source: Adapted from US Department of Commerce, 1971-1980.

Table 9.3 Temperature conditions, in °C

Location	January		July		1971-1980	
	Average	Range	Average	Range	Average	Range
Kharkiv	-7.9	-14.0/-1.7	19.9	17.6/23.1	7.3	5.6/8.2
Kiev	-5.7	-10.9/-5.4	18.8	16.9/22.0	7.7	6.5/9.6
Lviv	-4.1	-7.6/+1.2	17.0	15.9/19.8	7.1	5.8/7.7
Odessa	-2.0	-7.0/+2.4	21.1	19.9/23.4	10.0	9.2/11.5
Simferopol	-1.4	-7.0/+3.5	21.2	19.8/22.8	10.5	9.2/11.4

Source: Adapted from US Department of Commerce, 1971-1980.

Absolute winter temperatures can fall to –15°C in the southwest and to –40°C in the northeast. If there is little snow cover, a high risk of crop damage exists that generally increases from west to east, and from south to north. The vegetation period becomes shorter to the northeast, which has 160 days, while the southwest has 210 days, for a difference of nearly two months.

In regions with large temperature extremes, farm managers face the challenge of completing fieldwork within the optimal time frame. Machinery use must, of course, be adapted to these conditions. The risk of drought or an occasional precipitation deficit has to be met by using water-conserving farming systems.

Vegetation zones

The relatively homogenous parent material of mainly fluvioglacial and old alluvial materials in the north and northwest and *loess* deposits in the middle and south, and relatively flat topography and climatic conditions have allowed large natural landscapes or vegetation zones to develop.

Whether they are forest zone, forest steppe zone, or steppe zone depends greatly on the degree of humidity or aridity.

The forest zone stretches northward from above the 50th parallel on both sides of the Dnieper to the Desna-Seym river system, a tributary of the Dnieper. It is marked by mostly mixed forest vegetation, and in the northwest often by damp forest and moor vegetation (Polesye region). This zone covers about 20 percent of the country's area. The area converges with the forest steppe zone to the south and southwest. This is a transitional area stocked primarily with deciduous forests and showing increasingly steppe-like characteristics to the south (mostly long grass and meadow steppes).

The southern part of this zone contains large areas of alternating forests and steppe, and it covers about 34 percent of the country's territory. A virtually treeless vegetation area, the steppe zone, follows to the south. With decreasing precipitation, short grasses dominate. Semi-desert vegetation, primarily wormwood species, can be found in coastal regions crossing over to the Crimean Peninsula. The steppe zone covers about 40 percent of Ukrainian territory. Along with these large natural areas, there are special vegetation zones in the southern part of Crimea as well as in the Carpathian foothills.

The suitability of these vegetation zones for farming can be estimated by calculating their net primary production. This amounts to 60 and 70 dt/ha of produced organic substance for steppe and forest steppe vegetation; for summer green forest vegetation it amounts to 120 dt/ha. Climate and soil conditions can cause deviations, however. These vary in areas of steppe vegetation from 20 to 150 dt/ha, in forest steppe from 25 to 120 dt/ha, and in forest vegetation from 60 to 250 dt/ha of organic substance (Bartsch and Bürger, 1988). In Ukraine, these values lie at the upper end of the respective ranges.

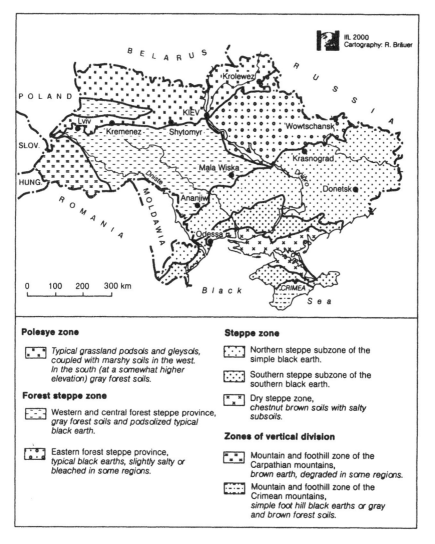

Polesye zone

Typical grassland podsols and gleysols, coupled with marshy soils in the west. In the south (at a somewhat higher elevation) gray forest soils.

Forest steppe zone

Western and central forest steppe province, gray forest soils and podsolized typical black earth.

Eastern forest steppe province, typical black earths, slightly salty or bleached in some regions.

Steppe zone

Northern steppe subzone of the simple black earth.

Southern steppe subzone of the southern black earth.

Dry steppe zone, chestnut brown soils with salty subsoils.

Zones of vertical division

Mountain and foothill zone of the Carpathian mountains, brown earth, degraded in some regions.

Mountain and foothill zone of the Crimean mountains, simple foot hill black earths or gray and brown forest soils.

Figure 9.2 Agricultural soil division

9.2 Land use

Soil varieties and prerequisites for agricultural production

Ukraine contains a large area of agricultural land. About 70 percent of the country's area is used for agriculture; over 75 percent of this is arable land, and 16 percent is forested (table 9.4).

To calculate agricultural production potential more accurately, soil fertility has to be added to climate and area variables. A strip of very fertile black soil - regarded as some of the best black soil in the world - stretches across almost the breadth of the country, converging with fertile gray forest soils in the north and simple or southern black earth in the south. This provides the country with relatively abundant and uniform, prime soil. Climatic and topographic factors have led to the formation of grass podsols and moor soils, and in some cases gley soils, in the north. Chestnut-colored soils with partially salty sub-soils have formed in the south, where precipitation levels are lower than evaporation levels. Podsol and chestnut-colored soils have lower yield potentials.

Table 9.4   Comparison of area utilized in Ukraine, 1995

Usage	Area (1,000 ha)	Percent
Total area	60,356.0	100.0
Farmland	41,973.4	69.5
Arable land[a]	30,922.9	73.7
Winter crops	665.1	1.6
Meadow	1,966.4	4.7
Pasture	4,555.0	10.9
Individual land use	3,864.0	9.1
Forested area	9,942.0	16.5

Note: [a] Figures reported here are a percent of total farmland, while forested area is a percent total area. The amount of arable land is in fact somewhat higher because mead-ows and individual land uses include some arable land.

Source: Adapted from Ministerstvo Statystyki, 1995.

Over time, land use has affected natural yield potentials of agricultural areas both positively and negatively. On the one hand, the potential has suffered from serious neglect by farmers and the clearing of large tracts of natural vegetation. This is evident from a negative humus balance, area and gully erosion (affecting 30 percent of arable land), soil compaction (of more than 50 percent of arable land), nutrient leaching (30 percent of the area has subnormal pH-levels) and concentration of harmful materials. A third of the arable land suffers from nutrient leaching, with three-fourths of this occurring in the forest steppe and steppe. In the southern dry regions, irrigation has lead to high salinity levels. Nearly the entire black soil region is in danger of eroding. On the other hand, drainage and irrigation have raised yields. Protective forests planted in the first half of the century have had only small positive effects.

Drained areas are mainly located in the damp parts of the forest zone; they cover about 3.3 million ha. In comparison, 2.45 million ha are irrigated. About 80 percent of these are in arid regions of the steppe. Aridity presents a substantial yield risk in this area. In practice, farmers expect reduced harvests as a result of drought every five years.

The Ukrainian Committee for Land Recourses drew attention to the deteriorating soil conditions in the early 1990s. According to its report, 12 million ha of black soil are in danger of eroding, and the damaged areas grow by 70,000 to 80,000 ha annually. In order to relieve damage caused largely by inappropriate farming techniques, the government issued a long-term program (1994 to 2000) to promote soil melioration. This program included reconstructing 295,000 ha of irrigation systems and 212,000 ha of drainage systems, as well as improvement measures for 60,000 ha of land. At present, no reliable information is available on results of the program.

Gross output varies significantly across administrative areas and vegetation zones. The highest gross production per ha of land was achieved not in the typical black soil regions, but rather in the western regions of Ivano-Frankivsk, Chernivsti, Transcarpathia and Lviv, followed by the central regions of Kiev and Cherkasy. Output in these regions exceeded the national average by 30-90 percent. The lowest production levels are found in the regions Kherson and Mykolayiv, northwest of Crimea, as well as in Luhansk in the east and in Zaporizhya, north of the Sea of Azov (Ministerstvo Statystyki, 1995).

Farming systems and production methods

State and collectively owned large-scale farms continue to dominate the agricultural sector with 83 percent of the land area and 40-50 percent of the livestock. The available information allows a simplified look at farming systems in Ukraine.

Most large production units grow crops for markets, and often also provide some value-added processing before crops leave the farmgate. These units are usually self-sufficient in the sense of having their own skilled laborers to repair equipment and construct buildings. Some of these farms specialized exclusively in vegetable, orchard or vineyard production, again usually in combination with value-added activities such as extraction of juices, processing of grapes, canning, etc. Other farms specialized in producing poultry (including layers, broilers and breeders), beef or hogs. Currently there are some 600 registered operations of this kind, although some have shut down or operate well below capacity.

A key characteristic of large-scale farms is that they traditionally provided social services to their members; in some rural communities, they represented the entire social support network. All of these units also provided services such as kindergartens and daycare for children. The relative importance of supporting activities (such as repair and maintenance crews) and social institutions account for the unusually large workforce of 10.7 workers/100 ha on these farms.

By virtue of their size, these large farms offer favorable conditions for mechanization and for becoming efficient operations; however, this will require that they shed all or most of their social service functions. Output of many farms remains sub-optimal today because of inadequate levels of mechanization and deteriorating buildings. Although some important processes, such as harvesting of grain and sugar beet, are fully mechanized, much of the other work is only poorly mechanized, or not mechanized at all in the case of transportation, loading and storage. In general, storage conditions are poor and losses high. Together with inadequately constructed facilities, current storage methods not only require large amounts of labor but also reduce the quantity and quality of stored products.

With current production methods, the regions' production potential is nowhere close to being reached. Serious shortcomings exist in these areas:

- Conditions and reliability of machinery and vehicles; repairs are often hampered by unavailability of spare parts, and limited investment in replacements;
- Poor quality of existing machinery (low precision in seed planting, high post-harvests losses, etc.);
- Lack or late arrival of fuel and lubrication, fertilizer and insecticide;
- Insufficient use of seed designated for specific locations;
- Continued weaknesses in the organization and motivation of workers, which affects the punctuality and quality of work.

In the case of livestock, most farms use relatively modern machinery for important tasks such as milking and feed distribution, but other chores such as raising young livestock and feed preparation continue to be carried out manually. A primary problem facing the livestock sector is feed management. Livestock is often given feed of lesser quality, leading to a low and unbalanced concentration of nutrients. The mixed feed industry all but fell apart after 1991; its rebuilding is being partly supported by foreign investment. Unsuitable and deteriorating facilities, outdated forms of livestock holding, and limited levels of mechanization contribute to high costs and low output.

Production performance

Gross agricultural production up to 1998 declined by more than 40 percent relative to 1986-1990 averages (table 9.5). The decline in livestock production is particularly pronounced, especially on state and cooperative farms. A growing amount of feed is set aside for payment in-kind and feed sales to cooperative members who keep their own livestock.

The fact that small farms have started to produce increasing shares of total output is partially the result of agricultural policies, although this was not necessarily the objective of the policies. In particular, large-scale farms pay higher taxes than small producers, so that more and more products are being sold on private markets. Large-scale farms are further disadvantaged by regulations that tie delivery of inputs to the sale of specific products, at unfavorable conditions, to buyers designated by authorities. This reduces their profitability (Koester, 1999). Even so, the total decline in production on large units was too large to be compensated for by the small rise in private sector activity. Unfavorable trends in livestock production continued after 1994, while favorable weather conditions boosted crop production in 1995 and 1997.

Table 9.5   Trends in gross agricultural output, 1986/1990=100, and percent of total accounted for by each sector

Product and sector	1991	1993	1995	1996	1997	1998
Crop output (index)	80.8	91.7	72.8	66.5	70.4	58.2
Cooperative (% of total)	53.8	45.4	60.9			
State farms	20.4	17.4				
Private sector[a]	25.8	37.2	39.1			
Livestock output (index)	91.4	71.7	58.2	52.1	45.7	46.8
Cooperative (% of total)	44.0	37.6	50.9			
State farms	22.2	19.6				
Private sector[a]	33.8	42.8	49.1			
Gross total output (index)	86.6	80.6	64.9	58.7	57.6	50.8
Large scale farms	-	-	-	52.5	47.8	45.0
Private sector	-	-	-	47.5	52.2	55.0

Notes: [a] Family farms and individual small scale farmers
 [b] Cooperative and state farms are not separately listed after 1995; after 1996, specific data for crop and livestock production are not available; some of the data are estmated.

Sources: Adapted from Ministerstvo Statystyki 1995 and 1998; FAO, 1999.

Crop production

By 1998, output of all major crops had declined (grains to 51.4 percent of 1990 levels; among grains, wheat fell to 54.2 percent, corn to 57.8 and sunflower seed, despite increased planted area, to 87.9, sugar beet and vegetable to 34.6 and 86.7 percent). Only potato production rose to 104.6 percent, after area planted increased. Yield, influenced by weather, does not exhibit a straight downward trend, as is the case with total production. Potential yields, however, have not been reached for years.

Compared to Western Europe, grain yield in Ukraine is only 34 percent, sugar beet 31 and sunflower seed 59 percent (Statistisches Jahrbuch, 1999). Compared to most other former republics of the USSR, Ukraine is achieving high yields, although they remain lower than those in neighboring Poland and the Czech Republic.

The gap between actual and potential yields can be estimated using empirical comparisons. For example, *Kolkhoz Ustimovka* (forest steppe zone), reported the following yields for 1993: 97 dt/ha for wheat, 50 dt/ha for peas, 75 dt/ha for barley, 50 dt/ha for oats, 39 dt/ha for buck wheat, 100 dt/ha for corn, and more than 600 dt/ha for sugar beet. These can be compared with national yields reported in table 9.6.

Table 9.6   Crop yields in dt/ha

	Avg. 1986-90	1991	1993	1995	1996	1997	1998
Grain	30.7	26.5	32.1	24.3	19.6	24.5	20.8
Winter wheat	36.4	30.3	38.0	30.1	23.2	28.5	26.9
Corn	35.4	32.6	28.4	29.2	27.4	32.6	25.3
Sugar beet	267.0	234.0	222.0	205.0	183.0	176.0	173.8
Sunflower seed	16.5	14.6	12.7	14.2	11.5	11.5	9.3
Potato	122.0	95.0	137.0	96.0	119.0	106.0	101.8
Vegetable	151.0	128.0	130.0	120.0	112.0	114.0	123.2
Fruits/berries	25.0	32.0	43.2	29.8	31.0	45.0	28.6

Sources: Adapted from Ministerstvo Statystyki, 1995 and 1998; Agra Food East Europe, various editions.

The Wheat Institute in Mironivka (forest steppe zone) recorded average yields of about 70 dt/ha when it tested new wheat varieties. In the field, these varieties yielded 40-62 dt/ha at various locations and on different soils, including podsols. Subsequent field trials for wheat and other crops conducted on Kolkhoz "40th *Anniversary of October*" demonstrated, using Ukrainian (Soviet) technology and West European farming methods, that a doubling of yield is possible within a short period of time with technological change and appropriate expertise (table 9.7).

In a German-Ukrainian project, field trials were performed from 1994 to 1998 on a 180 ha state farm. The objective was to determine the effects of three different farming methods on yield and profitability. Special attention was paid to a so-called "adapted technology," in which domestic tractors were fitted with German implements for planting, cultivating and harvesting, while taking exact yield measurements. The following yield increases were achieved over standard local methods:

Winter wheat	+14 percent
Corn	+67 percent
Sunflower seed	+39 percent
Sugar beet	+24 percent

Table 9.7 Kolkhoz "40th Anniversary" yields, Kiev region, in dt/ha

Crop	Ukrainian (Soviet) Technology	West European Technology
Wheat	40 – 44	75 – 82
Barley	30 – 35	55 – 65
Corn	40 – 42	90 – 103
Sugar beet	280 – 320	450 – 500
Rape seed	10 – 11	32 – 35
Peas	25 – 29	45 – 53

Source: Adapted from World Bank,1994.

The Ukrainian test farm was an efficient and well-managed operation that continually exceeded yields of neighboring farms by a substantial margin (Dieter-Gillwald et.al, 1997; Wagner, 2000).

According to the Ministry of Agriculture, only 40 percent of potential yields are being achieved in crop production. The main causes are a lack of fertilizer, agricultural technology, insecticides and other inputs. Other experts estimate that a sustained winter wheat yield of 60 dt/ha can be attained (Kommission für die Erforschung der Agrar- und Wirtschaftsverhältnisse des europäischen Ostens, 1997).

Farming conditions have changed substantially for only a few crops over the period 1991-1998. While total area farmed fell by 4 percent (annual average 1996/98 compared to 1991/93), grain area fell by 11 percent. Wheat area was reduced by 5 percent while cultivation of summer barley was extended by 18 percent. One reason for this change was increased demand for brewing barley. Sunflower farming was expanded (with declining yields) by about one-third to take advantage of international demand. Commitment of foreign companies to the Ukrainian oil and fat industry has also played an important role, even invigorating domestic demand in some regions. Reduced area of corn and sugar beet is largely the result of delivery problems in the agricultural input sector.

Area planted to potatoes and field vegetables essentially remained the same in the 1990s, largely because even in the planned economy these crops were traditionally produced on small farms as well as by Kolkhoz members or employees of state farms. Today they are typical subsistence goods and increasingly produced by other population segments in collective gardens and *dacha* areas.

Trends in livestock production

Despite favorable production conditions, abundant supplies of livestock feed from domestic and other sources within the former USSR, livestock output in Ukraine was always comparatively low. In the 1980s, livestock output exceeded that of many administrative units in the USSR with similar natural resources, but trailed behind that of Poland with its small farm structure. Overall, livestock production used 62-66 percent of the country's agricultural land.

Livestock production has declined drastically since the early 1990s. This is evident from rapidly falling inventories between 1991 and 1998, when cattle and hog stocks were only about half as large as in 1991, cow herds were a fourth smaller and the number of sheep declined by up to 70 percent. Milk production shrank by one-half and meat output fell to less than 40 percent of 1991 levels (table 9.8 and 9.9).

Table 9.8   Trends in livestock inventories, 1,000 head

	1990	1991	1993	1995	1996	1997	1998
Cattle	25,195	24,623	22,457	19,624	17,557	15,295	12,759
incl. cows	8,528	8,378	8,057	7,818	7,531	6,280	6,265
Hogs	19,947	19,427	16,175	13,946	13,144	11,236	9,473
Sheep and Goats	9,003	8,419	7,237	5,575	4,099	3,047	2,362
Poultry (millions)	255.1	246.1	214.6	164.9	149.7	105.0	122.9

Source: Adapted from Ministerstvo Statystyki, 1995; ZMP, 2000.

One reason for the poor recent performance of the livestock sector has been low yields of feed crops and pastures. Other reasons include a lack of specialization in the production of feed concentrate, which was also not correctly balanced in terms of nutrient content, improper feed storage and treatment, and performance-reducing housing of livestock. Another reason is that large amounts of feed are siphoned off to small-scale farms, as mentioned earlier. This also explains the low average milk yields of 1,646 kgs/cow on large-scale farms in 1998.

Productivity in the livestock sector is low when compared internationally. Although feed conversion rates are similar to those in other former states of the Soviet Union, they are falling further behind those of Hungary, Poland or the EU. Low productivity is associated with excessive feed consumption that, depending on the type of livestock, is 3 to 4 times higher than in EU countries and requires an estimated 80-100 percent more labor than in Poland or Hungary.

Table 9.9   Trends in livestock output and yields

	1990	1991	1993	1995	1996	1997	1998
Meat total							
(1,000 t sw*)	4,358	4,029	2,815	2,294	2,113	1,875	1,670
incl. Cattle and							
Calves	1,986	1,878	1,379	1,186	1,048	930	793
Swine	1,576	1,421	1,013	807	789	710	668
Poultry	708	654	362	235	218	186	200
Milk (1,000 t)	24,508	22,409	18,148	17,274	15,821	13,768	13,739
Eggs (bill.)	16.29	15.19	11.79	9.40	8.76	8.24	8.30
Wool (1,000 t)	29.8	26.6	20.5	13.9	9.3	6.7	4.6
Milk/cow (kg)	2,866	2,668	2,274	2,205	2,103	1,988	2,219
Eggs/hen	214	204	174	171	169	187	196

Note: * sw = Slaughter weight
Sources: Adapted from Ministerstvo Statystyki, 1995 and 1998; ZMP, 2000.

Agricultural zones and production characteristics

The country's agricultural area is divided into three zones in accordance with the vegetation zones described earlier (section 9.1). These zones include the following administrative units:

Forest Zone	*Forest Steppe Zone*	*Steppe Zone*
Ivano-Frankivsk	Kharkiv	Kherson
Lviv	Khmelnycky	Dnipropetrovsk
Riwno	Kiev	Donetsk
Zhytomyr	Poltava	Kirovohrad
Transcarpathia	Sumy	Luhansk
Chernihiv	Ternopil	Mykolajiv
Volhynia	Cherkassy	Odessa
	Chernivtsi	Zaporizhya
	Vinnytsya	

These relatively homogenous agricultural areas, organized into administrative regions, provided a foundation for state-control of agriculture in the former USSR. They are also an important working basis for the current agricultural administration, even though the zoning has been partially modified, based on two different versions. In the first, the province Transcarpathia is classified within the forest steppe zone. In the second version, Ivano-Frankivsk and Transcarpathia are both removed from the forest zone to create a fourth agricultural zone, known as the Carpathian zone (Krysalny, 1993).

Forest, forest steppe and steppe zones each stretch over 15, 20 and 25 million ha, respectively. Of these, 7.7 million ha (51 percent), 14.3 (72 percent) and 18.8 million ha (65 percent) are used agriculturally. The relationship of arable land to farmland is similar to that of farmland to total area across zones. Arable land takes up 59.8 percent of the area in the forest zone, 75.6 percent in the forest steppe zone and 78.1 percent in the steppe zone. According to data for the period 1982 to 1992, between 95 and 97 percent of arable land was cultivated annually. The share of uncultivated land is estimated to have risen slightly to about 6 percent in 1998.

The forest steppe and steppe zones are major grain producing areas. In the early 1990s, about 930 kgs of grains were harvested per capita; currently, only 600-700 kg are harvested per capita. Sugar beet production is concentrated in the forest steppe zone, and sunflower seed in the steppe zone, especially in the eastern region. Horticultural production mostly takes place in the steppe zone, especially Crimea and the Odessa region. Here, much of the land is irrigated. There are also several centers of horticultural production in the forest steppe zone, especially around Kiev and Kharkiv. Potato farming occurs mainly in the north of the country, in the forest zone as well as in northern parts of the forest steppe. These are also the major locations for fiber plant production (mostly flax).

Livestock production for slaughter, including poultry, is concentrated in the northern forest and forest steppe zones (Kiev, Vinnizja and Kharkiv). For the most part, this is the result of higher and more evenly distributed precipitation, which in turn increases rates of growth of livestock feed crops relative to other parts of the country. Production and marketing patterns in different regions are shown in table 9.10. These numbers exclude the production centers of Donetsk, Dnipropetrovsk and Crimea.

Table 9.10 Production and marketing of livestock products per ha by agricultural zone, 1997-1998

Type or group of production	Forest zone A	B	Forest steppe zone A	B	Steppe zone A	B
Total meat (kg sm)[a]	56	21	51	24	33	13
Hogs[b]	28	-	23	-	15	-
Milk (kg)	560	94	381	117	213	62
Eggs	249	43	223	73	169	70

Notes: [a] sm = Slaughtered mass   A = quantity produced
       [b] Estimated   B = quantity marketed

Sources: Calculated from Ministerstvo Statystyki, 1998; Kommission für die Erforschung, der Agrar- und Wirtschaftsverhältnisse des europäischen Ostens, 1997.

9.3 Changes in property and use rights

Legal foundation

Ukrainian political leaders opted for gradual transformation of the agricultural sector in the early 1990s. They feared that accelerated privatization of farms would run out of control, leading to a collapse of agricultural production and a de-capitalization of the agricultural sector. Some observers were concerned about rampant land speculation. Others pointed to weaknesses in Ukrainian agriculture in areas of technology and management, and recommended a slow reform process for this reason.

Various laws, ordinances and presidential decrees have had little if any impact on the implementation of new property and use rights, at least up to 1999. They have instead created regulatory uncertainty, because the new laws often contradict existing regulations or are themselves contradictory. There still are no laws that allow purchases, sales, inheriting or leasing of land.

President Kutchma signed a decree in December 1999 to reform public sector farms based on "principles of land ownership" (Decree of the President of the Ukraine, 2000). At present, it is impossible to judge the practical effects of this decree (Ukrainian Agrimarket Weekly Report, 2000). In addition, a so-called land law or "land law book" is being drafted that should be passed in 2001. This law not only deals with agricultural land use, but it also determines land rights for non-agricultural users. The law is expected to contain regulations for buying and selling land, and should create a basis for mortgage laws.

It appears, therefore, that land laws will be in place after 2001 that provide incentives for efficient agricultural production. Even so, it will take time for agricultural managers and producers to learn to work under the changed economic conditions and to take advantage of any market incentives that are created (Cramon-Taubade, 2000). It is important to note that private property was unknown for hundreds of years in Russia and most parts of Ukraine, the only exception being a few years before WW I, when a few farmers were given titles to private property; this was reversed in the Bolshevik Revolution.

The goal in Ukraine must be a profound modernization and improvement in the efficiency of agriculture, and not just its restoration. In order to achieve this, the marketing and processing sectors must be reorganized and given new regulatory foundations, and a viable producer credit system has to develop along with an efficient and modern input supply sector.

Types of organizations in the agricultural sector

Current agribusiness organizations in Ukraine are based on five laws issued in 1991, 1992 and 1997. The most important of these is the collective farm, which is made up of the collective property of its workers. This property was created following the de-nationalization of land (all land and mineral rights had been nationalized after the October Revolution of 1917).

These types of agricultural organizations existed in 1998:

- Collective farms consist of their members' collective property; decision-making authority rests with the full assembly or authorized assembly, with representation by proxy. Important questions, such as the locus of management control, decision authority of the board and procedures for expulsion of members remain unresolved.
- Agricultural producer cooperatives consist of their members' property; the full assembly votes using the "one member, one vote" principle. Rules exist for forming committees to resolve internal differences.

- Joint stock companies; decisions are made in the shareholders' assembly, where votes depend on the number of shares. A board of directors oversees management, while an internal committee deals with finances.
- Limited liability companies; members decide on company policy in the full assembly; votes depend on the amount of capital invested. A committee consisting of members selected by the assembly provides oversight.

By mid-1998 the following companies were registered officially, not counting the 6,676 collective farms (Kommission für die Erforschung der Agrar- und Wirtschaftsverhältnisse des europäischen Ostens, 1997):

- 903 farmers' unions
- 231 *Kolkhozes*
- 1,401 joint stock, limited liability and other corporations
- 323 leased farms
- 138 cooperatives
- 299 agricultural firms
- 377 other economic units.

In addition to these organizations, there are 3,525 state farms and some 35,000 family and subsistence farms (table 9.11).

Foreign investors generally do not consider firms that are based on collective property, including the collective farms, to be attractive investment opportunities. Yet outside capital is urgently needed to improve conditions on these farms. On these farms, duties and lines of authority are often so poorly defined that no one individual is or feels responsible for daily operations.

In many cases, members of collective farms lack the knowledge and experience to contribute in productive ways, and they are also not able to influence the performance of farm managers or to otherwise enforce their rights. According to the Institute of Postgraduate Education for Members of the Agro-Industrial Complex, 30 to 50 percent of all agricultural managers have absolutely no business expertise. Some claim that workers in agricultural companies are often "hostages of management's incompetence" (Puhachov, 1999*a*). Other organizational forms also lack clear legal foundations outlining their rights and responsibilities.

Importance of organizational forms and their development prospects

For statistical purposes Ukrainian farms are allocated either to the public or private sectors. Among the terms used to describe them are "agricultural companies" and "citizens' estates." According to the most common definition, the public sector includes:

- State farms (3,525 units in 1998);
- Collective firms in a broad sense, meaning all economic units based on the collective property of employees or shareholders (including joint stock, limited liability and other corporations).

Table 9.11 Trends in land use and livestock inventories by type of farm organization, 1990, 1994 and 1998

Organizational form	Number of farms	Average agricultural area (ha)	Share (%) Agricultural area	Inventory of Cows	Hogs
			1990		
Public sector farms	13,345	2,900	92.7	73.9	72.4
Collective farms	8,820	3,263	69.0	55.9	50.0
State farms	4,525	2,194	23.7	18.0	22.4
Private sector farms					
Subsistence farms*	9,206	0,29	6.4	26.1	27.6
Family farms	332	12.0	*na*	*na*	*na*
			1994		
Public sector farms	15,462	2,243	84.4	64.0	57.7
Collective farms	9,977	2,639	64.1	49.8	39.2
State farms	5,485	1,524	20.3	14.2	18.5
Private sector farms					
Subsistence farms*	11,057	0,48	13.0	35.8	42.0
Family farms	34,692	21,4	1.8	0.2	0.3
			1998		
Public sector farms	15,962	2,117	81.9	49.4	41.8
Collective farms	12,401	2,520	76.3	44.2	34.9
State farms	3,525	653	5.6	5.2	6.9
Private sector farms					
Subsistence farms*	11,560	0,51	14.6	50.1	56.0
Family farms	35,485	29,0	2.5	0.3	0.4

Note: *In 1,000s; *na*=not available.
    Note that data for the private sector are estimated; totals are not reported for Private sector farms because not all units are necessarily represented, and in some cases problems arise with definitions.

Sources: Adapted from Ministerstvo Statystyki, 1995 and 1998; Bouveyron, 1995; Cramon-Taubade, 1999.

The private sector includes all economic units belonging to individuals or families. It includes most family farms founded since 1991 and so-called household farms, remnants of the planned economy that are still referred to as "personal secondary farms" and whose numbers have increased slightly. Collective gardens form another special category. They cover a total area of 0.5 million ha. Approximately 6.1 million units are either sublet (collective gardens) or farmed as personal property. Approximately 53 percent of the population works these small plots for subsistence purposes. The main crops grown are potatoes, vegetables and fruit (Puhachov, 1999*b*).

The private sector accounts for more than half of gross agricultural product, and its share appears to be growing. This does not mean, however, that large-scale farms are ill-suited for Ukrainian agriculture, and that small-scale farms should necessarily receive preferential support (Bedszent, 2000). Large farms are in an excellent position to produce high quality grain, oil seed, sugar beet and other market crops, as well as livestock products. Their relatively small current share of total production volumes can be explained by the tax policy discussed earlier. On the other hand, small and mid-sized farms also have the potential to be highly competitive and their development should be supported, since certain products or product groups can be produced and marketed more efficiently by these farms. Furthermore, experience in highly developed countries shows that significant market opportunities exist for small farms near cities and population centers.

Marketing, processing and input supply

In the first years after the shift to a free market system, sales of agricultural products only changed slightly. Laws and ordinances passed from 1992-1994 to restructure the market system and to privatize purchasing and processing were executed slowly and inconsistently. This resulted in increasingly disorganized relationships between farmers, purchasers and the food industry, including the creation of a large number of competing marketing channels that could not be supported by the volume of commodities produced, and rapidly worsening profitability of these companies. This in turn led to payment defaults by several suppliers, resulting in further reductions in investments in storage, loading and processing facilities. As a result, these plants remain technically obsolete and many have been forced to shut down as a result.

Today, marketing occurs through diverse channels. In 1998 more than half of marketed oilseed and approximately one third of grains were sold through some form of barter trade; for sugar beet and potatoes, barter trade represented about a fourth of all sales. Private individuals receive a large amount of the produce, mostly as payment-in-kind. In local and sub-regional markets, primarily potatoes, fruits, vegetables, eggs and wool are being sold. Sales channels that were once controlled by processing plants now play an important role only for sugar beet and milk and dairy products, accounting for about one-third of the total amount sold of each.

The food industry's production index sank to 47 by 1995 (1990=100). By 1998, the index declined to 36. The dairy industry was especially hard hit, along with the slaughter and meat industries. There are a number of reasons for the drastic fall in production. First, processing plants are severely outdated, which has resulted in enormous losses during storage and processing of raw materials and finished products. Low quality of goods has created marketing problems domestically and especially in demanding foreign markets (Kommission für die Erforschung der Agrar- und Wirtschaftsverhältnisse des europäischen Ostens, 1997). A second factor is the general economic decline, accompanied by high inflation and a fall in purchasing power. This has increased the trend toward self-sufficiency of many households, in cities as well as in rural areas. The decline in sales has reduced profits and a number of operations have had to shut down. A third factor has been the year-to-year decline in supplies from farms, continually reducing raw materials available to the processing industry. Low purchase prices have led some private farmers to build their own small-scale plants to process agricultural products. Thus, an apparently inevitable shakeout of less efficient operations is underway.

Low and falling profitability has led to sharp declines in meat and dairy production. Even in the planned economy, profits in the meat industry were low and many farms operated at a loss for reasons discussed earlier. The problem has become more obvious since about 1993, with cuts in agricultural subsidies. Since 1991, a growing price squeeze on farmers has further reduced the profitability of livestock production (Ministerstvo Statystyki, 1998).

On the surface, privatization of the food industry has advanced significantly since reforms started: 95 percent of companies had been privatized by 1995. It should be noted, however, that the regulatory framework for privatization has not exactly enlivened this industry, nor promoted its modernization. Moreover, most privatized companies are joint stock corporations and the law provides for relatively high state (25 percent) and plant (51 percent) ownership shares, the remainder being reserved for a diverse group of shareholders (plant workers, family of management and others). Along with the lack of a stock exchange, this complicates the decision-making process and makes potential investors, especially foreigners, wary.

In addition, leadership structures that existed during the planned economy have been carried over in only slightly changed forms, and a considerable amount of continuity can be observed in personnel of companies and authorities. Partly as a result, markets for agricultural products and food tend to lack transparency, and competition among buyers is not intense, to the detriment of farmers. Alternatives for selling products are limited, and farmers are often forced to accept unfavorable prices (for example in dairy farming). Further, the total debt owed by processing companies to various agricultural operations is estimated at several million UAH (bfai, 2000c; Striewe, 2000; Zoria, 2000).

The supply of inputs to farms remains far below what is economically rational. Large shares of fertilizer, pesticides, fuel and similar products are still distributed by local authorities, which use their strong bargaining positions to secure cheap delivery of food to preferred customers. Many processing companies lack the capital needed for basic technological modernization, including steps to improve hygiene and protect the environment. These companies also need to be restructured and reorganized: there is an estimated excess of about 5,000 companies in this industry (in 1998), and many are unfavorably located. Knowledgeable observers argue that the companies need to be merged into larger, more productive economic units, which would allow them to specialize and to react with greater flexibility to changing market conditions. Flaws in the purchasing and processing sectors have also reduced Ukraine's ability to build up a competitive palette of exports.

Weakness in the Ukrainian agricultural and food sector is evident from low and declining agricultural exports. During 1996-1998, Ukraine managed to reach average export sales of only $43 US per ha, about four times less than neighboring Poland and ten times less than Hungary. An estimated 80 percent of goods are exported to Russia and other CIS countries, because there are no other buyers at prevailing prices. At the same time, imports have increased noticeably, with food industry products making up a rising share. In 1998, food products amounted to more than 52 percent of total agricultural and food imports (Ministerstvo Statystyki, 1998).

9.4 Forest fund and forestry

Forestry is relatively less important in Ukraine than in the other CEE countries. The forested area amounts to 15.6 percent (1995), which is about one-half that of other European countries. Total area of the so-called forest fund, measured in the forest inventory of 1995, was 10.78 million ha, of which 9.10 million ha were stocked wooded land. The relation of wooded land to other forestland of 87.2 : 12.8 is unfavorable. Numbers for 1988 were: forest fund of 9.94 million ha, including 8.62 million ha (86.5 percent) of wooded land (Ministerstvo Statystyki, 1998).

The distribution of forests is irregular due to the nature of the land. In the forest zone, the forested share amounts to 31 percent of total area, while it is 12 percent in the forest steppe zone. The steppe zone has few forests; here the percent of wooded area is only 3.5 percent. The most important tree species are conifers, oaks, beeches and birches; alders are abundant in the Polesye region.

Wood production reached a level of 9.7-10.6 million m³ in the 1990s. Productivity is only moderate, with a wood harvest of about 1.12 m³ per ha of forest. One reason is the relatively low age of many stands, which were severely damaged during WW II and have only gradually been renewed. In 1998, 45 percent of wood production was timber, about 11.7 percent lumber and 37 percent firewood. Along with wood, production of medicinal herbs, mushrooms, wild fruits, fish, honey, resin and other products play a role. A total of approximately 396.6 million UAH, or 1.3 percent of gross agricultural product, was earned in forestry in 1998. In 1998, almost 52 percent of forest output came from Zhitomir, Rivne, Kyjiv, Lviv, Ivano-Frankivsk and Chernihiv.

Wood processing (lumber, cellulite, paper industries) made up only 1.7 percent of national industrial production in 1998 (compared with 2.8 percent in 1985). The foreign trade balance for this industry is negative, and its share of total exports was only 1.9 percent in 1998 and 2.8 percent in 1999 (1st-3rd quarters). Imports amounted to 3.2 and 3.4 percent. Imports of cellulite goods are about two to three times higher than exports.

References

Agra Food East Europe Agra Ltd. (various editions), London.

Bartsch, H. and Bürger, K. (1988), *Naturressourcen und ihre Nutzung*, Gotha.

Bedszent, G. (2000), 'Ukraine: Hungrige Zeiten', *Zeitschrift des Europäischen Bürgerforums*, No. 74.

Bouveyron, C. (1995), *Main Indicators of Enterprises and Organizations*, TACIS, Project Report, Kiev.

Bundesstelle für Außenhandelsinformation (bfai) (2000a), *Wirtschaftstrends:Ukraine zum Jahreswechsel 1999/2000*, Köln.

Bundesstelle für Außenhandelsinformation (bfai) (2000b), *Ukrainische Konjunktur hellt sich auf*, Köln.

Bundesstelle für Außenhandelsinformation (bfai) (2000c), *Industrie der Ukraine nimmt neuen Aufschwung*, Köln.

Cramon-Taubade v., S. and Striewe, L. (1999), *Die Transformation der Landwirtschaft in der Ukraine: Ein weites Feld*, Wissenschaftsverlag Vauk, Kiel.

Cramon-Taubade v., S. (2000), personal communication.

Decree of the President of the Ukraine (2000), Translation of Presidential Decree by ISU UAPP, Kiev.

Dieter-Gillwald, I., Mechtel, M. and Wagner, H.-J. (1997), 'Die Konkurrenz von morgen?', *DLG-Mitteilungen*, 2, pp. 77-79.

FAZ GmbH (1995), *Länderanalyse:Ukraine*, Frankfurt/Main.

Food and Agricultural Organisation of the United Nations (1999), *Production Yearbook 1998*, Rome.

Koester, U. (1999), 'Bedeutung der Organisationsstruktur landwirtschaftlicher Betriebe für die Entwicklung des Agrarsektors in der Ukraine', Report prepared for the Federal Government and Deutsche Bank, Kiel.

Kommission für die Erforschung der Agrar- und Wirtschaftsverhältnisse des europäischen Ostens (1997), *Die Wettbewerbsfähigkeit der Agrarwirtschaft der Ukraine im Hinblick auf eine eventuelle Freihandelszone mit der EU ab dem Jahr 1998*, Gießen.

Krysalny, A.V. (1993), *The Ukraine and its Agricultural Complex*, Kiev.

Ministerstvo Statystyki (various years), Statystychny Shchorichnyk, Kiev.

Puhachov, M. (1999a), *Forms of economic organization in the Ukrainian agrarian sector*, Inter-Ministerial Commission for Agrarian Reform, Kiev.

Puhachov, M. (1999b), *Appraisal of the private agricultural sector*, Inter-Ministerial Commission for Agrarian Reform, Kiev.

Schubert, W. (1995), 'Bodennutzung und Betriebssysteme in der Ukraine', *Berliner Beiträge zur Agrarentwicklung*, Berlin.

Statistisches Jahrbuch über Ernährung, Landwirtschaft und Forsten (1999), Münster Hiltrup.

Striewe, L. (1998), 'Grain and Oilseed Marketing in Ukraine, Paper of the German Advisory Group on Economic Reform in Ukraine, Kiel.

Striewe, L. (2000), personal communication.

Ukrainian Agrimarket Weekly Report (2000), January 24-30, Kiev.

US Department of Commerce, World Weather Records, 1971-1980, Washington, D.C.

Wagner, H. J. (2000), personal communication.

World Bank (1994), *Ukraine. The Agriculture Sector in Transition*, Washington, D.C.

Zentrale Markt- und Preisberichtstelle GmbH (ZMP) (2000), *Agrarmärkte in Zahlen: Mittel- und Osteuropa 1999*, Bonn.

Zoria, W. (2000), personal communication.

EASTERN EUROPEAN COUNTRIES

10. Bulgaria

DIETER DRÄGER AND TANJA JAKSCH

10.0 Background to the transformation

Bulgaria has had four different governments since 1990, each with its own ideas about reform, and this has without question set back economic transformation. Although there is general agreement in the country on transformation goals, and the desirability of establishing a democracy and free markets, considerable disagreement exists about the nature and speed of reforms.

Economic decline in the late 1980s, and failure to induce rapid changes through shock therapy in the early 1990s, led to an economic collapse and reduced the supply of consumer goods to the population. The crisis continued until 1998, and intensified the political controversy over appropriate reforms. Political instability has meant that the regulatory framework required for successful transformation remains incomplete, and that privatization of state property, reforms of business and agriculture, and decentralization have been delayed. Selected recent macroeconomic trends are presented in table 10.1.

GDP declined by 40 percent between 1989 and 1994, industrial production by 45 percent and agricultural production by almost 40 percent. Retail sales sank by 64 percent and total exports by 75 percent, compared with 66 percent for agricultural exports (Bulgarisches Wirtschaftsblatt, 1999).

The current government, in office since 1995, wants to accelerate reforms, making them more efficient and at the same time socially tolerable. An anti-crisis program was developed to create a basis for stable economic growth. The government views the acceleration of privatization and the establishment of regulatory mechanisms as the main pillars of this program (bfai, 1998a; bfai 2000).

177

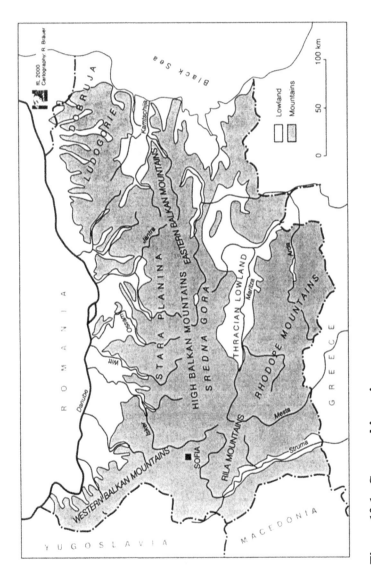

Figure 10.1   Geographic regions

Table 10.1 Trends in economic indicators

Indicator	1990	1991	1994	1995	1998	1999
GDP (real)*	-9.1	-11.7	1.4	2.5	3.5	2.4
Private sector share of GDP (in percent)	-	11.9	25.0	34.0	-	-
Industrial production*	-16.7	-22.2	8.5	4.6	-	-
Agricultural Production (Index/Average 1989-91)	-6.0*	4.5*	68.6	77.5	65.7	-

Note: *In percent over the previous year

Sources: Bulgarisches Wirtschaftsblatt, 7/1999; ZMP, 1999.

10.1 General setting

Geography and climate

Bulgaria's national territory stretches over 110,994 km². About 32 percent is lowland up to 200 m above sea level, while 36 percent is hills and highlands (200 to 500m). Elevations of 500 to 1,000 m take up 20 percent while 12 percent of the territory lies above 1,000 m (figure 10.1). Because the hills and mid- to high-elevation mountains generally have steep slopes, nearly 60 percent of the territory is vulnerable to erosion. This also applies to a large share of the area farmed. Protective measures taken to date have been inadequate and nearly 40 percent of the agricultural area has been damaged by erosion.

Bulgaria is exposed both to continental and maritime climate influences, which give it a typical transition climate. Most of the country has moderately cold winters and warm summers with an early spring warming. The average January temperature is between –1.7°C and 2.3, while the July average lies between 20°C and 25°C. Precipitation is relatively low, averaging 650 mm. In the major crop growing regions of the lowlands and hills, precipitation ranges from 45 to 500 mm (figure 10.2) and here irrigation is essential to raise yields.

About 3.6 million ha of the agricultural area (58 percent) is considered to be in need of irrigation, and by the end of the 1980s, 1.3 million ha had been developed for irrigation. Numerous reservoirs, covering 278,000 ha in 1990, have been constructed to ensure stable water supplies. Yet scientists have repeatedly argued that only a fraction of the area can be irrigated effectively. From 1990 to 1993, the amount of water used for irrigation declined from 1.9 billion m³ to 276 million m³.

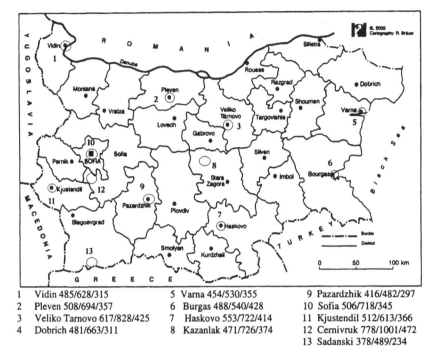

1	Vidin 485/628/315	5	Varna 454/530/355	9	Pazardzhik 416/482/297
2	Pleven 508/694/357	6	Burgas 488/540/428	10	Sofia 506/718/345
3	Veliko Tarnovo 617/828/425	7	Haskovo 553/722/414	11	Kjustendil 512/613/366
4	Dobrich 481/663/311	8	Kazanlak 471/726/374	12	Cernivruk 778/1001/472
				13	Sadanski 378/489/234

**Figure 10.2   Meteorological Stations and annual means of
precipitation, 1984-1993**
(1st number: 10-year average; 2nd number: Annual maximum
on 10-year average; 3st Annual minimum on 10-year average)

Population

Bulgaria has 9.4 million inhabitants, of which two-thirds live in urban
areas, and 33 percent in the country or rural areas (table 10.2). The average
population density is 76.2 inhabitants/km², ranging from 51.6 in the region
of Sofia to 89.9 in Plovdiv. The city of Sofia, including the immediately
surrounding administrative area, has 907 inhabitants/km². Administrative
divisions of Bulgaria are shown in table 10.3 and figure 10.3. (Eastern
Europe and the Commonwelth of Independent States, 1997).

Table 10.2 Territory and population

Republic / Regions	Territory 1,000 km²	Population in 1,000	Population (1,000)		Inhabitants per km²
			Urban	Rural	
Republic of Bulgaria	110,994	8,459.7	5,720.5	2,739.2	76.2
Regions:					
Sofia, city	1.31	1,188.6	1,137.7	50.9	906.7
Burgas	14.72	850.0	577.7	272.3	57.7
Varna	11.93	914.1	648.3	265.8	76.6
Loveč	15.15	1,009.2	653.7	355.5	66.6
Montana	10.61	626.2	359.6	266.6	59.0
Plovdiv	13.59	1,221.5	791.7	429.8	89.9
Ruse	10.84	765.7	420.3	345.4	70.6
Sofia	19.02	950.6	590.5	390.1	51.6
Haskovo	13.82	903.9	540.9	363.0	65.4

Source: Nacionalen statisticeski Institut, 1999.

Table 10.3 Bulgaria's administrative divisions

Republic / Regions	Communities	Total settlements	Cities	Villages	Single farm, small communities	Average population per village or city
Republic	278	5,336	238	4,446	652	616
Regions:						
Sofia, City	24	38	4	34	-	1,496
Burgas	21	485	26	450	9	605
Varna	30	524	23	500	1	532
Loveč	32	961	40	506	415	703
Montana	33	398	24	365	9	730
Plovdiv	34	574	34	430	110	999
Ruse	27	501	22	457	22	756
Sofia	50	918	40	841	37	464
Haskovo	27	937	25	863	49	421

Source: Nacionalen statisticeski Institut, 1999.

10.2 Agricultural policy

A primary goal of agricultural policy since 1991 has been the reinstitution of private property rights governing agricultural land ownership. About 5.3 million ha are to be returned. Additional tracts of land are destined for first time ownership and will be given primarily to landless farmers. The "Law on property and use of agricultural land" of February 22, 1991 and its amendments form the legal basis for this transfer.

Based on this law, citizens, the state, communities and private individuals may own agricultural land. A primary concern is reinstating property rights originally granted under the April 1946 "Law on land farmed by its owner." In 1946, about 99 percent of the land was owned by private individuals, each with an average of 4.8 ha. The reinstatement of property rights today is complicated somewhat by the fact that only a fraction of those entitled to the land remain active in agriculture or live in rural areas. Land is also often no longer easily transferable due to changes in its use. For example, buildings may have been erected on what was once farmland. Conducting land surveys, clarifying claims for replacement of property and compensation, and determining changes in value and conflicts with current land users all draw out the process of restitution, and thus the desired and necessary restructuring of state farms.

The law presently states that only landowners can decide how their land is to be used, which creates uncertainty for small-scale rural producers and new farms established on leased land. By 1998, 76 percent of claims to land had been declared to be legally valid. Remaining uncertainty about final confirmation of property rights - often settled in court is an obstacle to investments, including the renovation of facilities, extension of irrigation systems and the creation of competitive farm businesses.

The 1992 amendment of the land law provided for the liquidation of cooperative farms. At the end of 1994, 2,385 liquidation agents were employed to carry out this task. Only 290 of these agents were able to complete their task in the amount of time allotted, however, and more than 2,000 farms have incurred sizeable losses since 1992 while working under liquidation conditions. This is the result of a lack of credit and access toinputs, and a general climate of uncertainty. The reduction in livestock numbers through slaughter, which included much of the breeding stock, and the neglect of irrigation systems and cooperative orchards and vineyards, have led to significant declines in agricultural production (bfai 1998a; bfai 1998b).

In the spring of 1995, the new government ordered the liquidation agents to cease their activities. At the same time, accelerated return of land to owners and the use of leasing arrangments were intended to form the basis of a competitive restructuring of farms. As a result of current inheritance laws in Bulgaria, 91 percent of the agricultural land holdings consist of parcels ranging from only 0.1 to 1.0 ha in size. To counter the associated fragmentation of land into plots of unworkable size, leasing is viewed as an important means of consolidating the land. It is expected that small-scale farms, individual household farms and larger-scale single or multiple-owner farms will only be able to reach a viable scale of operation if they lease land or form cooperatives (Boevsky and Kramer, 1996).

Early results suggest that forming joint ventures under the new cooperative law is an economically feasible solution for the "new" owners of land (Bulgarische Wirtschaft, 2000). Two basic types of agricultural producer cooperatives have developed in Bulgaria. The first is cooperatives for joint farming, which draw on pre-WW II traditions of cooperative work. Members of these cooperatives have legally registered deeds, which are based on precise land measurements. The second type of cooperative consists of merged former Soviet-style cooperatives. Here members only have so-called "ideal shares" of land, which are recorded on paper and are not officially documented in a land register. These ideal shares were created to reward those long-term members of cooperatives who had not brought any land of their own into the cooperatives when they were first established under socialist rule.

Criteria used to divide profits in the latter type of cooperative are the amount of labor supplied, and the quality and quantity of the land and amount of capital brought into the cooperative. This can lead to disputes in terms of how profits are distributed. Along with members who work on the farm, this type of cooperative may include member who contributed land but do not work on the farms themselves. In addition, mixed forms of cooperatives exist, in which some workers do and others do not own parts of the land farmed (Boevsky and Kramer, 1996).

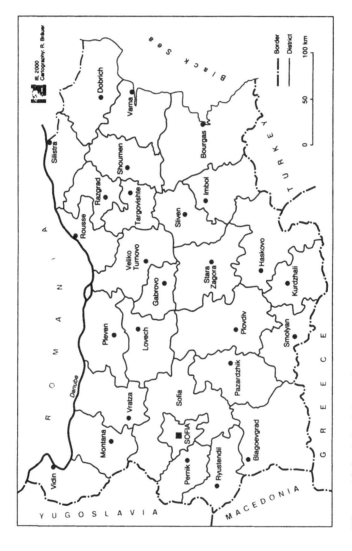

Figure 10.3 Administrative structure

10.3 Land use

Nine-tenth of Bulgaria's territory is occupied by agriculture and forestry (table 10.4).

Table 10.4 Land use patterns, 1998

Use	1,000 ha	percent
Territory	11,143	100
Agricultural area	6,203	55.8
Forestry area	3,877	34.6
Protected area (National Parks, green spaces, etc.)	383	3.5
Other areas (built-up areas, bodies of water, mining, unusable land)	680	6.1

Source: Nacionalen statisticeski Institut, 1999.

Settlements, roads, mining and bodies of water take up 6 percent. Just under four percent of the land is protected, two-thirds of this in the form of National Parks.

Future developments will show whether opportunities to adapt agricultural practices to a sustainable and efficient use of land resources are actually taken advantage of, after initial transformation problems are overcome. Important considerations include modernization of irrigation systems, protection against erosion and prevention of further soil humus reduction.

Agricultural land use

By legal definition, agricultural land includes all areas intended for agricultural production but excludes land in settled areas, even if the land is used for home gardening. Low quality, low-yielding pastures (*meri i pasishye*) take up a large share of agricultural land. They are found primarily in the mountain and foothill regions, and are often highly eroded. The boundaries between these low quality pastures and wasteland tend to be blurred. In 1994, farmland covered 75 percent of the agricultural area, or 42 percent of the territory.

While the agricultural area increased by 7 percent with the inclusion of over 650,000 ha of low-quality pastures in the 1960s and 1970s, arable land area fell by 8 percent. Area allocated to fruit crops, such as orchards and vineyards, increased significantly up to 1970, but then declined substantially. Higher-quality pastures and crop pastures play only a small role, and show little change over time.

Three aspects of structural change in agricultural land use stand out:

- The extensification of agricultural production onto more marginal lands has dominated historically, even though agricultural policy was always directed at agricultural intensification.. A clear increase in yield was only achieved for grains and oil seeds, but not for feed crops, vegetables, tobacco, fruit, grapes and grassland. The increase was mainly due to the use of improved varieties and chemicals, improvements in planting technology and irrigation. Total crop production expanded only slightly faster than the increase in agricultural area.
- In the early 1970s, Bulgaria developed a dual agricultural strategy: the stabilization and expansion of vegetables, fruit and tobacco exports, and expanded livestock feed production to increase the output of livestock products.
- In the early 1990s, significant and rapid changes in land use occurred, as a result of changing demand conditions, complications related to land and enterprise reform and deteriorating economic conditions. The large decline in livestock numbers went hand in hand with reductions in the amount of land used to raise feed crops. This reduction primarily involved high-yielding meadows, crop pastures and field feed crops; in contrast, the amount of low quality pastures remained constant in this period. Significant output declines have also occurred in orchards and vineyards. The area devoted to producing food and so-called luxury crops (such as tobacco and rose oil) rose from 46 percent in 1990 to 57 percent of the total agricultural area in 1998.

Table 10.5 Yield trends for selected crops, period averages (dt/ha)

Crop	1951-1955	1961-1965	1971-1975	1981-1985	1991-1994	1998
Wheat	14.7	18.1	33.8	38.6	31.8	30.0
Barley	16.9	20.5	30.9	36.3	32.2	26.8
Corn	14.1	25.1	39.7	47.0	32.3	31.6
Sunflowers	10.3	13.4	17.0	17.3	11.8	10.4
Crops' share of area planted (%)	65.0	62.0	63.0	60.0	67.0	70.0

Source: Nacionalen statisticeski Institut, 1990 and 1999.

The regional distribution of the agricultural area is a function of topography, precipitation, irrigation potential and population density. The regions of Varna, Ruse, Lovec and Montana in northern Bulgaria have the highest shares of agricultural area, at 51 percent to 60 percent of the territory. These regions are mainly lowlands along the Danube and elevated plains bordering the mountain foothills. The most important farming area is also located here, representing 61 percent of the country's total farmland. In the other regions, where mountains and foothills dominate, the share of agricultural area is below 40 percent of the total territory. This includes the regions of Plovdiv (with 29 percent) and Sofia (22 percent) and the Thrakish Plain, which extends through the regions of Plovdiv and Haskovo, continuing into the Burgas hills. This is the most fertile farming region of the country, and it contains about 20 percent of the arable land.

Permanent pasture covers 6 percent of the nation, with Sofia, Lovec, and Montana being the primary regional production centers. Orchards and vineyards cover an average of 5 percent of the nation's agricultural area. Of these, 40 percent are fruit and nut orchards, 54 percent vineyards, 0.9 percent strawberries and 7.1 percent unspecified multi-year crops. Apples dominate the fruits with 21 percent, followed by plums with 15 percent, cherries with 12 percent, peaches with 11 percent and apricots with 9 percent (Statistisches Bundesamt, 1991).

The following are regional concentrations of different fruits:

Apples	Plovdiv 41 percent, Sofia 15 percent of the total apple area;
Plums:	Lovec 44 percent, Plovdiv 21 percent of the total plum area;
Cherries:	Sofia 40 percent, Burgas 15 percent;
Walnuts:	Haskovo 26 percent, Ruse 25 percent, Lovec 21 percent;
Peaches:	Burgas 39 percent, Lovec 16 percent;
Apricots:	Ruse 56 percent, Lovec 16 percent.

Vineyards are found in all regions. Their area has been reduced by more than 30,000 ha, or about one-fifth of the total area, since 1990. In 1994 there were 116,000 ha of vineyards, with 113,700 ha listed as fruit bearing. Ten to 12 percent of vineyard production was in the form of table grapes. Concentrations occur in the regions of Burgas, with a 20 percent share, Plovdiv with 14 percent and Levec with 13 percent of the total (ZMP, 1993; ZMP 1995).

Arable land use

Substantial changes have occurred in Bulgarian farmland use, reflecting the policy goal of increasing and diversifying the country's food supply from domestic sources and expanding agricultural exports, especially to COMECON member states. This has led to increases in the production of livestock feed and reductions in grain farming. Although feed grain yields increased significantly, livestock output (especially swine and poultry) grew substantially faster in the 1970s and 1980s. This made it necessary to import grains and feed concentrates. Cattle, sheep and goats herds expanded only slowly.

The changing structure of farming since 1990 reflects a gradual reallocation of land in response to changing domestic demand patterns, as well as the abandoning of farms. A major change is the decline in crops produced to feed livestock, and the expansion of area planted to food. The planting of vegetables, potatoes and melons initially declined in tandem with bankruptcies of firms involved in marketing, processing and exporting these products. However, plantings have again risen since 1994.

Wheat dominates among grains, including legumes. It is the most important food grain, taking up 53 percent of the grains area. Area planted to wheat has expanded by 157,000 ha since 1990. The planting of rye and food legumes declined slightly, while that of rice fell sharply. Corn makes up about one half of the feed grain area. While area planted expanded up to 1992, the area devoted to corn, feed legumes and soybeans has since declined. Total area planted to oats, in contrast, has expanded recently.

Industrial crops are dominated by oil crops, and these are in turn dominated by sunflowers (based on 1994 data). Area planted to oil crops has expanded significantly since 1990 and they now take up the largest amount of land. This reflects the growing need for vegetables (including oils) and increasing export opportunities (in 1998, the output of 458,000 ha was exported). The planting of fiber crops decreased up to 1994, but rose by almost 50 percent to 14,000 ha in 1998.

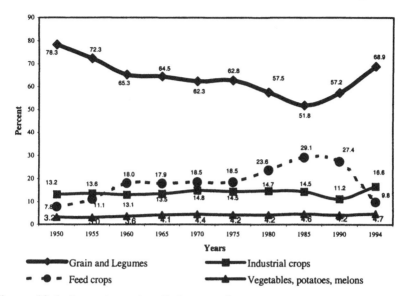

Figure 10.4 Long-term trends in cropping patterns

Sources: Nacionalen statisticeski Institut (1999), OECD-Report, 1994; ZMP,1995)

Tobacco is an important export crop, but its production has declined since 1990. Problems associated with marketing and processing, and difficulties of restructuring agricultural businesses are primary causes. The situation is similar for sugar beets. The average area planted to sugar beet in 1992/94 was only a third of that in 1989/1991. In 1998, the area planted sank further, to a third of that in 1992.

Vegetables make up one-half of the area planted to the crop group of vegetables, potatoes and melons. The most important vegetables are tomatoes, green bell peppers, onions, cucumbers and green beans. These vegetables, in processed form, are also important exports. Potato farming in 1999 returned to 1990 levels, after growing only slowly up to 1995. This crop makes up 30 percent of the area planted to the vegetables, potatoes and melons group. Melon farming also increased substantially. Overall, the area planted to vegetables has almost doubled in 1998 since the beginning of transformation. Household farms growing these products for their own use are a major source of this increase.

Table 10.6 Area allocated to industrial crops

Crop	Average 1992/1994 Area planted 1,000 ha	1998 Area planted 1,000 ha
Total	567.7	497.0[a]
Oil crops	493.0	459.0
Including sunflowers	480.0	453.0
Luxury good crops[b]	51.7	38.0
including tobacco	39.7	34.0
sugar beet	12.0	4.0
Medicinal/ethereal herbs	12.7	-
Fiber crops	10.3	-

Note: [a] Excluding medicinal and ethereal herbs and fiber crops
[b] These include crops such as tobacco and rose oil.

Source: Nacionalen statisticeski Institut, 1995; ZMP, 1999.

Table 10.7 Area allocated to vegetables, potatoes and melons

Crop	Average 1992/1994 Planted area 1,000 ha	1998 Planted area 1,000 ha
Total	151.0	185.0
Vegetables	75.0	127.0
tomatoes	19.1	28.0
green bell peppers	15.3	12.0
Potatoes	44.7	37.0
Melons	28.0	21.0
Other	3.3	-

Source: Nacionalen statisticeski Institut, 1995; ZMP, 1999.

Perennial feed crops accounted for almost two thirds of area planted in 1992/94 of this, 45 percent was alfalfa (lucerne) and 30 percent green and silo corn. Along with a pronounced decline in total area devoted to crops grown as livestock feed, the relative share of high-yield feed crops has declined noticeably. The area sowed with green and silo corn in 1998 was only a fifth of that in 1993.

Table 10.8 Area allocated to livestock feed crops

Crop	Average 1992/1994	1998
	Area planted 1,000 ha	Area planted 1,000 ha
Total	583.0	299.0
Perennial feed crops	363.0	-
Alfalfa	260.0	166.0
Green and silo corn	179.0	35.0
Single year grasses	11.3	-
Feed beets	2.9	-
Other	26.8	-

Source: Nacionalen statisticeski Institut, 1995; ZMP, 1999.

Table 10.9 Regional shares of area planted to individual crops (1997)

Crop	Northern Bulgaria	Southern Bulgaria	Southwestern Bulgaria
Wheat	63	32	5
Rye	13	62	25
Corn	85	12	3
Barley	44	52	4
Oats	56	27	17
Legumes	66	23	10
Sunflowers	69	30	1
Soybeans	97	3	0
Sugar beet	86	13	1
Tobacco	22	58	20
Vegetables	42	44	14
Potatoes	29	44	27

Source: Nacionalen statisticeski Institut, 1997; ZMP, 1998.

Northern Bulgaria, with the regions of Montana, Lovec, Ruse and Varna, and the extended lowlands south of the Danube and the mountain foothills, has 64 percent of the national area planted. Southern Bulgaria, with the regions of Burgas, Haskovo, and Plovdiv has a variable topography and only 31 percent of the area planted. The southwestern region of Sofia and the city of Sofia, a mountainous region in which farming is possible only in valleys, has more than 5 percent of the national area planted. Here, arable land only makes up 16 percent of the territory, and only one-half of the arable land was actually farmed in 1994 (ZMP, 1998; Statistisches Bundesamt, 1991).

Production of certain crops is heavily concentration within these regions. For example, 41 percent of the legumes are grown in Varna, 42 percent of the soybeans in Ruse, 100 percent of the rice and 75 percent of the peanuts in Plovdiv, 75 percent of the cotton and 41 percent of the tobacco in Haskovo, and 43 percent of the sugar beet in Lovec (figure 10.5).

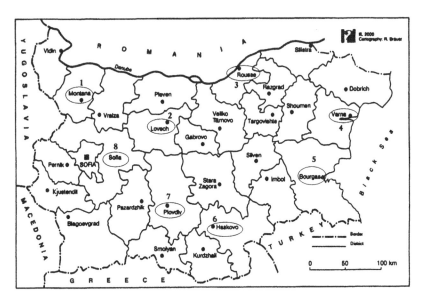

1	Montana: oats, sunflowers, melons	6	Haskovo: cotton, tobacco, walnuts
2	Lovech: corn, sugar beet, plums	7	Plovdiv: rice, rye, peanuts, potatoes,
3	Rousse: corn, soybeans, melons, apricots		apples, plums
4	Varna: legume fodder crops, wheat,	8	Sofia: oats, tobacco, potatoes, cherries
	soybeans, sunflowers		
5	Burgas: barley, sugar beet, peaches, grapes		

Figure 10.5 Concentrations of different crops

Livestock production

Since the beginning of the transformation, no agricultural sector has faced greater problems than the livestock and meat industry (table 10.10). The livestock production and processing sectors still require substantial restructuring, if they are to be internationally competitive.

Table 10.10   Overview of the livestock and meat industry

	1990	1996	1998*
Swine inventory	4,332	2,198	1,400
Breeding sows	381	234	150
Inventories of private owners	865	1,267	.
Including breeding sows	93	155	.
Hog slaughters	5,532	3,940	2,400
Meat production (1,000 t SW)	476	295	172
Meat consumption (1,000 t SW)	.	231	234
Cattle inventory	1,575	632	521
cows	617	371	321
dairy cows	606	370	320
Inventories of private owners	282	512	.
Cows	145	317	.
Meat production (1,000 t sw)	152	96	70
Meat consumption (1,000 t sw)	.	91	99
Poultry inventory	36,338	18,609	17,000
Layers	15,459	10,615	.
Ducks	600	200	.
Turkeys	605	600	.
Geese	400	300	.
Inventories of private owners	13,867	13,753	.
laying hens	8,554	7,782	.
Meat production (1,000 t sw)	182	99	95
Meat consumption (1,000 t sw)	107	33	.
Sheep inventories	8,130	3,383	2,516
Goat inventories	433	833	707
Inventories of private owners	2,978	3,976	.
Meat production (1,000 t sw)	86	71	42
Meat consumption (1,000 t sw)	.	51	54

Note: *Estimates based on FAS (faostat database, 1999, Rome).

Sources: ZMP, 1997, 1998, 1999, 2000.

With the break up of large-scale Soviet-style farms, livestock herds were divided among former employees of cooperatives and shareholders. The share of private cattle owners has since risen to 85.4 percent, compared with 59.2 percent for hogs, and 92.2 percent for sheep. Most of these owners (70 percent) have no more than 10-15 cattle or 20 swine each.

Following a poor harvest, livestock herds collapsed in the winter of 1996/97. While poultry and hogs numbers had stabilized by 1994 and 1995 relative to 1990 numbers, hog inventories subsequently fell by 30 percent through increased slaughtering, in response to rising feed prices. A good harvest in 1997 had the potential to stabilize declining stocks. The decline in stocks is now so advanced, however, that a recovery in the near future cannot be expected.

Increased imports are needed to meet domestic meat demand. This dependence may continue if the government is unable to provide credit to rebuild livestock inventories, and to improve producer confidence by assuring some degree of price stability. It is questionable, however, whether the country has the financial resources needed to support the development of viable and competitive firms by initially providing producer credits and implementing price stabilization mechanisms (Eulert, 1996; Ministry of Agriculture and Forestry, 1999).

The high cost of feed affects the quality of slaughtered animals. As a result of accelerated herd liquidations, the average slaughter weight of hogs was just 93 kg/animal in 1997 although an increase to 105 kg/animal is expected. In addition, the ratio of meat-to-fat varies considerably from animal to animal. The average slaughter weight of cattle reached 420 kg/animal in 1996, and remained essentially unchanged in 1997/98 (Spreer, 1997; OECD-Report, 1994).

Dairy industry

The dairy herd has declined drastically in Bulgaria with the political transition, falling in 1998 to one half the 1990 level, without a substantial change in productivity: 1990 yields were 3,063 kg/cow, compared with 3,148 kg/cow in 1998 (ZMP, 1998). Total milk production has declined by 30 percent, from 1,760,000 t in 1990 to 1,270,000 t in 1998. With the goal of exporting milk to the European market, the Bulgarian dairy industry is now primarily concerned with satisfying EU criteria related to quality and consumer safety (ZMP, various years).

Forestry

Forests cover about 35 percent of the territory. Of the 3.8 million ha of forests in 1993, 3.3 million ha are wooded areas. Pine tree stands in the mountain regions and eroded forest areas account for the balance. About 88 percent of the forest area is commercially used for wood production.

Deciduous forests dominate evergreen forests with 2.1 million ha (54 percent). The most important deciduous trees are oak, beech, poplar, robinia and lime. Conifers cover 1.2 million ha, with stands consisting of pine, spruce and silver fir.

References

Boevsky, J. and Kramer, W. (1996), 'Das bulgarische Genossenschaftswesen in der Transformation', *Berliner Beiträge zum Genossenschaftswesen*, 26.

Bulgarisches Wirtschaftsblatt (various years), Sofia.

Bulgarische Wirtschaft 2000, *Wirtschaftsblatt*, Sonderausgabe Expo, Sofia.

Bundesstelle für Außenhandelsinformation (bfai) (1998a), 'Wirtschaftliche Erholung dauert länger als erwartet', *bfai-Info Osteuropa*, 11, Bonn.

Bundesstelle für Außenhandelsinformation (bfai) (1998b), *Märkte der Welt 1997/98*, Köln.

Bundesstelle für Außenhandelsinformation (bfai) (2000), *Bulgarien: Wirtschaftsdaten aktuell*, Köln.

Eastern Europe and the Commonwealth of Independent States (1997), *Regional surveys of the world*, Rochester.

Eulert, E. (1996), *Bulgarien, Wirtschaftstrends zum Jahreswechsel (1995/96)*, Länderreport der Bundessstelle für Außenhandelsinformation, Bonn.

Ministry of Agriculture and Forestry (1999), Annual Report 1999, Sofia.

Nacionalen statisticeski Institut, (various years), *Statisticeski godischnik*, Sofia.

Nacionalen statisticeski institut, (various years), *Statisticeski izvestija*, Sofia.

Nacionalen statisticeski Institut (1999), *Statisticeski spravočnik*, Sofia.

Spreer, E. (1997), 'Deutsche Hilfe für Bulgariens Milchwirtschaf', *Deutsche Milchwirtschaft*, 4, Bonn.

Statistisches Bundesamt (ed.) (1991), *Länderbericht Bulgarien*, Wiesbaden.

Südosteuropa aktuell (1995), *Der Wandel des ländlichen Raums in Südosteuropa*, München.

OECD-Report (1994), *Bulgaria Livestock: Situation and Outlook*, Paris.

Zentrale Markt- und Preisberichtsstelle GmbH (ZMP) (1993), *Agrarmärkte Osteuropa*, Bonn.

Zentrale Markt- und Preisberichtsstelle GmbH (ZMP) (1995), *Agrarmärkte Osteuropa*, Bonn.

Zentrale Markt- und Preisberichtsstelle GmbH (ZMP) (1998), *Agrarmärkte Osteuropa*, Bonn.

Zentrale Markt- und Preisberichtsstelle GmbH (ZMP) (1999), *Agrarmärkte Osteuropa*, Bonn.

Zentrale Markt- und Preisberichtsstelle GmbH (ZMP) (2000), *Agrarmärkte Osteuropa*, Bonn.

Zentrale Markt- und Preisberichtsstelle GmbH (ZMP) (1998), *Vieh- und Fleischwirtschaft in Osteuropa*, Bonn.

Zentrale Markt- und Preisberichtsstelle GmbH (ZMP) (1997), *Milchwirtschaft in Osteuropa*, Bonn.

Zentrale Markt- und Preisberichtsstelle GmbH (ZMP) (various years), *Osteuropa-Agrarmärkte aktuell*.

11. Czech Republic

TANJA JAKSCH

11.0 Background to the transformation

Czechoslovakia, along with Poland, was one of the countries that consistently administered IMF shock therapy to its economy. The early adjustment period in the still-united Czechoslovakia was marked by hyperinflation as well as a decline in GNP and nominal wages. In 1993, after initial difficulties related to separation from Slovakia, a period of relative stability set in, and the Czech Republic was until 1998 considered to be a model of successful transformation.

In 1989, the government immediately introduced comprehensive economic reforms, which included elimination of price controls, liberalization of domestic and foreign trade, and privatization. Owing to fiscal restraint, the domestic currency devaluation, public deficits and growing foreign debt that were common in most transformation countries were avoided. Even the high joblessness prevailing in other countries did not appear in the Czech Republic until 1998, after hovering around only 3.2 percent in 1994. Since 1998, however, macroeconomic conditions in the Czech Republic have deteriorated. This has in turn affected the agricultural economy.

After World War II, the Czech government pursued the same path for agriculture as did other countries that came under socialist rule. Land reform led to the creation of large-scale farms, and small farms were combined into cooperatives or state farms. Cooperatives outnumbered state farms, with as many as 10,816 being created by 1960. By 1989, the number of cooperatives had fallen to 1,660 as the average amount of land operated by each cooperative increased. At this point, cooperatives farmed 61 percent of the agricultural land area, while state farms worked 26 percent (Filip and Schinke, 1994). In the process of dividing and reducing areas cultivated, the number of cooperatives rose by 5 percent in 1990, even as the number of members and employees declined by 5 percent. In 1991, the number of cooperatives grew by 20 percent. In comparison, the number of state farms rose by almost 30 percent to 257 between 1980 and 1990, while the number of employees was unchanged. In 1991, the number of state farms increased to 397.

Private farms were not mentioned in statistical publications after 1978, reflecting the imposition of policies in the early 1970s favoring the socialist sector. The main thrusts of agricultural policy at that time were to expand the adoption of technical innovations in agriculture, to perfect crop production as a basis for stable agricultural development, to increase livestock production through large-scale operations, to distribute and encourage the use of large implements, and to centralize the management and organization of farms. The agrarian-industrial-complex (AIC) stood in the foreground of all further development.

By the mid-1980s, it became clear that the goals envisioned by state planners for the agricultural sector were not attainable. This failure was due to the development and adoption of inefficient production methods, the fact that decision-making related to a complex agricultural system was heavily centralized, and to the spread of farming to regions where costs of production were prohibitive. Large-scale production technology was promoted in almost all agricultural sectors, leading to substantial increases in costs of production that were not accompanied by productivity gains. The major reason for this failure to achieve established goals was a compensation and wage system that was not linked to work performance.

In 1989, several agricultural reform attempts were made within the framework of rebuilding the economic system, following government declaration no. 187 in June 1988. This first reform, still in effect in 1990, increased the economic independence of farms, limited central edicts related to agricultural production, broke up monopolies, and established new state farms. However, unlike reforms in other sectors of the economy, reforms in agriculture met with little success.

The law of May 1990 on agricultural cooperatives returned rights over property used by cooperatives back to farmers and other citizens, who were also allowed to leave the cooperatives with their share of land. The equal legal standing of public and private property was recognized. The so-called land law regulating ownership of land and other agricultural property was passed in May 1991. However, the principal problems of Czechoslovakian agriculture were left unresolved(European Comission, 1998).

It was not clear whether cooperative farms should be transformed at all, and restitution in agriculture proved difficult. Farmers who had transferred their property to cooperative farms in the 1950s, or who were stripped of their property under questionable land reforms and legal decisions, were able to file for restitution. Original landowners could claim the land and buildings, along with any inventory (animals, machines, and supplies), but only if they intended to use the land for agricultural purposes. Land remaining unclaimed after the period of restitution is still being privatize (Department of information services, 1993; OECD, 1995; OECD, 1999).

A decisive breakthrough occurred with the transformation law of 1991. Together with the land law, this law permitted the thorough privatization of Czech collective agriculture. However, a cautious initial approach to privatization delayed the transformation by an entire year, and even today Czech agriculture continues to be dominated not by family farms but by cooperatives (figure 11.1). Since 1993, these cooperatives have operated within a new legal framework based on international standards for cooperatives. Cooperatives farm 54.5 percent of the total agricultural land, while private family farms own and operate 18 percent of the land; the remaining land continues to be under public ownership.

The Czech government's agricultural policy was tied to an extensive program of economic reform. As in other economic sectors, a system of supporting policies and institutions was intended to help the agricultural sector adjust. Various instruments already existed or were being created in 1995: state subsidies, guaranteed loans, agricultural commodity exchanges and quotas for milk and wheat (Anonymous, 1994; bfai, 1999).

Czech agriculture contributes about 10 percent of the county's total export volume. In addition to supplying the domestic market with affordable goods, a strategic goal of the Czech Republic is to increase traditional exports (hops, starch from potatoes, beef and apples for juice production) with protective measures imposed on imports.

Discussions over entry of the Czech Republic into the EU have been contentious. The Czech government has set import quotas on cheaper EU products to protect domestic producers (e.g., of apples). The EU retaliated by removing voluntary reductions on customs duties (for pork, poultry and fruit juice) and threatening further measures targeted at milk and dairy products. The EU-commission has criticized the let-up in convergence toward EU conditions on the Czech side, and it expects the Czech government to implement extensive area and production controls, to adopt the EU's subsidy system along with its veterinary and pesticide standards, and to create an integrated regional and rural developmental policy (Jaksch, et al., 1996; Ost-West Contact, various years).

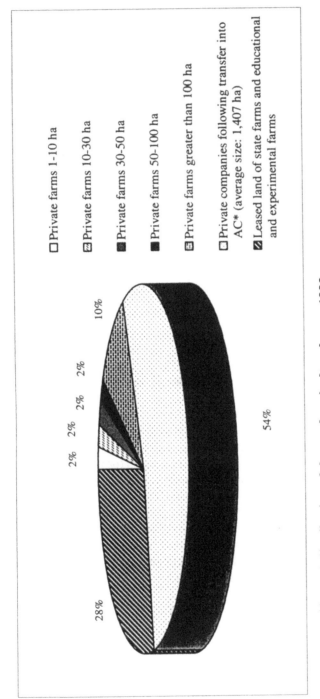

Figure 11.1 Size and distribution of the total agricultural area, 1993

Note: *Agricultural Cooperatives
Source: Ministerium für Landwirtschaft der Tschechischen Republik, 1999a; 1999b.

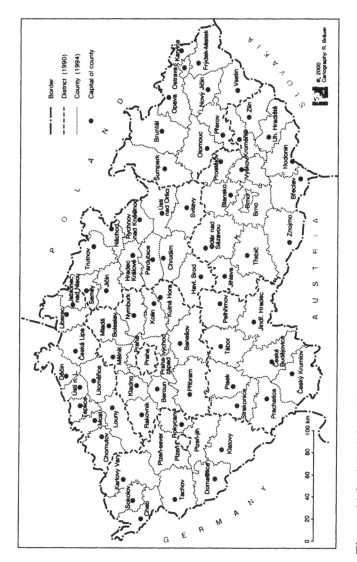

Figure 11.2 Administrative structure

11.1 General setting

Geography and climate

The Czech Republic is located in the center of Europe and has a land area of 78,846 km². It is surrounded by mid-sized mountains stretching from the Bohemian Forest in the west across the Ore Mountains, and bordered by the Ohre River Valley, the Sumava and Sudeten Mountains and the Moravian Karst to the southeast. The interior is covered with rolling hills and mountains, interrupted by *loess*-covered basins. The Czech Republic is divided into the regions of Northern, Western, Middle, Eastern, and Southern Bohemia, and Northern Moravia and Southern Moravia. The Republic lies in the transition zone between oceanic and continental climates. Maritime influences dominate in Bohemia and Moravia (Statistisches Bundesamt, 1988).

Population

In 1998, the Czech Republic had 10.3 million residents, with 1.2 million living in the capital of Prague. Ninety-four percent of the population is Czech, and 3 percent are Slovakian. The Republic has a population density of 131 inhabitants per km², which is considerably higher than Slovakia's. The rural areas of Southern and Western Bohemia have densities of only 61 and 80 inhabitants per km².

11.2 Land use in agriculture and forestry

Fifty-five percent of The Czech Republic's land area is used for agricultural purposes. One third (3.6 million ha) of the country is covered with forests. These are divided into harvestable forests and forests with special functions, such as forests in erosion and forest stream areas, recreational forests, green zones around cities and villages, state protective forest belts, and nature preserves or national parks. Northern and Western Bohemia as well as parts of Northern Moravia contain more than 45 percent forested land. Since 1980, the amount of agricultural land has declined marginally. Recent data reveal small changes in areas occupied by forests and agriculture in the past decades (Statistisches Bundesamt, 1988).

Little change has occurred since 1990 in the primary uses of land as arable land, meadows and pasture. Table 11.1 shows a slight decrease in arable land in favor of meadows.

Table 11.1   Land use in agriculture and forestry, 1989 and 1997 (in 1,000 ha)

Type of Use	1989	1997
Arable Land	3,271	3,095
Meadows and Pastures	833	953
Forest Area	2,579	2,627

Source: ZMP 1994, 1999.

In the long term, more effective production techniques and a decrease in consumption of some products are expected to result in a reduction of area cultivated (Filip and Schinke, 1994). According to government plans, land that is taken out of production will be reforested or used in water protection projects; vegetation will be planted on land that is sloping. Land will also be removed from agricultural uses under a new program for reclaiming land damaged by industrial emissions.

Agricultural land use

The largest share of agricultural land is arable land with 70 percent, followed by meadows and pasture. Arable land is primarily used to grow grains (56 percent), feed (26 percent), oil seed (8 percent) and tubers (6 percent) (figure 11.3).

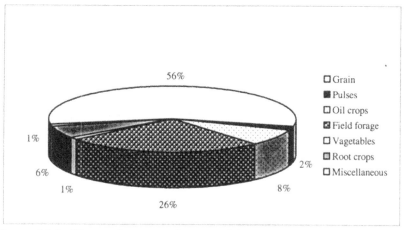

Figure 11.3   Share of crops and area cultivated, 1994
Source: Ministry of Agriculture, 1995.

Livestock production

As in the other transformation countries, livestock inventories have fallen
drastically since 1991, and in some cases have been cut in half since 1989
(tables 11.2 and 11.3).

Table 11.2   Changes in livestock inventory, 1990-1998

Livestock production	1991	1993	1995	1998
Cattle (in 1,000)	3,360	2,511	2,301	1,561
Cows	1,195	932	768	604
Swine (in 1,000)	4,569	4,052	3,805	3,817
Sows	323	295	318	298
Sheep (in 1,000)	343	196	134	94
Wool (in 1,000 t)	-	0.7	0.4	0.3*
Poultry (in 1,000)	30,756	24,974	27,875	29,010
Hens	27,160	25,522	26,489	27,845
Laying hens	14,894	12,556	12,303	12,280
Geese	.	194	158	153
Ducks	.	.	409	374
Turkeys	.	.	692	638
Laying performance per hen	245	242	261	268[a]
Egg production (in million)	3,500	3,100	3,047	3,600
Milk production per cow (kg)	3,712	3,824	4,117	4,837
Cow milk production (1,000 t)	4,124	3,350	3,031	2,716

Note: * 1996 data.
Source: ZMP, various years; Vydava Ministerstvo Zemedelstvi Ceske Republiky, various
    years.

Table 11.3   Changes in livestock production, 1991-1999

Animal production	1991	1993	1995	1998
Meat production[a]				
Total (1000 t lw)	1,270	1,420	1,090	.
Total (1000 t sw)	965	974	889	917
Cattle (1000)	3,360	2,511	2,031	.
Beef (1000 t lw)	436	373	323	310[b]
Pork (1000 t lw)	680	750	566	570[b]
Wool (1000 t)	.	0.7	0.4	0.3[b]
Slaughtered Poultry (1000 t lw)	208	156	180	178[b]
Laying performance per hen	245	242	261	268[b]
Egg production (mill.)	3,500	3,100	3,047	3,600
Milk production per cow (kg)	3,712	3,824	4,117	4,837
Cow milk production (1000 t)	4,124	3,350	3,031	2,716

Notes: [a] Excludes poultry   [b] Numbers are for 1996

Source: ZMP, various years; Vydava Ministerstvo Zemedelstvi Ceske Republiky, various
    years; Praha.

11.3 Looking ahead at possible developments in agriculture

Compared to other CEE countries, agriculture in The Czech Republic, makes up a relatively small share (6 percent) of GDP. Even so, the sector is important for exports and for supplying the population with food: in 1989 the food self-sufficiency rate was 94 percent for plant products and 104 percent for livestock. Further, adjustments in the agricultural sector to market reforms have largely been completed; this includes reducing the somewhat inefficient production of livestock, and limiting production that requires large amounts of labor and capital assets.

Grain production declined early in the transformation period, but expanded again after 1995. Now grains, along with sugar beet and potatoes, make up 60 percent of production. Most of the grain produced is wheat and barley. Corn production has also expanded during the last 10 years, and the traditional agricultural export crop, hops, continues to be grown. The production of rapeseed has doubled since 1989 as a result of the rise in rapeseed oil prices. The primary vegetables produced in the Czech Republic are red cabbage, onions, cauliflower and green bell peppers. Green beans, onions and cabbage are increasingly being exported (Agrarwirtschaft, 2000; Ministerium für Landwirtschaft der Tschechischen Republik, 1995).

The Czech Republic's jobless rate is lower than that in the other CEE states, and it is lower in rural areas than in urban areas. Two-thirds of the workforce has exited from agriculture since 1989. Agricultural efficiency is estimated to have increased by 11 percent since 1989, and production levels are equal to those of Western European countries with similar levels of asset ownership. Declines in net income and rising rural joblessness have led to an expansion of household farms. Seventy-three percent of the rural population owns or uses land for subsistence farming (Filip, 1994).

Despite expectations to the contrary, the agricultural economy of the Czech Republic has not yet stabilized. Gross agricultural production in 1997 (in 1989 prices) fell to 76.80 bn Kc, and in 1998 output in key production sectors failed to reach levels attained in the previous year. In particular, the index of revenues at market prices relative to the previous year was down for slaughtered cattle (98.3), slaughtered swine (98.5), grain (92.6) and sugar beet (86.1). In contrast, milk (112.3) and potato (123.3) revenues expanded (Lagemann, 1998).

Agricultural product prices rose by only 2.3 percent in 1998. While prices of animal products increased by 5.9 percent, prices for vegetable products fell 5.4 percent below the previous year's level, resulting in an almost identical price index in both production groups compared to 1994 (vegetable products 122.2; animal products 122.7).

The consumer price index for foodstuffs (including beverages and tobacco) rose to 105.4 remaining, as in the year before, below the general price index. In 1998, loans in the amount of 26.1 bn Kc were made to agriculture (2.9 percent of total loans) and 49.5 bn Kc (5.4 percent of total loans) to the food industry, including beverages and tobacco. This represented a slight reduction for the food industry, and a significant decline for the agricultural sector. Shortages of capital and credit, especially to replace machinery and equipment and to purchase mineral fertilizer and agricultural chemicals, will continue to pose a major constraint to developing the agricultural economy.

The credit situation has led to calls for protection of domestic producers from foreign competitors and for additional export subsidies. Czech farmers hope that the government will soon limit low-cost imports of sugar, pork, milk and other goods.

While the traditional agricultural sector struggles, the number of farmers engaged in organic farming has risen continually since 1990. Table 11.4 presents data on selected characteristics of organic farmers for 1995 (bfai, 1999; Cesky Statisticky Urad, 1999).

Table 11.4   Overview of organic farming, 1995

	Number	Area in ha	Average farm size in ha
Private Farmers	81	2,131	26.3
Cooperative Farms	23	4,809	209.1
Farming schools	3	669	223.1
Joint stock and limited liability companies	15	3,854	257.1

Source: Ministry of Agriculture, 1995.

11.4   Forestry

Czech forests are highly diversified. In addition to forests along the Dyje, Vltava and the Elbe, the Czech Republic has numerous mountain spruce forests and dwarf pine growth. The largest forest complexes are found in the foothills along the national borders, while the most sparsely forested areas are located in Moravia and Middle Bohemia. In the past, Czech forests have suffered from heavy industrial pollution, which has damaged an estimated 60 percent of the forested area.

The government in 1994 pledged to support a sustainable and balanced use of forests and passed a new forest law that takes into account newly established rights to private property. However, the profound changes in property rights have not entirely extended to the forestry sector. Almost all forest stands in The Czech Republic were state-managed until 1989, and currently about 50 percent have been privatized.

References

Anonymous (1994), 'Landwirtschaft wird von Genossen dominiert', *AGRA-EUROPE 50*, Bonn.

Anonymous (1995), Tschechien, in 'Presseschau Ostwirtschaft', 1 and 3, *Österrreichisches Ost- und Südosteuropa-Institut*, Wien.

Agrarwirtschaft (2000), *Die landwirtschaftlichen Märkte an der Jahreswende 1999/2000*, Frankfurt-Main.

Bundesstelle für Außenhandelsinformation (bfai) (1999), *Wirtschaftstrends–Tschechische Republik*, Köln.

Cesky Statisticky Urad (1999), *Okresy Ceske Republiky v Roce 1998*, Prague.

Cesky Statisticky Urad (1999), *Definitivni Udaje o Sklizni Zemedelskych Plodin v CR za Rok 1999*, Prague.

CSU (1995), *Daten zur Landwirtschaft nach Kreisen*, Prague.

Department of information services (1993), *Select Economic and Social Development Indicators of CR*, Prague.

European Commission (DG VI) (1998), *Agriculture Situation and Prospects in the Central and Eastern European Countries: Czech Republic*, May 1998, Luxembourg.

Filip, J. (1994), 'Entwicklungstendenzen der Agrarstrukturen in der Tschechischen und der Slowakischen Republik', vol. 199, *Giessener Abhandlungen zur Agrar- und Wirtschaftsforschung des Europäischen Ostens*, Berlin.

Filip, J. and Schinke, E. (1994), 'Agrarstrukturen in der Tschechischen Republik und der Slowakischen Republik vor und während der aktuellen Wirtschaftsumwandlungen, *Berichte über Landwirtschaft*, 72, Münster-Hiltrup, pp. 623-640.

Jaksch,T., Bork, H.-R., Dalchow, C., Dräger, D. (eds) (1996), *Landnutzung in Mittel- und Osteuropa*, Budapest.

Kurzinformationen von: Agra-Europe, Agra Food East Europe, Agrar Export Aktuell, Berliner Zeitung, dpa, East Europe Food and agriculture, Interfax, Prager Wirtschaftszeitung, Prager Zeitung , various issues.

Lageman, B. (1998), 'Die Osterweiterung der EU: Testfall für die „Strukturreife" der Beitrittskandidaten', *Berichte des Bundesinstituts für ostwissenschaftliche Studien*, No. 38, Köln.

Ministry of Agriculture of Czech Republic (1995), *Basic Principles of the Agricultural Policy of the Government of the Czech Republic Up to 1995 and for a Further Period*, Prague.

Ministerium für Landwirtschaft der Tschechischen Republik (1995), *Landwirtschaft der Tschechischen Republik*, Prague.

Ministerium für Landwirtschaft der Tschechischen Republik (1997), *Landwirtschaft der Tschechischen Republik*, Prague.

Ministerium für Landwirtschaft der Tschechischen Republik (1999a), *Situation in der Landwirtschaft der Tschechischen Republik 1996*, report, Prague.

Ministerium für Landwirtschaft der Tschechischen Republik (1999b), *Zum Bericht über den Zustand der Tschechischen Landwirtschaft für 1998*, Prague.

OECD (1995), 'Agricultural Policies, Markets and Trade in the Central and Eastern European Countries (CEECs): 4, Czech Republic, in Agricultural Policies, Markets and

Trade in the Central and Eastern European Countries', selected New Independent States, Mongolia and China, Monitoring and Outlook 1995, Paris, pp. 35-44.

OECD (1999), *Agricultural Policies in OECD Countries, Monitoring and Evaluation*, Paris.

Ost-West Contact, Das Wirtschaftsmagazin für Ost-West-Kooperation, various years, Münster.

Panorama of the Food Industry of the Czech Republic 1999, Prague.

Statisticky udajovy mesicnik CR (1993), Prague.

Statistisches Bundesamt (1988), *Statistik des Auslands: Länderbericht Tschechoslowakei*, Wiesbaden.

Statistisches Bundesamt (1989), 'Statistik des Auslands: Landwirtschaft', *Vierteljahresheft zur Auslandsstatistik*, 2, Stuttgart, pp. 72-106.

Vincentz, V. and Quaisser, W. (1998), *Wachstumsfaktoren in Transformationsländern*, München.

Vydava Ministerstvo Zemedelstvi Ceske Republiky: Situacni a Vyhledova Zprava, laufende Berichte (series) über einzelne Agrarprodukte, Praha.

Zentrale Markt- und Preisberichtsstelle GmbH (ZMP) (various years), *Agrarmärkte in Zahlen: Mittel- und Osteuropa*, Bonn.

Zentrale Markt- und Preisberichtsstelle GmbH (ZMP) (various years), *Osteuropa: Agrarmärkte–aktuell*, Bonn.

ZMP Zentrale Markt- und Preisberichtsstelle GmbH (ZMP) (1998), *Vieh- und Fleischwirtschaft in Osteuropa, Stand und Entwicklung in 17 ausgewählten MOE-Ländern*, Bonn.

12. Hungary

TANJA JAKSCH

12.0 Background to the transformation

Within the Soviet Union, Hungary was regarded as a model of efficient agricultural production, and it had by far the most productive agricultural sector of all socialist countries. Yields of major crops such as wheat, corn and sunflowers were close to West European levels. To a large extent, this success was the result of a *production systems* strategy, which had parallels to farming systems research of the late 1970s and early 1980s conducted in developing countries, and involved research and recommendations for agricultural production practices that were specific to local farming conditions.

Several waves of collectivization have passed over Hungarian agriculture, as they have in the other transformation countries. Socialist restructuring of agriculture began with land reform in 1945, when all large and mid-sized farms over 50 ha were parceled out to the rural population (Südosteuropa aktuell, 1995). During the 1956 revolution, many collective measures introduced during the previous decade were reversed, and nearly all farm cooperatives were dissolved. New forms of cooperative farms were not created until 1958; by 1960 all farmers were *de facto* members of these new cooperatives. Cooperative farms worked 76 percent of the total farming area, and state farms 20 percent. Only 4 percent of farmland at this time was privately held.

Between the late 1960s and late 1970s, Hungarian agriculture was liberalized to a much greater extent than was true in other socialist countries. Even so, members of cooperatives lacked incentives and were poorly motivated, because of real and perceived injustices in the system of compensation. At the same time, liberalization provided many rural residents with an opportunity to supplement their incomes through farming. In 1989, this private sector activity accounted for 36 percent of total agricultural output, 80 percent of slaughtered swine, one-fifth of corn and 23 percent of total milk production (Antal, 1995). Members and employees of cooperatives were able to produce this output "on the side", using only 4 percent of the total farmland, and receiving services and inputs in-kind as part of their compensation from the cooperatives in which they worked (ZMP, 1995).

Although large-scale farms historically had stronger roots in Hungary than family farms, as many as 320,000 smallholder applicants were given their land back in the privatization process. Ninety percent of cooperatives were transformed into new types of organizations, and out of 126 former state farms, only 25 stock companies now remain. This has led to widespread layoffs of former employees, and nearly 40 percent of Hungary's population now pursues some form of small-scale agricultural production activity to meet subsistence needs.

Just under 13 percent of the total workforce is directly employed in production agriculture. However, the emergence of small commercial farms has failed to prevent the jobless rate from rising to 80 percent in rural regions during the transformation process. In the Great Alföld, the Hungarian breadbasket, lack of employment opportunities has created an unprecedented rural exodus (Nepszabadsag, 1994; Magyar mezögazdasag, 1995).

Table 12.1 Changes in farmland management, 1989-1998

Legal form	Arable land		Farmland	
	ha	%	ha	%
May 1989				
State farms	689,839	14.6	944,716	14.6
Cooperative farms	3,849,224	81.7	4,911,183	75.7
Self-administrated	35,411	0.8	94,621	1.5
Private enterprises and other	138,204	2.9	533,381	8.2
Total	4,712,678	100.0	6,483,901	100.0
May 1998				
Companies	821,000	17.4	988,000	16.0
Cooperatives	1,259,400	26.8	1,482,700	23.9
Individual proprietorships	2,629,000	55.8	3,721,900	60.1
Total	4,709,400	100.0	6,192,600	100.0

Source: Research and Information Institute for Agricultural Economics, 1990; Central Statistical Office, 1999.

Not surprisingly, Hungary's agricultural and food industry has been exposed to tremendous changes since the initiation of political and economic transition in 1989/1990 (table 12.2). Agricultural land, which makes up more than 70 percent of total land area, has mostly been privatized. A number of enterprises that were profitable before transition have lost their ability to compete. Privately-held firms (proprietorships) are adapting and searching for economic opportunities in the continually evolving food system.

Agricultural production has declined by almost one-quarter, with livestock production falling by more than crop production. The index of gross agricultural output at one point fell to only 71 percent of that in 1989. Although agriculture as a whole is recovering, progress is slow and the sector presently produces only 6 percent of GDP. Paralleling these trends, food system employment has declined dramatically. In 1989 about 900,000 people worked in the food industry, compared with only about 300,000 now.

Table 12.2   Trends in selected economic indicators

Indicator	1989	1991	1994	1999
Agricultural share of value added (%)	13.8	10.0	12.8	6.0
Index of agricultural production (1979-1980=100)	113.6	114.7	92.0	77.0
Official jobless rate (%)	0.3	1.9	10.0	9.5

Sources: ZMP, 1995 and 2000; OECD, 1995.

To date, ambitious expectations of conquering new markets remain largely unfulfilled. In the past, Hungarian agricultural exports amounted to about $2.5 billion annually, which reflects the importance of agriculture in the national economy. More than half of these exports went to the EU, primarily Germany. After a slight decline in 1997, Hungarian agricultural and food exports reached 1.04 billion Euros, accounting for 7.2 percent of all Hungarian exports 1998 to the EU. The by far most important exports are meat and meat products, valued at 365 million Euros (bfai, 1999; bfai 2000).

To summarize, even as Hungary's economic performance improved continually during 1998, and early 1999, agricultural output declined. Agriculture and forestry now account for 6 percent of GDP and employ less than 8 percent of the workforce (Bravermann et al., 1993).

12.1   General setting

Hungary has an area of 93,000 km² and in 1994 had 10.3 million inhabitants. Population density declines from the west to the east. Hungary is divided into 19 administrative *comitats* (figure 12.1) and three major geographical regions: the Great Alföld, Transdanubia, and Northern Mountains. The Great Alföld comprises almost half of Hungary. Smaller geo graphic regions such as Sarköz and Drava Valley stretch toward Transdanubia. The Danube forms the western border of this plain, while the central mountains border it to the north. Transdanubia lies to the west of the north-to-south running Danube Valley. It consists of larger areas of plains, hills and mountains. The basin of the Little Alföld, stretching southward into Transdanubia, separates alpine foothills on Hungary's western border from the Transdanubian mountains. Finally, the Inner Carpathian volcanic crest forms the northern Hungarian border.

Hungaria's climate has a continental character that intensifies from west to east. Average annual temperature is between 8 and 11 °C, and average temperatures in the north and south differ by only 3 °C. Average precipitation is 200 to 500 mm in April to September, and western parts of the country receive more precipitation (600 to 800 mm) than eastern parts. The least amount of precipitation falls on the plains. On the far side of the Thiess River, some areas averaged less than 500 mm of rainfall in the last 50 years (Pecsi and Sarfalvi, 1962). Soil quality and climate profoundly influence farming patterns in Hungary. The relatively dry climate favors cultivation of plants with high drought tolerance.

12.2 Land use

Table 12.3 shows changes in land use over the last 14 years. The share of arable land fell during this time by 4 percent to 65.8 percent of total area, while land used for forestry expanded by more than 100,000 ha. During the last 20 years, agricultural land area has declined by more than 20,000 ha in each of the following regions: in Transdanubia in three of nine *comitats–Komárom-Esztergom, Somogy* and *Zala*–and in two of nine *comitats* in the Great Alford–*Bács-Kiskun* and *Szabolcs-Szatmár-Bereg* (Research and Information Institute for Agricultural Economics, 1996). While cooperative and state farms had 95 percent of the farming area in 1989, private owners and new cooperatives have 80 percent of the land today (figure 12.2).

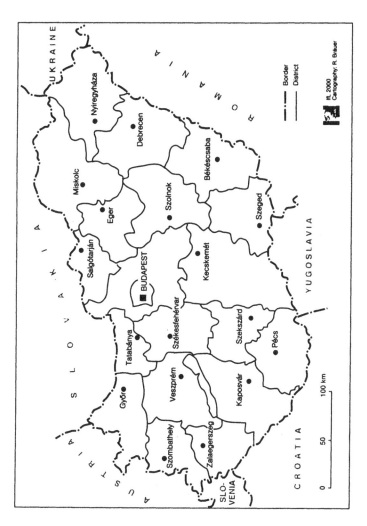

Figure 12.1 Administrative borders in Hungary

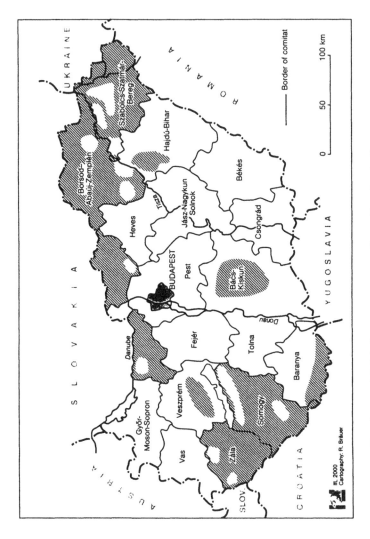

Figure 12.2 Regions with high percentages of small private farms

Table 12.3 Land use, in 1,000 ha

	Agriculture	Forests	Roads and residences
1981 to 1985 (average)	6,498	1,678	1,060
1998	6,195	1,767	1,346

Source: Research and Information, Institute for Agricultural Economics, 1999.

Agricultural land use

Agricultural land use differs greatly from region to region, reflecting natural conditions. Agriculture dominates in the seven comitats of the Great Alföld, *Bács-Kiskun, Békés, Csongrád, Hajdú-bihar, Jász-Hagykun-Szolnok, Pest* and *Szablocs-Szatmár-Bereg.* These areas comprise more than one-half of all agricultural land in Hungary. Horticulture and vineyards are important in sandy areas of the Danube and Thiess, as well as on southern slopes of western Transdanubia, in Baranya, the Little Alföld between Danube and Thiess, and in the central mountains.

Forest stands are also unevenly distributed among regions. While mountainous regions are highly forested (around 75 percent of the land), the plains have almost no trees, with only 2 percent of the area covered with forests (Pecse and Sarfalvi, 1962). Major changes in land use have occurred since 1989 only in the case of horticultural products (table 12.4). Changes in other categories of land use have been small.

Table 12.4 Changes in agricultural uses of land, 1,000 ha

Use	1989	1994	1998
Arable land	4,713	4,716	4,820
Horticulture	339	35	35
Orchards	94	94	90
Vineyards	141	132	130
Pastures	1,197	1,148	1,148

Sources: Research and Information Institute for Agricultural Economics, 1990, 1996; ZMP, 1999.

Uses of arable land

The share of arable area in the Great Alföld is 65-75 percent, while in hilly areas the share hovers around 50 percent, and in forested areas around 45 percent. Twenty-seven percent of arable land has a high organic matter content and 85.5 percent of soils have a humus horizon of more than 100 cm, as well as favorable supplies of water and nutrients (Biopotential of Hungary, 1983).

Farmland privatization has allowed members of cooperatives to withdraw all of their own land from the cooperative, which has in turn led to the creation of private farms that in some cases contain large tracts of land with good soil conditions. This is especially true in Gyor-Moson-Sopron and Vas in western Transdanubia. Other regions with farmland of exceptionally high quality include Fejér and Tolna.

Cropping patterns

Wheat and corn cover almost half of all farmland in Hungary, with the remainder largely accounted for by livestock feed and oil seeds. Table 12.5 shows absolute and relative areas allocated to different crops in 1989, 1994 and 1998. To a large extent the changes in crop production reflect declining livestock numbers.

Table 12.5 Land allocated to selected crops, 1989-1998

	1989		1994		1998	
Crop	1,000 ha	Share (%)	1,000 ha	Share (%)	1,000 ha	Share (%)
Arable land	4,710	100.0	4,714	100.0	4,820	100.0
Grains	2,817	59.8	2,895	61.4	2,566	53.2
wheat	1,242	26.4	1,060	22.5	1,174	24.3
corn	1,085	23.0	1,200	25.2	1,023	21.2
barley	283	6.0	425	9.0	369	7.7
Oil seed	509	10.8	470	10.0	492	10.2
sunflowers	356	7.6	419	8.9	452	9.4
Potatoes	44	0.9	58	1.2	53	1.1
Sugar beet	120	2.5	106	2.2	80	1.7

Sources: ZMP, 1994 and 1999; Anonymous, 2000.

Area planted to sunflowers has increased by nearly 100,000 ha since 1989. In particular, cultivation of sunflowers, which are drought tolerant and do not demand high-quality soils, has expanded into areas with sandy soils. The primary planting area lies in the southeast of the Great Alföld. During the 1980s, Hungary evolved into an important sunflower producer and processor. By the end of the decade, it was the sixth-largest producer of sunflower seed oil, and the fifth-largest producer of seeds world-wide. The increase in area planted, together with the introduction of improved technology and expansion of processing capacity, have helped Hungary become the fourth largest sunflower oil exporter in the world.

Potatoes cover only 1.1 percent of arable land in Hungary. The most important farming areas are in the acidic sandy soils of Nyirség and Somogy. Only 1.7 percent of arable land is planted with sugar beet, mostly in the Little Alföld, but also in Somogy and foothills of the Matra mountains. Feed crop production is concentrated in western Transdanubia and the northern mountains.

Yields

As mentioned earlier, Hungary's agriculture was highly productive in the Soviet era, matching yields of western European countries for wheat, corn, barley and sunflowers. Table 12.6 shows yield trends for selected crops between 1980 and 1998. Drought conditions and structural change initially reduced yields and output levels of some crops by as much as 25 percent. This trend was reversed in 1997, however, and yields of major crops, with the exception of sunflowers, have now surpassed 1989 level. Significant yield differences exist within planting regions. In the case of wheat, this difference is as high as 36 dt/ha (Fejér 60 dt/ha, Szabolcs-Szatmár-Bereg 24 dt/ha). The maximum difference in corn yields between regions is 30 dt/ha.

Table 12.6 Yield trends for selected crops in dt/ha

Crop	1980	1989	1991	1994	1998
Grain	46.3	52.4	51.9	45.9	46.4
Corn	61.1	62.2	67.1	38.5	59.5
Barley	36.6	46.9	43.6	36.7	35.4
Sunflowers	21.0	19.5	20.0	16.0	16.8
Sugar beet	388.0	439.8	371.0	319.0	419.6
Potatoes	182.0	186.0	157.0	127.0	188.5

Sources: Research and Information Institute for Agricultural Economics 1989, 1993, 1996; ZMP, 1999; Magyar Statisztikai Zoebkönyv, 2000; Central Statistical Office, 2000.

Livestock production

Dramatic reductions in livestock herds have occurred in Hungary since 1990, as is true in all of the transformation counties. Swine inventory has dropped by more than a third and that of cattle by almost one-half (table 12.7). In 1998, output of meat, milk, eggs and wool were significantly lower than in 1989 (table 12.8).

While Hungary is without question competitive in terms of crop production, significant changes are needed to achieve efficiency levels comparable to EU levels in the case of livestock production. Since 1990, milk production per cow increased slightly from 4,800 to 4,993 liters in 1998, while egg-laying performance rose from 174 to 207 eggs per hen.

Table 12.7 Trends in livestock inventories, 1,000 head

Inventory	1989	1993	1998
Cattle	1,571	999	873
Dairy cows	630	450	407
Swine	8,000	5,001	5,479
Chicken	50,011	36,512	30,557

Sources: Research and Information Institute for Agricultural Economics, 1990; ZMP, 1999; Magyar Statisztikai Zoebkönyv, 2000; Mezögazdasagi elemiszeripari statisztikai zsebkönyv, 1990.

Table 12.8 Trends in livestock production, 1989-1998

Factor	1989	1993	1998
Meat production (1,000 t slaughter weight)	2,260	875	871
Milk (1,000 t)	2,779	2,304	1,993
Eggs (million)	4,576	4,211	3,200
Wool (t)	8,764	4,100	3,000

Sources: Research and Information Institute for Agricultural Economics, 1991; ZMP, 1999; Idöszaki Tajekoztatoy. Mezögazdasagi termeles, 2000; Mezögazdasagi Statisztikai Evkönyv, 1999.

12.3 Outlook

Agriculture has traditionally been an important part of Hungary's economy. In 1990 it employed 20 percent of the national workforce and contributed 15 percent of GDP. The agricultural sector has also been affected more profoundly by economic transformation than have other sectors. Loss of markets in the Soviet Union has had a particularly strong negative impact, and compounded the problems associated with restructuring. As a result, the relative importance of crop and livestock production has also changed profoundly. The share of income from livestock production has dropped to 41 percent of 1989 levels.

Structural change is taking much longer than initially expected. To a large extent, the expected turnaround has failed to materialize because of a lack of capital and continued general economic and political uncertainty.

Further, lack of experience and the perception that market prospects are dim, have kept many of the 320,000 private landowners from establishing their own enterprises. These new owners include heirs whose ancestors had farmed the land, and many (such as teachers) have no previous farming experience. Many members of cooperatives are also not prepared to take their land out of cooperatives to strike out on their own. To date, only about 15 percent of members of cooperatives are estimated to have removed their land, although as noted earlier regional differences exist.

At the same time, those newly transformed cooperatives that have lost land generally lost their higher-quality land, which the new owners often lease to domestic or foreign companies or farmers for larger amounts of money; the average leasing price is about $50/ha annually. This means that some of the cooperatives, which used to farm an average of 4,500 ha each, are forced to operate on a few hundred hectares of mediocre or even poor soils (Entwicklung und ländlicher Raum, 2000). With their limited stocks of capital and financial reserves, these cooperatives are simply unable to compete in the bidding war over land. To date, this leasing system is not entirely regulated, and it favors landowners over existing cooperatives. Cooperatives with large livestock herds also must compete with foreign investors for land to produce the large amounts of livestock feed they require, and most lack the funds needed to achieve efficient scales of operation. Furthermore, these acquisitions compete with other investments, including upgrades of machinery and equipment.

In the period immediately following liberalization, land prices failed to reflect true opportunity costs because a market for land had not existed in the planned economy. In the early 1990s, foreign companies and foreign farmers were able to purchase land inexpensively by working through shell corporations set up in Hungary. At that time, Hungarian land could be bought at one-fifth the price of comparable land in certain EU countries. In the meantime, the number of foreign owners mostly in western Hungarian *comitats* bordering Austria and the Burgenland - has grown rapidly.

The conservative national government in power between 1990 and 1994 regulated land purchases under law 1994/LV, according to which only Hungarian nationals were allowed to buy land up to 300 ha. Foreign nationals and companies were only permitted to lease land up to 300 ha for up to 10 years. As soon as this law was implemented, however, loopholes were detected and exploited. In particular, foreigners signed leasing contracts with clauses securing their right to purchase the land as soon as the law changes. This is expected to occur as privatization continues, and the rights of ownership of the land would then be transferred to the foreigners. About one-fifth of the land in Györ-Moson-Sopron (northwest Hungary) is now controlled by foreign interests, whether overtly or covertly. The situation is similar in border *comitats* Vas and Zala (Europäische Kommission, 1997; bfai, 1993).

The estimated 1.5 million small-scale, subsistence-oriented farms are an important element of Hungarian agriculture. These farms, which are expected to become increasingly important, largely exist because such a high share of household budgets is allocated to food (50 percent of average family income). This lifestyle may become even more widespread, because 20 percent of Hungary's population lives at or below basic subsistence levels and the real cost of food remains high. In other words, many families can only survive in the current environment by growing their own food.

Other potential sources of income, along with subsistence farming, include the manufacture of labor-intensive niche products (such as decorative flowers mounted behind glass frames). Labor-intensive activities such as these create sensible part time jobs in the agricultural sector that are family-based and build on existing Hungarian traditions.

Despite the current adjustment problems, prospects for transformed cooperatives and most state farms appear to be good. According to Varga (Varga, 1997), phasing out the large-scale farms involved in mass production to meet EU requirements would weaken Hungary's competitive position. In the future, opportunities for state farms may exist in conducting R&D as well as in plant and animal breeding. Cooperatives are also expected, in addition to reducing their size, to provide other services such as input supplies and output marketing. Thus, cooperatives are now being asked to diversify again and become vertically integrated, after first being instructed to shed these functions during privatization. Since cooperatives have experience in this area, albeit under different management structures and incentives, taking on these functions should not be difficult.

Products such as grains, meat and wine are currently being subsidized to expand exports. Hungarian speciality crops will increasingly be protected and promoted in the future (for example wine in Tokaj, bell pepper production in Kalocsa and Szeged, and onion production in Makó). Hungary hopes that these so-called *Hungarica* will compete effectively with mass-produced, generic agricultural goods, especially within the EU.

With modern inputs and improved technology, Hungary is likely to once again reach former yield levels for important product groups. Notable attempts are also under way to develop agriculture in accordance with natural local conditions. The organic movement in Hungary presently includes 25 large-scale farms and several cooperatives, producing wine, hogs and other commodities on 18,000 ha of land (Europäische Kommission, 1997; Monthly Report, 2000).

References

Agra Food East Europe. Agra Europe Ltd., London, various issues.

Antal, Z.(1995), 'Die Umwandlung der Landeigentumsverhältnisse in Ungarn in den Jahren 1991-1993',*Südosteuropa aktuell*, 19, München.

Anonymous (1983), *The Biopotential of Hungary. Present and Future*, 53 pp.; Budapest.

Anonymous (1994), 'Nem scokken, hanem nö azö inflacio', *Nepszabadsag*, 105: 19, Budapest.

Anonymous (1995), 'Okok es következmenyek', *Magyar mezögazdasag*, 21: p. 7, Budapest.

Anonymous (2000), *Die ungarische Landwirtschaft und Lebensmittelindustrie in Zahlen*, Budapest.

Bravermann, A., Brooks, K. and Csaki, Cs. (1993), *The Agricultural Transition in Central and Eastern Europe and the former USSR*, 314 pp., Washington D.C. (The WorldBank).

Bundesstelle für Außenhandelsinformation (bfai) (1993), *Ungarn*, 16 pü., Köln.

Bundesstelle für Außenhandelsinformation (bfai) (1999), *Wirtschaftstrends. Ungarn zum Jahreswechsel 1999/2000*, Köln.

Bundesstelle für Außenhandelsinformation (bfai) (2000), *Ungarn. Wirtschaftsdaten aktuell*, Köln.

Central Statistical Office, 1998 (1999). Budapest.

Central Statistical Office 1999 (2000), Budapest.

Entwicklung und ländlicher Raum (2/2000), *10 Jahre Transformation*, Frankfurt/Main.

Europäische Kommission, Generaldirektion Landwirtschaft (1997), *Lage und Aussichten der Landwirtschaft in den mittel- und osteuropäischen Ländern: Ungarn*, Brüssel.

Idöszaki Tajekoztatoy. Mezögazdasagi termeles 1999 (2000), Mezögazdasag, *Központi Statisztikai Hivatal*, Budapest.

Magyar Statisztikai Zoebkönyv 1999 (2000), *Központi Statisztikai Hivatal*, Budapest.

Mezögazdasagi elemiszeripari statisztikai zsebkönyv 1989 (1990), *Központi Statisztikai Hivatal*, Budapest.

Mezögazdasagi Statisztikai Evkönyv 1989 (1999), *Központi Statisztikai Evkönyv*, Budapest.

Ministerium für Landwirtschaft (1990), *Landwirtschaft und Nahrungsmittelindustrie 1989*. Budapest (Statistische und Wirtschaftsanalytische Zentrale).

Monthly Report 6/2000. The Vienna Institute for International Economic Studies, Vienna.

OEDC (1994) (1995), *Review of Agricultural Policies: Hungary*, 222 pp., Paris.

OECD (1995), *Wirtschaftsberichte: Ungarn*, 233pp.; Paris.

Pecsi, M. and Sarfalvi, B. (1962), *Die Geographie Ungarns*, 384 p., Budapest (Corvina).

Research and Information Institute for Agricultural Economics (1989) *Agriculture and Food Industry 1990*, Budapest.

Research and Information Institute for Agricultural Economics (1990) *Agriculture and Food Industry 1991*, Budapest.

Research and Information Institute for Agricultural Economics (1991) *Agriculture and Food Industry 1991*, Budapest.

Research and Information Institute for Agricultural Economics (1993) *Agriculture and Food Industry 1992*,-115pp., Budapest.

Research and Information Institute for Agricultural Economics (1996), *Agriculture and Food Industry 1995*, Budapest.

Research and Information Institute for Agricultural Economics (1999) *Agriculture and Food Industry 1998*,-115pp., Budapest.

Südosteuropa aktuell (1995), *Der Wandel des ländlichen Raums in Südosteuropa*,- 45 pp., München.

Varga, G. (1997), 'Privatisierung und Umstrukturierung der ungarischen Landwirtschaft und ihre Folgen: Privatisierungsprozess, Rechtsformen und Betriebsstrukturen im Agrarbereich der mittel- und osteuropäischen Länder', Beiträge zum Seminar am 26./27.11.1996 in Halle/Saale, Institut für Agrarentwicklung in Mittel- und Osteuropa, Halle/Saale.

Zentrale Markt- und Preisberichtsstelle GmbH (ZMP) (1994), *Agrarmärkte Osteuropa*, Bonn.

Zentrale Markt- und Preisberichtsstelle GmbH (ZMP) (1995), *Agrarmärkte Osteuropa*, Bonn.

Zentrale Markt- und Preisberichtsstelle GmbH (ZMP) (1999): *Agrarmärkte Osteuropa*, Bonn.

Zentrale Markt- und Preisberichtsstelle GmbH (ZMP) (2000): *Agrarmärkte Osteuropa*, Bonn.

13. Poland

HERMANN MERTENS

13.0 Background to the transformation

The labor strikes of 1980 and 1981, the founding of the labor union *Solidarnosc*, and discord between citizens and political leaders set the stage for economic reforms in Poland. The last communist Government, led by Prime Minister Rakowski, in 1988-89 crafted several laws establishing preconditions for the transition to a market economy: a law that permitted private exchange, the Banking Act of 1989, which paved the way for private banks, and others (Olszynski and Vogel, 1991).

In September 1989, the first post-war government not dominated by Communists came to power under Prime Minster Mazowiecki. This government carried out a shock treatment drawn up by finance minister Balcerowicz, which not only created free markets but also initiated fundamental political changes. Major elements of the so-called Balcerowicz Plan included:

- elimination of state planning and directives
- liberalization (de-control) of almost all prices
- making it easier to form private enterprises
- privatization of state-owned and quasi-cooperative economic entities[1]
- liberalization of foreign trade
  (*Source*: Olszynski and Vogel, 1991; Vincentz, 1994).

Based on developments to date, it appears that a non-gradual transformation strategy was, in principle, appropriate for Poland. After stagnation in 1989, and rapid decline of GDP in 1990 and 1991, slight improvements in economic conditions were recorded in 1992. By 1998, GDP was 22.3 percent higher than in 1989. Between 1990 and 1998, privatization was initiated and in many cases completed for 6,129 former state-owned enterprises. In 1998, two-thirds of all output originated in the private sector.

The contribution of private firms to overall industrial output has increased visibly, due mainly to the growth sectors of communications technology, computer and office technology, rubber and plastics, and the motor vehicle industry. The share of services in GDP increased from 15.5 percent in 1990 to 25.5 percent in 1997.

Polish agriculture dominated by family farms even during the years of state-control went through substantial changes in the form of state farm restructuring, privatization of cooperative farms and discontinuation of state marketing of agricultural products. However, because of its structural backwardness, agriculture is still a weak element of the economy. Negotiations about Poland's accession to the European Union (EU) are, as a result, likely to be complicated.

13.1 General setting

Territory, population and administrative structure

Poland covers an area of 313,895 km², including the so-called inner sea waters. Land area together with internal bodies of water is 312,685 km² (GUS*a*, 1995). The resident population was 38.65 million at the beginning of 1999, for an average population density of 123.6 residents per km². Natural population growth is essentially zero (GUS*a*, 1999).

During the administrative reforms of 1975, Poland was subdivided into 49 *voievodships*, with 2,489 municipalities *(gminy)*. Subsequent administrative reforms took effect on January 1, 1999. Poland is now subdivided into 16 *voievodships* with 373 districts *(powiaty)* - 65 of which are urban - as the newly established middle level of administration. Municipalities *(gminy)* remain as the smallest units of government. According to official statistics, Poland has 1,604 rural, 318 urban and 567 mixed municipalities. The new administrative structures were established with the intent of giving regions more autonomy and of creating more efficient administration and planning (figure 13.1).

In 1975, several *voievodships* were aggregated for regional planning purposes to create macro-regions (as of 1982 there were nine such macro-regions) that, however, had no administrative power (Kapala, 1988). While these macro-regions are no longer used by government agencies, we refer to them here when it is convenient (Gawlikowska-Hueckel, 2000).

Geography and climate

Most of Poland is classified as lowland: 75 percent of the total area is less than 200 m above sea level, and only 3 percent is above 500 m. To the south, Poland has a small share of the Carpathian and Sudetic Mountain ranges (GUS*a*, 1992).

Poland lies in the transition zone between a cyclonal westerlies climate and continental climate of the upper middle latitudes (Schonwiese and Krüger, 1994). Mean air temperatures from 1981 to 1990 were between 8.9°C in western Poland (Szczecin) and 6.4°C in the extreme east (Suwalki). At higher elevations (between 200 and 500 m), mean annual temperatures are between 0.8 and 1.5°C lower, with declining means towards the east and in the foothill regions.

Despite the relatively uniform topography, climate conditions for agriculture vary widely within Poland. This is largely a function of the growing season, which ranges from 190 days in southern parts of the country and the Baltic Ridge, to more than 230 days in Dolni Slask, the Sandomierz Basin and the Poznan region (Wöhlke, 1991).

For most of the country, annual precipitation averaged 500 to 700 mm between 1951 and 1980. More than 800 mm of rainfall is received only in a narrow strip in southern Poland that is not important agriculturally (GUS*a*, 1992). Figure 13.1 shows a particularly dry area, about 30-300 km wide, alongside the Poznan-Warszawa line. Most of the 16 percent of the territory receiving less than 500 mm of precipitation annually is concentrated in that zone. Some smaller regions (e.g., upper reaches of the river Notec) receive less than 450 mm (Starkel, 1991). In addition, significant variations in the amount of precipitation occur between the Baltic Ridge and the southern hilly and mountainous regions starting at the Katowice-Kielce-Rzeszow-Lubaczow line where, based on the long-term average, prolonged dry periods are expected every second year (Wöhlke, 1991).

Economic structure

Located on the main transit routes between Eastern and Western Europe, and between Scandinavia and southeast Europe, Poland is well-positioned geographically to be integrated into international exchange of goods and services. Poland's state planners failed to utilize the country's strategic location, however, and it is not apparent that structural change in the last decade has moved the country any closer to using this advantage.

In 1997, industry contributed 25.8 percent, building and construction 7.0 percent, trade (including repair services) 18.5, agriculture

GDP (GUS*a*, 1998). In 1997, employment totaling 15.94 million was spread as follows across economic sectors:

Sector	%
Industry	23.6
Building and construction	5.9
Trade incl. repair services	12.9
Transport, storekeeping, postal services and telecommunications	5.4
Agriculture, forestry and hunting	27.4
Service sector[2]	24.7

Source: GUSa, 1998.

Polish researchers believe that reforms of the administrative system have created new prospects for regional development that more accurately reflect local conditions. The economic potential of the new administrative units and their appeal to foreign investors were reappraised in light of administrative reforms. A 1999 report by IBnGR ranked *voievodships* according to five degrees of attractiveness (A = most, E = least attractive):

Voievodship	Rank
Mazowsze, Slask	A
Pomorze Zachodnie, Pomorze, Dolny Slask, Wielkopolska	B
Malopolska, Ziemia Lubuska, Lodz	C
Warmia-Mazury, Kujawy-Pomorze	D
Podkarpacie, Podlasie, Opole, Lublin, Swietokrzyski region	E

Sources: Adapted from Gawlikowska-Hueckel, 1999b

In this ranking, the attractiveness of *voievodships* to foreign investors was based on:

- development of transport and transportation infrastructure
- degree of development of regional markets
- level of industrial development
- degree of privatization
- employment situation
- business environment (such as availability of financial services, fairs and exhibitions)
- potential for tourism, and environmental conditions.

Figure 13.1   Administrative structure and population density by
voievodships

The high ranking of the Slask *voievodship* is due mainly to the heavy concentration of industrial production in that region. This concentration, however, is also associated with heavy pollution from mining operations and industrial plants, and production here may not be sustainable.

Conclusions about the development potential of different *voievodships* can also be drawn from their share in total exports, and their exports to the EU. Rapid growth is expected to occur in Warszawa and Poznan (Kuklinski and Szul, 1990), based on the fact that in 1997 the Mazowsze and Wielkopolska *voievodships* alone accounted for 58 percent of exports of electronic products (Gawlikowska-Hueckel, 1999a). Mazowsze, Slask, Wielkopolska and Dolny Slask are the primary exporters to the EU. Ziemia

Lubuska ranks near the top in per-capita exports, owing in part to its proximity to the EU (Gawlikowska-Hueckel, 1999a).

Gawlikowska-Hueckel points out that Poland has two East-West infrastructure corridors, and that regions along these corridors have excellent development potential. The corridors run from Warszawa in Central Poland to the border crossing Frankfurt/Oder or Swiecko, and from Krakow (Tarnow) to the border crossing Zgorzelec/Görlitz in the South.

Earlier research by IbnGR (on 49 *voievodships*) suggests that regional economic disparities have not diminished since 1990. Pronounced regional differences are most obvious in eastern Poland. Using the 21st meridianroughly the eastern edge of Warszawa as the dividing line, eastern regions account for nearly 30 percent of the land area, but only 20.5 percent of the population, and as little as 12 percent of industrial output. These regions also contain 31 percent of the country's farmland and 38.4 percent of the agricultural labor force.[3]

In 1996, these regions contributed 22 percent of Poland's agricultural market production. They have only five cities (out of a national total of 42) with more than 100,000 inhabitants, and 16 (out of 50) municipalities with a population of between 50,000 and 100,000. About nine of the former *voievodships* in that area have good potential for producing organic products, however, and six or seven former *voievodships* have the types of natural amenities needed to develop a tourist industry. General structural economic weakness in these areas remains a major barrier to fulfilling this potential (Gawlikowska-Hueckel, 1999b).

Status of economic reforms and commercial indicators

Local and foreign observers both have a generally positive view of economic trends in Poland since 1993. They point to beneficial structural change in the national economy (table 13.1), increasing capital investment (in particular, from foreign companies), declining unemployment rates, infrastructure improvements, as well as optimistic expectations of managers and improved financial positions of many companies. Administrative reforms, as mentioned above, along with reforms of the health and social insurance systems are seen as steps towards achieving greater economic efficiency and flexibility.

Table 13.1 Trends in major economic variables

	1991	1992	1993	1994	1995	1996	1998
Gross domestic product (1990=100)	92.4	94.8	98.4	103.5	110.8	117.4	131.4
Industrial output (1990=100)	88.1	90.6	96.4	108.1	118.5	128.4	149.9
Agricultural output (1990=100)	98.4	85.9	91.7	83.2	92.1	92.7	98.7
Rate of inflation (consumer prices in %)	60.4	43.0	35.3	32.2	27.8	19.9	11.8
Rate of umemployment (%)	11.4	14.3	16.4	16.0	14.9	13.2	10.4
Budget deficit (% of gross domestic product)	3.8	6.4	3.3	3.6	3.3	3.4	2.4
Capital investment (1990=100)	95.8	96.2	98.4	106.4	124.6	148.5	217.7
Trade balance (in $ million US)	-618.0	-2,726.0	-4,691.0	-4,329.0	-6,155.0	-12,697.0	3,667.0

Note: * Based on annual averages.

Sources: Adapted from GUSa, 1995; 1998; Rzadowe Centrum Studiow Strategicznych, 1999.

The marked economic slowdown in 1998 and declining economic growth during the first six months of 1999 did not change this favorable image of Poland. Higher growth rates are expected in the future. Negative factors include a continued high rate of inflation, negative trade balance and labor problems in northern Poland.[4]

Serious weaknesses in the Polish economy are also apparent in the context of present negotiations surrounding the country's accession to the EU. This applies particularly to inefficiencies in primary industries due to delayed privatization (especially in mining, where privatization was started only in 1999 and will not yield positive results for some time), and manufacturing weakness, which some observers believe accounts for Poland's growing trade deficit. The structural retardation of the agrarian sector is particularly problematic, however, and adjustment to EU requirements will have far-reaching political, economic and social implications for this sector.

At the end of 1998, 2,790 companies were still state-owned, while another 6,129 formerly state-owned companies were in the process of being privatized, with the 15 National Investment Funds established in 1995 playing a crucial role in the privatization process. In 1997, about 69 percent of the employed worked in the private sector, which accounted for 67.2 percent of GDP, 64.2 percent of industrial output, and 93.6 percent of construction activity. Private companies accounted for 76 percent of imports and exports and 94.3 percent of domestic trade (GUS*h*, 1998; Rzadowe Centrum Studiow Strategicznych, 1999). By the end of September 1995, the *Agency for Agricultural Fiscal Property* (AWRSP), which was entrusted with the privatization of former state farms, had taken over all state farms.

13.2 Land use

Land use policy of the Polish state

In 1989, almost one-half of all land in Poland (71 percent of farmland and 17 percent of forestland) was privately owned (GUS*a*, 1992). In October 1991, 15 months after the adoption of the Great Privatization Act, the Polish legislature (*Sejm*) approved a special law outlining terms for privatizing state farms and other agricultural property or assets then in state hands. These rules were designed to:

- make farmland available to strengthen family farms
- restructure state farms, many of which were inefficient, into efficiently managed enterprises.

AWRSP (the Agency for Agricultural Fiscal Property) was created to carry out this Act. The agency took over land and other assets as well as liabilities of former state farms, in addition to land in the State Land Fund, which included land that had been abandoned (mostly by family farmers). Sixteen regional offices carry out the agency's work (Wietersheim and Ulatowski, 1994; AWRSP, 1994).

All liquidated state farm property had been taken over by the end of September 1995. By the end of 1998, 3.75 million ha had been transferred to the AWRSP from 1,666 former state-owned production units, along with 0.59 million ha from the State Land Fund, and 0.12 million ha of other land. Other tangible assets taken over included more than 327,000 apartments. Table 13.2 shows how the agency disposed of the land.

Land held by former state farms was disposed of as follows:

Rented out	68.6%
Sold	16.2
Publicly operated	5.5
Not farmed[a]	7.3
Transferred free of charge[b]	2.1

Notes: [a]Mostly land with low productivity or unfavorable location, most of which is better suited for non-agricultural uses.
[b]Primarily given to municipalities, state forestry enterprises and church institutions.

Source: Guzewicz, 1999.

Table 13.2 Disposition of land taken over by the AWRSP by December 1999 (in 1,000 ha)

Type of Land	
Land sold	727.9
Land transferred without payment	147.8
Land transferred to farms or companies	12.9
Still in the AWRSP land fund	3,757.3
Of which: rented out*	2,810.5
publicly operated	207.6
under temporary management	416.9

Notes: *About 2,540 thousand ha of the total is farmland, and 74,800 ha went to foreign companies.

Source: Guzewicz, 1999.

About 310,000 hectares of former state farmland were sold to family farmers, and about 550,000 ha were rented to them. As a result of these purchases and other transactions, the share of family-owned farmland increased from 72.1 percent to about 76.7 percent between 1985 and 1995 (GUSa, 1998; Ostrowski, 1999). In 1997, 92.0 percent of all farmland was being farmed by the private sector: 82.9 percent by family farms, 6.6 percent by large private farms, and 2.5 percent by cooperative farms. In comparison, 20 percent of all farmland was still being worked by public farms in 1990.

By 1998, about 5,300 large farms had emerged from the former state farms, with various forms of ownership arrangements and business organizations. Of these, 335 operations were either owned or funded by foreigners. About 5,000 large farms were primarily specialized in commercial crops (wheat, rapeseed, sugar beet and seed). At the same time, the volume of livestock production remains low and continues to decline (Guzewicz, 1999).

AWRSP's work is closely aligned with that of the *Agency for the Restructuring and Modernization of Agriculture* (ARiMR). This agency was created in December 1993 to provide subsidized loans for the modernization of agricultural production, processing operations and service agencies; and to deliver high-quality vocational training, extension and technical information. Moreover, the agency provides funds to improve agricultural infrastructure and to support small traders in rural areas.

In addition, the state's land use policy goals include (Marzecka, 1995):

• accelerating reforestation of marginal, barren and waste lands
• restricting the use of valuable farmland for non-agricultural uses
• alleviating damage to agricultural land from erosion and human activity
• making conservation and landscape protection efforts more efficient.

These goals are supported by the Act of February 3, 1995 to protect agricultural and forestland, which also facilitates changes in land use, restructuring of farms, improvement of agricultural infrastructure and creation of non-agricultural jobs in rural areas (Bekas, 1996). Against the background of Poland's accession to the EU, both AWRSP and ARiMR actively encourage larger, more efficient family farms. According to the *Institute for Agricultural and Food Economics* (IERiGZ), however, the two agencies have yet to meet these goals (IERiGZ, Raporty Rynkowe *l*, 1999).

Land use by voievodship

Table 13.3 shows changes in land use between 1980 and 1997, which are comparable to those in countries at similar levels of economic development. Farmland accounts for about 60 percent of the national territory. According to IERiGZ forecasts and the *Institute for the Development of Rural Areas and Agriculture* (IRWiR), the amount of land farmed will decline significantly over the next 35 years, while land in forests and shrubs will increase. By 2030, farmland is expected to comprise only 48 percent of the national territory, while forests and shrub lands will have increased to 40 percent (Rykowski, 1995). Reforestation will be concentrated mainly on marginal land and on sites damaged by pollution. Other sources forecast that forestland will increase to about one-third of the total.

Regional land use patterns differ considerably across Poland. In the industrial and mining *voievodship* Katowice, only about 49.5 percent of the land is used for farming, while the share of forestland is slightly below the national average. Here the share of roads, settlements and mining land in total land use is uncommonly high (10 percent). In four of Poland's nine macro-regions (Center-West, Center, Capital, and Center-East), farmland accounts for more than 60 percent of the total land. Eight former *voievodships* have more than 35 percent of their territory covered with forests (in Krosno the share is as high as 48.6 and in Zielona Gora 48.7

percent), while Plock (12.3) and Skierniewice (13.7 percent) are sparsely wooded (GUS*g*, 1998).

Table 13.3 Types of land use

	1980	1997
Total area (km²)	312,680.0	312,685.0
Farmland (%)	61.1	59.5
Forests and shrubs	28.0	29.1
Water	2.6	2.7
Traffic areas	3.1	3.1
Settlements	2.7	3.4
Waste land	1.5	1.6
Mining land	0.1	0,1
Other	0.9	0.5

Source: Calculated from GUS*a*, 1998.

Land use for agriculture and forestry

The current farmland classification and appraisal system was introduced in the mid-1930s for taxation purposes (Zwolinska, 1995). The system contains six quality classes each for arable land and grassland, beginning with class I (the best soils). Classes III, IV and VI are further broken down into IIIa, IIIb; IVa, IVb; and VI, VIz sub-classes. VIz contains very poor soils that are designated for reforestation. These classes correspond to coefficients (from 0.15 for class VI to 1.75 for class I) that are used to create aggregate quality indices for farms or larger geographic units. The average index value for Poland is 0.79 (GUS*c*, 1998).

So-called valuation figures for agrarian production areas (hereafter referred to as *agrarian values*) are used for regional planning purposes. These values are based on analyses by the *Institute of Agronomy, Fertilization Research and Soil Science* in Pulawy and take into account soil quality, agroclimatic conditions, water regime and topography of a site. With a national average of 1.0, the agrarian values range between 0.692 (former *voievodship* Nowy Sacz) to 1.29 (former *voievodship* Krakow). Figure 13.2 reveals the generally low productivity of soils compared to those of neighboring countries to the south and west. Only 0.4 percent of Polish farmland is class I, and 2.9 percent is class II; about 40 percent of soils are in classes IVa and IVb, which are mostly low-quality soils (Rojewski, 1977).

Table 13.4 Farm and forest lands by *voievodship*[a] (in 1,000 ha)

Voievodship	Farmland 1,000 ha	%[b]	Grassland 1,000 ha	%[c]	Forest land 1,000 ha	%[b]
Dolny Slask	1,167	58.6	245	21.0	564	28.3
Kukawy-Pomorze	1,158	64.4	138	11.9	401	22.3
Lublin	1,715	68.4	336	19.6	545	21.7
Ziemia Lubuska	556	39.8	138	24.9	682	48.8
Lodz	1,260	69.3	221	17.5	366	20.1
Malopolska	880	58.2	287	32.6	436	28.8
Mazowsze	2,391	67.3	562	23.5	783	22.0
Opole	582	62.0	84	14.5	251	26.7
Podkarpacie	943	52.7	301	31.9	644	35.9
Podlasie	1,202	59.7	403	33.5	591	29.3
Pomorze	913	50.0	181	19.8	655	35.8
Slask	652	50.5	162	24.8	391	31.8
Swietokrzyski	728	62.5	151	20.8	320	27.4
Warmia-Mazury	1,305	54.0	399	30.6	702	29.0
Wielkopolska	1,893	63.6	301	15.9	755	25.3
Pomorze Zachodnie	1,113	48.7	228	20.5	792	34.6

Notes: [a]Rounded; *voievodships* according to the administrative structure on January 1, 1999.
[b]Reference base = national territory.
[c]Reference base = farmland area.

Source: Calculated from GUS (Polska w nowym podziale terytorialnym), 1998.

Figure 13.2 shows that the ten *voievodships* with agrarian values above 1.1, with one exception (Elblag), are located in southern Poland. With the exception of Zamosc, these areas generally also suffer from heavy pollution.

On average, four (Krakow, Tarnow, Tarnobrzeg and Przemysl) of nine southern and southwestern *voievodships* with agrarian values above 1.1 have unfavorable agrarian structures, including a large share of small farms with less than 2.1 ha each, few large farms, and pronounced fragmentation of farmland (the latter primarily in Krakow and Tarnobrzeg). As a result, production for markets in these areas is well below the potential, and the number of farms that can be modernized is limited.

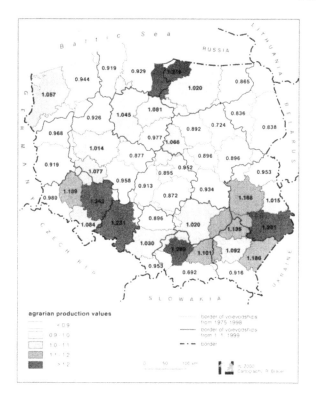

Figure 13.2 Agrarian values by *voievodships*

Agricultural land use

Poland's agricultural land included a large share (76.5 percent) of arable land in 1998, 22 percent grassland, and 1.4 percent permanent crops, which are mostly orchards. During the last 25 years, arable land has declined by almost 1 percent, while grassland and permanent crops have increased accordingly (GUS*a*, 1980; 1999).

Table 13.6 shows the increasing share of grains in total area cropped, from about 54 percent in the late 1970s to an average of 70 percent in 1996-1998. The large share of rye fields (which averaged more than 40 percent during 1971-95) has declined to about 25 percent of grain fields, while oats still account for about 6.5 percent. Wheat production is increasing, averaging 29.3 percent of grain area during 1996-1998, and mixed grains and triticale are more widely grown (16.6 percent and 7.2 percent of grain fields, respectively, in 1998).

Table 13.5 Share of major crops in total crop area by macro-region

Macro-Region	1979-1980				1997-1998					
	Grains total	Potato	Sugar beet	Rape & beet	Grains Total	Wheat	Rye	Potato	Sugar beet	Rape & beet
North										
A	50.9	11.9	2.3	3.5	73.3	26.6	18.4	6.7	2.5	7.6
B	10.0	7.7	7.9	21.6	10.9	13.4	10.5	5.8	8.1	25.3
North-East										
A	56.4	15.5	1.1	1.4	73.8	15.2	17.3	9.5	1.1	2.5
B	11.2	10.1	3.6	8.8	10.8	7.5	9.7	9.4	3.4	8.2
South-West										
A	50.6	10.5	4.5	4.7	71.6	32.9	13.4	6.2	4.1	7.8
B	8.7	6.0	13.4	25.3	9.3	14.5	6.7	5.4	11.4	22.7
Center-West										
A	53.1	14.1	5.1	1.9	72.6	17.8	19.6	6.7	5.3	3.2
B	18.8	16.4	30.8	20.8	22.0	18.3	22.8	13.7	34.3	22.1
Central Region										
A	55.4	20.7	2.8	0.5	68.4	10.6	29.0	16.1	2.4	0.6
B	9.2	11.3	8.0	2.6	8.8	5.6	14.3	14.0	6.6	1.6
Capital Region										
A	57.7	23.1	1.5	0.2	70.3	8.7	31.5	15.3	1.5	0.4
B	12.2	16.0	5.3	1.4	11.1	4.6	19.0	16.3	5.0	1.4

Table 13.5 continued

Macro-Region	1979-1980				1997-1998					
	Grains total	Potato	Sugar beet	Rape & beet	Grains Total	Wheat	Rye	Potato	Sugar beet	Rape & beet
Center-East										
A	59.5	18.6	6.0	0.4	72.1	26.4	12.4	10.2	5.6	1.3
B	9.6	9.8	16.6	2.2	9.6	11.9	6.3	9.2	15.9	3.7
South										
A	50.6	17.2	3.2	3.3	66.4	27.2	10.5	9.8	3.5	5.2
B	7.2	8.0	7.7	14.4	7.2	9.9	4.3	7.1	8.0	12.5
South-East										
A	53.3	18.1	1.8	0.4	60.5	24.6	9.8	16.6	2.0	0.6
B	13.2	14.7	7.7	3.2	10.3	14.2	6.4	19.1	7.3	2.4

Notes: A = Percent of total crop area in the macro-region concerned.
B = Percent of national crop area.

Sources: Adapted from GUS*a*, 1980; 1981; 1998; GUS*i*, 1997; GUS*k*, 1998.

Table 13.6   Changes in crop area and shares, 1977-1980 and 1996-1997

Crops	1977-80		1997-99	
	1,000 ha	%	1,000 ha	%
Cropping area total	14,606	100.0	12,555	100.0
Grain	7,897	54.1	8,726	69.5
Rye*	3,012	38.2	2,277	26.1
Potatoes	2,395	16.4	1,290	10.2
Sugar beet	493	3.4	397	3.2
Rapeseed and beet	309	2.1	443	3.5
Field forage	2,647	18.1	933	7.4
Field vegetables	264	1.8	245	1.9
Other	601	4.1	519	4.2

Note: *Percent relative to the grain area.

Sources: Adapted from GUS (1978-1981 annually); GUS*a*, 1992; 1998; 1999.

Compared to the 1970s, less land is now devoted to sugar beets and forage crops. Potato areas have declined to 10.5 percent of the total land, a trend that is likely to continue as more mixed feeds are used for animal production and private households reduce their consumption. Demand for potatoes is forecast to decline in the medium term to between 15 and 20 million tonnes annually, while domestic consumption averaged 29 million tonnes annually between 1991/92 and 1993/94. Area cultivated to rapeseed has varied since the late 1980s (ranging between 0.35 and 0.57 million ha), with an equilibrium expected at about 0.45 million ha.

Table 13.5 shows regional differences in the changing relative importance of different crops. The increasing share of area used for grain, sugar beets and rape production in the Center-West region is noteworthy. Domestic consumption of fruits and vegetables is relatively high, and both fresh and processed products are also exported. Table 13.7 shows the main fruit and vegetable producing *voievodships*.

**Table 13.7 Field vegetable and fruit production by *voievodship*,
1997-1998 averages as a percent of national totals**

	Vegetables		Fruit
Voievodship	crop area	output	output*
Warszawa	7.0	9.8	4.0
Katowice	3.2	4.2	
Kielce	5.0	5.9	8.6
Krakow	5.0	4.6	4.0
Lublin	4.0	3.1	8.6
Nowy Sacz			3.2
Plock	4.1	3.1	
Poznan	4.1	4.3	
Radom	3.6	3.6	
Tarnobrzeg	3.2	3.4	8.7

Note: *Figures only for 1997.

Sources: Adapted from GUS*f*, 1997; 1998.

Economic and ecological agricultural land use problems

Most agricultural land in Poland is fragmented among many small farms. In 1989, 56.2 percent of the 2.7 million family farms[5] had three or more plots. This is one of the most important problems facing the country in terms of efficient land use. According to one survey, the total number of plots in Poland lies between 10.4 and 11.9 million (GUS*c*, 1990), although more recent data suggest a much higher number: 24 million plots, or 12 plots per family farm (Szot, 1995). Small farm sizes and the splintering of farmland are also serious obstacles to efficient use of farm machinery, services and technical extension,[6] as well as to efficient product marketing.

Moreover, Polish family farms tend to be highly diversified, as is evident from (among other factors) relatively low marketed surpluses: 57.2 percent of output was sold in 1991 and only 56.8 percent in 1998. This also suggests a strong subsistence orientation[7] (GUS*a*, 1992; 1999). According to the 1996 General Agricultural Census, only about 46 percent of the more than 2 million family farms produced for market, and about 44 percent produced only or largely for own-consumption (with market production of less than US$ 930 per farm). Data were not available for more than 10 percent of family farms. According to the same survey, only 8 percent of family farms specialize in producing a single crop (i.e., at least 60 percent of their revenue is derived from a single product or product group), a finding consistent with that of other reports (Skawinska, 1993; Berkowska et al., 1995). Small farm size and the fragmentation of farmland in Poland also make irrigation and drainage prohibitively expensive. In addition to maintenance work needed on about 100,000 ha each year, about 29 percent of all land requiring irrigation still needs to be equipped with such systems (GUSc, 1998).

At the same time, the future role of large farms in Poland is also somewhat uncertain. There are some indications such as sales patterns of farm machinery dealers, growing interest of foreign investors in larger scale production units, integrative activities of some processing and export companies that many farms will adopt modern management principles and become profitable. This will most likely occur in the *voievodships* Bydgoszcz, Legnica, Lezno, Opole, Pila, Poznan, Szczecin, Torun and Wroclaw in western Poland, and Bialystok and, possibly, Zamosc in the east (the latter oriented towards exporting to Baltic and several CIS states). Many large farms, especially public enterprises and sole proprietorships, continue to face serious financial difficulties (Guzewicz, 1999). Another concern for long-term soil quality is the often singular focus of large farms on commercial crops (mainly grains and rape).

Ecological problem As mentioned above, heavy pollution occurred in many parts of the regions with good soils in the early 1990s. Since then substantial improvements were made in some of these regions. Table 13.8 summarizes major environmental data for ten *voievodships* with agrarian values above 1.1.

Table 13.8 **Selected environmental data on *voievodships* with agrarian values above 1.1 (1997)**

Voievodship	Agrarian value	Wastewater (1,000 m³/km²)	SO₂ output (t/km²)	Industrial waste (t/km²)
Elblag	1.219	0.47	0.28	0.35
Krakow	1.290	4.65	2.86	2.21
Legnica	1.189	0.43	0.88	15.61
Lublin	1.168	0.59	0.75	0.94
Opole	1.231	0.33	0.60	0.31
Przemysl	1.186	0.20	0.06	0.11
Tarnobrzeg	1.135	6.82	0.30	0.43
Tarnow	1.101	0.02	0.37	0.17
Wroclaw	1.243	0.48	0.57	0.21
Zamosc	1.281	0.05	0.06	0.06

Source: Calculated from GUSa, 1998.

The relatively poor environmental conditions in some *voievodships* specializing in fruit and vegetable production are noteworthy. Of the *voievodships* shown in table 13.6, only Novy Sacz and, to some extent, Kielce are largely pollutant-free, while Katowice, Lodz and Warszawa are heavily polluted: here SO_2 pollution levels are 8.6, 4.4 and 3 times the national average, respectively.

In 1983, a government resolution declared 29 areas to be ecologically at-risk. Until the early 1990s, large amounts of ecological data were collected and published for these areas. More current data are not available, but information from some former *voievodships* which are almost identical to the previously defined at-risk areas suggests that pollution from industrial wastewaters, dusts, gases and solid waste products remains high. Only Gdansk and Legnica-Glogow lie partly below the Polish average, following a substantial reduction in environmental pollution. Nineteen of the 29 at-risk areas are in southern Poland, where soils are excellent and agricultural potential is high.

Other factors affecting farmland and forestland include:

- degradation caused by human activity
- erosion
- changing land use patterns
- radioactivity and
- water regime.

Soil degradation occurs mainly in several *voievodships* in southern Poland and in Konin and Pila. Two of the affected *voievodships* (Opole and Tarnobrzeg) have agrarian values above 1.1 (figure 13.3), but degraded sites account for less than two percent of farmland in these regions. On average over the last decade, these degradation processes have mostly affected less valuable soils. During 1995-1998, steps toward re-cultivation and reestablishment of farming were taken on 2,778 and 1,802 hectares, respectively (GUS*c*, 1998; GUS*a*,1999).

Nationwide, the risk of erosion is not high. Some 19.8 percent of the territory faces medium or strong risks of wind erosion. The *voievodships* Ciechanow, Konin, Plock, Sieradz and Skierniewice in central Poland with their limited forest stands are especially affected, with up to 40 percent of the land being at risk.

Medium to high risk of water erosion exists on 28 percent of the land. Sheet erosion primarily threatens southern *voievodships,* especially in their foothills and mountains, and southeastern districts of Przemysl, Rzeszow and Zamosc. Przemysl and Zamoc rank among the most fertile regions, and here risk of gully erosion is high to very high for 10 percent of the land. In the highly fertile *voievodships* Tarnobrzeg and Tarnow, between 11 and 21 percent of the land is exposed to gully erosion (GUS*e*, 1995; 1998).

According to Ministry of Agriculture estimates, irrigation and drainage systems in 1994 existed on 6.68 million hectares of farmland, including 4.73 million ha of arable land and 1.95 million ha of grassland. Most of that land (65.5 percent) was drained. Altogether about 70.7 percent of the land needing irrigation or drainage has been ameliorated; this proportion has increased by about 5.5 percentage points over the last ten years (GUS*a*, 1998).

Data on land use changes show that the amount of farmland declined only slightly over the last 38 years: between 1960 and 1998, 51,680 ha or 0.27 percent of land farmed in 1980 was put to other uses (GUS*e*, 1995; 1998*e*). In the future, farmland area will decline more rapidly as a result of reforestation programs and anticipated adjustments to EU conditions and regulations. Radioactive soil pollution is not excessive relative to EU conditions, suggesting that the Chernobyl disaster had little if any impact on Poland. Further, regional variations in soil pollution within the country are small (GUS*a*, 1996).

13.3 Environment, agricultural production and rural areas

With political and economic transformation, Polish citizens have become more aware of the environment. Restructuring of industrial production, introduction of low-input technologies and steps toward improved wastewater disposal have contributed to significant reductions in pollution from large industrial and municipal entities. However, agricultural and other rural emission sources, most of which are small and dispersed, remain inadequately covered by both prevention and remediation efforts. Surface water and groundwater resources are contaminated from unlined manure pits, manure dumps, liquid manure and slurry pits, and refuse disposal sites. Additional pollution occurs from improper heating systems and small manufacturing businesses that are promoted by local authorities with the goal of reducing unemployment in rural areas; in particular, pollution associated with these efforts contributes to acidification of farmland.

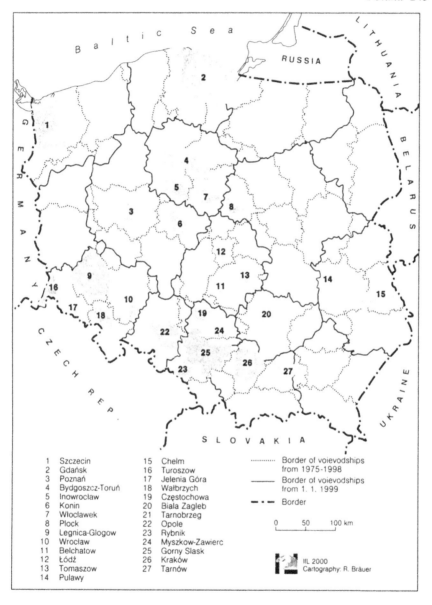

1	Szczecin	15	Chelm
2	Gdańsk	16	Turoszow
3	Poznań	17	Jelenia Góra
4	Bydgoszcz-Toruń	18	Wałbrzych
5	Inowrocław	19	Częstochowa
6	Konin	20	Biala Zagleb
7	Włocławek	21	Tarnobrzeg
8	Płock	22	Opole
9	Legnica-Głogow	23	Rybnik
10	Wrocław	24	Myszkow-Zawierc
11	Belchatow	25	Gorny Slask
12	Łódź	26	Kraków
13	Tomaszow	27	Tarnów
14	Pulawy		

············· Border of voievodships
from 1975-1998

———— Border of voievodships
from 1. 1. 1999

–·–· Border

0   50   100 km

IfL 2000
Cartography: R. Bräuer

Figure 13.3   Ecologically At-Risk Areas

Controlled refuse disposal sites are available for only one-third of all farms, and sewage treatment in rural areas is in its infancy. So far, only 5.8 percent of rural households have been connected to sewage treatment plants. Some households have properly installed sewage storage facilities, but the content of these facilities is sometimes illegally discharged onto nearby grounds, because sewage trucks are in short supply and user fees for disposal are high. Most rural households discharge their sewage directly and it eventually seeps into the groundwater. Centralized water supplies have been expanded considerably in recent years, and in 1999 about 75 percent of rural households were connected to such systems, leading to a sharp increase in water consumption. As a result, proper wastewater disposal has become an urgent concern. The World Bank estimates that only about 10 percent of Poland's 2 million farms have storage facilities for farmyard or liquid manure.

Surface waters and groundwater resources are therefore often polluted by harmful substances leaching into the ground, or by microorganisms. Organic manures are often applied in excessive amounts, which also contributes to heavy groundwater pollution (Kalbarczyk, 1999; Papuga, 2000). These conditions are not only hazardous to rural residents, but also limit the agricultural sector's prospects for producing and marketing organic foods, and for developing rural tourism.

Inputs and yields

During the period of state-control, input use in Poland differed significantly from that in other COMECON countries. This was particularly true for mineral fertilizer. During the early 1980s, use of NPK in the COMECON countries was 75 kg/ha higher than in Poland. Between 1986 and 1989, when Poland recorded its historic peak of 187 kg NPK/ha, application rates were 55 kg/ha higher in Czechoslovakia and 90 kg/ha higher in East Germany. Not surprisingly, yields in Poland were on balance lower by 33 percent for grains than those in neighboring countries (table 13.9).

Table 13.9   Yields of selected field crops 1981-1985, 100 kg/ha

	Grain	Sugar beet	Potatoes
East Germany	43.6	302	241
Czechoslovakia	45.5	352	188
Poland	30.1	337	189

Source: Statistitscheskij eshegodnik strantschlenow SEW, 1986.

In the process of transformation, input use in agriculture changed significantly. First, during 1991-1995, average annual use of mineral fertilizer declined to 42 percent of 1981-1985 levels (178 kg/ha). Although application rates later increased, the annual average of 88 kg/ha during 1996-1998 was less than one-half that of the early 1980s.

Second, the significant differences in mineral fertilizer application rates that existed under state-control between socialized (large) farms and family farms have declined considerably. In 1981-1985, state farms used almost 87 percent more fertilizer than family farms. Between 1996 and 1998 large farms most of which emerged from state farms used about 55 percent more mineral fertilizers than family farms. Third, differences in fertilizer input among family farms are now greater than in the 1970s and 1980s. The difference between *voievodships* with the highest consumption levels and those with the lowest was 2.5:1 during the first half of the 1980s, and between 5.5:1 and 3.6:1 in 1996-1998.

Compared with 1980-1985, use of other yield-increasing inputs has declined as well: by about 50 percent for pesticides, 40 percent for certified seed grain and 80-85 percent for seed potatoes. Here again, regional differences are considerable. In general, farms in northern, western and southwestern parts of the country in some cases use 5 to 10 times more certified seed than farms in the East and, especially, the southeast (IERiGZ, Raporty Rynkowe *h*, 2000).

However, average yields in 1996-1998 were no lower than those in 1981-1985. Indeed, yields of all major field crops, including vegetables, increased by between 6 and 40 percent (except for rapeseed, which suffered from severe winter killing in two consecutive years). This suggests that, with transition to free markets, farmers are making more efficient use of yield-increasing inputs than was true in the state-controlled system.

Even so, overall yield levels are lower than in EU countries. Table 13.10 shows total output and yields of major field crops between 1996 and 1998. Poland presently attains only 45-55 percent of grain, potato and rape yields, and 75 percent of sugar beet yields of EU countries with similar climatic conditions (Statistisches Jahrbuch, 1998).

Significant differences also exist in the degree of mechanization of farm labor. Shortages of machinery and equipment account for generally low levels of mechanization (table 13.11).

One-half of all family farms have one or more tractors, but about 810,000 farms using one-fifth of the land farmed by families have neither tractors nor draft animals. The stock of farm machinery and equipment remained unchanged in 1997 and 1998, and sales declined markedly in these years. Milk coolers are an exception: the number of units owned in 1998 exceeded those owned in 1996 by 130 percent.

Table 13.10   Total output and yields of field crops, 1996-1998

Crop	1996		1997		1998	
	Output 1,000 t	Yield 100kg/ha	Output 1,000 t	Yield 100kg/ha	Output 1,000 t	Yield 100kg/ha
Total Grains	15,298	29.0	25,399	28.5	27,159	30.7
Wheat	8,576	34.6	8,193	32.1	9,537	36.2
Rye	5,653	23.4	5,299	23.1	5,663	24.7
Barley	3,437	30.4	3,866	31.1	3,612	31.7
Triticale	2,130	30.6	1,841	29.2	2,058	32.4
Mixed grains	3,520	27.9	4,105	28.7	4,274	29.3
Potatoes	17,217	203.0	20,776	159.0	25,949	200.0
Sugar beets	17,846	394.0	15,886	379.0	15,171	379.0
Rape	449.0	15.9	595.0	18.7	1,099	23.6
Field vegetables	5,104	-	4,936	-	5,919	-

Source: Adapted from GUSa, 1997 – 1999.

Table 13.11   Units of farm machinery and equipment, June 1996[a]

	Number (in 1,000)	Family farms[b]	No. per 100 ha farmland
Tractors	1,303	1,211	8.57
Grain combines	97.0	82.1	1.12[c]
Potato combines	76.5	73.9	5.70[c]
Beet combines	27.0	25.3	5.96[c]
Self-propelled choppers	5.5	2.1	0.12[d]
Pick-up balers	104.7	97.9	0.57
Milking machines (cans)	294.2	289.4	0.35[e]
Milking machines (pipeline)	7.4	5.0	0.01[e]
Milk coolers	28.4	24.4	0.03[e]

Notes: [a] Data from Agricultural Census 1996.
[b] Partly estimated.
[c] Calculated per 100 ha of respective crop.
[d] Calculated per ha of grassland plus field grass and fodder legumes.
[e] Per commercial dairy farm.
Sources: Adapted from Pawlak and Zalewski, 1998; GUSa, 1999; IERiGZ, Raporty Rynkowe *g*, 1999; Raporty Rynkowe *h*, 2000.

Although there are large numbers of some types of grain combines, dung and fertilizer spreaders and potato planters per unit area, fieldwork mechanization rates remain low. In 1997, combine harvesters were used on only 65 percent of grain fields, 40 percent of sugar beet fields and 33 percent of potato fields. Tractor-drawn implements were used for spreading 70 percent of fertilizer and seeding 50 percent of grains and rapeseed (Szemberg, 1999; Pawlak and Zalewski, 1998).

Machine milking amounts to 50 percent of all milking activity, and automated hog watering to 15 percent, but all other animal husbandry labor is mechanized at rates of less than 10 percent. Small farm size, fragmentation of farmland and the limited use of private contractors are significant barriers to increased mechanization.

Along with limited mechanization and low levels of farm specialization, labor input is relatively high. Even family farms using tractors for their entire field work average 21 full-time workers per 100 ha of farmland. The following labor input per 100 kg of product was calculated from accounting records of 1,200 farms in 1996:

Wheat	1.75 man-hours
Potatoes	1.22 man-hours
Sugar beet	0.64 man-hours
Hogs (live weight)	34.00 man-hours

It should be noted that family farms that maintain records are usually above-average operations (Pokrzywa and Augustynska, 1998).

Livestock production

Polish agriculture is heavily specialized in livestock production. This applies especially to family farms, 72 percent of which have large animals (including sheep). About 64 percent (1996-1998 average) of marketed output in Poland is in the form of animal products mostly milk, live hogs and poultry meat. Total and per capita outputs of major animal products are shown in table 13.12.

However, most farms practice animal husbandry inefficiently and products often fail to reach quality standards of markets in advanced countries. Compared with the EU average, for example, labor and feed input per unit product is high. The share of top-quality raw milk is about 50 percent below EU standards, and Poland is also 10 percentage points behind West European suppliers in terms of lean meat proportions of slaughter hogs. Poultry-for-slaughter is an exception, as quality standards here no longer differ notably from those of West European producers. The production of waterfowl, particularly geese, is a Polish specialty for which strong demand exists in some EU countries.

Table 13.12 Total and per capita animal production

Product	1996	1997	1998	Family farm share (%)[b]	Per capita output (1998)
Meat[a] total	3,106	3,021	3,274	88.1	84.7 kg
(1,000 t)					
Beef	388	402	418	90.2	10.9 kg
Veal	47	44	54	97.8	1.4 kg
Pork	2,072	1,895	2,053	87.9	53.1 kg
Poultry	390	474	520	85.1	13.4 kg
Milk (million l)	11,355	11,770	12,178	93.1	305 liters
Eggs (billion)	7.06	7.66	7.66	79.6	198 pieces

Notes: [a] Live carcass weight including fat and offal.
    [b] Reference period 1997.
Sources: Calculated from GUSa, 1997; 1998, GUSe, 2000.

Milk, hog, poultry and egg production levels differ greatly among regions. This is reflected especially in different concentrations of production per unit area. Beef production is not concentrated in any specific region. *Voievodships* with output well above the national average (140 percent) are found in all parts of Poland, and the six major beef-producing *voievodships* account for only 22 percent of the national total.

Slaughter hog production is concentrated (34 percent) in six *voievodships* around Poznan: in four of these, output is between 2.4 and 4 times the national average. Regional concentration is even stronger for poultry meat production. The six top districts produce 36 percent of the national total; nine of 49 (former) *voievodships* account for one-half of national output. In three administrative units, output per hectare exceeds the national average by 100 to 130 percent. Poultry meat production is concentrated in regions to the north and east of the capital and in western and southwestern Poland.

Milk production presents a highly heterogeneous picture. Six of the 49 former *voievodships* account for 22 percent of national output and for 31 percent of milk supplies to dairies with five or more employees. Surprisingly, with only one exception, these are regions in which average milk yield per cow is 0.5 to 9.5 percent below the national average. These regions form a semicircle to the north, east and southeast of the capital. In 1998, administrative units with higher milk yields per cow (above 4,000 l/year) contributed only 14.8 percent to national output and supplies to dairies.

Small herd size is a defining feature of Polish dairy farms, with an average size on family farms of only 2.6 animals. Low skills levels of dairy farmers, inadequate breeding and hygiene in stalls, low input of concentrates and major deficiencies in feed management explain low milk yields and slow productivity growth. From 1992 to 1998, annual milk yield per cow only increased from 3,015 to 3,477 liters.

Recently, Polish scientists forecast growth in dairy cow numbers and the structure of dairy herds, projecting in three different scenarios a total of 3.46 and 2.93 million cows and 962,000 and 698,000 dairy farmers, respectively, by the year 2010. Scenario III predicts that by 2010 farms with more than four cows each will produce 86 percent of the country's total milk output and 94 percent of market production (Smolenski, 1998).

Hog farming is also spatially dispersed. About 1.03 million family farms, and between 1,200 and 1,500 large (including cooperative) farms, kept hogs in 1996. Family farms have 16.5 hogs on average, and more than 70 percent of all hog farms have fewer than 20 head. In 1998, this latter group accounted for one-quarter of all hogs on family farms (GUS*i*, 1997; GUS*k*,1998). Large-scale hog farming is concentrated in regions of northern Poland and in former *voievodships* Poznan, Opole and Zielona Gora in the West and south-west of Poland.

Many factors contribute to modest productivity levels, among them inadequate hygiene in pigpens. Nearly one-half of all pigpens are more than 40 years old, poorly maintained and rarely upgraded, and hogs are often kept in simple farm buildings together with other farm animals. In addition, breeding improvements find their way into farming practice only slowly, and use of mixed feeds is rare on hog farms. While only 18 percent of total output of the mixed-feed industry was formulated for hogs in 1998, some 72 percent of protein concentrates and other feed additives were designated for hogs. On average, only 22.5 percent of hog rations are estimated to be nutritionally well-balanced (IERiGZ, Raporty Rynkowe *m*, 1998).

The concentration both of regions and of farms is high for poultry meat production. Over 80 percent of the output is produced by an estimated 2,000 to 4,000 family farms. This sector stands out for its use of mixed feeds, modern forms of stock keeping, intensive breeding and rapid introduction of research findings into farming practice and, especially, vertical integration (IERiGZ, Raporty Rynkowe, various years).

More than one third of *egg* production originates from small producers with extensive production of 130 to 180 eggs per hen annually. Intensively operated egg farms, most of which are located close to urban areas, produce between 250 and 310 eggs per hen.

Rural economic adjustment

Conditions in Polish agriculture lag from far to very far behind those in EU countries in terms of crop yields, animal performance, quality standards for farm produce, labor productivity, working conditions, specialization, organization of the marketing system, provision of services and cooperation among farms. A major obstacle to quickly improving these conditions is the large rural labor force. This includes 4.84 million agricultural workers counted in the 1996 agricultural census about 740,000 of whom according to farm managers interviewed were "not really needed" for agricultural production, but were employed, sometimes temporarily, for social and family reasons and 611,000 workers who were recorded as unemployed in rural areas in November 1997 (GUSc, 1998; GUS, Aktywnosc ekonomiczna ludnosci Polski, 1998; Szemberg, 1999).

Family farms in 1996 employed 35.5 persons, or 24.9 full-time workers, per 100 ha of farmland (GUSc, 1998). Regional differences are considerable: some *voievodships* in southern and southeastern Poland have more than 50 people working per 100 ha, but this number is sometimes 10 or lower in northern and northwestern regions. Constraints to employing these surplus workers include the limited capacity of services and manufacturing in regions with excess labor to absorb workers, and barriers to commuting or migration into areas offering non-agricultural jobs.

Another serious obstacle to rapid modernization is a lack of capital for farming. Only crude estimates are available of capital investments needed to modernize and align agriculture with EU market requirements. During negotiations with EU authorities on Poland's accession in the fall of 1999, a total investment of at least 25 billion zlotys over three years was mentioned (Boss-Rolnictwo, No. 46, 1999). However, when a government program for adjusting the Polish dairy industry to EU conditions was presented, investment for this sector alone (including the processing sector) was estimated at 16 billion zlotys. Hence, investment needs for all branches of agriculture combined will be much higher. But even 25 billion zlotys represent three times the amount invested in 1996-98 (Boss-Rolnistwo, No. 5, 2000).

Substantial funds have to be provided not only to modernize agriculture, but also the sectors associated with agriculture. In 1998 and 1999, the Polish Government adopted three programs, which provide not only for restructuring and adjustment of agriculture to EU markets, but also for modernizing rural areas. These are:

- A medium-term strategy for developing agriculture and rural areas
- A coherent structural policy for developing rural areas and agriculture
- A pact for agriculture and rural areas.

Proposed are both short-term measures, especially market stabilization and greater tariff protection, and longer-term measures for accelerating the alignment of the agricultural and food industry with EU markets and legal conditions, and for improving the industry's competitive position. This includes the intensification of basic and advanced training and of agricultural extension, an improved organization of information, better working and living conditions in rural areas, and development of technical and social infrastructures. Initiatives to create non-agricultural jobs in rural areas, including small towns, are considered to be vitally important, as they are expected to eventually increase farm-level labor productivity.

13.4 Strategic considerations

Poland's considerable agricultural potential is presently nowhere near being fully reached. Even when 3.1 million ha of farmland representing soils class VI (the poorest) and about one third of class V soils are excluded Poland's farming sector would still be able to increase its output of major crop and animal products by 30-70 percent, if 90 percent of 1996-1998 yields of German farms were achieved.

Further, such an increase in agricultural production would only be achieved on market-oriented, highly specialized farms with modern equipment and depending on the product sufficient scale. If this transformation were successful, the number of farms would decline to about 0.5 million, and the number of agricultural workers would drop to 600,000-800,000 full-time workers. This would eliminate at least 3.5 million workers from farming, a process that would be difficult to manage economically and socially.

With the above combination of facts limited prospects for marketing and expansion and high labor surpluses only one development strategy would appear to be sensible: moderate expansion of production with a careful but continual labor force reduction. This would be combined with attempts to increase, more so than in the past, value added of agriculture, food industry and marketing, taking full advantage of Polish agriculture's strengths.

These strengths include Poland's labor cost advantage, which is likely to continue for some time, large stretches of unpolluted land, and the biological quality of many agricultural raw materials and food products (Seremak-Bulge, 1998 and 1999). Profits could be earned based on the following:

- An increase in organic production of agricultural raw materials and food products
- A clear move to more natural products of animal and plant origin

- An emphasis on niche products
- The extended cultivation of industrial crops
- Output increases through gradual change from conventional techniques to more productive and efficient farming methods.

These structural changes in primary agricultural production have to be accompanied by shifts in the processing industry to technologies that are both environmentally sound and that preserve the dietetic value of raw foods. Moreover, a high rate of innovation must be achieved for a wide range of processed products; this also applies to production and processing of other (non-food) products. In the end, the success of such a strategy depends on more effective marketing of Polish products both at home and abroad.

The implementation of such a strategy, therefore, depends on a wide range of pre-conditions that must exist outside of agriculture. Such a transformation of the agrarian system is not feasible in certain regions of the country, particularly those with natural disadvantages (heath, swamp forest zones, riverside forest regions and foothill mountain ranges). In these regions it would be sensible to encourage with assistance from central and regional authorities and perhaps with EU financial support extensive agriculture based on indigenous crops and production practices.

In addition, vast regions of Poland still offer a potential for developing nature-based tourism, i.e., vacations on farms or in areas with scenic amenities. This also offers alternative employment and income prospects for farm families. However, realizing this potential requires that certain preconditions are met, particularly the reduction of pollution from agriculture and from rural households. Other contingencies include the redevelopment of many villages and refurbishment of local facilities, so that these regions become attractive to tourists. An appropriate tourist infrastructure (including hotels and restaurants) also still needs to be developed. All of these steps have to be incorporated into realistic regional development plans, such as those that are presently being drawn up in Poland.

Against this background, a strong regional differentiation in agriculture is evident, but has been given little attention so far. Trends in marketed output per hectare of farmland since the mid-1980s reveal that the gradual introduction of free market principles has increased regional differences in the productive efficiency of farms. The author attempted to obtain comparable data on market production per hectare across regions.[8] When comparing 1985-1989 with 1996-1998 data, a ratio of about 2.3:1 to 2.9:1 is calculated for means of the five best and the five poorest *voievodships* in the 1980s, while the 1996-1998 ratio is as high as 4:1 (GUS, Rocznik

Statystyczny, various years). In the 1980s, two or three *voievodships* had market production rates that fell short of two thirds of the national average, compared to eleven in the 1996-1998 survey.

The agricultural development potential of former *voievodships* is ranked here using the following variables: market production per hectare of farmland, aggregate indices of major crop and animal products, labor productivity (annual mean of market production per full-time worker), per-hectare capital investment, share of market-oriented farms, and share of market-oriented farmers who believe their farms can be expanded.[9]

This regional analysis of agricultural development potential would be incomplete without also considering the stage of development and role of the food industry in various administrative units of Poland. Between 1992 and 1999, output and investment in Poland's food industry increased by 79 percent and nearly 90 percent, respectively. At the end of 1998, foreign investments of more than US $4.5 billion had flowed into the industry, representing one-quarter of all foreign investment flows into Poland. Processing industry advances, however, vary among sub-sectors and regions. We consider only those sub-sectors that process large quantities of primary agricultural products, including the slaughter and meat industry, the dairy sector, milling industry and bakeries, the sugar industry, and fruit and vegetable processing.

Table 13.13 Estimated farm development potential by *voievodship*
(A = excellent; E = poor development potential)

Category A	Leszno, Opole, Poznan
Category B	Bydgoszcz, Kalisz, Lomza, Lodz, Pila, Plock, Torun, Warszawa
Category C	Ciechanow, Elblag, Gdansk, Gorzow, Koszalin, Legnica, Olsztyn,Ostroleka, Siedlce, Skierniewice, Szczecin, Walbrzych, Wloclawek, Wroclaw, Zielona Gora
Category D	Biala Podlaska, Bialystok, Konin, Jelenia Gora, Katowice, Kielce, Krakow, Lublin, Piotrkow Trybunalski, Radom, Sieradz, Slupsk, Suwalki, Zamosc
Category E	Bielsko-Biala, Chelm, Czestochowa, Krosno, Nowy Sacz, Przemysl, Rzeszow, Tarnobrzeg, Tarnow

Sources: GUSa, 1997; GUSd, 1998; GUSb, 1999; Michna, 1999.

The degree of concentration is relatively low in these industries. About 19,000 companies are now registered, 9,500 of which are in the slaughter and meat, dairy and milling business. The ten largest firms in each branch account for 15-25 percent of output (GUS*f*, 1999; BOSS-Rolnictwo, No.

48, 1998). The seven or eight largest fruit and vegetable processing companies have a 60 percent market share.

Based on industry surveys and company news releases, relatively few companies strategically choose, interact with or influence their supplies. This would include no longer buying from inefficient farms and favoring or even investing in farms that demonstrate growth potential, which would reduce uncertainty associated with obtaining raw materials so that these firms could also plan more effectively. Most successful in this respect have been several meat, dairy, and fruit and vegetable processing firms (BOSS-Rolnistwo, No. 17, 1999; IERiGZ, Raporty Rynkowe *f*, No. 16, 2000), but few if any comparable activities are evident in other food industry sub-sectors.

These activities have also reached a significant scale in only a few *voievodships* (defined using the administrative structure in effect until 1998). The food industry plays a minor role in western and northwestern *voievodships* (up to about 100 km east of the border, except for Szczecin and Zielona Gora), in some regions in southern and eastern parts of the country, and in the central *voievodships* of Czestochowa and Piotrkow Trybunalski.

The processing industry is well-developed in *voievodships* Warszawa, Katowice, Poznan and Bydgoszcz, but it is narrowly focused on meat and dairy products in Bialystok, Kielce, Lomza, Olsztyn, Ostroleka, Siedlze and Tarnow. The most viable fruit and vegetable processing companies are concentrated around Warszawa, primarily in the former *voievodship* Radom. It is also noteworthy that some highly profitable companies are located in regions (such as Kielce, Krosno, Przemysl and Suwalki) where agricultural development potential is low due to small farm size, low levels of market orientation, and limited skills of farmers.

13.5 Land use for forestry

Forested areas accounted for 28.2 percent of Poland's national territory in 1998, which was 3.5 percent less than the European average and far less than the share of forests in all neighboring countries, except for the Ukraine. The slightly smaller percentage relative to the European average is in part explained by decades of destructive clear-cutting that started at the beginning of the 20th century and lasted well into World War II.

In 1945, forested area was estimated at only 6.47 million ha or 20.7 percent of national territory. Since then, woods have increased to 8.81 million ha as a result of reforestation, with a maximum of almost 278,000 ha added between 1961 and 1965. Reforestation declined markedly during the 1980s, but has again increased since the early 1990s.

Almost 83 percent of forests are under public ownership (1998). Of the 7.3 million ha that are publicly owned, 94.7 percent are managed by the state forest enterprise (UstF) within the Ministry of Environmental Protection, Natural Resources and Forestry. Other public wooded areas, except those owned by municipalities, are managed by nature conservation authorities as national parks, or by other agencies (GUSg, 1998, MOS, 1991).

The Forestry Act took effect on January 1, 1992. It defines UstF's duties and forms the legal basis for managing all forests, and for all forms of ownership, protection and reforestation. Both UstF and state authorities are concerned about the condition of forests, which have endured largely uncontrolled human interference. Efforts are underway to slow the process of forest degradation (Rykowski, 1995).

In terms of forest health, Poland ranks near the bottom of European countries (Kolk et.al, 1994). Widespread occurrence of the nun-moth *(Lymantria monacha)* in 1982 placed particular stress on forests. The damage report of 1994, which was prepared under the International Cooperation Program for assessing and monitoring impacts of air pollution on forests, identified a high and lasting level of forest damage in Poland, with the most severe damage recorded in Slask (United Nations Economic Commission for Europe, 1994). The report mentions declining air pollution, particularly of SO_2 and nitrogen oxides, but also points out that until 1994 forest health had declined further, although at a slower rate than earlier (table 13.14).

Table 13.14   Trends in forest defoliation rates in selected European countries (percent of defoliation classes 2-4 in total forest stands)

Country	Defoliation			
	Coniferous trees		Deciduous trees	
	1990	1997	1990	1997
Czech Republic	46.9	71.9	37.6	26.5
Germany	15.9	19.8	23.8	18.6
Lithuania	22.9	13.9	15.8	15.9
Belarus	57.0	41.2	45.0	23.0
Slovakia	55.5	42.2	31.3	23.3
Poland	40.7	36.8	25.6	35.8

Source: GUSg, 1998.

Another conspicuous fact is the significant difference in shares of private forests in total forest area; this share is usually much smaller in northern and western districts that became part of Poland after World War II, than in regions that have been part of Poland since 1918. Not only has forested area in Poland increased significantly since World War II, but the species composition has also changed in favor of deciduous trees (table 13.15).

Table 13.15 Forest area by *voievodship*, 1998[a]

Voievodship	Forest area (1,000 ha)[b]	Share of total forest land (%)	Share of forests in region (%)	Share of coniferous trees (%)[c]	Private forest share (%)
Dolny Slask	569.6	6.4	28.6	73.5	2.2
Kujawy-Pomorze	402.7	4.5	22.4	86.5	9.9
Lublin	548.7	6.2	21.8	67.0	38.0
Lubuska	683.9	7.7	48.9	85.0	1.1
Lodz	368.6	4.1	18.2	81.5	31.8
Malopolska	438.7	4.9	29.0	71.5	42.4
Mazowsze	783.0	8.8	22.0	79.0	41.0
Opole	251.2	2.8	26.7	84.0	3.0
Podkarpacie	467.3	7.3	36.1	60.5	14.1
Podlasie	594.0	6.7	29.4	73.0	31.0
Pomorze	655.8	7.4	35.8	80.0	10.0
Gorny Slask	393.6	4.4	32.0	81.0	19.3
Swietokrzyska	320.6	3.6	27.5	83.0	24.7
Warmia-Mazury	704.2	7.9	29.1	73.0	4.5
Wielkopolska	759.8	8.5	25.5	84.5	9.4
Pomorze Zachodnie	796.4	8.9	34.8	76.0	1.1
Poland total	8,918.1	100.0	28.5	77.3	16.9

Notes: [a]Administrative structure since January 1,1999
[b]Areas including field trees and bushes
[c]Estimates

Sources: Calculated from GUSc 1998, GUSg, 1998; GUSb, 1999.

Due to large variations in the spatial distribution of mining, primary industry and urbanization, overall forest conditions in Poland differ widely among regions. In general, forests to the south are in poor condition, while those along the Baltic Sea coast and in eastern regions are healthier. Table 13.17 shows trends in selected forest-treatment measures.

In 1994, the UstF's Director General directed that seven silvicultural research sites were to be established throughout Poland to develop and test site-specific techniques for developing sustainable forests. If successful, these techniques will be put into practice (Rykowski, 1995).

Table 13.16 Comparison of species composition and age structure of forests, 1945 and 1997 (percent of total forest area)

Species composition and age structure	1945	1997
Coniferous trees	87.0	77.3
Pine and larch	77.5	69.0
Spruce	8.8	5.8
Deciduous trees	13.0	22.7
Oak, ash, maple species, elm	4.1	6.0
Red beech	3.3	4.2
Birch, robinia	2.2	6.0
Alder	2.8	5.3
Age groups		
I (1 - 20 years)	23.2	14.0
II (21 - 40 years)	22.8	24.6
III (41 - 60 years)	18.5	21.8
IV (61 - 80 years)	13.1	17.6
V (81 years and more)	14.3	17.0
Clearings, other areas with little growing stock	8.1	3.2

Sources: GUSg, 1995; 1998.

Table 13.17 Trends in selected silvicultural measures (1,000 ha)

Measure	1966-1970	1971-1975[a]	1980	1985	1990	1994	1996	1997
Forest renewal[b]	5	...	79.4	61.4	57.3	53.9	50.9	40.8
Reforstation	35.3	18.8	13.6	6.7	6.8	13.3	17.5	18.3
Improvements	...	...	33.1	27.7	23.9	22.7	22.5	16.3
Maintenance	111	111	580.3	519.7	449.3	359.1	374.4	347.1

Notes: [a]Five-year average
[b]Partly estimated

Sources: GUSg, 1995; 1998.

Care and preservation of forest and landscape health have been encouraged by establishing protected areas, the number and size of which have increased substantially since the early 1980s. Since 1990, for example, the number of National Parks and protected landscape areas increased from 5 to 22 and from 215 to 429, respectively. National Parks and protected landscape areas are heavily forested. For details see table 13.18.

Table 13.18 Protected areas and forests

Type of area	Number	Total area (1,000 ha)	Share of forests (partly estimated)
National Parks	22	305.7	61 %
Nature reserves	1,215	141.2	33 %
Landscape parks	120	2,482.2	31 %
Protected landscape areas	429	6,480.1	48 %
Protective forests*		3,400.0	-
voiev. Zielona Gora		229.7	-
voiev. Krosno		183.0	-
voiev. Katowice		161.6	-

Note: *Woodland managed by the state forest enterprises, serving mainly for preventive water protection, soil protection and recreational purposes.

Sources: GUSg, 1995; 1998.

Wood harvesting, processing and trading

Harvesting of wood at a rate below natural annual growth rates is a key component of Poland's forestry policy. In this manner, forest timber stocks, which in 1997 amounted to 1.61 billion m³ (1.29 bn m³ softwood), are to be increased and their age structure improved. In fact, between 1989 and 1997, timber stocks grew by 14 percent (GUSg, 1999). Ten percent of timber stocks are in private forests (GUSg, 1999).

In recent years, the forestry sector has contributed 0.4 percent of GDP and accounted for 0.54 percent of employment. In comparison, the wood-processing sector makes a larger contribution. In Polish industry statistics (PCN), the latter sector includes the timber and wood products industry, pulp and paper industry, and the furniture industry (including the toy industry, etc.). During 1996-1998, these branches on average produced 8.2 percent of the country's industrial output and employed 10.5 percent of the industrial labor force (including mining and power generation) (GUSf, 1998; 1999). The growth in sales of these three branches in the last few years was remarkable: from 1995 to 1998, total processing industry sales increased by 32.5 percent, but that of the furniture and toy industry increased by more than 70 percent, the timber industry by 38 percent, and the pulp and paper industries by 42 percent (GUSf, 1999).

Lumber, fiberboard and chipboards, paper and cardboard, seating and office furniture are primary wood-processing industry products.

Voievodships Slupsk, Gorzow, Koszalin and Olsztyn are regional centers of lumber production, contributing 28 percent of national output. Fiberboard production is more concentrated, with more than 80 percent produced in Zielona Gora, Gdansk, Czestochowa, Pila and Przemysl. About one third of national output of composite particleboard comes from Poznan and Suwalki. The paper industry is concentrated in Bydgoszcz, Elblag and Ostroleka; cardboard comes mainly from Bydgoszcz, Warszawa, Bielska Biala, Katowice and Opole; and Bydgoszcz, Olsztyn, Poznan and Ostroleka are furniture industry centers (GUS*b*, 1998).

These industries and the forestry sector have recently become more important in Poland's trade balance. In 1994, they accounted for 10.1 percent of export value, while agriculture and the food industry contributed about 12.2 percent. According to official sources, the wood industry's share increased to 15.1 percent in 1998,[10] and the import-export ratio declined from 1.7:1 to 1.4:1 (GUS*h* 1995; 1998). Seating and other furniture, paper and cardboard and derived products, and lumber were the main exports, most of which were shipped to EU and CIS countries (75 percent and 17 percent in 1998, respectively) (GUS*h*, 1998).

Paper (including cigarette paper) and cardboard comprise 25 percent of Poland's imports, followed by goods produced from these raw materials. Other major imports are furniture, toys and sports equipment, and chip and fiber boards. About 70 percent of these imports come from EU countries, and 14 percent from CEE countries. In addition, some developing countries are major suppliers of furniture and toys (GUS*h*, 1998).

Table 13.19 Forest conditions by forest and landscape zones, 1997

| Forest and landscape zone[a] | Forest stands[b] by grade of damage (percent) | | | | | | | | | Degree of defoliation | | |
| | 0: No damage | | | 1: Endangered | | | 2-4: Medium to severe damage; dead trees | | | | | |
	A	B	C	A	B	C	A	B	C	A	B	C
Poland total	10.9	9.9	14.1	52.5	53.3	50.1	36.6	36.8	35.8	2.79	2.80	2.75
Sudety	2.9	2.8	3.0	29.7	25.9	42.0	67.4	71.3	55.0	3.61	3.68	3.39
Gorny Slask	1.9	2.4	0.2	26.8	28.0	23.0	71.3	69.6	76.8	3.49	3.45	3.61
Karpaty	1.5	1.7	1.3	49.4	40.6	61.4	49.1	57.7	37.3	3.21	3.40	2.95
Malopolska	5.7	4.6	11.2	48.3	48.5	47.4	46.0	46.9	41.4	3.04	3.08	2.87
Mazowsze-Podlasie	13.8	13.4	15.0	53.0	52.1	56.2	33.2	34.5	28.8	2.77	2.80	2.67
Mazury-Podlasie	21.5	19.2	27.4	51.8	55.5	42.4	26.7	25.3	30.2	2.49	2.48	2.55
Wielkopolska-Pomorze	14.4	13.9	17.0	60.9	62.8	50.6	24.7	23.3	32.4	2.47	2.44	2.66
Wybrzeze Baltyckie	16.5	11.8	25.4	66.3	71.6	56.0	17.2	16.6	18.6	2.34	2.38	2.27

Notes: A = Total; B = Coniferous; C = Deciduous
[a]Names of zones based on Polish forest statistics
[b]Refers to stands 40 years and older
Source: GUSg, 1998.

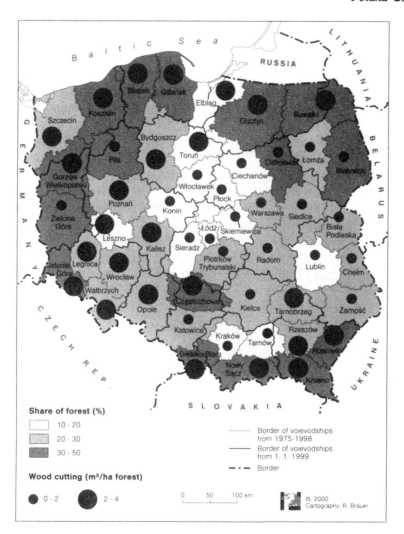

Figure 13.4 Forestland and woods

13.6 Rural socioeconomic conditions

Poland's rural population generally lives under less favorable conditions than, for example, rural populations in the Czech Republic, Hungary and parts of Slovakia. Differences between urban and rural areas also appear to be more pronounced in Poland, and there is substantial evidence that the rural disadvantage has increased since 1989. Important regional differences exist, however. Socioeconomic conditions are relatively favorable in the new *voievodships* Pomorze, Wielkopolska and Dolny Slask, but they fall far short of the national average in eastern, north-eastern, south-eastern and southern parts of the country (Klodzinski and Wilkin, 1999).

Presently, 38.4 percent of the population lives in rural areas, with two facts distinguishing Poland from other CEE transformation countries:

- Most villages are small, with average populations of 259 (including sections, abodes, etc.). This figure is less than 200 in northwestern, northeastern and central Poland (Suwalki is an extreme case, with only 110 inhabitants per rural settlement) and in regions north and northwest of Warsaw, but it is between 300 and 780 in most regions in the south and southeast (GUS*a*, 1998).
- Most villages remain almost purely agrarian. According to the general agricultural survey of 1996 and periodic general statistics, 74 percent of all rural households derived their livelihood either fully or partially from farming in 1996 (including smallholdings of less than 1 ha). This share was as low as 30-40 percent in western and northwestern *voievodships*, and between 75 and 82 percent in some eastern and southeastern regions. Approximately 65 percent of the employed in rural areas work in farming (GUS*a*, 1998; GUS*d*, 1998).

It has become obvious, furthermore, that farm earnings are falling behind earnings of the non-farm rural population, suggesting that farmers are losing out in the transition to a market economy (Wos, 1999).

During the first two years after transformation (1990-1991), real income per farm dropped by 60 percent compared with only a 10 percent drop for the rest of the population. Earnings growth resumed in 1992, with farm workers benefiting roughly to the same degree as other socio-economic groups (Wos, 1999).

Since 1997, the rural population has continued to experience significant earnings losses. According to official surveys, 1998 family farm household income per capita was 22 percent below that of non-farm households (including the unemployed and recipients of other transfer payments), and it was 31 percent below per capita income in households in which heads were blue-collar workers, non-manual employees or self-employed. It is important to note that transfer payments such as pensions and retirement income made up 20 percent of rural household income, but only 10 percent of income for other households. Accordingly, agricultural workers earn about 35 percent less than services and industry employees[11] (calculated and estimated from GUS*a*, 1998; GUS*b*, 1999).

Substantial regional variation also exists in farm incomes. In 1997, for example, farm households in the former eastern *voievodships* Biala Podlaska, Chelm, Lublin and Zamocz earned only 80 percent of national average farm income, while farmers around Poznan earned 122 percent. For part-time farms, total income per capita in 1997 was estimated to be 14 percent below that of full-time family farms (GUS*b*, 1999).

Income differences relative to other sectors are not the only indication that rural areas and farmers are lagging behind their urban counterparts. The high rate of hidden unemployment on family farms also has to be noted. This unemployment is hidden because these individuals are forced to stay on their farms to produce food for their subsistence needs, and they are unable to find better-paying work elsewhere. The number of these unemployed is estimated at between 740,000 and 906,000 persons, depending on the source (Szemberg, 1999; Rosner, 1999).

Large numbers of people of retirement age, who account for about 15 percent of all workers, are forced to work on their own or their childrens' farms because their retirement income is insufficient to cover their subsistence needs. The share of these elderly exceeds 20 percent of the workers on family farms in eleven *voievodships*, including Zielona Gora, Jelenia Gora and Walbrzych, and most administrative units in the southeast macro-region (GUS*b*, 1998).

Other disparities include infrastructure deficiencies in rural areas along with poorer living conditions (Ministerstwo Rolnictwa i Gospodarki Zywnosciowej, 1994). According to the 1988 National Census, per-capita total floor space was slightly larger in rural than in urban homes, but actual living space (room space) per person was lower in rural homes. At that time, rural houses were on average also older than urban houses: 61.1 percent of residential buildings in cities had been erected since 1960, compared to only 44.9 percent in rural areas. Additionally, interior walls in many rural residences consist of combustible materials (GUS, Gospodarka mieszkaniowa, 1994).

Rural areas also lag behind urban areas in the use of water pipes, flushing toilets, bathrooms, central gas supply and central heating (table 13.20).

More recent data do not show any notable reductions in regional disparities. Lower-income *voievodships* with a mostly agrarian orientation (Biala Podlaska, Bialystok, Kielce, Radom, Siedlce and Zamosc) in many cases have only two-thirds to three-quarters of the facilities average of other rural areas, while those in western and northern parts of Poland (including Elblag and Gdansk) as well as Bielska Biala and Katowice in the south are mostly well above that level.

Table 13.20 Amenities of urban and rural households, 1998

	Availability (in percent)	
Equipment	Rural	Urban
Central water supply	81.0	97.3
Water closet	61.2	89.0
Bathroom	65.5	87.4
Central gas connection*	14.7	76.4
Central geating	53.5	79.6

Note: *In rural areas, altogether 68.8 percent of the households have gas hook-up,
      including burners operated with mobile tanks (Piecek, 1999).

The lack of telephones in rural areas with large variations between
regions directly impedes the modernization of agricultural production and
marketing. In 1993, 2,500 rural settlements still had no phone; 4.03
telephones were available per 100 rural residents (590,000 in absolute
terms). This implies access to less than one telephone for every three
family farms. In 1996, the number of telephones had increased to 6.72 per
100 residents, but 500 settlements were still not connected to the telephone
net. By 1997, this figure had increased to 8.36, although regional
differences remain significant: villages in the former *voievodship*
Warszawa averaged 22.5 telephones per 100 residents, but the eastern and
south-eastern *voievodships* Siedlce and Przemysl had only 3.9 and 5.1
respectively (GUS*b*, 1998).

The deficiencies outlined above impede the modernization of Polish
agriculture for a number of reasons. They not only directly explain the slow
pace of the modernization process and of full integration of the agrarian
sector into the national economy, but they also indirectly hinder job
creation efforts in rural areas and encourage the out-migration of young
people. Therefore, specific rural development programs, such as those
being prepared by the Ministry of Agriculture and Food Industry, warrant
special attention (Duczkowska-Malysz, 1995).

Notes

[1] Officially, the so-called cooperative sector included cooperative farms, including most
     dairies, consumer cooperatives, agricultural procurement and marketing cooperatives,
     and several food industry companies as well as importers and exporters (e.g., the
     HORTEX company).

[2] The service sector includes hotels and restaurants, financial sector, real estate,
     information and consulting, health care, public administration, municipal and private
     services, education.

3   Calculations are based on the total labor force, including part-time workers.

4   This refers to the former administrative districts of Koszalin, Slupsk, Elblag, Olszt and Suwalki, with unemployment rates between 17.8 and 20.5 percent (December 1998).

5   The 1989 survey also included units with less than 1 ha of farmland.

6   According to Polish agricultural extension workers, only about 10 percent of family farms receive extension services (Rylski, 1995).

7   Wilkin distinguishes between so-called peasant and market-oriented farming (Wilkin, 1990).

8   Some of these numbers are estimates, as official comparable data concerning market production by *voievodship* are only available for some years.

9   As only limited data are available on successor operations of former state farms, the influence of these operations on the situation in the various administrative units is considered only to a limited extent.

10   Data on Poland's foreign trade are recorded both by the National Bank and by customs authorities; in part, the numbers differ significantly. Additional problems arise from the use of several different industrial classification systems.

11   These numbers are based on surveys of nearly 1,700 farm households. It is doubtful whether they are truly representative in view of the great variation in employment and incomes in rural areas. For 1997, for example, Wos (1999) reports only 69 percent as the income level of farm households. Publications of Instytut Ekonomiki Rolnictwa i Gospodarki Zywnosciowoj also indicate that the income situation is worse than that implied by the above data.

References

Agencja Wlasnosci Rolnej Skarbu Panstwa (AWRSP) (1994), *Biuletyn towarzystwa obrotunieruchomosci*, T.O.N. AGRO, Warszawa.

Bekas, E. (1996), 'Fundacja Programu Pomocy dla Rolnictwa', *Biuletyn informacyjny*, 1, Warszawa (Eigenverlag des MRiGZ), pp. 14-16.

Berkowska, E., Rasz H. and Stankiewicz, D. (1995), *Przemiany agrarne w Polsce w swietle stowazyszenia Polski z Unia Europejska*, 72 pp., Warszawa (Kancelaria Sejmu).

BOSS-Rolnistwo, Tygodnik o rolnictwie i gospodarce zywnosciowej Boss Informacje ekonomiczne, No. 48/1998; No. 17/1999; No.46/1999; No. 5/2000.

Duczkowska-Malysz, K. (1995), 'Development of Rural Areas', *Zagadnienia ekonomiki do rolnej*, Zeszyt 6, dodatck, pp. 23-35.

Gawlikowska-Hueckel, K. (1999*a*), *Ocena Konkurencyjnosci Wojewodztw: Struktura Handlu Zagranicznego*, Instytut Badan nad Gospodarka Rynko, Gdansk.

Gawlikowska-Hueckel, K. (1999*b*), *Atrakcyjnosc Inwestycjna nowych Wojewodztw*, Instytut Badan nad Gospodarka Rynkowa, Gdansk.

Gawlikowska-Hueckel, K. (2000), Personal Communication.

Glowny Urzad Statystyczny (GUS) (Central Statistical Office), various years, Warszawa.

    GUS*a*   Rocznik Statystyczny Rzeczypospolitel Polskiej (Rocznik Statystyczny starting from 1998).

    GUS*b*   Rocznik Statystyczny Wojewodztw.

    GUS*c*   Rocznik Statystyczny Rolnictwa.

    GUS*d*   Powszechny Spis Rolny 1996 Systematyka i charakterystyka gospodarstw rolnych 1998.

    GUS*e*   Maly Rocznik Statystyczny Polski 2000

GUS   Ochrona Srodowiska.
GUS*f* Rocznik Statystyczny Przemyslu.
GUS*g* Lesnictwo.
GUS*h* Rocznik Statystyczny Handlu Zagranicznego.
GUS*i* Wyniki spisu rolnego 1997.
GUS*k* Uzytkowanie gruntow. Powierzchnia zasiewow i poglowie zwierzat gospodarskich w 1998.

Glowny Urzad Statystyczny (GUS)(1998), *Aktywnosc ekonomiczna ludnosci Polski,* Warszawa.

Glowny Urzad Statystyczny (GUS) (1994), *Gospodarka mieszkaniowa w 1994 roku,* Warszawa.

Glowny Urzad Statystyczny (GUS) (1998), *Polska w nowym podsiale terytorialnym,* Warszawa.

Guzewicz, W. (1999), 'Przeksztalcenia w rolnictwie wielkoobszarowym', in A. Wos (ed), *Analiza produkcyjno-ekonomicznej sytuacji rolnictwa i gospodarki zywnosciowej w 1998 roku,* Instytut Ekonomiki Rolnictwa i Gospodarki Zywnosciowej, Warszawa, pp. 257-266.

Instytut Ekonomiki Rolnictwa i Gospodarki Zywnosciowej Ministerstwo Rolnictwa i Rozeoju Wsi Agencja Wlasnosci Rolnej Skarbu Panstwa (IERiGZ), *Raporty Rynkowe,* Warszawa,

a Handel zagraniczny produktami rolno-spozywczymi, (2000), No. 11.

b Rynek cukru (2000), No. 17.

Rynek drobiu i jaj (1999), No. 16; (2000), No17.

d Rynek miesa (2000), No.18.

e Rynek mleka (1999) (1999), No. 17; (2000), No.18.

f Rynek owocow i warzyw (2000), No. 16, No.17.

g Rynek rzepaku (1999), No.16.

h Rynek srodkow produkcji i uslug dla rolnictwa (2000), No.17.

i Rynek zboz (2000), No 18.

k Rynek ziemniaka (2000), No. 18.

l Rynek ziemi rolniczej (1999), No. 2.

m Rynek pasz (1998), No. 6.

Kalbarczyk, S. (1999), 'Ekologia i ochrona srodowiska w Polsce', *Boss Informacje ekonomiczne,* Warszawa.

Kapala, A. (1988), *Polen,* Klett, Stuttgart.

Klodzinski, M. and Wilkin, J. (1999), 'Rural Development in Poland: Barriers and Priorities', *Wies i Rolnictwo,* 2 (103) , Supplement, pp. 11-22.

Kolk, A., Sierota, Z. and Malecka, M. (1994), *Ocena wplywu zagrozen biotycznych (szkodnikow lesnych i chorob infekcyjnych) na stan lasow w Polsce w latach 1970 – 1992,* Biblioteka Monitoringu Srodowiska, Warszawa.

Kuklinski, A. and Szul L. R. (1990), 'Powstanie nowej przestrzeni przemyslowej w Polsce', *Gospodarka Narodowa,* 2/3, Warszawa, pp. 24-27.

Marzecka, H. (1995), 'Organiczenie przeznaczania gruntow rolnych na cele nierolnicze', *Biuletyn Informacyjny,* 6 and 7, Ministerstwo Rolnictwa i Gospodarki Zywnosciowej, Warszawa.

Michna, W. (1999), 'Regionalne zroznicowanie czynnikow wytworczych, produkcji rolniczej, zrodel utrzy mania ludnosci wiejskiej oraz infrastruktury obszarow wiejskich', *Analize produkcyjno-ekonomicznej sytuacji rolnictwa i gospodarki zywnosciowej w 1998 roku,* Warszawa.

Ministerstwo Ochrony Srodowiska (MOS) and Zasobow Naturalnych i Lesnictwa (1991), *The act concerning forests,* Warszawa.

Olszynski, J. and Vogel, O. (1991), *Polen auf dem Weg zur Marktwirtschaft*, Deutscher Instituts-Verlag, Köln.

Ostrowski, L. (1999), 'Rynkowy i nierynkowy obrot ziemia rolnicza', *Analiza produkcyjno-ekonomicznej sytuacji rolnictwa i gospodarki zywnosiowej w 1998 roku*, Instytut Ekonomiki Rolnictwa i Gospodarki Zywnosciowej, Wrszawa, pp, 192-202.

Papuga, J. (2000), 'Gdzie rolnik Wyrzuca smieci', *Boss-Rolnictwo*, No. 4 (523), report, Warszawa.

Pawlak, J. and Zalewski, A. (1998), *Rynek Maszyn rolniczych w Polsce*, Instytut Ekono-miki Rolnictwa i Gospodarki Zywnosciowej, Warszawa.

Piecek, B. (1999), 'Wiejskie obszary problemowe pod katem widzenia infrastruktury', in M. Klodzinski (ed), *Typologia wiejskich obszarow problemowych*, Instytut Rozwoju Wsi i Rolnictwa, Warszawa, pp. 39-57.

Pokrzywa, T. and Augustynska, A. (1998), *Produkcyjno-ekonomiczna sytuacja gospodarstw prowadzacych rachunkowosc rolna w latach 1994-1996*, Instytut Ekonomiki Rolnictwa i Gospodarki Zywnosciowej, Warszawa, pp. 89-96.

Rojewski, M. (1977), 'Potencjal wytworczy gospodarki rolnej', in T. Rychlik (ed.), *Ekonomika Rolnictwa*, Panstwowe Wydawnictwo Rolnicze i Lesne, Warszawa.

Rosner, A. (1999), 'Spatial Diversification of Socio-Economic Structures in Poland and Systemic Changes in the Economy', *Wies i Rolnictwo*, 2 (103), Supplement, pp. 75-80.

Rykowski, K. (1995), 'Trwaly rozwoj lasow w Polsce', Ministerstwo Ochrony Srodowiska, Zasobow Naturalnych i Lesnictwa, Warszawa.

Rylski, M (1995), Personal Communication.

Rzadowe Centrum Studiow Strategicznych (1999), 'Ocena sytuacji spoleczno-gospodarczej w 1998r. wraz z elementami prognozy na 1999 rok', Warszawa.

Schonwiese, C.-D. and Krüger, L. (1994), *Klimatologie*, Ulmer Verlag, Stuttgart.

Seremak-Bulge, J. (1998), 'Zalety i slabosci polskiego rolnictwa', *Zagadnienia Ekonomiki Rolnej*, No. 5-6, Warszawa.

Seremak-Bulge, J. (1999), 'Wyzwania dla polskiego rolnictwa, jakie niesie integracja z UniaEuropojska', *Biuletyn informacyjngi*, 9 , Agencja Rynku Rolnego, Warszawa.

Skawinska, E. (1993), *Regiony problemowe w przekroju Rolniczym, Uniwersytet Mikolaja Kopernika*, Torun.

Smolenski, Z. (1998), 'Przeobrazenia spoldzielni mleczarskich i koncepcje nowych zasad oraz symulacyjne scenariusze rozwoju popytu ipodazy produktow mleczarskich', in E. Skawinska (ed.), *Uwarunkowania rozwoju mleczarstwa polskiego w procesie integrowania Polski z Unia Europejska*, part II, Uniwersytet Mikolaja Kopernika, Torun, pp. 121-138.

Starkel, I. (1991), *Geografia Polski Srodowisko przyrodnicze*, Panstwowe Wydawnictwo Naukowe, Warszawa.

Statistisches Jahrbuch über Ernährung, Landwirtschaft und Forsten, 1998, Landwirtschafts-verlag, Münster-Hiltrup.

Statistitscheskij Jeshegodnik stran-tschlenow SEW (1986), Moskwa, 1986.

Szemberg, A. (1999), 'Mechanizacja indywidualnych gospodarstw rolnych', in A. Wos, (ed), *Analiza produkcyjnoekonomicznej sytuacji rolnictwa i gospodarki zywnosciowejw 1998 roku*, Instytut Ekonomiki Rolnictwa i Gospodarki Zywnosciowej, Warszawa, pp. 203-214.

Szot, E (1995), 'Matka Zywicielka' , *Rzeczpospolita 181*, 16, Warszawa.

United Nations Economic Commission for Europe (1994), *Forest Conditionsin Europe: Results of the 1993 Survey*, 1994 Report, Brussels, Geneva.

Vincentz, V. (1994), *Untersuchungen der Binnenhandelssysteme und Möglichkeiten ihrer marktwirtschaftlichen Ausgestaltung am Beispiel Polen, Tschechische und Slowakische Republik, Ungarn, Russische Föderation und Estland*, Osteuropa- Institut, München.

Wietersheim, V. and Ulatowski W. (1994), 'Polnisches Gesetz über die Privatisierung der Landwirtschaft', *Wirtschaft und Recht in Osteuropa*, 10, Beck-Verlag, München, Frankfurt/M. pp. 383-388.

Wilkin, J. (1990), *The peasant factor in the history of the socialist economy*, unpublished, Warszawa.

Wöhlke, W. (1991), *Länderbericht Polen*, Bundeszentrale für politische Bildung, Bonn.

Wos, A. (1999), 'Makroekonomiczne uwarunkowania rozwoju sektoru zywnoscioweg', in A. Wos (ed.), *Analiza produkcyjno-ekonomicznej systuacji rolnictwa i gospodark zywnosciowej w 1998 roku*, Instytut Ekonomiki Rolnictwa i Gospodarki Zywnoscioej, Warszawa, pp. 1-26.

Zwolinka, M. (1995), personal communication.

14. Romania

DIETER DRÄGER AND TANJA JAKSCH

14.0 Background to the transformation

The transition to democracy and free enterprise in Romania has been riddled with conflict, along with political instability, economic decline and rising inequality. Now, political conditions are gradually stabilizing, and the legislative and executive branches are beginning to establish themselves with some degree of authority. The parliamentary majority has developed and partially implemented a reform plan. Elements of this plan include liberalizing prices and trade, introducing a new tax system, creating private banks, privatizing firms and increasing public fiscal discipline, as required by the IMF and World Bank in exchange for loans.

Table 14.1 shows the degree of economic disruption that occurred in Romania early in the transformation process. GNP has increased after initial sharp declines in 1993 and 1994, when it sank to about 87 percent of the 1989 level. Per capita GNP, measured in terms of inflation-adjusted purchasing power parity, was $2,791 at its lowest point, in 1992, compared with $3,086 in 1984 (Radocea, 1995).

Table 14.1   Changes in selected economic indicators*

Indicator	1989	1990	1991	1992	1993	1994	1998
Gross national product	na	-5.6	-12.9	-13.6	1.3	3.4	-1.6
Gross agricultural product	na	-2.9	1.0	-13.9	12.4	0.2	16.0
Index of agric. production (1979-81 = 100)	98.8	88.2	88.7	72.0	84.0	88.4	91.3
Industrial production	na	na	-22.8	-21.8	1.3	3.3	na
Private consumption, (nominal)	1.3	21.3	na	-17.5	-1.3	8.3	Na
Consumer prices	na	5.1	174.5	210.9	256.1	137	59.1

Note: *Data are percent change over previous year except where noted. *na:* not available.
Source: OstWirtschaftsReport, 2000.

14.1 General setting

Territory, population and administrative structure

Covering 238,391 km², Romania has the largest land area of any country in southeastern Central Europe. Thirty-one percent of the territory is covered by mountains (eastern, southern and western Carpathian Mountains), 36 percent by highlands and hill country (Carpathian foothills, Transilvanian highland, Moldavian plateau, Dobrudscha massif), and 33 percent is covered by lowlands and river plains (Tisza lowland, southern Romanian lowland and the Danube delta) (figure 14.1). The moderate climate allows for a wide array of land uses.

Administratively, Romania is divided into 41 districts, 260 cities and 2,688 rural communities. Each district has an average size of 5,814 km². The average population size of cities is 47,500 residents, compared with 3,876 residents in the average rural community (Radocea, 1995).

Figure 14.1 Regions of Romania

Romania's population has doubled since the beginning of the century. The largest increases occurred between 1950 and 1980, averaging about 200,000 people per year (Südosteuropa aktuell, 1995). In the 1980s, annual population growth averaged 100,000. Since 1990, the population has decreased annually by 150,000 as a result of drastic reductions in natural growth and sharp increases in emigration. In 1998, Romania had a total population of 22.5 million.

In 1950, three-quarters of the population was living in rural areas. This share had dropped to 45.7 percent by 1990, and 45.5 percent by 1993. The absolute decline in the rural population was 1.7 million from 1950 to 1990, or some 14 percent. The urban population increased during this period by 8.5 million or 207 percent. Average population density is 95.7 inhabitants per km² (1993 data), and varies significantly across districts (figure 14.2, table 14.2).

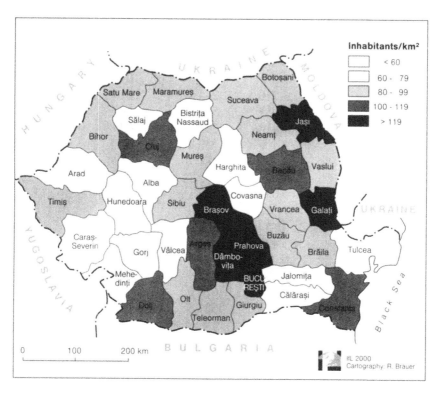

Figure 14.2 Administrative structure and population density

Table 14.2 Area and population by district, 1992

District	Area (km²)	Inhabitants (1,000)	Inhabitants/ km²	Rural population share
Alba	6,242	412.7	66.3	45.0
Arad	7,754	486.8	62.9	48.0
Arge	6,826	679.4	99.8	54.2
Bacau	6,621	739.2	111.4	49.9
Bihor	7,544	638.6	84.7	51.4
Bistrita-Nasaud	5,355	328.0	61.0	63.3
Botosani	4,986	463.2	92.5	60.9
Brasov	5,363	645.0	119.9	23.7
Braila	4,766	393.6	82.3	34.0
Buzau	6,103	517.6	84.7	59.5
Caras-Severin	8,520	375.6	44.2	43.7
Calarasi	5,088	339.8	66.6	60.6
Cluj	6,674	729.0	110.3	32.8
Constanta	7,071	743.0	105.9	26.3
Covasna	3,710	234.5	62.9	47.3
Dâmborita	4,054	560.3	138.6	68.9
Dolj	7,414	761.2	102.8	51.0
Galati	4,466	639.8	143.5	40.4
Giurgiu	3,526	311.7	88.9	69.9
Gorj	5,602	395.7	71.6	58.3
Harghita	6,639	349.1	52.5	54.3
Hunedoara	7,063	549.4	77.6	24.9
Jalomita	4,453	305.6	68.8	59.1
Jasi	5,476	811.7	148.2	49.6
Maramures	6,304	541.7	85.7	47.1
Mehedinti	4,933	332.4	67.4	52.4
Mures	6,714	610.6	90.0	48.7
Neamt	5,896	581.3	98.1	59.6
Olt	5,498	524.8	95.2	61.0
Prahova	4,716	878.5	185.4	47.7
Satu Mare	4,418	401.4	90.7	53.8
Sllaj	3,834	266.8	69.0	59.6
Sibiu	5,432	449.5	83.4	32.0
Suceava	8,553	704.4	82.1	64.4
Teleorman	5,790	484.4	83.6	66.1

Table 14.2 continued

Timis	8,697	691.0	80.5	39.5
Tulcea	8,499	270.7	31.9	51.1
Vaslui	5,318	464.0	86.8	56.2
Vâlcea	5,765	439.1	76.0	61.3
Vrancea	4,857	394.9	81.0	61.3
Municipiul Bucuresti	1,821	2,343.1	1,293.0	11.0
Total	*238,391*	*22,789.0*	*95.7*	*45.7*

Source: Comisia nationala pentru statistica, 'Annarul statistica al Romāniei', various
   years; Hasegann, 1957.

Fourteen districts have a low population density (of fewer than 80
inhabitants/km²), averaging 61 inhabitants/km². These districts cover 35
percent of the territory, and 51 percent of their population is rural. They are
mostly mountainous regions. Another nineteen districts have a medium
population density (80-100 inhabitant/km²), averaging 90 inhabitants/km².
These districts cover 49 percent of the territory and 52 percent of their
population is rural. They include the Carpathian foothills, a part of the
highland areas, and the lowlands.

Eighty districts have a relatively high population density, averaging
187 inhabitants/km². They cover 16 percent of the territory and have a rural
population of 34 percent. These are the regions in central and eastern
Romania with large cities and industrial centers such as Bucharest, Dluj,
Brasov, Iasi and others. Romania's districts are listed in table 14.3 along
with selected characteristics.

Table 14.3 Romania's administrative divisions, 1992

Population size group	Number of communities	%	Inhabitants/ size group	%	Average population per rural community
up to 1,000	36	1.4	26,012	0.2	723
1,000 – 1,999	337	12.5	540,491	5.2	1,604
2,000 – 4,999	1,696	63.1	5,697,520	54.7	3,359
5,000 – 9,999	589	21.9	3,788,158	36.4	6,432
Over 10,000	30	1.1	366,035	3.5	12,201

Source: Comisia nationala pentru statistica, 'Annarul statistica al Romāniei', 1993.

14.2 Agricultural policy

Before 1989, agriculture was subject to a high degree of state control. Large-scale state public enterprises used nearly 70 percent of agricultural inputs. They operated on about 30 percent of the total farmland and managed 50 percent of swine and poultry inventories. Cooperatives farmed another 60 percent of all farmland but used only 21 percent of inputs. Livestock inventories held on these farms included 49 percent of all cattle and 36 percent of all sheep. Family farms used 9 percent of the inputs and farmed about 10 percent of the farmland. Livestock inventories held by family farms included 33 percent of cattle, 29 percent of swine, 47 percent of sheep and 36 percent of poultry stocks (Latzo, 1995).

Since 1989, three key agricultural policy issues have been at the forefront: changing basic conditions in agriculture; using a moderate degree of state intervention to stabilize production; and developing rural villages in such a way that they serve as a social buffer by absorbing workers released from agriculture. Important agricultural policy steps designed to change basic conditions in agriculture include a rapid and thorough restructuring of the centrally planned agricultural sector, promoting the development of small-scale farms and re-privatizing farmland. According to the "land fund law of 1991," land that had been brought into a cooperative during collectivization is to be returned as private property to the original owners or their heirs. Data from 1993 show that 79 percent of those entitled had received their land, but only 3.7 percent were actually provided with documentation that proved their ownership of the land.

The large amount of time needed to reorganize and implement rights to the land is a major hindrance in the restructuring of farms, because family farms are presently so small (about 2 ha each) that any operations seeking to achieve an efficient scale need to buy or lease additional land. The fragmentation of land ownership under privatisation is largely responsible for the small size of these units. Along with traditional small-scale farms and family farms, many new forms of cooperatives have emerged either out of former cooperative farms or as newly created entities. In 1998, private farms accounted for 72 percent of total agricultural area and 84 percent of arable land. The remaining land is state property and is presently used primarily by state farms that have yet to be privatized. The private sector accounts for an estimated 63 percent of crop and 37 percent of livestock production.

Now, vibrant but mostly unregulated leasing activity is starting to allow the consolidation of some of the land, even though an official land register or market for land do not exist at this time. Leasing activity is expanding because the lack of capital makes it impossible for most farmers to purchase land outright. In this changing agricultural structure, corporate farms hold an important position. They include former state farms, so-called "mechanization stations," which under socialism leased out or repaired agricultural equipment, and firms that constructed and maintained irrigation or drainage facilities. These corporations are still state-owned and operated, but they are targeted for takeover by private large-scale agricultural enterprises.

The process of agricultural change has resulted in a dominating share of very small farms, which produce food for own-consumption needs. The agricultural policy vision is for a plural structure to develop, in which family farms, cooperative farms and large private farms co-exist, but where large farms produce and market a larger share of the total than is currently the case. These large farms will include former state farms with relatively modern equipment for producing wine, poultry and hogs (Dumitru, 1994).

Structural changes in the agricultural input supply and food marketing industries lag far behind those occurring at the farm-level. Here, state enterprises continue to dominate, often monopolizing purchasing and sales and setting prices. The Romanian government expects privatization based on *coupons* distributed to individuals to accelerate structural change in the food system and to increase agricultural sales.

Today, the government considers support of agriculture to be a primary economic and political concern. A short-term goal is to eliminate food shortages, while longer-term goals include self-sufficiency and expanded agricultural exports. An annual government plan announces application rates established by public agencies for agricultural chemicals and, even today, sets agricultural production targets along with guidelines for providing subsidies and interest rates on loans.

In the 1970s and 1980s, individuals working on their own farms or in the cooperative sector suffered economically because the government supported only the state farm sector. Low income, hard manual labor and lack of infrastructure investment all contributed to a rural exodus and an imbalance in the demographic structure. The policy of "systemizing the territory" was particularly disastrous. This included concentrating the rural population in central villages and "agro-cities," often through forced resettlement. Between 6,000 and 8,000 villages were to be forcibly evacuated, but these plans were quickly dropped following the demise of Ceaucescu's dictatorship in 1989.

In 1993, 10.4 million people or 45.5 percent of the population lived in rural areas. Statistics reveal their relatively poor standards of living: only 14.3 percent of living quarters had external or internal water supply, only 10 percent were connected to external or internal sewage systems, and only 2 percent had central heating. Over 400,000 rural inhabitants still do not have electricity. Poor and crumbling rural infrastructure is an important reason why not more urban families have left cities to return to rural areas.

Distinct change has occurred in the social structure of the rural population. As noted above, the re-privatization of land, often with multiple heirs, has fragmented agricultural plots. Over 50 percent of the private land belongs to retirees, people living in cities or people not involved in agriculture. The average area of land owned by this group is only about 1.5 ha per owner (Eurostat, 1999).

The private farms that existed even during the Ceaucescu regime own nearly 1.5 million ha of land, with an average of 4 ha per farm. The dominant rural social group is, therefore, the small-scale private farm. Their production is primarily intended for own-consumption rather that for market sales. Along with small-scale farms, many families have been forced to become engaged in agriculture to meet their own consumption needs, even though they had lived in cities and lack previous farming experience (many of these are retirees). Unlike the situation in the US, where off-farm employment is widespread, there are very few non-farm jobs in rural areas of Romania, and the number of non-farm workers living in rural areas has historically been negligible.

These changes in the social structure are part of the transitions occurring during the transformation process. However, the many small and fragmented farms are inconsistent with the type of modernization needed to increase incomes, productivity and investments in rural areas. New policies and strategies are needed that create jobs in a more diversified rural economy that is not exclusively based on agriculture.

14.3 Land use

Land use statistics do not reveal the tremendous structural changes that have occurred in the last decades. The share of land used agriculturally has ranged between 61 and 63 percent since 1960, while the share of wooded land increased from 27 to 28 percent. The share of land covered by water increased from 3 to 3.8 percent as a result of the construction of dams and canals, mostly affecting areas that were not previously used for farming or forestry. Other uses of land that have expanded include construction, roads and mining.

In Romania, the most pronounced changes in land use occurred in the second half of the 19th Century, and the first half of the 20th Century. One-hundred and fifty years ago forests, primarily oak and spruce, covered 60 percent of Romania's current territory. Before World War II, extensive wood exports led to deforestation along rivers, and in hills and lowlands, resulting in fundamental changes in the landscape and land structure. The largest share of these deforested areas was used for agricultural purposes, especially as arable land, a substantial part became covered with shrubs, and only a small portion was replanted.

In the mid 19th Century, about 2 million ha of land were used for farming. By 1916, this number had grown to 6 million, and by 1938 it was 9.4 million ha. The share of grain farming was as high as 90 percent of the total arable land in some periods. This one-sided use of agricultural land was the result of highly profitable grain exports. Along with wood and grain exports, the sale of crude oil gained importance early in the 20th Century. Exports of natural resources earned sizeable profits for landowners and foreign investors, which were generally not reinvested locally and the mostly rural population remains impoverished.

Changes in the organization of agriculture, industrialization and state development of natural resources reduced some of these economic and social concerns after 1945. Increasing centralization and undemocratic leadership soon reversed these positive developments, however. We mention these developments here because the reform processes underway since 1989 operate, and have to be viewed, in the context of this historical legacy. Table 14.4 shows current land use patterns.

Table 14.4 Land use in Romania, 1992

Type of area	1,000 ha	percent
Territory	23,839.1	100.0
Arable land area	14,790.1	62.0
Wooded area	6,681.8	28.0
Water area	892.8	3.8
Built-up area	630.5	2.6
Roads	393.4	1.7
Other	450.5	1.9
Protected areas*	1,250.3	5.2
Preserves	402.3	3.0
National parks	396.8	1.6
Nature reserves	151.2	0.6

Note: *The protected areas are included in the areas listed above.

Source: Comisia nationala pentru statistica, 1995.

Regional differences in agricultural and forested areas are considerable. In the lowlands and highlands, agricultural use dominates, mostly in the form of farming. The Carpathian mountains are mainly used for forestry. Sixty percent of total forested area is located here, a further 30 percent is in the highlands and hill country, and 10 percent in the lowlands. Tree inventories include 31 percent beech, 31 percent conifers and 18 percent oak.

In official Romanian statistics, three types of forested land area are distinguished: Existing forests and other areas with forest vegetation (for example protected forest strips); land containing wooded areas that are being prepared for forestation as well as other areas used for forestry; and wooded areas including tree and shrub forests that are not harvested. These areas measured, respectively, 6,681, 6,367 and 6,249 thousand ha in 1993.

Forestry output has declined since 1990. In 1993, reforested area was only 10,347 ha, a reduction of 75 percent compared to 1989. Forest maintenance activity declined by 40 percent during this period, as fewer resources were available for such efforts. A total of 13.6 million m³ of timber was harvested in 1993, representing 5.9 million m³ or 30 percent less than in 1989. Even so, forestry remains an important sector in Romania, employing some 77,000 people. Along with the production of raw materials and fuel, the regeneration and care as well as the expansion of forests in the south and southeast of Romania are likely to become more important.

Agricultural land use

Table 14.5 shows patterns of agricultural land use since 1989. The historically largest amount of farmland was measured in 1987, at 15.09 million ha, or 63 percent of the total territory. This represented an increase of 540,000 ha over 1960. In just two years (1987-89), farmland area declined by 330,000 ha, as a result of the dramatic changes leading up to the political upheavals of 1989. These included the forced relocation and concentration of people to rural "cities" by the communist party, which adversely affected the use of farmland. Since then, the amount of farmland has once again increased slightly.

Arable land makes up 63 percent of agricultural land or 39.2 percent of the territory. After a slight increase between 1960 and 1986, the amount of arable land fell to 9.46 million ha in 1989, and it has since declined further by 122,000 ha.

Orchard and vineyards cover 4 percent of arable land. By the mid-1970s these areas had extended to over 760,000 ha, falling continuously thereafter until 1990. By 1993, however, the area had again expanded by 9,000 ha. Permanent pasture covers 33 percent of farmland area, and has changed only minimally over the decades.

Table 14.5 Patterns of farmland use

	1989		1990		1992		1998	
Land Use	1,000 ha	%	1,000 ha	%	1,000 ha	%	1,000 ha	%
Farmland	14,759	100	14,769	100	14,790	100	14,789	100
Arable land	9,458	64.1	9,450	64.0	9,357	63.3	9,336	63.1
Orchards & vineyards	596	4.0	591	4.0	603	4.1	--	--
Meadows	1,448	9.8	1,465	9.9	1,481	10.0	4,899*	33.1*
Pastures	3,257	22.1	3,263	22.1	3,349	22.6	--	--

Note: * Meadows and pastures combined.

Source: Comisia nationala pentru statistica, 'Informaţii statitice operative', various years; ZMP, 1999*a, b.*

Romania has a balanced variety of production conditions due to its topography, soil types and climate, giving a country of this size an unusually broad spectrum of farming possibilities. The territory can be divided into three land use zones, based on simplified topographical divisions.

Lowlands (up to 200 m elev): These include the Muntenia, Oltenia, the Danubian Delta, the Tisza Plain, several valley basins and waterlogged meadows. The primary soil varieties are black earth and brown forest soils. The average annual temperature is 10°C in the southern lowlands and 8°C in the northern and western lowlands. An average of 450 mm of precipitation fall in the south and southeast, although droughts are common in the summer and early fall. In other lowland areas with precipitation levels of 500 to 600 mm, droughts are less frequent.

Arable land dominates in the lowlands. In some districts of Muntenia, arable land makes up 95 percent of the agricultural land, and over 80 percent of the total territory. In areas with greater rainfall, permanent pastures increase from the southwest to the northwest, with the share of arable land amounting to over 70 percent.

Highland and hill country (200 to 800 m elev.): This group includes the large areas of the Transylvanian highlands, the Moldavian plateau and the Carpathian foothills. The predominant soil varieties are podsols and brown forest soils. Average annual temperature is between 7 and 8 °C, and precipitation is 600 to 700 mm. The share of arable land ranges from 50 to 70 percent. The share of pastures is also high -40 percent in Transylvania and the Carpathian foothills, and 30 percent on the Moldavian plateau.

Vineyards and orchards cover an above-average area in the Carpathian foothills.

Mountains (above 800 m elev.): These are the east, south and west Carpathian mountains. The major soil varieties are skeletal-podsols. The region has an average annual temperature of 5 to 6 °C and average annual rainfall of 900 to 1,000 mm, providing sufficient conditions for agriculture except in the high mountains. Pastures dominate the agricultural structure. Farming is widespread in the lower elevations and in river valleys.

Table 14.6 characterizes regional land use patterns in selected districts. The applicability of this data is limited because each district's territory is not always identical to the characteristic landscape. This grouping also does not take economic and demographic factors into account. Despite these limitations, the obvious structural differences reveal a tendency towards adapting land use to local natural conditions. The question remains, however, whether this adaptation is optimal from a socioeconomic or ecological point of view.

Table 14.6   Regional land use characteristics, in percent, 1997

	Territorial share		Share of agricultural land		
Landscape/District	Arable land	Forested area	Farm-land	Meadows & pastures	Vineyards & orchards
Lowlands					
Timis	81	13	77.2	20.7	2.1
Dolj	79	11	82.3	12.1	5.5
Calarasi	85	4	97.7	1.1	1.2
Highlands					
Mures	61	32	55.4	42.9	2.7
Jasi	69	18	66.2	28.0	5.8
Prahova	59	32	52.6	37.3	10.2
Mountains					
Suceava	41	53	51.9	46.7	1.4
Covasna	50	45	46.5	52.8	0.7
Caras-Severin	47	48	29.6	66.5	3.9

Source: Comisia nationala pentru statistica, 'Informaţii statitice operative', 1998.

Arable land use

Depending on the crop, patterns of arable land use have fluctuated notably over time (table 14.7). From 1989 to 1992, area planted fell by more than 900,000 ha (about 10 percent) as a result of land privatization and the break-up of collective farms. By 1994, the area had increased by 311,000 ha. Since 1990, area planted consistently lay below arable land area by 2.4 percent and substantial changes have occurred in cropping patterns.

Table 14.7   Area planted to different crops, in percent

Crop	1989	1990	1991	1992	1993	1994
Grains, legumes	64.4	62.1	66.7	65.6	70.5	71.9
Industrial crops	15.7	9.7	9.9	11.9	9.2	9.0
Potatoes, vegetables and melons	6.5	5.8	5.2	5.5	.6	.4
Feed crops	11.7	20.7	16.9	16.2	14.2	13.6
Other	1.7	1.7	1.3	0.8	0.5	0.1
Total	100.0	100.0	100.0	100.0	100.0	100.0

Source: Comisia nationala pentru statistica, 'Informaţii statitice operative', 1995.

An increase over time in the share of grains and legumes is evident along with a fall in the share of industrial crops, feed crops, vegetables, and potatoes. Absolute amounts of areas planted to different crops are shown in table 14.8.

Table 14.8   Area planted to different crops, 1,000 ha

	Average 1989-1991	Average 1992-1994
Arable land	9,444	9,347
Planted area	9,482	9,098
Grains, legumes	6,101	6,310
Industrial crops	1,123	898
Potatoes, vegetables, melons	548	498
Feed crops	1,554	1,334
Other	156	58

Note: Area planted may exceed farmland area due to multiple cropping within a year.

Source: Comisia nationala pentru statistica, 'Informaţii statitice operative', 1995.

The increase in grains accounted for only a third of the decrease in the other crops; the other two-thirds were caused by a reduction in area planted. Crop combinations varied greatly as well, although they do reveal certain trends. The share of corn has increased in the grains and legume category (see table 14.9). Area planted to corn increased in absolute terms from 2,592 ha (1989-1991 average) to 3,144 ha (1992-1994 average). Recently, an average of 50 percent of grains area and 35 percent of all farmland was planted with corn, indicating its dominant role in the country's overall crop production.

Table 14.9 Grains and legume cropping patterns, in percent

Crop	1989	1990	1991	1992	1993	1994
Corn	43.1	42.3	42.0	57.1	47.5	45.7
Wheat and rye	37.2	39.4	36.2	25.3	35.7	37.1
Barley	12.1	12.8	16.6	10.8	9.9	12.0
Oats	1.7	2.5	3.4	5.2	5.6	-
Rice	0.8	0.7	0.4	0.3	0.2	-
Beans	3.1	1.2	0.8	0.8	0.5	-
Peas	1.5	0.9	0.6	0.4	0.5	-
Other	0.5	0.2	-	0.1	0.1	-
Total	*100.0*	*100.0*	*100.0*	*100.0*	*100.0*	*100.0*

Source: ZMP, various years.

With the exception of sunflowers, area cultivated to all industrial crops declined, especially fiber-crops, tobacco, soybeans and rapeseed. Sugar beet planting was also reduced. The planting of sunflowers rose from 435,000 ha (1989-1991 average) to 595,000 ha (1992-1994 average), reaching 66 percent of total planted area to industrial crops. Shares of other crops were: soybeans 11.4 percent, sugar beet 15.1 percent, medicinal and aroma crops 3.5 percent, fiber crops 1.5 percent, other oil and fiber crops and tobacco 2.5 percent.

In the group comprising potatoes, vegetables, and melons, the share of vegetables and melons rose, taking area away from potatoes. The average planted area for these crops was 239,000 ha of potatoes or 48 percent of the total, 215,000 ha of vegetables or 43 percent, and 44,000 ha of melons or 9 percent. In vegetable farming, 23 percent of the land went to tomatoes, 16 percent to dry onions, 16 percent to cabbage, 10 percent to bell peppers and 35 percent to a variety of other vegetables.

Cultivation of feed crops rose during the 1980s, but started to decline in 1991. In 1994, after a dramatic decline in livestock inventories (table 14.10), production still lay above the 1980s average.

The share of clover and other legumes, as well as one- and multi-year grasses, rose by 9 percentage points to 80 percent of the primary area allocated to feed crops (1992-1993). The share of silage, primarily corn, and feed beets consequently fell to 20 percent. Due to significantly varying local conditions, various farming patterns and concentrations have emerged for different crops or crop groups in certain areas (see tables 14.11 and 14.12).

**Table 14.10 Cropping patterns of crops used as livestock feed
(1,000 ha)**

Crop	1989	1990	1991	1992	1993
Field crops	1,149	1,962	1,552	1,442	1,305
multi-year grasses	665	814	823	706	722
Meadows	1,448	1,465	1,468	1,481	1,489
Pastures	3,257	3,263	3,310	3,349	3,363
Grains used for feed (GF)	5,854	6,690	6,330	6,272	6,157
GF/arable land (%)	39.7	45.3	42.8	42.4	41.6
Permanent pasture/GF (%)	80.4	70.7	75.5	77.0	78.8

Source: ZMP, various years.

Table 14.11 Cropping patterns in selected districts

Landscape/District	Crop group share of the planted area				
	Grains, legumes	Industrial crops	Potatoes, vege-tables, melons	Feed crops	Other
Lowlands					
Timis	69.3	9.9	4.3	15.7	0.8
Dolj	76.2	9.4	4.9	8.8	0.7
Calarasi	69.2	17.0	2.3	10.4	1.1
Highlands					
Mures	73.6	1.3	5.9	16.6	2.5
Jasi	67.3	5.1	5.5	21.7	0.4
Prahova	78.0	4.8	5.4	10.9	0.4
Mountains					
Suceava	48.2	2.9	18.3	30.3	0.3
Covasna	42.5	2.6	19.3	35.2	0.4
Caras-Severin	74.2	3.0	5.9	16.4	0.5

Source: Comisia nationala pentru statistica, 'Agricultura si silvicultura României
1980-1993', 1995.

To illustrate, corn is grown in every district of the country, while production is concentrated in the Moldavian plateau, the southern Romanian lowlands, the Tisza plain and the Dobrudsha. Fifty percent of the corn is grown in 13 districts. The same is true for concentrations of wheat. Barley and oats are concentrated in the Carpathian mountains, the Transilvanian highlands, and the Tisza plain. Legume farming is concentrated in the Moldavian plateau, the Dobrudsha, and in the southeastern Romanian lowlands. Concentrations of soybean production are also found here, while sunflower production (figure 14.3) stretches over the entire southern Romanian lowlands, where it makes up an above-average share of the cropping pattern.

Table 14.12 Share of planted area of selected crop groups, 1993

Crop	Share of the national average (percent)	Districts with above-average shares (in percent)
Corn	33.5	Vaslui 44, Mehediuţi 41, Botoşani 37, Galaţi 37
Wheat, Rye	25.2	Mehediuţi 35, Dolj 34, Olt 34, Galaţi 31
Barley	7.0	Covasna 17, Harghita 16, Mureş 13, Timiş 12
Sunflowers	6.4	Teleorman 14, Jalomiţa 12, Călăraşi 12, Constanţa 12
Soy beans	0.8	Călăraşi 4, Brăila 3, Botoşani 2
Sugar beet	1.1	Botoşani 2.4, Jaşi 2.3; Mureş 2.3; Bistriţa-Năsăud 2.3
Potatoes	2.7	Covasna 17, Harghita 17, Maramureş 15, Suceava 15
Vegetables	2.4	Municipial Bucureşti 6, Valcea 5, Hunedora 5, Dâmboviţa 4, Gorj 4
Feed crops	14.2	Covasna 35, Braşov 33, Harghita 31, Suceava 30

Source: Comisia nationala pentru statistica, 'Agricultura si silvicultura României 1980-1993', 1995.

Concentrations of sugar beet farming occur in the northern and northwestern highland regions as well as in the Tisza plain and the southeast of the country. Potato farming (figure 14.4) is concentrated in arable regions of the Carpathian mountains, the Carpathian foothills and in Transylvania, amounting to 60 percent of the potato area. Concentrations of horticultural crops can be found in foothills of the southern Carpathian mountains, Oltenia and the Tisza plain. Production of feed for livestock uses an above-average share of land in districts of the Carpathian mountains and the Transylvanian highlands.

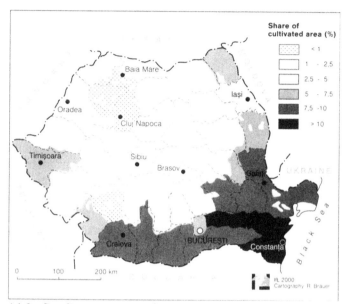

Figure 14.3   Sunflower production patterns

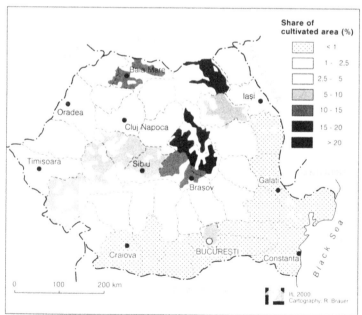

Figure 14.4   Potato production patterns

Livestock production

As is true in the other transformation countries, livestock production has gone through tremendous changes (tables 14.13 and 14.14). Sheep inventories alone fell by 5 million, or almost one third, from 1991 to 1998. The downward trend continued in 1998, mostly affecting inventory growth. For the next five years, average yearly increases of 1 percent for cattle and 4 percent for poultry are expected.

Within the livestock production sector, only milk output increased substantially between 1989 and 1998. By 1998, 25 percent more milk was produced than in 1990. The main source of this growth has been a sustained increase in yields, from 2,200 in 1990 to 3,203 kg/cow in 1998. Meat production, on the other hand, declined during the same period by about 30 percent. Within the meat production sector, pork ranked at the top with 53 percent.

Table 14.13 Production of livestock and livestock products

	1989	1990	1991	1992	1993	1994	1998
Head/per 100 ha farmland	63.8	59.2	54.1	49.5	43.7	42.0	--
Meat production kg/capita	65.2	70.5	68.7	58.8	57.5	54.9	52.9
Milk production kg/capita	197.4	222.5	201.1	180.7	173.6	172.8	246.0

Source: ZMP, various years.

The generally low output of the livestock sector is evident from per capita production data. Averages for 1997-98 were 52.9 kg of meat (slaughter weight), 246 liters of milk, 227 eggs, and 0.97 kg of wool. Food intake in Romania is also relatively low by European standards. Food products derived from livestock covered only 22 percent of actual average daily consumption in Romania of 2,597 kcal in 1996-1997.

14.4 Outlook

Romania is one of Europe's underdeveloped regions. Food industry products make up 9 percent of all exports and while this industry figures prominently in the Romanian government's goal of reaching the country's full industrial potential, it has so far failed to play a significant role. Low productivity, inability to meet international quality standards, low capacity utilization, and poor locational choices that have resulted in higher costs of goods have become obvious problems during the drastic recent changes following political and economic reforms (European Commission, 1998).

As market reforms continue, simply privatizing the economy and liberalizing trade are not sufficient. Policy directed at raising the competitiveness of Romanian agriculture and the food industry is urgently needed. This includes encouraging technological modernization and addressing questions of optimal size structure of farms (Probst, 1996).

There are two paths for achieving the concentration of land that is needed to assure efficient operation of farms: through cooperatives in which farmers presently work 12 percent of the land with an average area per farm of 451 ha, or through informal mergers of family farms that share agricultural implements and attempt to achieve economies of scale, without having any particular legal status. The latter group is eligible to participate in public programs designed to support individual farms, and they currently work 8 percent of the arable land and average 103 ha per farm. Fully 68 percent of the arable land area is under the control of small family farms that have emerged after the state and collective farms were dissolved.

State farms work the remaining 12 percent of the arable land with an average area of 3,657 ha per farm. These include large-scale industrial complexes for livestock production, which are not unlike confined animal feeding operations (CAFOs) in the US.

Romania's Law no. 54/98 created a legal foundation for the establishment of a land market, and it includes regulations governing lease arrangements. According to this relatively new law, family farms (which currently average 5 ha each) can purchase up to 200 ha of land. However, because family farms have virtually no access to credit and remain strapped for capital, land purchases are expected to increase only slowly.

Table 14.14 Livestock production in Romania

Commodity	1991	1993	1994	1995	1996	1997	1998
Total meat production (1,000 t slaughter weight)[a]	1,539	1,405	1,374	1,220	1,261	1,249	1,131
Meat consumption	1,545	1,364	1,322	1,236	1,238	-	-
Cattle							
Inventory (incl. buffalo)	5,381	3,683	3,597	3,481	3,496	3,436	3,303
incl. dairy cows	1,893	1,806	1,792	1,784	1,798	1,769	1,826
Beef and buffalo meat production (1,000 t sw)[b]	205	252	258	227	229	223	183
Swine							
Inventory (1,000 head)	12,003	9,852	9,262	7,758	7,960	8,235	7,273
incl. breeding sows	951	972	678	576	590	584	529
Pork production (1,000 t sw)	850	808	768	718	729	684	624
Sheep							
Inventory (1,000 head)	14,062	12,079	11,499	10,897	10,381	9,663	8,938
Milk production (1,000 t)	405	420	393	396	376	371	--
Wool per sheep (kg)	--	2	2	2	2	2	--
Wool (1,000 t)	35.5	26.0	25.1	24.3	23.2	21.6	20.3
Goats							
Inventory (1,000 head)	1,005	805	776	745	705	654	610
Milk production (1,000 t)	4,312	1,031	968	945	882	--	--
Poultry/eggs							
Total inventory (1,000 head)	--	87,725	76,532	70,157	80,524	78,478	68,915
incl. layers	--	--	37,981	36,233	38,574	38,883	30,421

Table 14.14 continued

Commodity	1991	1993	1994	1995	1996	1997	1998
Geese	4,500	4,500	4,400	4,300	4,200	4,200	4,200
Ducks	--	4,800	4,600	4,500	4,500	4,500	4,500
Turkeys	950	900	900	900	500	900	900
Poultry (slaughter; 1,000 t sw							
Exports (1,000 t)	282	301	269	277	293	254	258
Imports (1,000 t)	1.2	3.1	5.0	0.9	0.9	--	--
Yield per hen	32.0	36.8	39.0	24.1	3.2	--	--
Production (million)							
incl. eggs	7,177	5,633	5,407	5,567	5,783	5,117	--
Milk							
Milk production/cow (kg)	6,659	5,316	5,091	5,263	5,459	--	--
Cow milk production (1,000 t)	2,203	2,440	2,848	3,034	3,096	3,116	3,204
Horses	4,312	4,486	5,066	5,424	5,488	5,,360	5,425
Inventory (1,000 head)	670	721	751	784	806	816	825

Notes: [a] Includes poultry and innards
[b] Includes innards

Source: ZMP, 1999a, b.

References

Comisia nationala pentru statistica (various years), *Informaţii statitice operative*, seria agricultura, Bucureşti.

Comisia nationala pentru statistica (various years), *Annarul statistica al Romănie'*, Bucureşti.

Comisia nationala pentru statistica (1995), *Agricultura si silvicultura Romăniei 1980-1993*, Bucureşti.

European Commission, D6 VI Working document (1998), *Agricultural Situation and Prospects in the Central European Countries – Romania*, Brussels.

Eurostat, Themenkreis 3 (1999), *Beschäftigung und Arbeitsmarkt in den Ländern Mitteleuropas: Länderprofil Rumänien, Brüssel.*

Dumitru, D. (1994), 'Process formirovanija novoi agrarnoi struktury v Rumynii', *Agrarnye preobrazonanija: opyt i perspektivy*, Materialy meždunarodnoj konferencii, 3.-5. ijunja 1993, Orel.

Hasegann, M. (1957), *Geografia ewkonomică a Republicii Populare Romine*, Bucureşti.

Latzo, A. (1995), 'Aspekte der Entwicklung in Rumänien', *Berliner Europa-Forum*, Sonderheft III, pp. 14-18.

Operative Informationen der Nationalen Kommission für Statistik, in http://www.cns.ro/Indicatori/

OstWirtschaftsReport, No. 3, February 11, 2000, Düsseldorf.

Probst, J. (1996), *Rumänien, Wirtschaftstrends zum Jahreswechsel 1995/1996*, Länderreport der Bundesstelle für Außenhandelsinformation, Berlin.

Radocea, N. (1995), 'Romania – Stadiul actual al dezvoltării economice şi sociale', *Revista Romana de statistica*, Statistisches Bundesamt, Länderbericht Rumänien, Wiesbaden, pp. 1-138.

Südosteuropa aktuell (1995), *Der Wandel des ländlichen Raums in Südosteuropa*, -123 pp, München.

Zentrale Markt- und Preisberichtsstelle GmbH (ZMP) (1993), *Agrarmärkte Osteuropa*, Bonn.

Zentrale Markt- und Preisberichtsstelle GmbH (ZMP) (1995), *Agrarmärkte Osteuropa*, Bonn.

Zentrale Markt- und Preisberichtsstelle GmbH (ZMP) (1998), *Agrarmärkte Osteuropa*, Bonn.

Zentrale Markt- und Preisberichtsstelle GmbH (ZMP) (1999a), *Agrarmärkte in Zahlen. Mittel- und Osteuropa 1999, Tier- und Pflanzenproduktion 1999*, Bonn.

Zentrale Markt- und Preisberichtsstelle GmbH (ZMP) (1999b), *Agrarmärkte Osteuropa*, Bonn.

Zentrale Markt- und Preisberichtsstelle GmbH (ZMP) (2000), *Agrarmärkte Osteuropa*, Bonn.

Zentrale Markt- und Preisberichtsstelle GmbH (ZMP) (1998), *Vieh- und Fleischwirtschaft in Osteuropa*, Bonn.

15. Slovakia

TANJA JAKSCH

15.0 Background to the transformation

After Slovakia (or the Slovak Republic) became an independent state, and the former Soviet currency union was dissolved, macroeconomic developments were less favorable than in the neighboring Czech Republic. A new government was elected in 1998, and a four party ruling coalition was subsequently formed, which included the former opposition. This coalition inherited more difficulties than expected. New data show that state finances and the economy in general were in even worse shape than was previously known.

Slovakia's international reputation is based on images of an authoritarian government, the meshing of politics and economics, as well as discrimination against Hungarian minorities. Political and economic instability over the next few years could further damage the country's image. Since 1998, GNP growth has slowed and domestic price stability has faltered. Exchange rates are no longer fixed, the value of the Slovakian Crown (Sk) has declined by 12 percent and food prices have escalated. The rate of inflation has risen to 8.1 percent, and the jobless rate increased last year to 14 percent (OstWirtschaftsReport, 2000).

The new Slovakian government considers the goals of stemming economic decline, joblessness and the fiscal deficit; privatizing the banking sector; and investigating and reversing "illegal" privatization activities to be of primary importance. Opening the country to foreign capital is seen as a first step in reaching these goals. In the near term, however, a further slowing of GNP growth is expected, along with a rise in the jobless rate and higher rates of inflation (Jaksch et al., 1996; Ost-West-Contact, various years).

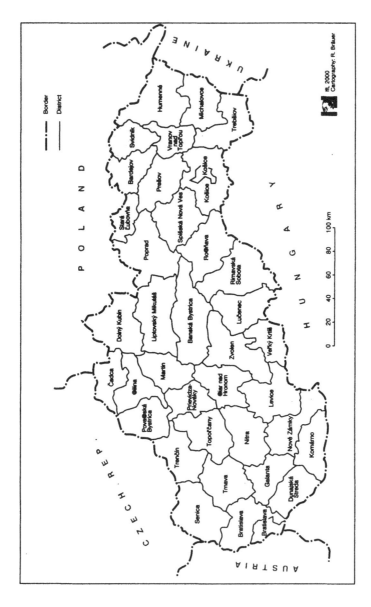

Figure 15.1 Administrative districts

15.1 General setting

Geography and climate

Slovakia lies east of the line formed by Znaim, Brünn and Ostravia. It has an alpine mountain range, stretching from the Little Carpathian Mountains to the Low and High Tatra, the Slovakian Ore Mountains and the Forest Carpathian Mountains. Slovakia has a share of the Hungarian plain in the Little Alföld, in the southern Carpathian foothills. Climate is mostly continental. The Little Alföld has a relatively mild climate with average annual temperatures of 11°C. Yearly precipitation climbs to 2,000 mm in the mountains, and averages 900 mm in the central region, which is some 400 mm above annual precipitation in the western and eastern regions.

Administrative structure and population

Slovakia was formed in 1993, following the separation of the Czech and Slovak Federal Republics. The 5.4 million inhabitants are distributed over 49,035 km²; 83.6 percent are of Slovakian nationality. At 12 percent, Hungarians make up the largest minority population. Average population density is 108 inhabitants/km². Central Slovakia is the most sparsely populated part of the country, with fewer than 90 inhabitants/km². Administratively, Slovakia is divided into 38 districts (figure 15.1).

15.2 Agriculture

Selected indicators of the general economic climate facing agriculture are reported in table 15.1. In 1997, agriculture contributed 4.4 percent of GNP (4.8 percent including forestry, fishing, and hunting) and employed 8.9 percent of the total workforce of 183,000. Agricultural production (based on constant 1995 prices) was 56.05 billion Sk (down 1.0 percent from the previous year), with crop production making up 41.6 and livestock production 58.4 percent of total output.

In 1998, total proceeds and profits from agriculture fell 3.5 percent relative to 1997 levels, largely as a result of low producer prices for crops, especially grains. Agricultural sector losses increased in 1998, and only about 55 percent of farms earned profits, compared with 58 percent a year earlier. Joint stock companies and limited liability corporations had relatively favorable returns, with 77.2 percent reporting a profit. Only 43.5 percent of cooperative farms could make the same claim (ZMP, 1999; Agra Food East Europae, various years).

Table 15.1 Selected economic indicators

Indicator	1990	1991	1995	1998
GDP over previous year (%)	3.5*	-16.3	6.5	4.4
Jobless rate (%)	0.8	11.8	13.1	14.0
Foreign trade balance, mn. $	-342.0	-324.0	93.0	-2,170.0

Note: * Data for Czechoslovakia.

Source: ZMP, 1994; 1995; 1999; Bundesstelle für Außenhandelsinformation (bfai), 1993.

Bohemia and Moravia were among the highly developed industrial areas of Europe, while Slovakia was an underdeveloped agrarian region of the first Czechoslovakian Republic (1918 to 1938). Widespread industrialization in the Slovakian part of the country was launched only after 1948, and then only the sectors important to COMECON were promoted. Industrialization efforts in Slovakia concentrated on weapons and heavy machinery manufacturing, which are sectors with limited prospects today. Between 1948 and 1989, 13.8 percent of the workforce moved out of agriculture. While 34 percent of the workforce was employed in agriculture and forestry in 1960, this share had fallen to 14 percent by 1991.

In 1989, Slovakia had 633 cooperatives and 68 state farms, with the latter on average farming twice the area farmed by cooperatives (table 15.2). The process of privatization began in 1990, as it did in the Czech Republic. Since then, 986 new agricultural enterprises have been created, including cooperative farms, joint stock companies and limited liability corporations. In terms of output and area, state and cooperative farms continue to dominate the agricultural sector, although the number of private farms has expanded dramatically (Wolz and Blaas, 1998).

Large-scale farms were sub-divided and adapted to local conditions during privatization. As in the Czech Republic, little incentive or desire exists under current conditions for rural households to rely on farming as their main source of income, although 71.2 percent of the agricultural workforce owns farmland as a result of restitution. There are presently about 21,700 individual small farms, covering 7 percent of total farmland, and consisting mostly of fragmented plots used for subsistence farming. Only 7,500 family farms are considered to be commercial ventures (Filip and Schinke, 1994).

Table 15.2   Changes in enterprises numbers and sizes by legal form

Legal form	1989 Number	1989 Average size (ha)	1997 Number	1997 Average size (ha)
Cooperative farms	633	2,654	977	1,732
State farms	68	5,162	72	5,729
Private farms	2,000	-	7,585	15.0

Source: Filip and Schinke, 1994; ZMP, 1999.

15.3   Land use

Overall land use in Slovakia has largely remained unchanged during the last decade. The share of farmland is almost 50 percent, while that of forested area is 40.5 percent.

Table 15.3   Land use, in hectares

	1990	1995	1998
Farmland	2,448,600	2,446,000	2,443,000
Arable land	1,509,500	1,483,000	1,473,000
Meadows and pastures	831,000*	835,000	843,000

Note: *1992

Source: Statisticka rocenka slovenske respubliky, 1991, 1993; ZMP 1995, 1999.

Agricultural land use

Agricultural land use includes a high percentage of forest and small grain areas in central Slovakia, a dominant farming center in western Slovakia, and primary grazing areas along with wine and tobacco regions in eastern Slovakia.

Structure of agricultural land use

Since the 1970s, changes in farmland in Slovakia have varied by region. Farmland in the region around Bratislava increased by 37 percent while it declined by 3 to 8 percent in other regions.

Uses of arable land have changed accordingly. While the amount of arable land decreased in central and eastern Slovakia by about 80,000 ha each, it increased by 20 percent in the Bratislava region (table 15.4).

Table 15.4 Changes in arable and farmland use by region in ha, 1970-1990

Region	Ratio of farmland / arable land		
	1970	1980	1990
Bratislava	12,500 / 10,500	17,900 / 13,300	17,100 / 12,800
Western Slovakia	984,700 / 820,300	963,900 / 814,800	956,000 / 812,000
Central Slovakia	870,700 / 368,400	746,900 / 286,800	740,900 / 283,700
Eastern Slovakia	823,800 / 483,500	748,000 / 401,300	734,500 / 400,900

Source: Statisticka rocenka slovenske respubliky, 1991.

Crop production

Many farming trends of previous years continued in 1998. Area planted to grain expanded (except for corn which saw a reduction of 19 percent), as did planting of oil seed–mostly sunflowers and rapeseed. As in previous years, the decline in area planted to potatoes and legumes continued, and for the first time this was coupled with a dramatic reduction of sugar beet area–by 10,000 ha or almost 21 percent of area planted in 1990.

Yields and output of sunflowers and legumes have increased while the stabile year-to-year rise in corn yields was not sustained. Legumes production has stabilized, and small increases in area cultivated, yield and quantity harvested were expected for the main crops of peas and beans in 1999 (Manegold, 2000).

Whether or not similar development will occur with leguminous feed crops is questionable. Declines in sugar beet area and output, together with the reduction in sugar content of beets (from 15.4 percent in 1997 to 14.0 percent in 1998), have led to a drop in sugar production from 218,000 t in 1997 to 170,000 t in 1998 that should continue in 1999. Potato farming has experienced especially severe reductions since the beginning of the transformation period. Harvested area and production were only 52.4 and 55.3 percent of 1990 levels.

Western Slovakia produces more than 60 percent of total national crop output. The central and eastern regions produce almost 90 percent of potatoes, while western Slovakia produces 75 percent each of national sugar beets and corn output (Ministerstvo Podohospodarstva Slovenskej Republiky, various issues).

Table 15.5 Area planted to selected crops, 1,000 ha

Crops	1990	1995	1998
Total grain	938.0	849.0	868.0
including wheat	418.0	438.0	432.0
barley	191.0	235.0	253.0
corn	151.0	121.0	118.0
Oil seed	71.7	115.0	142.4
Including Rape	31.8	61.2	61.2
Potatoes	55.2	41.3	28.8
Sugar beet	51.3	34.9	38.2

Source: ZMP, 1996; 1999.

Livestock production

Declining domestic demand, coupled with a lack of credit and high cost of capital that makes it impossible for many farmers to modernize their stalls, have caused a reduction in livestock herds (table 15.6). After 10 years, milk performance matches levels reached before 1980. Egg-laying performance has not yet returned to 1989 levels. The decline in meat supplies was caused by drastic reductions in livestock herds, and increases in poultry production have failed to compensate for these declines (table 15.7).

Table 15.6 Livestock inventories, 1989-1998 (1,000 head)

	1989	1995	1998
Cattle	1,623	929	750
Swine	2,708	1,985	1,593
Sheep	621	428	420
Poultry	16,585	13,382	14,492

Source: ZMP, 1995; 1999; European Commission, 1998.

Table 15.7 Livestock performance, 1989-1998

Livestock (and unit)	1989	1995	1998
Milk/cow (liters)	3,654	3,292	3,970
Eggs/hen	249	228	227
Meat production (1,000 t l.w.)			
beef	212	108	104
pork	382	287	267
poultry	111	86	111

Source: ZMP, 1995, 1998, 1999.

15.4 Development prospects in the context of transformation

In the midst of problems associated with transferring property rights, and incomplete economic restructuring, organic farming is expanding in Slovakia. With public subsidies amounting to 4,000 Sk/ha, 36 agricultural enterprises were farming a total of 15,000 ha using organic principles in 1991; this included 31 cooperative farms mainly growing grains. In the medium-term, Slovakian agriculture has the potential to reach former production levels as institutional arrangements and property rights are clarified. Agricultural know-how and a favorable climate could allow selected regions of Slovakia to compete with Hungary on agricultural export markets (European Commission, 1998).

The structure of farming in the future is likely to become more varied. Small farms with up to 5 ha each will dominate in number, while cooperatives will continue to account for large shares of output (Filip and Schinke, 1994). One stated goal is to expand the on-farm processing of goods, which would imply a lower degree of specialization. Between 15 and 30 percent of farms are to participate in this effort in the long-term. The overall Slovakian agricultural policy objective is to ensure a stable supply of food and to gradually improve the population's nutrition levels; this includes reaching a self-sufficiency rate of 90 percent for major agricultural products.

It appears that most agricultural production in the short-term will take place on cooperative and other larger farms, even as trends toward self-sufficiency and direct marketing accelerate. Small farms will retain their importance as sources of secondary income and for meeting subsistence needs over the next few years. In addition to developing markets through guaranteed purchases, subsidies and export promotion, public funds will be provided to turn hillsides into green areas, to reforest areas with poor soils and to plant non-food crops on polluted soils (Kurzinformationen, various issues; Ministry of Agriculture, Food, Forestry and Water Management, 1997).

References

Agra Food East Europe, Agra Europe (London) Ltd., various issues.

Bundesstelle für Außenhandelsinformation (bfai) (1993), *Wirtschaftstrends – Slowakei*, various issues, Köln.

European Commission (DG VI) (1998), *Agriculture Situation and Prospects in the Central and Eastern European Countries: Slovak Republic*, Luxembourg.

Filip, J. and Schinke, E. (1994), 'Agrarstrukturen in der Tschechischen Republik und der Slowakischen Republik vor und während der aktuellen Wirtschaftsumwandlungen', *Berichte über Landwirtschaft*, 72, Münster-Hiltrup, pp. 623-640.

Interfax, http://www.maximov.com/interfax/interfax_website.htm

Jaksch,T., Bork, H.-R.; Dalchow, C. and Dräger, D. (eds) (1996), *Landnutzung in Mittel- und Osteuropa*, Budapest.

Kurzinformationen von: Agra-Europe, Agrar Export Aktuell, Agrarny Trh, Berliner Zeitung, dpa, East Europe Food & Agriculture, Food & Agriculture report Hospodarske Noviny, various issues.

Manegold, D. (2000), 'Die landwirtschaftlichen Märkte an der Jahreswende 1999/2000', *Agrarwirtschaft*, 49 (2000), No. 1, 'Aspekte gemeinsamer Agrarpolitik 1999', Frankfurt-Main.

Ministerstvo Podohospodarstva Slovenskej Republiky: Situaena a Vyhuadova Sprava.-Bratislava, (various issues).

Ministry of Agriculture, Food, Forestry and Water Management of the Slovak Republic (1997), *Report on Agriculture and the Food Industry in the Slovak Republic 1997 (Green-Report)*, Bratislava.

Ost-West-Contact. Das Wirtschaftsmagazin für Ost-West-Kooperation (various years), Presseschau Ostwirtschaft, Münster.

OstWirtschaftsReport (2000), No. 3, February 11, Düsseldorf.

Statisticka rocenka slovenske respubliky (1991), Bratislava.

Statisticka rocenka slovenskej republiky (1993), Bratislava.

Statisticky Urad Slovenskej Republiky (various years), Statisticka Rocenka Slovenskej Republiky, Bratislava.

Wolz, A. and Blaas, G. (1998), 'Die Transformation der landwirtschaftlichen Produktions-strukturen in der Slowakei und ihre zukünftige Entwicklung', *Berichte über Landwirtschaft*, 76, 2, Münster-Hiltrup, pp. 309-323.

Zentrale Markt- und Preisberichtsstelle GmbH (ZMP) (1994), *Agrarmärkte in Zahlen: Mittel-und Osteuropa*, Bonn.

Zentrale Markt- und Preisberichtsstelle GmbH (ZMP) (1995), *Agrarmärkte in Zahlen: Mittel-und Osteuropa*, Bonn.

Zentrale Markt- und Preisberichtsstelle GmbH (ZMP) (1996), *Agrarmärkte in Zahlen: Mittel-und Osteuropa*, Bonn.

Zentrale Markt- und Preisberichtsstelle GmbH (ZMP) (1999), *Agrarmärkte in Zahlen: Mittel-und Osteuropa*, Bonn.

Zentrale Markt- und Preisberichtsstelle GmbH (ZMP) (various vears), *Osteuropa: Agrarmärkte – aktuell*, Bonn.

Zentrale Markt- und Preisberichtsstelle GmbH (ZMP) (1998), *Vieh- und Fleischwirtschaft in Osteuropa. Stand und Entwicklung in 17 ausgewählten MOE-Ländern*, Bonn.

16. Land Use for Forestry

ALBRECHT BEMMANN

16.0 Introduction

Forest is the most widespread form of vegetation on the planet. It has global ecological (Anonymous, 1991*a*) and regional economic importance (Brabänder, 1994). Industrialization and exponentially rising populations have increased pressure on this ecosystem, resulting in the destruction and overexploitation of forests in some parts of the world. Early industrial development and resulting wood shortages in Central Europe led to the introduction of conservation principles in forestry at the beginning of the 18th century (Kurth, 1994), although early societies were also careful in exploiting forests (Köpf, 1995/96).

With progressive human influence on the environment, an attempt was made to apply principles of sustainable use to all human interactions with nature (Harboth, 1993, Voss 1994; van Dieren, 1995). Since the Commission for Environment and Development reported to the United Nations General Assembly in the fall of 1987 (Anonymous, 1988), the words "sustainable development" have become commonplace in environmental politics. A more or less worldwide consensus on the need for sustainable development was reached at the 1992 UN Conference in Rio de Janeiro (Anonymous, 1992). Sustainable means, in this case, development that meets needs of the present without denying future generations the chance to fulfill their needs (Anonymous, 1988).

In parallel to intensifying discussions about global sustainable development, forestry scientists were continuing their work on the concept of sustainability (Janssen, 1990; Glück, 1994; Volz, 1995; Oesten, 1995; Klay, 1995; Schmithüssen, 1995; Moiseev, 1980 and 1992; Daly, 1991). In forestry the term was initially applied only to the production of wood. Since then, it has been broadened to incorporate all goods and services connected with forests. Conflicts over worldwide conservation and use of forests continue to this day (Herkendell and Pretzsch, 1995).

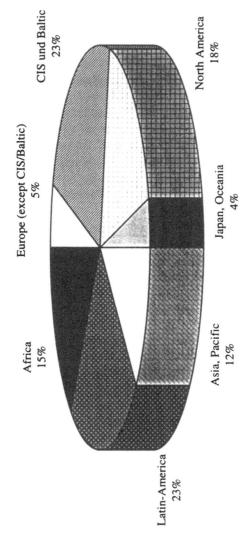

Figure 16.1 Share of total forest, by region of the world

Source: UNIECE, http://www.unece.org/trade/timber/tim-fact

16.1 Forest conditions

CEE forests cover an area of 950 million ha, making up about 20 percent of the world's forests (figure 16.1). Total wood supply in this region is approximately 90 billion m³, or 25 percent of worldwide supply. Within CEE, 94 percent of forests and 90 percent of wood supply are located in the Russian Federation (Bemmann, 1995).

Forested area in CEE countries (excluding the Russian Federation) amounts to 62.4 million ha, or more half the area found in the EU (table 16.1). The Russian Federation has a forested area more than 6 times larger than that of the EU. The rate of 0.30 ha per person in the CEE countries (excluding the Russian Federation) is below the EU average. The Russian Federation, with nearly 6 ha per person, is well above the average, and far above the rate in the most forested counties of the EU, Finland and Sweden.

Large differences exist in the degree of forestation of individual CEE countries (table 16.2). Forests cover over 30 percent of the land in the Russian Federation, Estonia, Latvia, Slovenia, Croatia, Slovakia, Georgia and White Russia. These are the most densely-forested countries in this region. Moldavia, Armenia, Ukraine and Hungary are, with less than 20 percent, the least densely forested countries.

Forests in the Russian Federation are important because of their expanse. While the Russian Federation contains almost all forms of the earth's vegetation, from semi-desert to arctic desert (figure 16.2), most of the territory is covered by the boreal forest zone, the Taiga.

Of the 814 million ha of forest in the former USSR,

23 million ha (2.8 percent) are wooded tundra
646 million ha (79.4 percent) are Taiga, with 104 million ha of this located in the sparse North Taiga forests
52 million ha (6.4 percent) are mixed forest
37 million ha (4.5 percent) are deciduous forest
21 million ha (2.6 percent) are wooded steppe
9 million ha (1.1 percent) are in the steppe
1 million ha (0.2 percent) are in the semi-desert
13 million ha (1.7 percent) are in the desert
10 million ha (1.3 percent) are in the grassland and sparsely wooded meadow zones.

Table 16.1 Total area and Population of the CEE Countries and EU

Country/Region	Total Area 1000 km²	Population 1000 Inhabitants	Inhabitants / km²	Forest Area 1000 Hectares	ha/capita	Forestation, average %
	EU = 1	EU = 1	EU = 1	EU = 1	EU = 1	
CEE countries, excl. the Russian Fed.	2,286 *0.7*	205,107 *0.6*	90 *0.78*	62,426 *0.5*	0.30 *0.8*	27.3
Russian Federation	17,075 *5.3*	147,976 *0.4*	9 *0.08*	868,588 *6.4*	5.87 *16.3*	50.9
CEE Total	19,361 *6.0*	353,083 *1.0*	18 *0.16*	931,014 *6.9*	2.68 *7.4*	48.1
European Union	3,236 *1*	371,485 *1*	115 *1*	135,475 [3] *1*	0.36 *1*	41.9

Note: Numbers in italics are values relative to the European Union.

Source: http://www.unece.org/trade/timber/tim-fact; Statistical yearbooks, various years; Anonymous 1991*b* and 1996; Personal communications.

Table 16.2 Forestry statistics for several CEE

Countries and -the EU (level 1995)	Total area	Population	Forest area	Stocked wodded area	Forestation	Wood supply		Wood growth		Wood harvest	
	1.000 km²	Mill	Mill ha	Mill ha	%	Mill. m³	m³/ha	Mill m³/a	m³/ha*a	Mill m³/a	m³/ha*a
Estonia	45,2	1,5	2,2	1,9	42,0	287	148	9,5	4,9	3,8	2,0
Latvia	63,7	2,5	2,9	2,1	33,0	489	229	16,5	7,7	6,9	3,2
Lithuania	65,3	3,7	2,0	1,9	29,1	353	188	11,9	6,3	6,0	3,1
Poland	312,7	38,7	8,8	8,5	27,2	1.607	190	30,5	3,6	23,0	2,7
Czech Rep.	78,9	10,3	2,6	2,5	31,7	608	239	18,8	7,4	13,5	5,3
Slovakia	49,0	5,4	2,0	1,9	38,8	378	197	10,2	5,3	5,3	2,8
Slovenia	20,3	2,0	1,1	1,1	54,0	228	208	6,0	5,5	('96) 2,3	2,1
Hungary	93,0	10,2	1,7	1,6	17,2	317	198	11,5	7,2	6,7	4,2
Russia	17.075,2	147,1 ('98)	868,6 ('98)	766,8	44,9	82.000	107	822,0	1,1	('98) 88,6	0,1
Bulgaria	110,9	8,4	3,8	3,3	30,0	456	140	12,3	3,8	5,1	1,5
Romania	238,4	22,2	6,3	6,3	26,4	1.341	215	25,9	4,1	14,5	2,3
Ukraine	603,7	50,7	9,2	8,6 (6,2)	15,9	1.320	154	24,4	3,9	('96) 10,4	1,2
White Russia	207,6	10,2	7,4	7,0 (6,0)	35,5	921	132	21,7	3,6	('96) 15,7	2,2
EU (15)	3.236,0	371,5	135,5	102,8	31,8	11.820	115	382,0	3,7	278,1	2,7

Source: UNIECE http:/www.unece.org/trade/timber/tim-fact; Statistical yearbooks, various years; Anonymous, 1996, personal communication.

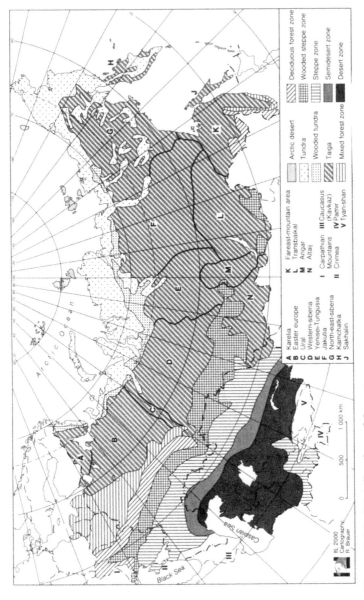

Figure 16.2 Distribution of forest zones

The total forested area of the Russian Federation has changed little in the 1990s. The area covers 1.18 million ha, 767 million ha of which are stocked,[1] so that 45 percent of the country's total area is forested. This is an important finding because recent publications have maintained that Siberian deforestation and foreign firms are destroying the Russian Forest (Iszleib, 2001). Around 400 million ha of the total forested area is not stocked. This includes agricultural areas (crops, grazing lands, orchards), bodies of water, forest roads, moor, fallow land and glaciers.

The area of stocked forests under the jurisdiction of the Federal Forest Service[2] has increased by about 13 million ha (table 16.3). However, forest expansion only partially accounts for this growth. Equally important factors include administrative assignment of stocked forests to the Federal Forest service as well as improved inventory methods, especially in heavily forested areas in the east of the country.

The distribution of forests varies greatly among regions of the Russian Federation (table 16.3). Only 20 percent of stocked forests lie on the European side of the country, while 80 percent are on the Asian side. The European north as well as Siberia and the far east have especially vast forests expanses. The age structure of these forests (stocked forest areas, major tree species of forestry groups I, II, III) is such that almost 50 percent are over-aged and ready for hewing, and only around 18 percent are young stock. These differences are even more pronounced in regional comparisons (figure 16.3). Differences in age structure can be traced back to the varied forest usage in the European part of the country - especially in central regions and the north - as well as in Siberia and the far east. Total wood supplies in forests of the Russian Federation add up to 84 billion m^3, of which 74.3 billion m^3 are under jurisdiction of the Federal Forest Service (table 16.4). Wood supplies analogous to stocked forest areas are concentrated in various regions of the country and have expanded in the 1990s.

Of all major tree groups, conifers dominate with over 500 million ha for 70 percent of stocked forest area. Of these, the Larch (Larix spp.) varieties dominate with 263 million ha representing 37 percent of stocked forest area. They occur in Siberia and the far east. By area, the next most prominent varieties are Scots pine (Pinus sylvestris L.) with 115 million ha, spruce (Picea abies, Picea obovata) with 76 million ha, Siberian spruce (Pinus sibirica) with 40 million ha and fir (Abies spp.) with 14 million ha. Deciduous trees cover an area of 138 million ha. Birch varieties (Betula spp.) cover 93 million ha and aspen (Populus tremula) 20 million ha. Shrub varieties cover an area of 72 million ha.

Table 16.3 Forested areas administered by the Federal Forest Service of Russia, by region, million ha, 1993 and 1998

	Total forested area		Stocked area	
*Region**	1993	1998	1993	1998
North	98.1	98.3	69.4	71.1
Northwest	8.3	8.7	6.3	6.8
Center	14.5	14.5	12.9	13.1
Volga-Vyatka	11.6	11.7	10.5	10.7
Central Black Earth	1.4	1.3	1.2	1.2
Volga	4.8	4.9	4.0	4.1
North Caucasus	3.6	3.6	3.0	3.1
Ural	35.2	35.6	29.5	30.6
West Siberia	137.1	138.1	78.8	81.1
East Siberia	297.4	297.7	216.3	218.9
Far East	498.3	495.9	273.7	277.8
Region Kaliningrad	0.3	0.3	0.2	0.2
Russian Federation	1,110.5	1,110.6	705.8	718.7
European part & Ural	177.7	178.9	136.9	140.9
Asian part	932.8	931.7	568.9	577.8

Note: *North: Republic Karelia, Republic Komi, Regions Archangelsk, Vologda, Murmansk; Northwest: Regions St. Petersburg, Novgorod, Pskov; Center: Regions Bryansk, Vladimir, Ivanovo, Kaluga, Kostroma, Moscow, Oryol, Ryasan, Smolensk, Tver, Tula, Yaroslavl; Volga-Vyatka: Republics Mari El, Mordvinia, Chuvashia, Regions Kirov and Nishni Novgorod; Central Black Earth: Regions Belgorod, Voronesch, Kursk, Lipezk, Tambov; Volga: Republiken Kalmückia Chalmg Tangch and Tatarstan, Regions Astrachan, Volgograd, Pensa, Samara, Saratov, Ulyanovsk; North Caucasus: Republics Adygeya, Dagestan, Kabardino-Balkaria, Karachayevo-Cherkessia, Nordossetia and Chechenia-Inguschetia, Regions Krasnodar and Stavropol, Gebiet Rostov; Ural: Republics Baschkortostan and Udmurtia, Regions Kurgan, Orenburg, Perm, Yekaterinburg, Chelyabinsk; West Siberia: Republic Altai, Region Altai, Regions Kemerovo, Novossibirsk, Omsk, Tomsk, Tyumen; East Siberia: Republics Buryatia, Tuva, Chakassia, Region Krasnoyarsk, Regions Irkutsk and Chita; Far East: Republic Sacha (Yakutia), Jewish Autonomous Region, Autonomous Region of Chukchen, Regions Primorsk and Chabarovsk, Regions Amur, Kamchatka, Magadan, Sachalin.

Source: Cejchan et al., 1999.

Total (645.9 million ha)

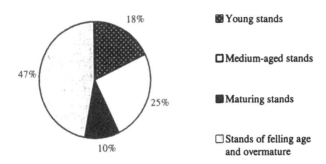

- 🔳 Young stands
- ☐ Medium-aged stands
- ▉ Maturing stands
- ☐ Stands of felling age and overmature

European part (140.4 million ha)

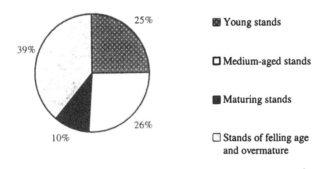

- 🔳 Young stands
- ☐ Medium-aged stands
- ▉ Maturing stands
- ☐ Stands of felling age and overmature

Asian part (505,6 million ha)

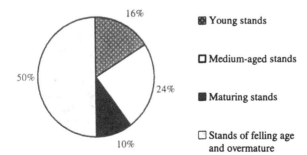

- 🔳 Young stands
- ☐ Medium-aged stands
- ▉ Maturing stands
- ☐ Stands of felling age and overmature

Figure 16.3   Forest age structure in Russia

Source: Anonymous, 1999.

Each year, 10 million ha of forest are surveyed through remote satellite reconnaissance (in comparison, 20 million ha were surveyed at the end of the 1980s). These are primarily sparsely populated, remote regions in northern Siberia and the far east. Although this remote survey is repeated every 30-35 years, forests in many parts of Siberia and the far east have only been surveyed once. Ground-level inventory methods have recorded about 62.5 percent of total forested area in the Russian Federation. Annual wood growth in forests of the Russian Federation is about 800 million m^3 (Cejchan et al., 1998).

Forests of the Russian Federation can be divided into three economic groups: protective forests (group I), forests with protective and useful functions (group II) and industrially useful forests (group III). Forests in group I cover 269 million ha, or 22.9 percent of total forested area (table 16.5). This group includes about 15 subgroups. The most extensive are subtundra forests (88.5 million ha), forests near spawning grounds in rivers and lakes (59.4 mill ha), forests along rivers and lakes (29.4 million ha) and forests in nature reserves and National Parks (25.7 million ha). These forests mostly have a protective function and are of scientific, historical or cultural importance. Industrial wood production is not permitted within this group.

Forests in group II cover 90 million ha (7.6 percent of the total forested area), with 67.9 million ha being exploitable. These forests are found mainly in densely populated areas and around cities. They have protective as well as recreational functions but are also important for wood production. They may only be logged with machinery and equipment that is not harmful to forests.

Forests in group III cover 819.3 million ha (69.5 percent of the total forested area). Of these, 253.2 million ha are exploitable, and 279.5 million ha are reserve forests. Most forests in this group are in northern regions of the European part of the county, in Siberia and the far east. These forests are primarily reserved for wood production and can be logged with industrial technology and large machinery.

The main threats to these forests are large forest fires, human damage - especially near industrial areas, and insect attacks. Forest fires are a natural part of the boreal forest ecosystem in the Russian Federation, as they are in Canada and Scandinavia. How much forest burns - whether naturally or due to human activity - is not known. According to Dixon and Kankina (1993), the average area affected annually by forest fires was 4 million ha from 1971-1986 and as high as 7 million ha from 1986-1991. Not all forest fires are the same, however: not every fire destroys the affected area. It is important to distinguish between fires that simply burn and fires that burn to the ground. In the boreal ecosystem, about 80 percent are surface fires and 20 percent crown fires. The weather can also cause year-to-year differences. In dry years, 12-15 million ha are affected by fire, while in years with high precipitation in summer months, fewer than 2 million ha burn. The fire hazard varies from region to region and from vegetation to vegetation. About 80 percent of all fires occur in Siberian forests and particularly the far east.

Table 16.4 Development of logging and wood supply in forests administered by the Federal Forest Service of Russia 1993-1998, by region

Region	Logging (mill. m³)			Wood supply (mill. m³)		
	1993	1998	Increase or reduction (%)	1993	1998	Increase or reduction (%)
North	38.7	23.8	-38.5	6,997	7,125	+1.8
Northwest	5.6	5.9	+5.4	1,028	1,210	+17.7
Center	14.6	7.3	-50.0	2,137	2,368	+10.8
Volga-Vyatka	12.4	7.4	-40.3	1,409	1,538	+9.2
Central Black Earth	0.7	0.1	-85.7	181	181	±0.0
Volga	3.7	1.7	-54.1	540	586	+8.5
North Caucasus	0.8	0.2	-75.0	513	533	+3.9
Ural	24.9	11.4	-54.2	4,098	4,261	+4.0
West Siberia	17.6	5.0	-71.6	9,519	9,788	+2.8
East Siberia	35.9	17.6	-51.0	26,116	26,329	+0.8
Far East	19.2	8.2	-57.3	20,450	20,362	-0.4
Kaliningrad region	0.1	0.0	-100.0	41	40	-2.4
Russian Federation	174.2	88.6	-49.1	73,028	74,321	+1.8
European part and Ural	101.5	57.8	-43.1	16,943	17,842	+5.3
Asian part	72.7	30.8	-57.6	56,085	56,479	+0.7

Source: Cejchan et al., 1999.

Economic development has led to deforestation of large areas since the 1930's. Many new cities were built (without proper sewage systems or infrastructure), along with hydroelectric dams. Further, rivers have been diverted and lakes drained for irrigation. Large industrial firms are to this day damaging forests with their emissions. Although causes of the damage are known, as are the companies with high emissions, the situation as a whole has deteriorated because funds are lacking to install pollution reduction equipment such as scrubbers (von Maydell and Cejchan, 1994).

**Table 16.5 Organization of forests under the Federal Forest
Service, by group and protective category
(as of January 1, 1998)**

Group and protective category	Total forest area (1,000 hectares)	Stocked forest area (1,000 ha)
Protective forests, group I	269,284	156,580
Forest in group II with protective and useful functions	90,044	75,925
including:		
exploitable forests	67,874	66,874
Industrially useful forests in group III	819,272	534,306
including:		
exploitable forests	253,157	253,157
reserve forests	279,464	175,375
Total forests, all groups	1,178,600	766,811

Source: Cejchan et al., 1999.

About 50,000 ha of forest have died on the *Kola Peninsula* since the 1930's, and an even larger area has suffered lasting damage. Smelting complexes and heavy industry in and around the cities of Nikel, Montshegorsk, Zapelyassry, Murmansk, Apatiti and Kandalaksha are polluting the environment with sulfur oxide, heavy metal dust, contaminated water and other chemicals. An improvement in the situation is not in sight.

The destruction of forests around Norilsk, along the lower course of the Yenisey, has been even more severe. The coal and heavy metal industry has killed off or permanently damaged several million ha of forest. Processing of non-ferrous metals and iron ore has discharged about 30,000 tons of dust and heavy metal oxides into the atmosphere, along with 2.3 million tons of sulfur oxide annually.

In the region of Tyumen, the largest oil and natural gas drilling region of Russia, environmental destruction is severe. An estimated 1 million tons of oil leak through defective pipelines into the soil and water. Flares burn off 12-15 billion m^3 of associated gasses at about 500 locations. Toxic waste is stored in about 5,000 tunnels.

The southern Ural region around the city of Chelyabinsk has been a developed economic center since the beginning of Russian industrialization in the middle of the 19th century. Forests around the cities of Asbest, Magnitogorsk, Nishni, Tagil, Pervouralsk, Yekatarinenburg and Chelyabinsk are being damaged by high sulfur dioxide emissions. Some observers believe that if this development is allowed to continue, the entire southern Ural region may become an industrial desert.

Damage associated with the increasing number of nuclear power plants built since the 1950s and with test reactors in partially 'closed' cities, along with accidents during nuclear tests conducted by the military, have contaminated large areas with radioactivity. About 3.5 million ha of forest (in 23 administrative areas of the Russian Federation) are radioactively contaminated (Muchamedscin et al., 1999). In addition, large amounts of radioactive water are discharged into rivers and lakes. Over five decades, thousands of people have been exposed to radiation. Managing forests in contaminated areas is problematic. There is also the additional danger that forest fires carry contaminated material into the atmosphere. These materials may be transported thousands of kilometers by air currents and contaminate clean areas when they fall as precipitation.

16.2 Changes in forest property rights

Points of departure

The transformation of CEE countries from planned to market economies involves fundamental changes in property ownership. Property was formerly owned exclusively by the state or cooperatives in some of these countries, and past experience with property ownership by individuals varied considerably across the countries. The current state of privatization ranges from an entirely new beginning in the Russian Federation and Baltic counties, where the concept of private property was largely foreign, to the resumption of past patterns in Poland and Slovenia, for example, where more property was traditionally held in private hands (Roggemann, 1996; Manssen and Banaszak, 1998).

The manner in which privatization is approached, the course it takes, and the results it produces will determine whether transformation succeeds. CEE countries have each followed different paths in their historical, political and economic developments. Consequently, they each had different points of departure at the beginning of the transformation, depending on their degree of modernity, and economic and educational levels. No generalizations could, therefore, be made about how transformation should be handled, especially in terms of privatization. Western analysts have tried to push the transformation and privatization processes forward without complete knowledge of the current situation and ignoring cultural and historical developments of individual countries.

It can be argued that the present political-economic situation in the CEE countries can be fully understood only within the context of historical developments since the Middle Ages. Furthermore, Western support for the current transformation process will be more effective with this understanding, along with an understanding of past intellectual developments (Altmann, 1988; Vranitzy, 1998; Küpper, 1999; Thanner, 1999).

CEE countries such as Estonia, Latvia, Lithuania, Poland, the Czech Republic and Hungary can be considered part of the Western tradition, having "only" been tied to the Soviet system for several decades. On the Balkans, in contrast, the 500-year rule of the Ottoman Empire still has a strong influence on Bulgaria.

Russia, more than other transformation countries and especially more than Western European countries, has taken a completely different course of development. Kraus (1993) places the historical roots of Russian development in Constantinople, in the eastern Roman Empire. A peculiar economic system developed out of this, which has made change to a system of free enterprise difficult even to this day (Saizew, 1998):

- The ethical basis of Russian civilization was Russian Orthodox belief.
- The Russian Orthodox Church never developed economic, business or career ethics.
- Anti-capitalist thought has existed in Russia for hundreds of years. Rulers were sovereign, like owners of an empire. Ties between property and power, administration and justice, along with the crown's monopoly on business and trade and its manipulation of the economy, impeded growth of private enterprise.
- Private property was despised, and considered to be the highest form of injustice. Only the products of working the land (soil), and not the land itself, should be considered private property. From an equity perspective, property can only be derived from work.

These beliefs set by the Russian Orthodox Church in the Middle Ages continued seamlessly after the Revolution of 1917 under atheistic auspices. Even today, after experiencing unsuccessful attempts to shape property ownership according to Western examples and movement toward democracy, many have been calling for a return to old Russian traditions of property (Völzing, 1997; Royen, 1999).

In this context, Schumpeter (Schwedberg, 1995) argued that:

- Economic events occur within the course of history
- Economic facts are not isolated data but are imbedded in social reality

- Most failures in economics occur because the economist lacks competency in economic history.

As a result of varied developments of cultural history in each country and economic policies since 1990, and the influence of Western analysts, social development and formation of private property have progressed along different paths. CEE countries today are more diverse, therefore, but also more full of contradictions than they were 10 years ago.

Trends and changes in property

The transfer of state or social and collective property to private property is underway in all CEE transformation countries, even if by different means (sale, restitution or vouchers) and speeds. Privatization of forests is, together with privatization of land and other natural resources, a sensitive area. Reflecting differences in cultural history, views on privatization of natural recourses also vary. But there is widespread consensus among countries on the following points:

- State forestry representatives point out that sound economic arguments (including sustainability, avoiding mono-culture, promoting public interests) exist for not privatizing forests completely.
- New private owners of small and very small forest areas prefer not to combine their land into forestry partnerships. Prior negative experiences with state regulation and manipulation are important reasons.
- New owners of forests are not attached to their property because they have not lived and worked there. They lack knowledge of ecological relationships and forestry. These new forest owners have participated in privatization of public property (for example, in Lithuania, see Kupstaitis, 1999), but will be unable to benefit in the near future because of poor general economic conditions in their countries (Thoroe, 1992).
- New forest owners seek quick returns on their assets (and investments). Privatization will lead to logging without regard to regeneration of timber stocks.

In the Baltic countries property ownership has changed several times this century (Kupstaitis, 1999; Roering, 1999, *d*, *e*, *f*), the most drastic being the complete dissolving of property rights after Soviet occupation in 1940, or after WW II in 1945. All three countries agree - this is covered in their constitutions and related laws - that property ownership should be restored to that existing in 1940, and include the return of forests. This type of restitution is difficult for several reasons and not only in the Baltic States. The process will certainly stretch over many years, because:

- Documents and proof of property as well as property markers are basically non-existent
- Land use has changed drastically during the last 50 to 60 years. This applies to forested areas and especially to agricultural areas that were deforested by the Soviet Union.

In Estonia, privatization of industry, agriculture, and forestry was consistent from the beginning. By the end of 1998, 19 percent of forests were returned, i.e., privatized, 47 percent were state-owned, and 34 percent were in the process of restitution (Kaimre et al., 1999). In early 1999 there were about 40,000 private owners of forests who owned over 400,000 ha. The largest percentage belongs to operations with forested areas of 5-20 ha. The average area is around 10 ha.

The Estonian government's goal is a ratio of 1.3 million ha (59 percent) of private forest to 0.9 million ha (41 percent) state forest (Kaimre et al., 1999). Forestry production is regulated by the forest law of December 9, 1998, which builds on concepts of sustained yield and multiple uses.

In Latvia, 44 percent of forests are currently in private hands, but not all owners are in the land register. About 250,000 private owners manage these forests, each with an average of about 5.6 ha and with all the disadvantages of small size for management. The legal basis for lasting and multifunctional forest management are the laws "On the management and use of the forest" (24 March 1994), "On the use of state forests" (20 March 1995), and "Regulations on material responsibility in offences against regulations on management and use of forests" (25 July 1995).

In Lithuania, property ownership also changed many times before Soviet occupation (Kupstaitis 1999; Roering, 1999e). But here the basis for restitution is now the property ownership that existed in 1940, the year of the Soviet occupation. Lithuania began to create a legal foundation for new property structures on February 12, 1990 with the "Law on Property Fundamentals". This law and the constitution of Lithuania guarantee the equality and unhindered existence of various forms of property ownership.

According to the forestry law of November 22, 1994, there are only two forms of property ownership in Lithuania: state property and private property. Heated discussions continue in Lithuania over the desirable amounts of each type of property. The "Program for development and expansion of wood and forest management" of July 1, 1996 calls for a dominant 70 percent share for state forests and 30 percent (630,000 ha) for private forests. The "Decision on the verification of land of importance to the state" of October 23, 1997 establishes a private forest share of 53.4 percent. A forecast by the Ministry of Land and Forest Management - also in 1997 - provides for a private forest share of 40 percent. In this process, state forestry representatives for the most part maintain that a large proportion of forests as well as all structures of forest management should remain in state hands. Others (Kupstaitis, 1999) believe that only former private forests should be returned to private ownership.

The size of the forest area eligible for privatization is 800,000 ha. This includes forest on land of former private property owners. Most are *kolkhoz* and *sovkhoz* forests with an area of 560,000 ha. In comparison, private forest areas only amounted to 250,000-300,000 ha in 1940. Other forests were private property until 1940, but were used for agricultural purposes (mostly grazing) and were razed after WW II.

Poland takes a special place among CEE countries in terms of property ownership (Fritz 1996; Bemann 1997; Roering 1999*c*). A forest area comprising 17 percent of the total area has been in private hands since 1947. Concentrated in southern Poland, the forest parcels are for the most part small, averaging 1.7 ha, and they are distributed among approximately 844,000 owners.

In the Czech Republic, forests are being restituted according to ownership patterns dating back to 1948. In this context, problems similar to those in the Baltic States are emerging. In Bohemia and Movaria the share of private forests in the total was especially high, at about 90 percent, and some owners had very large tracts of land (Gross, 1999; Roering, 1999*a*).

In Slovakia, forest ownership patterns are complicated by historical developments, which make privatization more difficult. In the mid-1990s, about 11 percent of the forests were privately owned, while 21 percent consisted of so-called *Urbarial* and *Kompossesorats* forests, which have for centuries been considered communal property. Since all property in Slovakia is passed on to children, the number of new owners of this property is large and many of them have no ties to their forest property (Roering, 1999*b*; Tutka 1999).

Between 1945 and 1990, state- and cooperatively-managed forests in Hungary emphasized different outputs (Lengyel, 1999). State forestry dominated in lumber production as well as in recreation and conservation. Cooperative forests produced disproportionate amounts of firewood and employed large numbers of workers. Today, a third of private forests (11.8 percent of all forests) lack expert managers or management in general. The forest service's control board is an administrative rather than executive organ and, therefore, cannot guarantee preservation of these forests.

Evidence for this is the 150,000 m³ of timber felled illegally form 1992-1996. These areas were not reforested (Lengyel, 1999).

In Bulgaria changes in property ownership during and since the 500 years of Ottoman rule (1376 to 1878) have caused special problems for forest privatization. It was not until 1878 that the then-Principality of Bulgaria began developing a structure of forest ownership such as the one that has existed since the middle ages in Central Europe. This structure was broken up in 1847 and is now being built up again.

Privatization will occur through restitution according to property rights of 1947, although forests in nature reserves are excluded. At that time, average area of private forest was 1.2 ha. Average area after restitution will fall to 0.4 ha, because there are an estimated 3 legitimate heirs per property (Halatcheva, 1999). In addition, there are almost no registries of forest owners, and information on 1947 property lines is incomplete because only private forests over 50 ha were officially recorded and registered. About three-quarters of those who can claim restitution live away from the forest and no longer feel attached to it.

Forests in Romania covered a total area of 6.7 million ha in 1947. The property structure was 23 percent private forests (1.51 million ha), 49 percent communal forests (33.1 million ha), and 28 percent state forests (1.87 million ha). In 1948, all forests in Romania were taken over by the state. In 1996 privatization of forests was allowed for the first time (in the post-1989 period) in the reworked law *Codul silvic*. Considerable controversy has surrounded the restituting of forests since early 1990. A *land return program* in 1991 was intended to return 350,000 ha of forest to 500,000 former owners (Ionascu, 1998). In 1998, about 4.3 percent (276,000 ha) had been restituted to former owners and 0.7 percent (22,400 ha) given back to communities. Restitution has been associated with a series of offences against new forestry laws (such as overuse of timber) (Ionascu, 1999).

The Russian Federation takes a special place among CEE countries in terms of changes in property ownership. The following decisions are anchored in the Russian constitution of December 12, 1993: "... land and other natural resources can be private, state, municipal, or other forms of property" (Article 9), and "... citizens and their associations have the right to own land" (Article 36) (Anonymous, 1993).

Although the constitutional foundation exists, political antagonism in Russia has prevented a law regulating land use from being implemented (Article 36, para. 3). Opponents and proponents have argued intensely over liberalization of property rights, and regulations in selected regions of the Russian Federation are legally controversial (Grossmann, 1999). In debates over Russian forestry laws in January 1997, the question of forest ownership was debated most heavily. The Duma decided that the so-called forest fund and forests of the Russian army are and remain federal property. These contradictions are strengthened by presidential decrees (Petrov and Bemmann, 1998; Petrov, 1998).

A part of the forest fund can be transferred to private persons for their use. This can occur through leasing, concession or free of charge (to agricultural forest enterprises) for up to 49 years or short-term for up to one year. Complete privatization of forests in the near future, according to all known discussions, is not in sight.

16.3 Forest use

Despite economic setbacks, CEE countries also need to satisfy the requirements of sustainable forest management. A suitable solution in the conflict between environmentalists and forest owners must be found, and at the same time the wood industry and its economic interests must be supported. As is true in Western Europe, forests in CEE can be harvested at a higher rate than is presently the case. The supply of wood in CEE (excluding Russia) grows at about 4 m³ per hectare annually; half of this growth is harvested. The yearly growth rate in Russia is only 1.2 m³ per hectare per year, but less than 0.3 m³ is cut (table 16.2).

These statistical averages, however, gloss over the type of forest management. Differences are partially due to varying economic conditions. But in all transformation countries, new laws have been passed with the goal of a sustainable, ecological and for the most part - except for Russia - multifunctional forest management. A definite trend exists toward environmentally-oriented forest and wood management in the Baltic states, Poland, the Czech Republic, Slovakia and Hungary. The Latvian forest laws of 1994 emphasize, along with the use of forest resources, ecological benefits of forests. Forests were accordingly divided into three groups: 74 percent economic forests, 10 percent protective forests and 16 percent forest reserves.

Important steps have also been taken in sparsely forested Hungary to use and preserve natural forest resources. The accomplishments of Hungary's forestry sector can be measured in terms of the growing supply of wood: 156 million m³ of wood in 1966, compared with 311 million m³ in 1990. Planting of an additional 15,000 ha of forest was planned to the year 2000. Hungary intends to increase the share of forests in total area from 17 percent at present to 22-25 percent.

The governments of Belarus, Ukraine, Romania and Bulgaria generally fail to encourage or practice sustainable forestry techniques. In Russia, with its vast forest expanses, no substantial improvements can be expected in forest and wood management in the near future because of on-going economic slowdown. Even so, it is noteworthy that a few private enterprises have emerged in the wood sector during the last few years. These firms are challenged by the fact that they use outdated technology as well as high energy prices, which make it prohibitively expensive to transport logs.

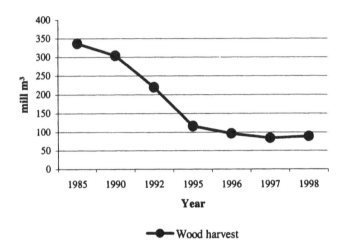

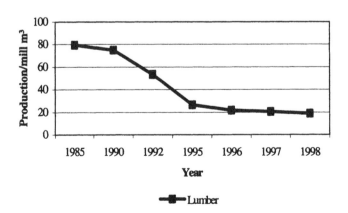

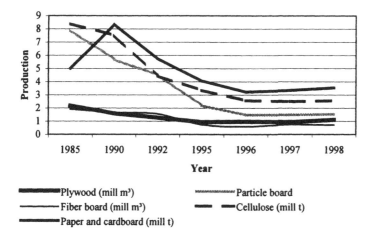

Figure 16.4 Wood harvest and wood production in Russia 1985-1998

Source: FAO, 2000.

Although the available wood supply amounts to 500 million m³ per year, actual annual felling has diminished since the beginning of the 1990s, reaching about 85-90 million m³ in 1998. Similar decreases in production can be seen in all branches of wood processing (figure 16.4). From 1990 to 1998:

- wood harvests declined by 70 percent
- lumber production declined by 75 percent
- plywood and fiberboard production declined by 73 percent and 57 percent. (FAO, 2000)

From 1990 to 1995 cellulose and paper production declined by 66 percent and 57 percent (Bemmann and Beiguelman, 1996). Wood production appears to have bottomed out in the late 1990s, and some regions have even experienced a turnaround.

To find a way out of the crisis, Russia's government is promoting a forest and wood management program. Although the importance of forests for the environment is repeatedly mentioned in the program, a key goal is to strengthen the economic contribution of this sector. The program's main aims are:

- Forming an effective nucleus of competitive businesses for domestic as well as foreign markets
- Protecting the social security of workers, especially those who are let go in the wake of restructuring or liquidation of a business
- Improving ecological conditions in areas with large numbers of forest and wood management businesses
- Accelerating investment in sub-sectors that have a large share of competitive products in the domestic and foreign markets
- Analyzing and evaluating prospects for wood products, developing a market information system for businesses and regions, as well as at the federal level
- Ensuring that wood processors located near furniture factories and other sources of demand operate at full capacity.

16.4 Forestry products certification

Most wood produced worldwide is used generically and inefficiently, coupled with low valuation of the raw material. At the same time, deforestation in many counties especially in tropical regions is continuing at great speed and unsustainable, uncontrolled uses of forests are significant. To avoid further destruction of forests and to ensure sustainable management, market oriented, regional and international approaches are necessary. One market-oriented approach is certification: An informational and regulatory system that combines economic *and* ecological interests (Neugebauer, 1995). Approaches to certification have been developed by various organizations since the 1990s.

- *CSCE-seminar of experts on sustainable developments of boreal and temperate forests* ("Montreal Process") for boreal forests and forests in temperate or wet temperate zones outside Europe (initiated by the Conference on Security and Cooperation in Europe CSCE).
- *European Process on Criteria and Indicators for Sustainable Management* ("Helsinki Process") for boreal forests and forests in temperate or wet temperate regions of Europe, continued in the PEOLOG.[3]

Environmental groups consider these political processes to be too slow. These groups seek certification according to self-imposed standards as the instrument for achieving sustainable forest management worldwide. The most prominent representatives of this movement are the *World Wide Fund for Nature (WWF)* and *Greenpeace International.* Interest groups for wood trade, wood processing industry, forest owners and unions increasingly take part in discussions on the introduction of certificates, which are considered as the intersection of interests of wood producers, wood processors and consumers of wood products (table 16.6 and 16.7).

Among all ecological processes, certification has persisted according to standards of the *Forest Stewardship Council* (FSC, founded in 1993, headquartered in Oaxaca, Mexico) (table 16.8). The global uniformity of the principles underlying this process has extended its influence beyond the limits of the Pan European Forest Certification (PEFC). But the FSC has received criticism, especially from representatives of small structured private forest owners in Europe. Important points are the feared loss of autonomy due to external regulations and expenses for which owners would not be compensated.

One particularly controversial point was that a part of the managed area (usually 10 percent) should be removed from production as a so-called "reference" area. In Germany, state and communal forests operators larger than 1,000 ha must presently remove 5 percent of their area from use, while in Sweden property owners with more than 20 ha are affected (Ripken, 1999). Poland has no specific regulations.

Table 16.6 Positions of nations with major forested areas on a forest agreement, and their forest areas and loggings

	For a Forest Agreement			Against a Forest Agreement	
	Forest area* (1.000 ha)	Logging (1994) (1.000 m³		Forest area* (1.000 ha)	Fellings (1994) (1.000 m³)
EU-States	87.806	278.758	US	295.990	491.748
Canada	494.000	187.951	Brazil	488.000	275.303
Russia	765.912	160.900	India	68.500	293.979
Malaysia	22.304	46.037	Australia	145.000	21.560
Indonesia	111.774	187.089	New Zealand	7.470	.
Total	*1.481.796*	*860.735*		*1.004.960*	*1.082.590*

Note: *According to the FAO definition: Areas covered with natural tree growth or plantations intended for forestry purposes, including forest areas that are temporarily unstocked but are expected to revert to forest. At least 20 percent is stocked with plants that normally grow higher than 7 m and are able to produce wood.

Source: Schneider, 1998; Statistisches Bundesamt, 1997.

Table 16.7 European membership in important Sustainable Forest Management processes

	Helsinki-Process	PEFC		FSC		
		Member	National work group	National work group	Certified forests	Buyer-Groups
Albania	x					
Belgium	x	x	x	x	x	x
Bulgaria	x					
Denmark	x	x	x	x		
Germany	x	x	x	x	x	x
Estonia	x	interested				
European Union	x					
Finland	x	x	x			
France	x	x	x	in Planning		in planning
Georgia	x					
Greece	x		in planning	in planning		
Great Britain	x	planned	in planning	x	x	x
Ireland	x	x	x	in planning		in planning
Iceland	x					
Italy	x	planned			x	
Croatia	x					
Latvia	x	x	x	x		
Liechtenstein	x					
Lithuania	x		in planning			
Luxembourg	x	planned	in planning	in planning		

Table 16.7 continued

Country						
Moldawia	x					
Monaco	x					
Netherlands	x	interested		in planning	x	x
Norway	x	x	x	in planning		
Austria	x	x	x			x
Poland	x		in planning		x	
Portugal	x	x	x			
Romania	x		in planning			
Russian Federation *	x					
Sweden	x	x	x		x	
Switzerland	x	interested	x	in planning	x	x
Slovakia	x					
Slovenia	x	x	x			
Spain	x	x	x	in planning		x
Czech Republic	x	x	x		x	x
Turkey	x					
Ukraine	x					
Hungary	x		in planning			
Belarus	x		in planning			

Note: *also member of the Montreal Process
Source: Iszleib, 2001.

Table 16.8 Development of FSC-standard certified forests

Country	Certified forest area (hectares)		Comparison 1999 to 1998 (% change)	Stocked forest area (1,000 hectares) FAO 1995	Share of all certified forests (%)
	1998	1999			
Belgium	10,282	4,342	42.2	709	0.6
Germany	.	23,615	.	10,740	0.2
Great Britain	6,063	16,161*	266.6	2,390	0.7
Italy	11,000	11,000	100.0	6,496	0.2
Netherlands	12,084	69,064	571.5	334	20.7
Poland	1,724,729	2,324,013	134.7	8,732	26.6
Sweden	3,155,900	8,875,979	281.3	24,425	36.3
Switzerland	.	2,112	.	1,130	0.2
Czech Republic	10,441	10,441	100.0	2,630	0.4
Europe	*4,930,499*	*11,336,727*	*229.9*		
Total:	8.972.217	17.346.605	193.3		

Note: *As of December 12, 1999 all state forests, comprise 800,000 hectares.

Source: Iszleib, 2001.

Certification according to international or national norms, such as the ISO or EAMS, has not been successful. One reason is the delayed development of norms adapted to forest management. There only appears to be an interest in ISO 14001 ff in Canada, where national norms CSA - Z808-96 and Z809-96 - developed at considerable expense - have met with little success.

Poland has taken the lead among CEE countries in terms of certification. Large areas of state forest have already been certified, although the process and execution of the certification has received international criticism. In most other countries, discussions on certification and the first steps are just beginning, although authorities are still waiting to see what will happen.

Russian legislators have introduced obligatory certification, but the lack of enforcement has made them meaningless in practice. The discussion is now dominated by the notion that agencies responsible for forest inventory should take over certification. At the same time, the Russian WWF is involved in intensive efforts to publicize FSC certification and to persuade forestry authorities to introduce it. In November 1998 and October 1999, international conferences took place in Petrozavodsk on independent certification for wood exports and in the Barents Lake region on sustainable forest management. They were prepared cooperatively by Russia's Federal Forest Service, the governments of Finland, Canada, and Norway, as well as forestry NGOs, and supported by the World Bank and others.

Those meeting here for the first time included representatives of Russian forestry, the forest industry, forest and wood enterprises; federal and regional governmental organizations such as the Ministry of Finance, the Forestry administration, and the State Committee on the Environment; certification and advisory businesses; researchers; the Organization of Indigenous People of the North, Siberia, and the Far East; and international and national NGOs (Ptichnikov, 1999). Since official state agencies continue to resent the western environmental groups, administrators of public forests are likely to join the PEFC-process.

16.5 Conclusions

Developments in CEE countries, with the exception of Russia, are similar to earlier developments in Western and northern European countries, in terms of changes in forested areas and forest conditions and management criteria. Those sustainable forest management practices that are already in place are likely to be continued. Environmentally sound forest management can be achieved with the help of foreign investment. A divide seems to be forming in this process: While the Baltic States, Poland, the Czech Republic, Slovakia and Hungary have shifted their forestry sectors towards sustainability, this is not the case in Belarus, Ukraine, Rumania and Bulgaria.

As a result of economic difficulties in Russia, a substantial improvement in forest and wood management is not to be expected. Even so, basic principles of competitive, sustainable forestry and environmentally sound wood production are known and accepted. In some regions of the country they have even been implemented.

The CEE countries - except for Russia, Belarus and Ukraine, have taken the first successful step toward free enterprise, each in their own manner. This also applies to changes in property ownership in forest and wood management. If this opening to free enterprise continues and the EU's *Acquis*-criteria are adapted, Bulgaria, Estonia, Latvia, Lithuania, Poland, Romania, the Czech Republic, Hungary and Slovakia will have no difficulty with forest and wood management when considered for entry into the EU. In the years to come, the management of restituted, small private forests will be one of these countries' main problems in formulating forestry policies and strategies. Management of private forest property is also an increasingly important issue in the US.

Based on the available evidence, Russia may need a longer time to change to democracy and free enterprise than some of the other countries. This is also true for structural changes in land ownership, including forests, which have only just begun.

Notes

[1] Forest with a timber density of more than 30 percent, and 40 percent where the stock is still young.

[2] The total forested area in Russia is comprised of forests administered by the following institutions:
Federal Forest Service (94.1 percent of all forests)
Ministry of Agriculture (3.2 percent)
State Committee of Environmental Protection (1.7 percent)
Ministry of Defense (0.5 percent)
Other institutions (0.5 percent)
The Federal Forest Service and the State Committee for Environmental Protection were dissolved in May of 2000 and merged into the Ministry for Resources.

[3] Third Ministerial Conference on Forest Protection in Europe, Lisbon June 2-4, 1998.

References

Altmann, F.-L. (1998), 'Wirtschaftswissenschaften und Osteuropaforschung', *Osteuropa*, No. 8/9, pp. 814-820.

Anonymous (1988), *Unsere gemeinsame Zukunft*, Bericht der Weltkommission für Umwelt und Entwicklung, 349 pp., Berlin

Anonymous (1990), *Volkswirtschaft der UdSSR*, (russian), Moscow.

Anonymous (1991a), *Protecting the Earth. A Status Report with Recommendations for a New Energy Policy*, Volume 1, 672 pp., Volume 2: 1008 pp., Bonn.

Anonymous (1991b), *Forest Fund of the UdSSR*, (russian), Moscow.

Anonymous (1992), 'Bericht der Bundesregierung über die Konferenz der Vereinten Nationen für Umwelt und Entwicklung im Juni 1992 in Rio de Janeiro', Eine Information des Bundesumweltministeriums, 76 pp., Bonn.

Anonymous (1993), 'Verfassung der Russischen Föderation vom 17. Dezember 1993', (russian), *Rossiskaja Gaseta*, 25. December 1993.

Anonymous (1996), *Statistical yearbook Russia*, Moscow.

Anonymous (1999), *Forest Fund of Russia*, (russian), Statistischer Sammelband, 649 pp., Moscow.

Bemmann, A.(1995), 'Osteuropa mit Russland', in J. Herkendell, and J. Pretzsch (eds), *Die Wälder der Erde*, München, pp.77-95.

Bemmann, A. and Beiguelman, A. (1996), 'Aktuelle Entwicklungschancen der Zellstoff- und Papierindustrie Russlands', I, *Holz-Zentralblatt*, No. 103/104, pp. 1569-1570, II, *Holz-Zentralblatt*, No. 107, Stuttgart, pp. 1622.

Brabänder, H. D. (1994), 'Der Wert des Waldes der nördlichen Hemisphäre aus ökonomischer Sicht', *Holz-Zentralblatt*, No. 153, Stuttgart, pp. 2584-2587.

Cejchan, S., Filiptschuk, A.N. and Strakhov, V.W. (1998), 'Wälder und Holzvorräte Russlands – Ergebnisse der nationalen Walderfassung von 1993 und holzwirtschaftliche Entwicklung 1980-1996: Aktuelle Probleme der Forstwirtschaft in der Russischen Föderation', *Mitteilungen der Bundesforschungsanstalt für Forst- und Holzwirtschaft*, Hamburg, No. 191, pp. 13-30.

Cejchan, S., Filiptschuk, A.N., Schröder, H.-J. and Strakhov, V.W. (1999), 'Holzvorräte Russlands unvermindert groß', *Holz-Zentralblatt*, Stuttgart, No. 151, pp. 2070, 2072.

Ceplaev, V.P. (1965), *Die Forstwirtschaft der UdSSR*, (russian), (Lesnaja promyshlennost) pp. 408, Moscow.

Daly, H. (1991), 'Elements of environmental macroeconomics', *Ecological Economics.The Siecnce and Management of Sustainability*, New York, pp. 32-46.

Dieren van, W. (ed.) (1995), *Mit der Natur rechnen*, Der neue Club-of-Rome-Bericht: VomBruttosozialprodukt zum Ökosozialprodukt, 338 pp., Basel, Boston Berlin.

Dixon, R.K. and Krankina, O.N. (1993), 'Forest fires in Russia. Carbon dioxide emissions to the atmosphere', *Canadian Journal Forest Research*, Ottawa, No. 4, pp. 700-705.

FAO (2000), http://www.fao.org

Friz, H. (1996), 'Analyse und Bewertung der polnischen Forstwirtschaft und des Rohholzmarktes unter besonderer Berücksichtigung der Staatsforsten „LasyPanstwowe', Diplomarbeit TU Dresden, Tharandt, (unpublished).

Friz, H. and Bemmann, A. (1997), 'Entwicklungstendenzen in der Forstwirtschaft Polens',*Holz-Zentralblatt*, No. 123, Stuttgart, pp. 1888-1890.

Glück, P. (1994), 'Entstehung eines internationalen Waldregimes', *Centralblatt für das gesamte Forstwesen*, Wien, No. 2, pp. 75-92.

Gross, J.(1999), 'Transformationsprobleme der Forstwirtschaft in der Tschechischen Republik', presentation at the TU Dresden on May 12 (unpublished).

Grossmann, M. (1999), 'Russisches Bodenrecht, Warten bis zum Jahr 2000', *OSTinWEST* No. 15, pp. 64-67.

Halatcheva, M. (1999), 'Privatisierung von Staatswald in Ostdeutschland und Bulgarien', presentation, Tharandt (unpublished).

Harborth, H.-J. (1993), *Dauerhafte Entwicklung statt globaler Selbstzerstörung*, (Editionsigma),.134 pp., Berlin.

Herkendell, J. and Pretzsch, J. (1995), *Die Wälder der Erde: Bestandesaufnahme und Perspektiven*, 340 pp., München.

Ionascu, G. (1998), 'Forest Fund Situation in Romania', presentation at FAO- Congress, Timisoara, 1998.

Ionascu, G.. (1999), 'Stand der Forstwirtschaft in Rumänien'. *Allgemeine Forst Zeitschrift/Der Wald*, No. 23, München, pp. 1214-1215.

Iszleib, M. (2001), 'Nachhaltigkeit der Waldbewirtschaftung in Nordwest-Russland', Diss. A, TU Dresden, Tharandt.

Jansson, G. (1990), 'Nachhaltige Forstwirtschaft – zukunftsweisende Nutzung naturnaher Ökosysteme', *Forstarchiv*, No. 6, Hannover, pp. 219-225.

Kaimre, P., Karoles, K. and Meelis, T. (1999), 'Transformation in der Forst- und Holzwirtschaft Estlands', in A. Bemmann and W. Grosse (eds), *Transformationsprozess in der Forst- und Holzwirtschaft einiger mittel- und osteuropäischen Länder* (in press).

Klay, A. (1995), 'Gedanken zur nachhaltigen Nutzung natürlicher, erneuerbarer Ressourcen', *Schweizerische Zeitschrift Forstwesen*, No. 2, Zürich, pp. 115-131.

Köpf, E.U.(1995/1996), 'Nachhaltigkeit: Prinzip der Waldwirtschaft – Hoffnung der Menschheit? Scheidewege', *Jahresschrift für skeptisches Denken*, Baiersbronn, pp. 307-317.

Kraus, W. (1993), *Zukunft Europa. Aufbruch durch Vereinigung*, Frankfurt a. M.

Küpper, H. (1999), 'Rechtskultur und Modernisierung in Ostmitteleuropa', *Osteuropa*, No. 4, pp. 337-353.

Kupstaitis, N. (1999), 'Eigentumsveränderungen in der Forstwirtschaft Litauens im 20. Jahrhundert und deren sozioökonomische Auswirkungen', Diss., Tharandt.

Kurth, H. (1994), *Forsteinrichtung: Nachhaltige Regelung des Waldes*, 592 pp., Berlin.

Lengyel, A. (1999), 'Eigentumsveränderungen in der Forstwirtschaft Ungarns und derenAuswirkungen im 20. Jahrhundert', Diss., Tharandt.

Manssen, G. and Banaszak, B. (1998), *Wandel der Eigentumsordnung in Mittel- und Osteuropa*, Berlin.

Maydell von, H.-J. and Cejchan, S. (1994), 'Forst- und Holzwirtschaft der GemeinschaftUnabhängiger Staaten-GUS (ehemals Sowjetunion), Die Russische Föderation', part 5 *Mitteilungen der Bundesforschungsanstalt für Forst- und Holzwirtschaft*, No.179, 272 pp., Hamburg.

Moiseev, N.A. (1980), *Die Reproduktion von Waldressourcen*, (russian), 263 pp., Moscow.

Moiseev, N.A. (1992), 'A system of forest management, based on the principle of forest sustainable multiple use', *Proceedings form IUFRO International Conference Integrated sustainable Multiple-use forestmanagement under the market system '*, September 6-12, 1992, Puschkino, pp. 21-33.

Muchamedschin, K.D., Tschilimov, A.I. and Snytkin, G.V. (1999), 'Zertifizierung von Waldressourcen nach dem Parameter Radioaktivität als Grundlage für eine Waldnutzung in radioaktiv kontaminierten Gebieten' (russian), *Lesnoe chosjaistvo*, No. 4, Moscow, pp. 10-11.

Neugebauer, B. (1995), 'Qualifizierung und Zertifizierung', in J. Herkendell and J. Pretzsch (eds), *Die Wälder der Erde*, München, pp. 218-225.

Oesten, G. (1995), 'Zur forstökonomischen Diskussion über das Leitbild einer nachhaltigen Waldwirtschaft', *Forst und Holz*, No. 6, Hannover, pp. 171-175.

Petrov, V.N. (1998), 'Forstpolitik und Waldschutz', (russian), St. Petersburg.

Petrov, V.N. and Bemmann, A. (1998), 'Grundlagen der gegenwärtigen Forstpolitik Russlands', *Allgemeine Forst Zeitschrift/Der Wald*, No. 10, München, pp. 536-538.

Ptichnikov, A. (1999), *Wälder Russlands: unabhängige Zertifizierung und nachhaltige Nutzung*, (russian), WWF Russia, Moscow.

Ripken, H. (1999), 'Noch unentschieden: Der Kampf um die Zertifizierung', *Forst und Holz*, No. 9, Hannover, pp. 257-263.

Roering, H.W. (1999a), 'Die Forstwirtschaft der Tschechischen Republik', *Arbeitsbericht des Institutes für Ökonomie*, Bundesforschungsanstalt für Forst- und Holzwirtschaft, Hamburg

Roering, H.W. (1999b), 'Die Forstwirtschaft der Slowakischen Republik', *Arbeitsbericht des Institutes für Ökonomie*, Bundesforschungsanstalt für Forst- und Holzwirtschaft, Hamburg.

Roering, H.W. (1999c), 'Die Forstwirtschaft Polens', *Arbeitsbericht des Institutes für Ökonomie*, Bundesforschungsanstalt für Forst- und Holzwirtschaft, Hamburg.

Roering, H.W. (1999d), 'Die Forstwirtschaft Lettlands', *Arbeitsbericht des Institutes für Ökonomie*, Bundesforschungsanstalt für Forst- und Holzwirtschaft, Hamburg.

Roering, H.W. (1999e), 'Die Forstwirtschaft Litauens', *Arbeitsbericht des Institutes fürÖkonomie*, Bundesforschungsanstalt für Forst- und Holzwirtschaft, Hamburg.

Roering H.W. (1999f), 'Die Forstwirtschaft Estlands', *Arbeitsbericht des Institutes für Ökonomie*, Bundesforschungsanstalt für Forst- und Holzwirtschaft Hamburg.

Roggemann, H. (ed.) (1996), *Eigentum in Osteuropa*, Berlin.

Royen, Ch. (1999), 'Der Westen und Russland – Lehren aus der Krise', *Osteuropa*, No. 1, pp. 79-88.

Saizew, S. (1998), 'Über die russische Wirtschaftskultur', *Osteuropa-Wirtschaft*, No. 1, pp. 36-70.

Schneider, T.W. (1998), 'Der internationale forstpolitische Dialog 5 Jahre nach Rio', *Allgemeine Forst Zeitschrift/Der Wald*, No. 6, München, pp. 314-316.

Statistisches Bundesamt (1997), *Statistisches Jahrbuch für das Ausland*, Wiesbaden.

Schmitthüsen, F. (1995), 'Walderhaltung als A ufgabe einerinternationalen Zusammenarbeit', *Schweizerische Zeitschrift Forstwesen*, No. 2, Zürich, pp. 79-85.

Statistical yearbooks (various years).

Swedberg, R. (1995), 'Schumpeters Vision der Sozioökonomie', in K.S. Althaler, E. Matzner, M. Prisching and B. Unger (eds), *Sozioökonomische Forschungsansätze*, Marburg, pp. 15-42.

Thanner, B. (1999), 'Systemtransformation: Ein Mythos verblasst. Der tiefe Fall Russlands: Von der Plan- zur Subsistenzwirtschaft', *Osteuropa-Wirtschaft*, No. 2, pp. 196-225.

Thoroe, C. (1992), 'Welche Vorteile bietet das Privateigentum? Privatisierung in der Forst- und Holzwirtschaft', UNECE-Arbeitstagung, Bonn-Röttgen, June 15-18, pp. 18-36.

Tinchev, V. (1999), Personal communication.

Tutka, J. (1999), 'Transformation in der Forst- und Holzwirtschaft der Slowakei', in A. Bemmann and W. Grosse (eds), *Transformation in der Forst- und Holzwirtschaft einiger mittel- und osteuropäischer Länder*, (in press).

UNIECE, , http://www.unece.org/trade/timber/tim-fact.

Völzing, J.A. (1997), 'Wer profitiert von der Privatisierung in Russland', *Osteuropa-Wirtschaft*, No. 3, pp. 301-314.

Volz, K.-R. (1995), 'Zur ordnungspolitischen Diskussion über die nachhaltige Nutzung der Zentralressource Wald', *Forst und Holz*, No. 6, Hannover, pp. 163-170.

Voss, G. (1994), *Sustainable development. Leitziel auf dem Weg in das 21. Jahrhundert*, 147 pp., Köln

Vranitzky, F. (1998), 'Ein neuer Gesellschaftsvertrag', *Osteuropa*, No. 7, pp. 645-651.

17. Prospects for the Future

TANJA JAKSCH, ROSEMARIE SIEBERT AND
STEPHAN J. GOETZ

In the Former Soviet Union, agriculture was a sector of exceptional stability relative to other sectors of the economy. Even in the late 1980s, the notion that the agricultural sector and its socialized, large-scale units of production would ever change was unimaginable.

Since 1990, political and economic changes in many of these countries have been profound and they have occurred quickly, paving the way for the implementation of economic and agricultural policies in line with those currently pursued in the European Union. A number of transformation countries have formed partnerships with EU nations through association contracts. However, these fundamental changes cannot proceed without at least some degree of friction. For a number of countries, important questions surround the future of agriculture, and how agricultural development will affect society, the economy and the environment. In large parts of rural Central and Eastern Europe, 60 percent of the population now lives under the official poverty level. The agricultural sector in most of the transformation countries consists of small-scale farms pursuing subsistence farming.

A fundamental question is, what will be the fate of rural areas of Central and Eastern Europe? Is it possible to integrate these areas into the overall economic and social development processes of these nations, with a productive and modern agricultural sector as one supporting pillar? Or will this region be cut off from the rest of society and marginalized? Past lessons from around the world suggest that agriculture has an important role to play in the economic development of a country. Whether that role is the same in each of the CEE countries remains to be seen. Furthermore, it is unclear to what extent non-agricultural job growth will occur in rural areas. It will be interesting to examine where industries locate, once they have freedom in making location decisions, relative to their locations in the planned economy.

333

Most of the countries discussed in the book are likely to seek to join the EU, creating significant problems for the continent that will likely also affect the US. Countries with a significant agricultural export potential, such as the Ukraine or Romania, could export mass-produced commodities such as grains, oil seed and oil, or sugar, possibly with the benefit of export subsidies. Other CEE countries will likely enter the European market with more highly processed goods, displacing local products.

Russia, with its vast territory that stretches over two continents, is likely to remain outside the EU. Without foreign support, rural areas could be marginalized, as suggested above. This would mean that Russia, with its enormous market potential, could cease to be a trading partner for many countries. As do the other transformation countries, Russia needs assistance in the form of agricultural production and marketing expertise rather than imports of food or food aid from the EU and the US. The question then is, which specific goods or commodities will be exported, and which imported, under free or nearly free market conditions, and how competitive will the domestic input supply and processing industry become?

In looking to the future of the individual transformation countries and trying to gauge what is possible, it is important to focus on the existing natural resources, which we have attempted to do in this volume, and to consider the following historical pre-conditions that surround the emergence of the agro-food-sectors in the individual countries.

- The agricultural conditions that existed before the establishment of a planned socialist economy varied significantly across these countries. The village community in Russia (called *Mir*) has existed for centuries and is so anchored in the thoughts and actions of the rural population that its most important features - the periodic redistribution of farmland - was retained in some areas even up to 1925-1926. In contrast, the Czech Republic as well as large parts of Poland have protected private property through a land registry for a long time.
- Central planning lasted 74 years in the Soviet Union and "only" 40 years in Hungary, for example, with the introduction of elements of a free market after 1970.
- Enormous differences existed, for example, between the former Soviet Union and Hungary in the political status and importance of the agricultural and food sectors in the individual countries.[1]

The different relative importance of the agricultural and food sectors in the national politics of these countries has the following implications:
- Different parts of the marketing system, such as shipping, storage and processing, are in very different stages of development. Centralized

resource allocation in the Soviet Union, Romania and Bulgaria, in particular, benefited production agriculture at the expense of other sectors.

- Significant differences existed in the degree of control exercised over the agricultural and food sector, that is, in the role market forces had in terms of the type of pricing, incentives, consumer price flexibility, and so forth. The greatest degree of control, and thus generally the greatest inefficiency was found in the Soviet Union, Romania and Bulgaria. Market forces were most strongly developed in Hungary, where prices were partially established by markets and systems of production were heavily commercialized.
- Systems of agricultural education varied widely across these countries.
- The degree of party and administrative intervention in farm operations and farm-level decision-making differed considerably.

These particularities have left a lasting impression on the attitudes and views of individuals both inside of and outside the agricultural and food sector. It is conceivable that such social-psychological factors, perhaps more so in rural areas, will change only after relatively long periods of time (lasting many years).

The diverse natural conditions that exist within these countries also play a determining role in future paths of development, even within a single country. In Russia, relatively independent economic regions are developing which, because of the large expanse of the country, lack close ties to the rest of the economy.

The people of Central and Eastern Europe have abandoned the battered and run-down ship of Soviet state socialism and jumped into a churning sea of economic and social transformation. They hope that acceptance onto the EU luxury liner will solve their complex economic and social problems. Given the strong desire to join the EU, this is an opportune time to re-orient these countries toward a sustainable form of agriculture, to the extent that this is viewed as a desirable goal. More specifically, Western nations may consider using this opportunity to encourage these countries to develop and implement environmentally sound production practices in their agricultural sectors.

Note

[1] The Soviet Union's agricultural and food sector was oriented primarily towards internal markets; many commodities were exported to close political allies. The domestic food problem was viewed in a purely quantitative manner, and it received little attention from party and state leaders so long as domestic needs were more or less met. Furthermore,

food quality was rarely a concern, except perhaps for products that were destined for larger cities, since none of the food was exported outside the union. Hungary, in contrast, attempted to continue its historical patterns of promoting and expanding agricultural exports even under Soviet rule. Since at least the late 1960s, a change in emphasis towards modern and demand-oriented supplies of higher-value foods and luxury goods (replacing unprocessed raw commodities) was apparent in Hungary both for domestic goods and for exports.

Index

For Product Safety Concerns and Information please contact our EU
representative GPSR@taylorandfrancis.com Taylor & Francis Verlag GmbH,
Kaufingerstraße 24, 80331 München, Germany

Printed and bound by CPI Group (UK) Ltd, Croydon, CR0 4YY
01/05/2025
01858349-0003